ANREALAGE A&Z

TABLE OF CONTENTS

ANREALAGE A&Z

RIZZOLI
NEW YORK

Introduction

That day, my brother did not wake up.
Even when morning came, he never stirred.

My father and mother, grandfather and grandmother were rushing around the house. I sensed something ominous in the air.

There was nothing I could do.

I listened intently to the grownups' conversations, but I couldn't understand what they were saying. I could only stare as they rushed past me.

The only thing I knew was that something had happened.

I wondered how much time had passed.

A small coffin was brought into the house.
My brother was changed into white clothes.

His face was pale.

Many people came to the house.
Still, my brother did not wake up.

I wondered what was wrong with my brother.
Why won't he wake up?

My brother, who was four years younger than me, died that day. It was a sudden death.

I had just turned four years old.

I felt as if the world I was in were a mirage.

To be alive was ordinary, but to die was unusual. That was the day I first learned about the ordinary and the extraordinary in life.

To be alive in this world was ordinary. To disappear from this world was extraordinary. I discovered how vague the line that separated the two could be.

Why did I wake up, but my brother did not?

What separated me from my brother?

I had never understood why I was allowed to live. I had never even tried to understand it.

At least not until I began making clothes when I turned nineteen.

That day from when I was four years old will stay with me forever. It is the original landscape of my heart.

What separates A from Z?

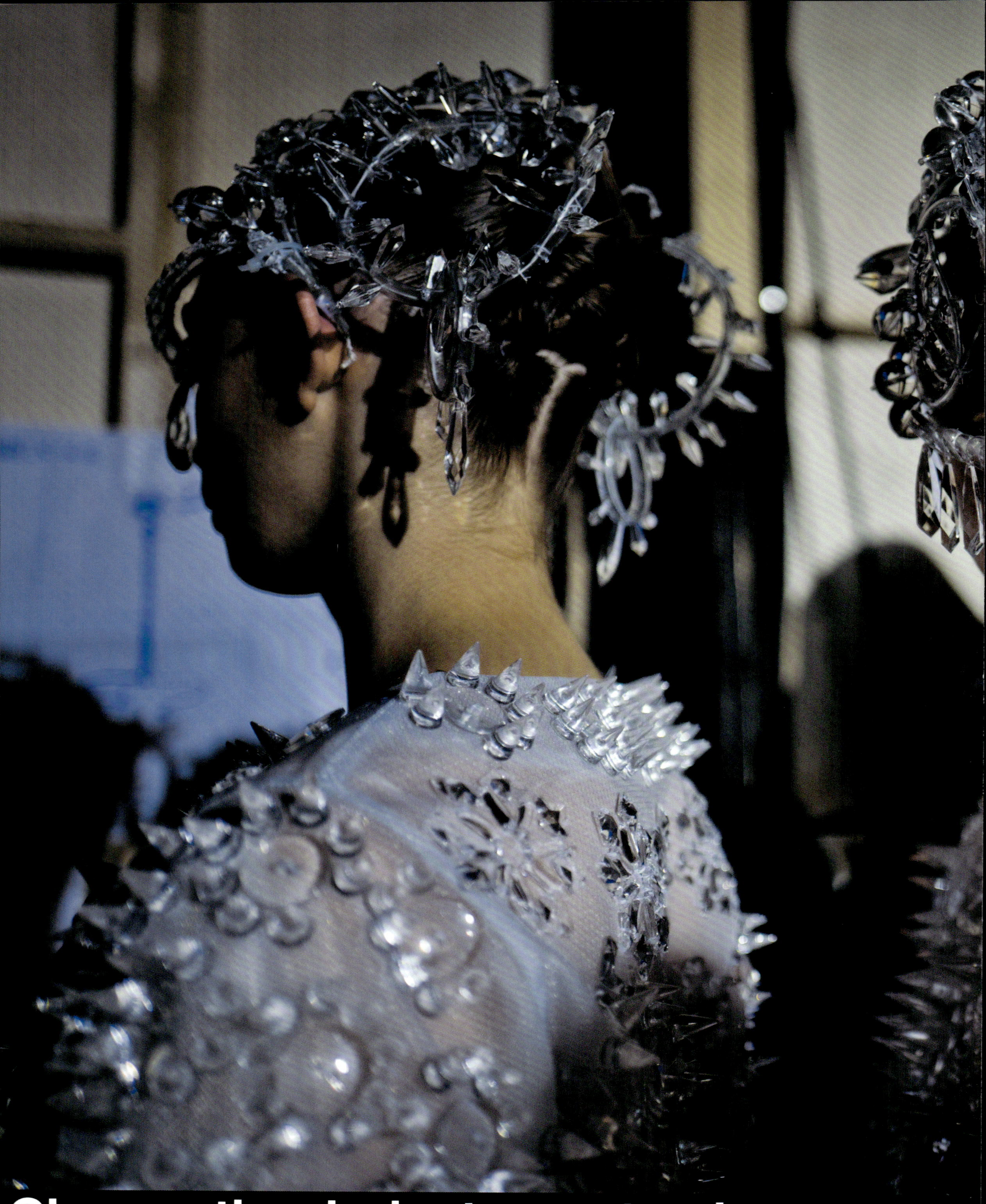

Change the dark stream to clear:

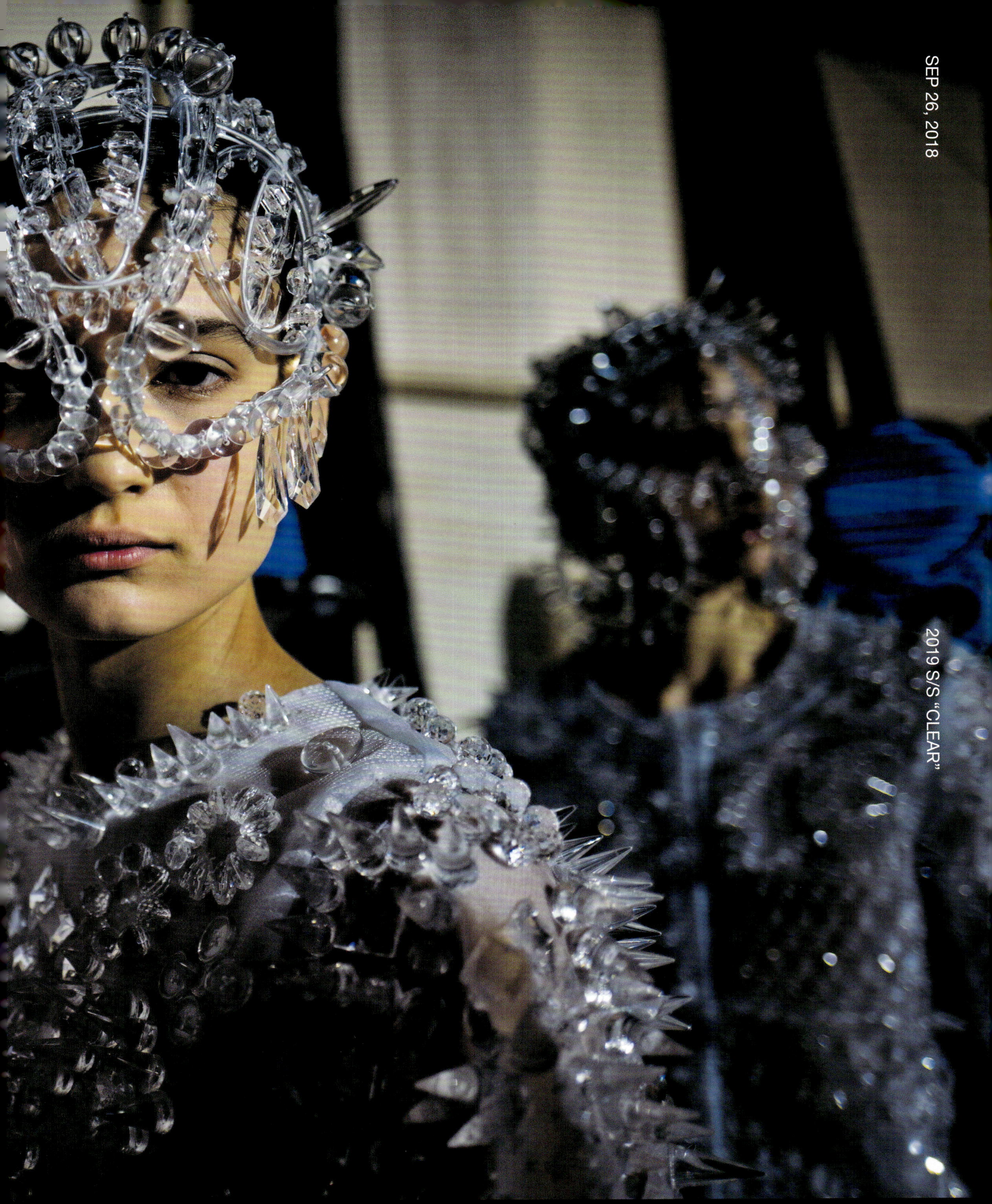

SEP 26, 2018

2019 S/S "CLEAR"

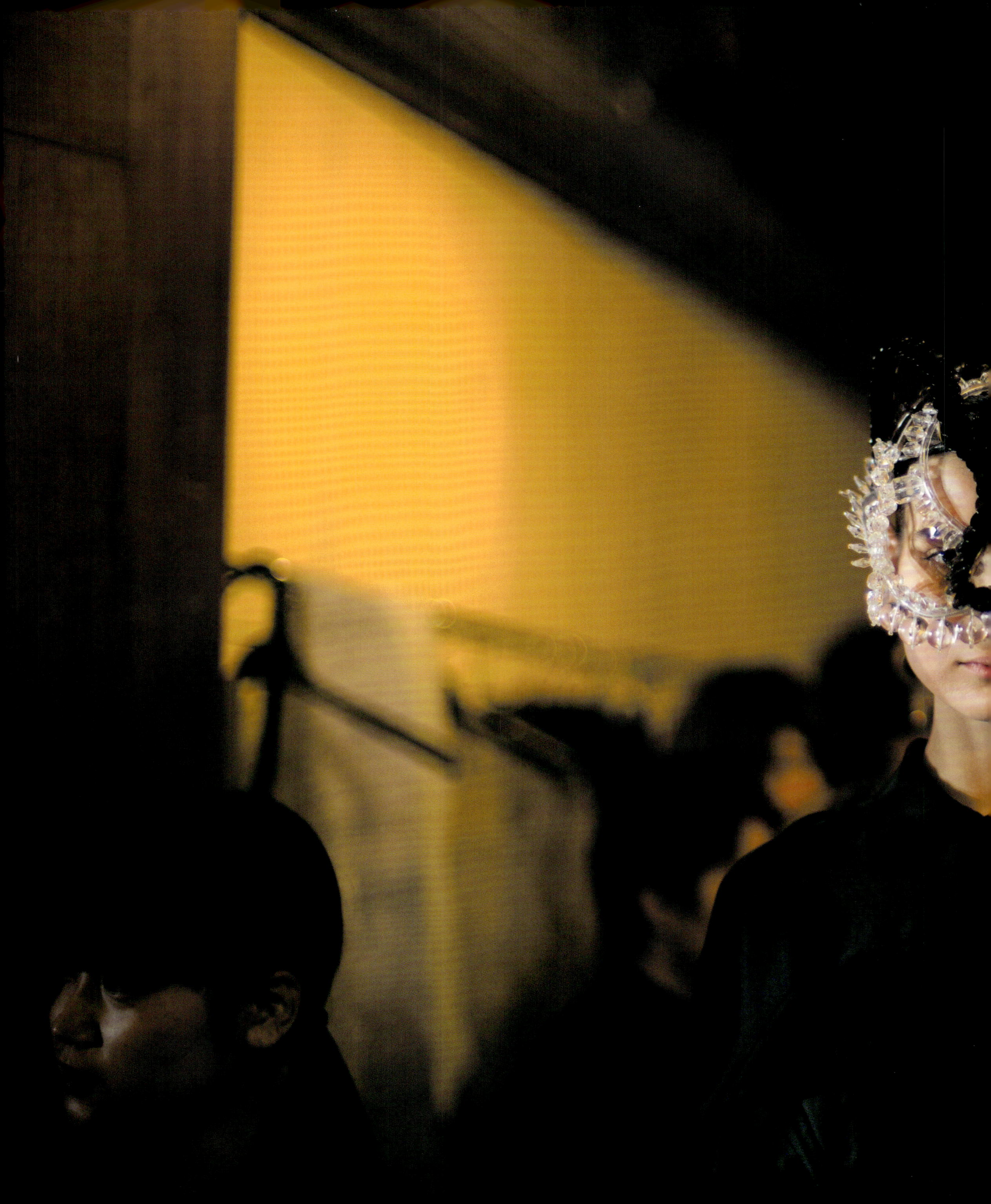

The visible becomes invisible, and the i

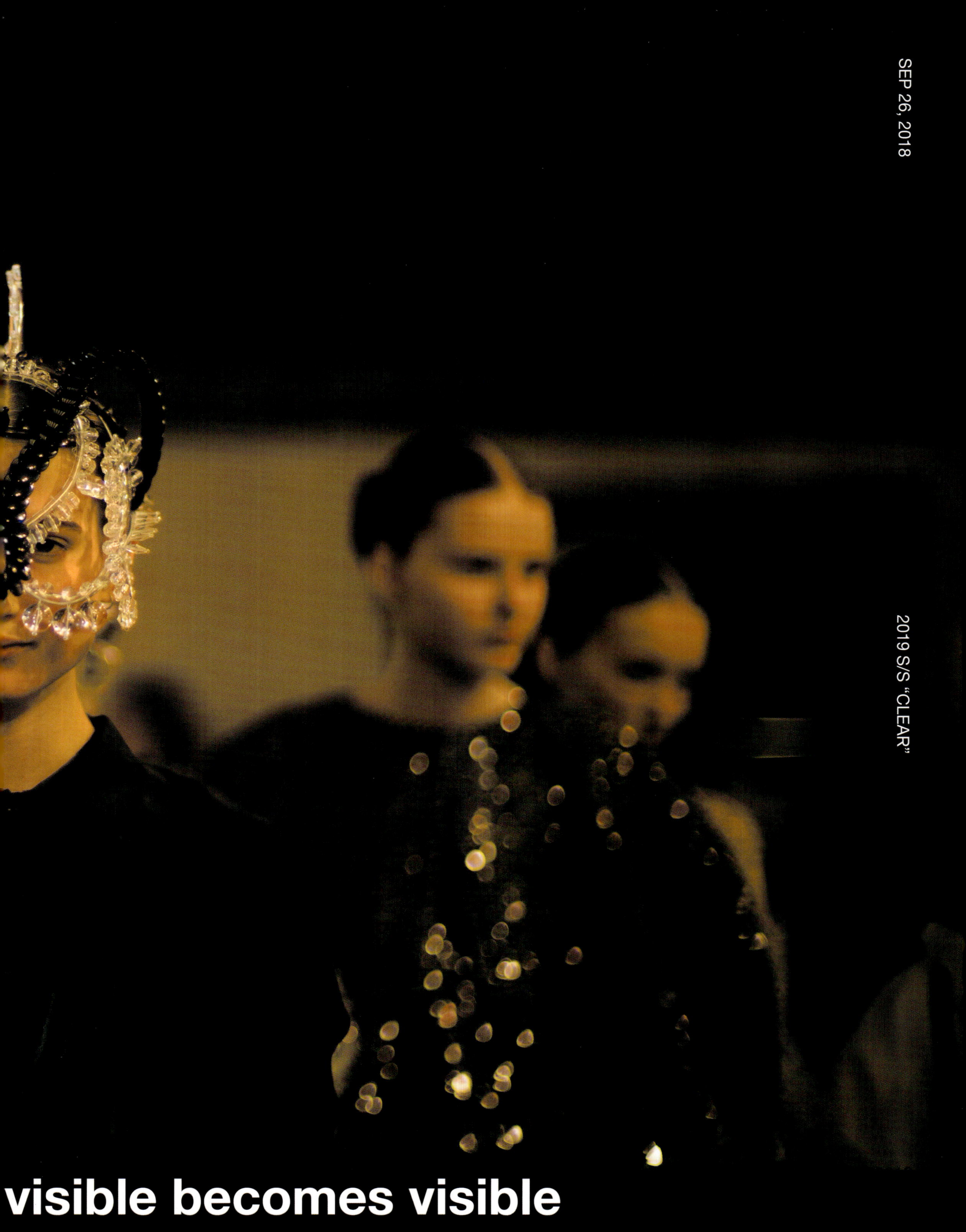
SEP 26, 2018
2019 S/S "CLEAR"
visible becomes visible

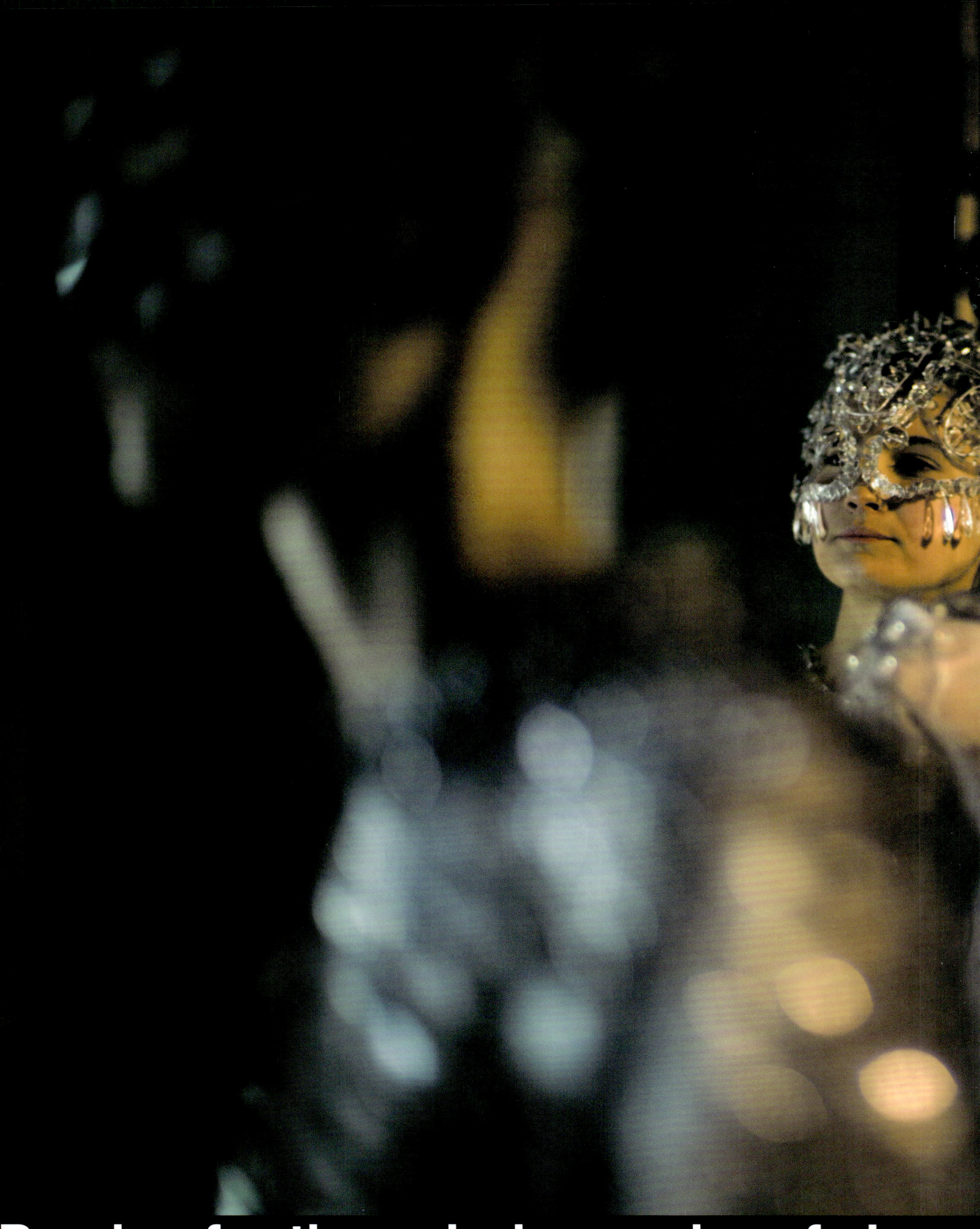

Praying for the colorless color of clear

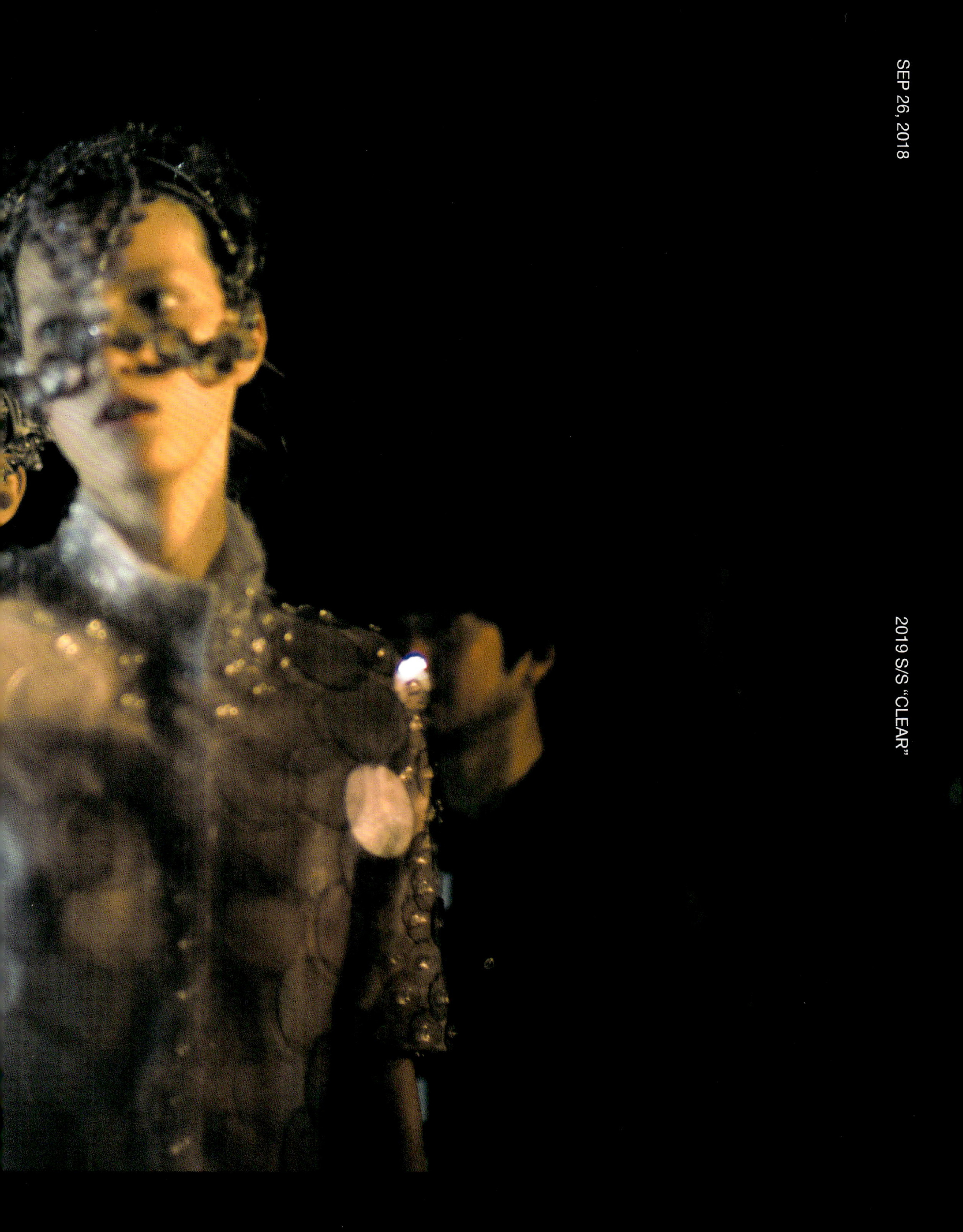

SEP 26, 2018

2019 S/S “CLEAR”

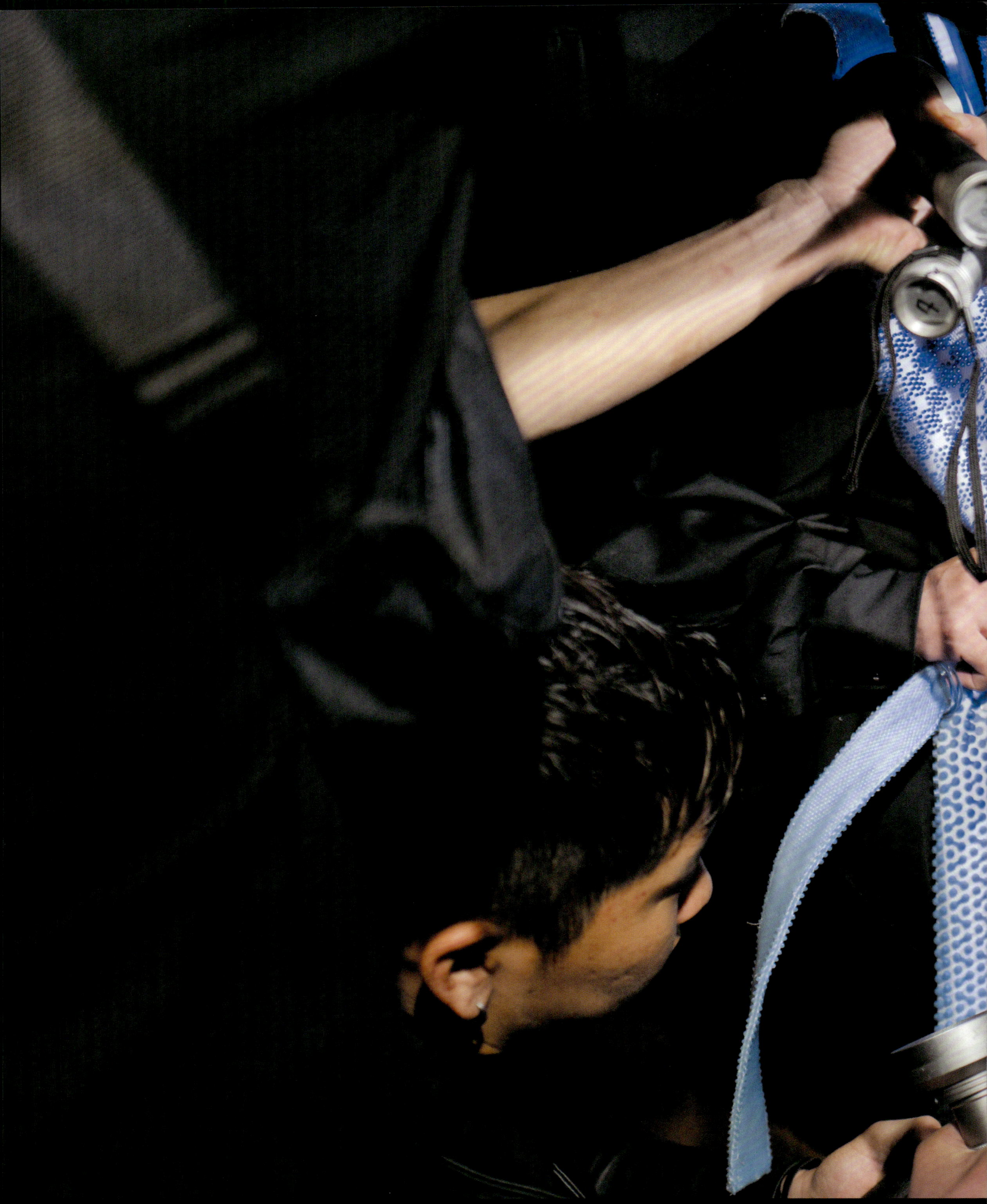

Technology is a double-edged sword

SEP 26, 2018

2019 S/S “CLEAR”

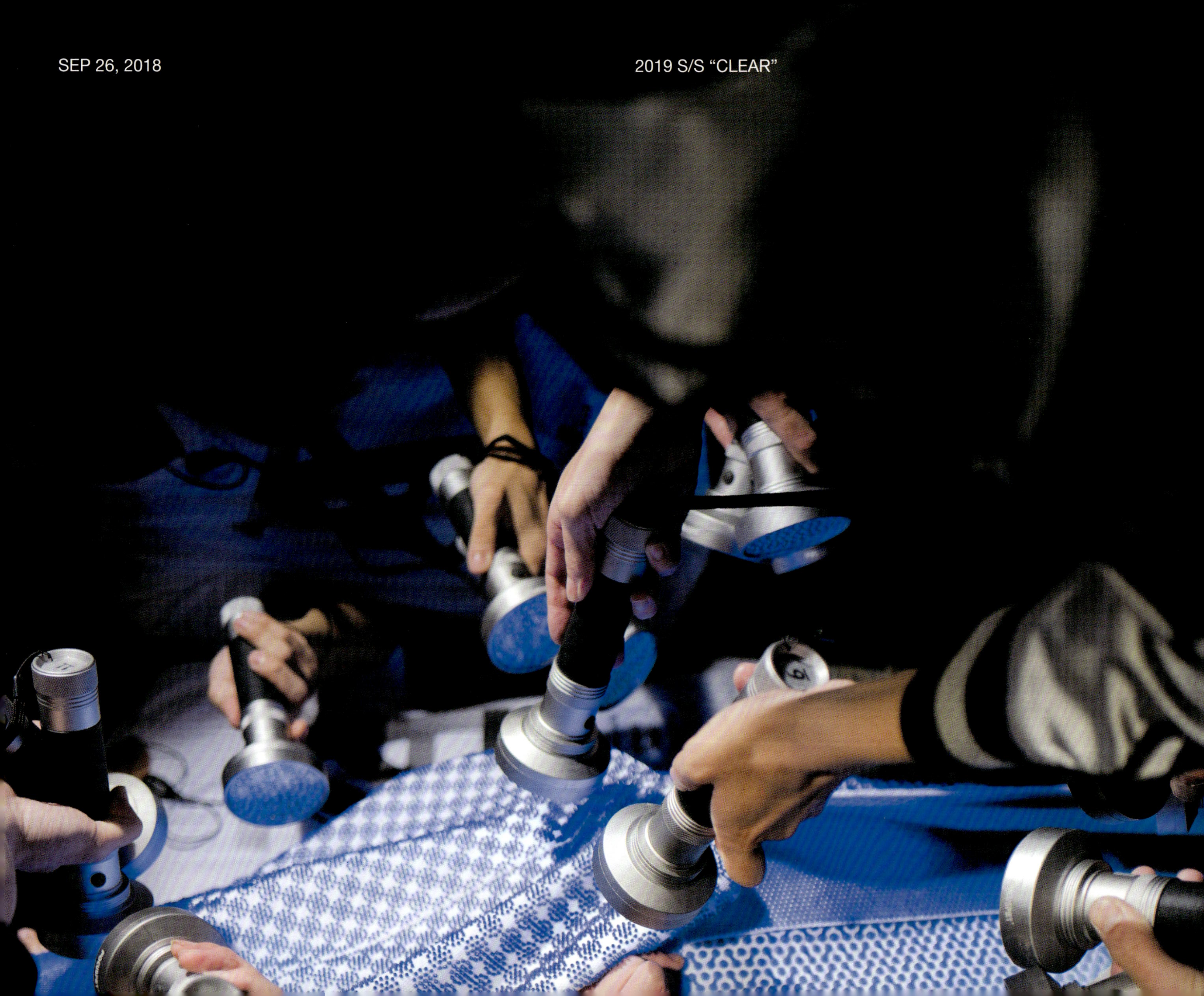

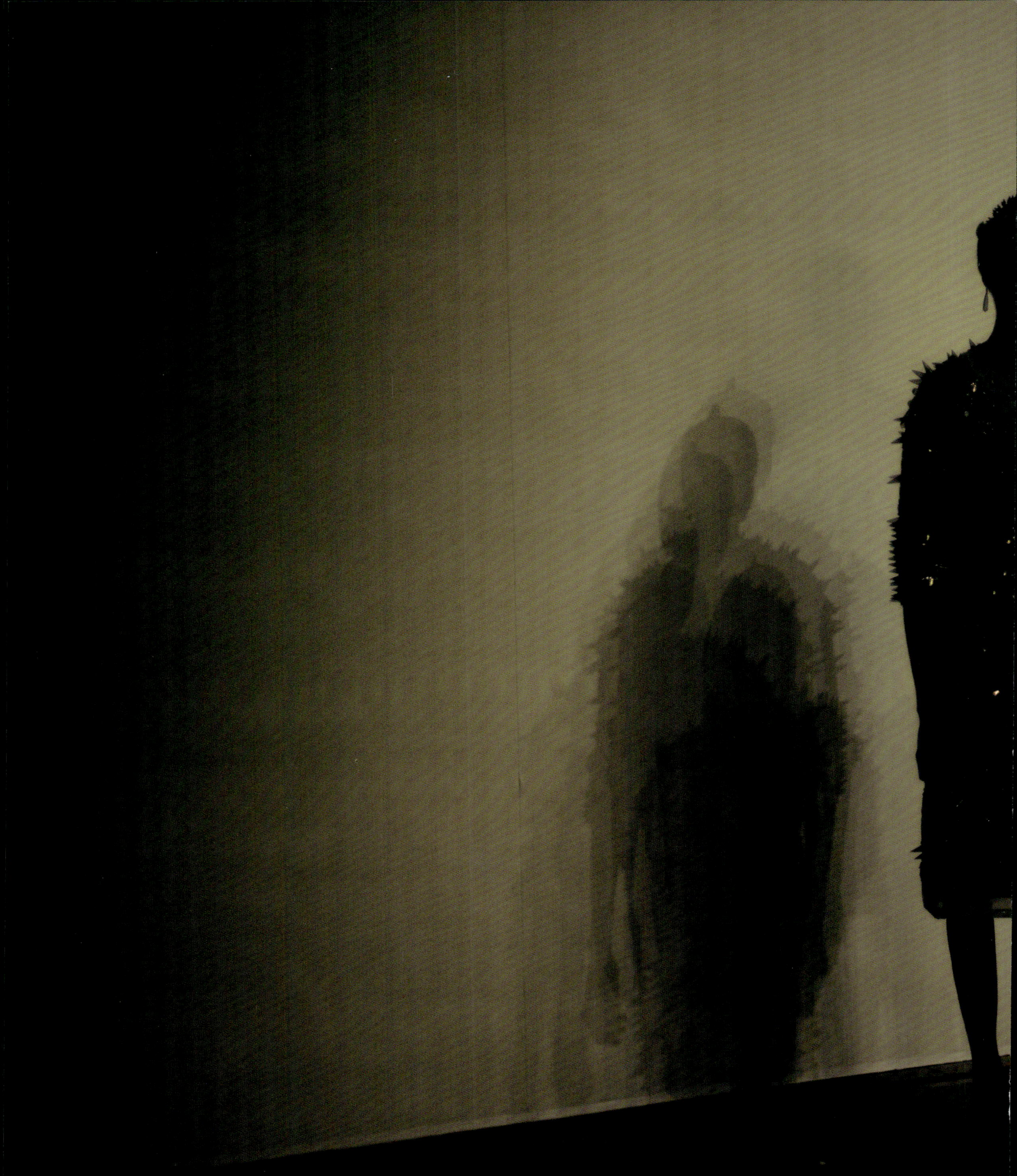

It advances fashion, but at the same tim

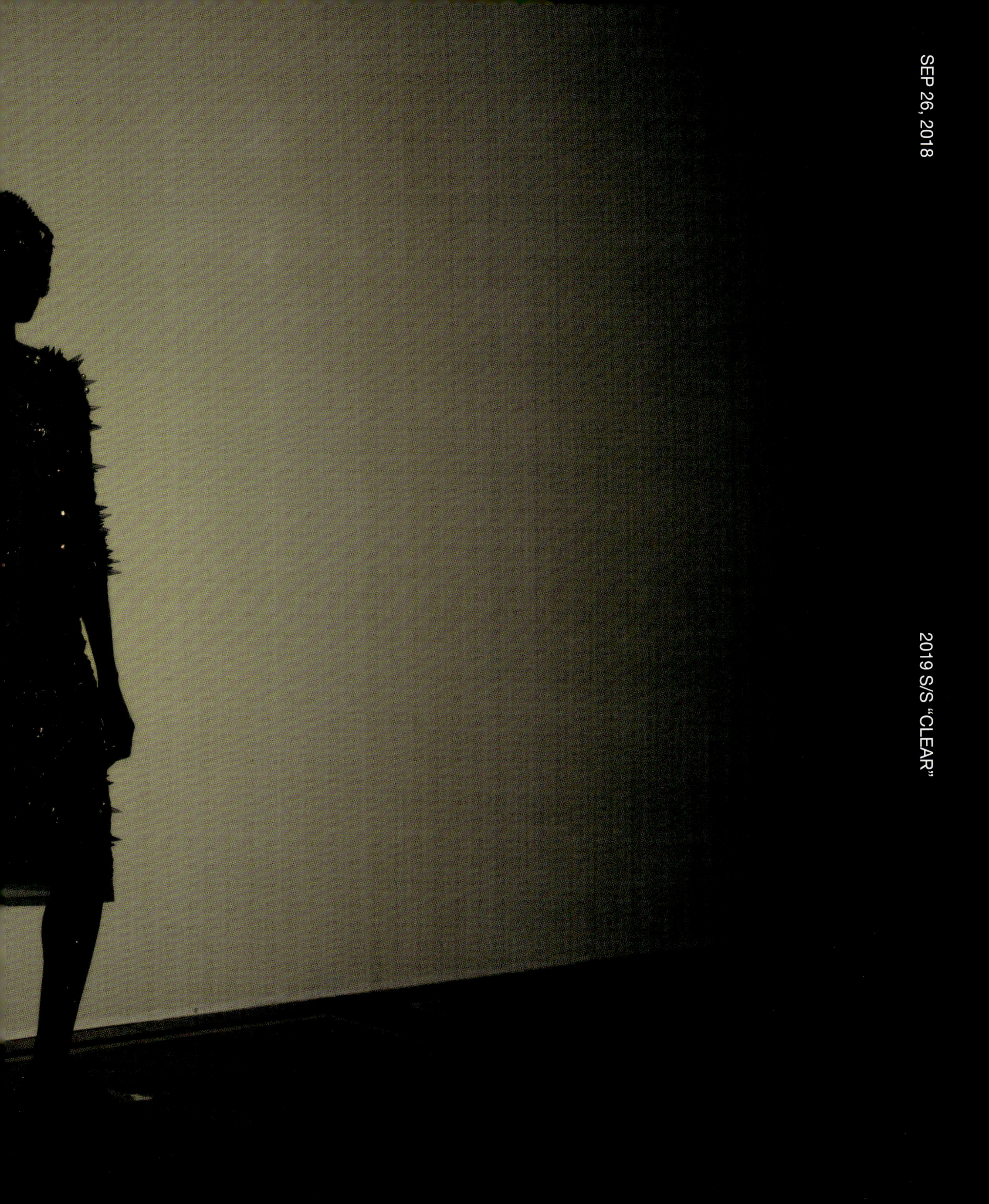

SEP 26, 2018

2019 S/S "CLEAR"

e it threatens to destroy fashion

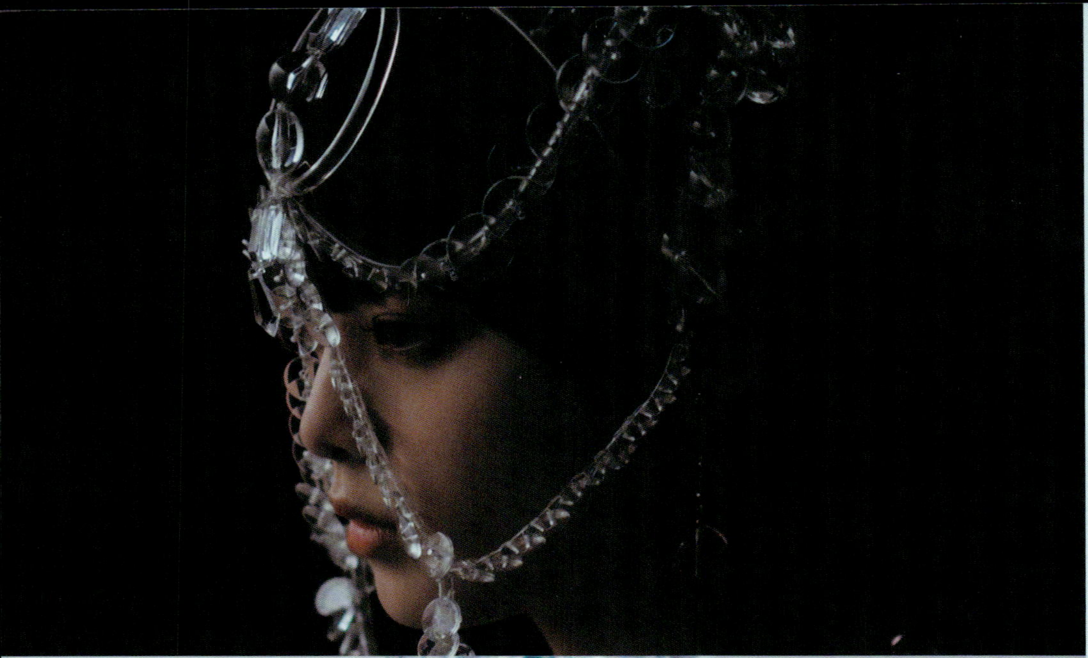
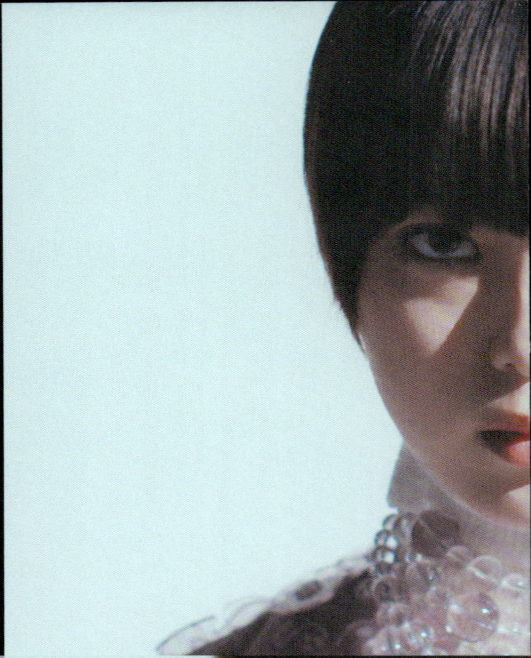
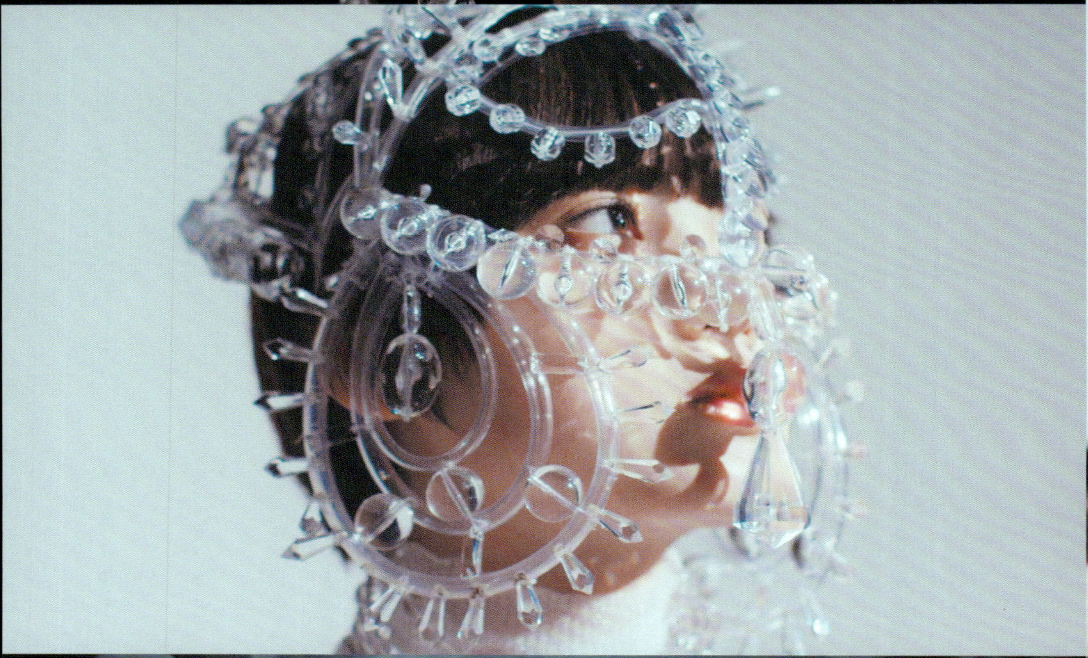
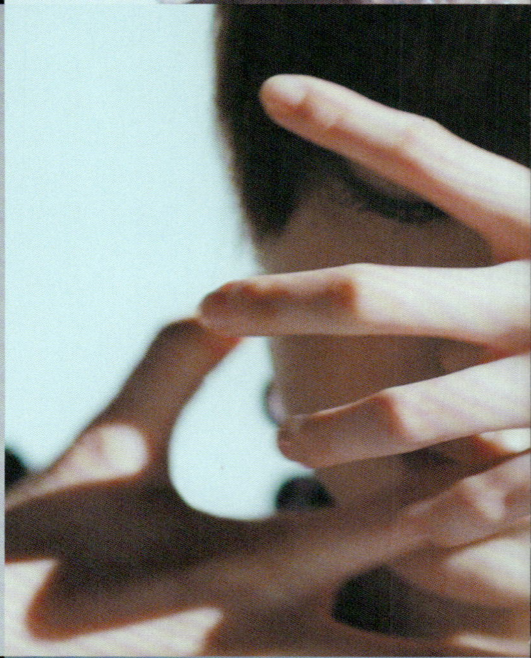
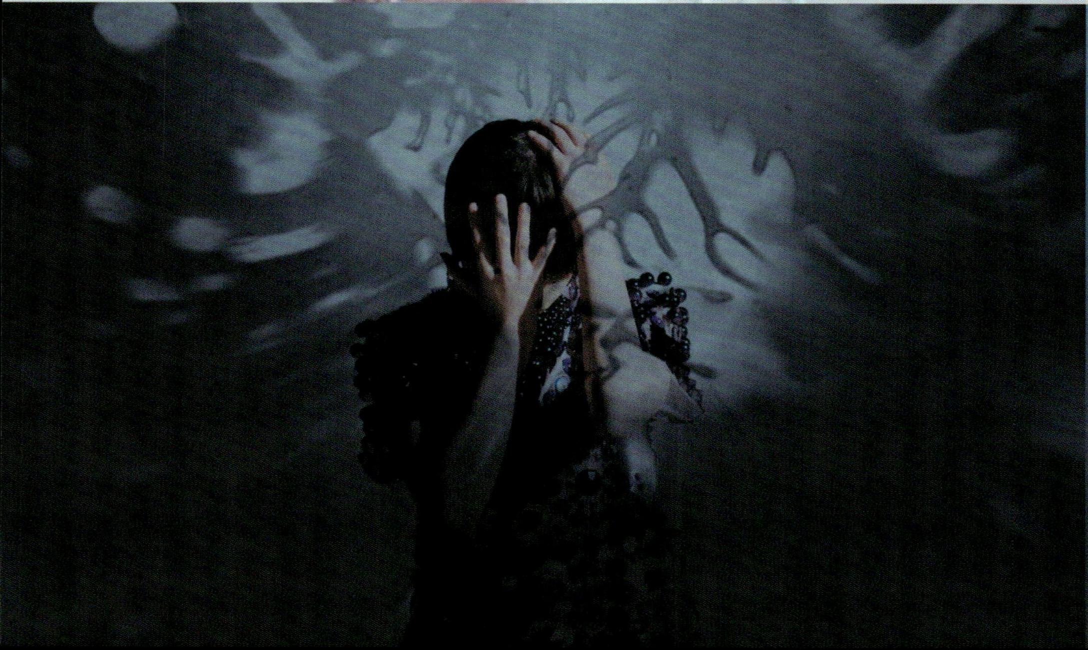

I need to continuously update myself to

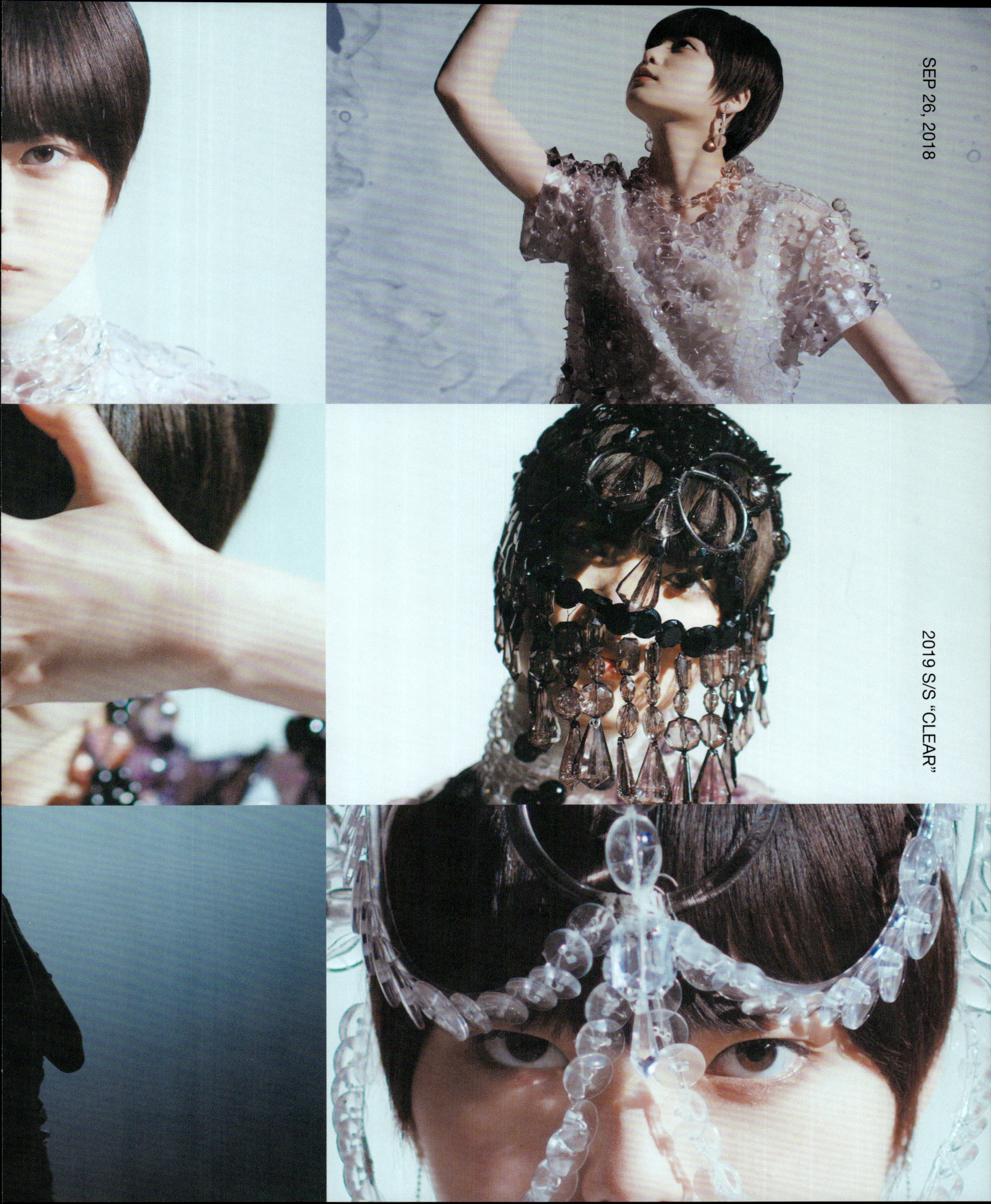

survive in the world of fashion

Shadow

Driven into a Corner

It will be the worst fashion show of my life.
It might be better to stop the show itself.
All will be lost if I don't do something...

It was September 23, 2014, the day of my Paris debut that I had long dreamed about. With my S/S 2015 collection about to open in a few hours, I was in despair inside the venue at the Beaux-Arts Salle Melpomene. From white to black. I will turn white clothes into black in an instant. I had prepared an electrifying performance for the collection I had entitled, *Shadow* (Japanese title: *Hikari [Light]*). It was supposed to be a showcase of clothing that utilized a photochromic dye that changes its color when exposed to light. I was planning to give the audience a surprise and innovation unlike anything they've seen before in the history of Paris Fashion Week. I was convinced that the application of the technology would be met with a thunderous applause. With each passing second, the pre-show rehearsal time was running out.

The color that was supposed to change did not.
The white clothes that were supposed to turn black did not.

I'll have to show the plain white clothes as they were. I would have to explain later that the color was supposed to change. I had to give up on the element of surprise.

I was driven into a corner.
Why did I come to Paris...? This will be the end of me.

I had brought over the lighting equipment from Japan and repeatedly tested them inside the venue. The photochromic material changed its color only slightly. The white clothes, that were supposed to turn black, refused to change. They only turned a little gray. The material, which responds to ultraviolet light, worked perfectly when I tested them in Tokyo. Perhaps because of the difference in voltage in Tokyo and Paris, the amount and quality of UV light produced by the Japanese lighting equipment in Paris were different.

I only had three days until the opening of the show. In haste, I visited a large store that handled lighting equipment and purchased fifty lights. I tripled the lighting intensity at the venue. Still, the clothes did not turn black. The lights available in Paris only emitted a minimal amount of UV rays so as not to cause adverse effect on the human body.

The effect of fifty lights was still too weak. There was nothing else I could do.

The Final Rehearsal

Keisuke Kanda, the designer whom I have called my *shisho* (mentor) and whose path I had followed since I was in university, walked over to me. He had arrived in Paris three days ago to support me and had attended the final rehearsal. With an hour left before the show, no matter how we operated the lighting equipment, the main clothes of the show would only turn from white to gray.

"If they only change to gray, I don't think it's necessary to show gray clothes," I said.
"Morinaga," my mentor said. "Even if they only turn gray, why not show the audience that the colors do change?
There's no need to stop."

My mentor and I argued further.

"Morinaga, listen carefully. Did you want to make black clothes? No. You wanted to make shadows appear on clothes. Are shadows always pure black? No. Shadows can be gray."

My mentor's words woke me up.

"Even if the clothes don't turn entirely black, I can still make shadows. Shadows can be made on the clothes by arranging how we light the models. If the models stand so that their bodies overlap in front of the light, shadows would appear on the clothes of the model standing behind. The title of the show is *Shadow*."

I had solidified my idea.

The show was meant to present shadows, not black. We changed the direction of the show from black to shadow. We had less than an hour. The model rehearsal began.

Four pieces of lighting equipment were placed in the center of the rectangular stage. At the center of the stage was a space that measured 1.8 meters in radius, and we illuminated only that part from four sides.

Two models took their positions in the designated space and were irradiated with intense light. It was the final test. The white coat gradually turned gray. I got goosebumps all over me while watching it. The staff who didn't know about the photochromic material marveled at the sight. *Why do the clothes change colors when they enter that space? What happened?*

I thought this could be an amazing show. My mentor stayed by my side. Still, my anxiety did not completely disappear.

Wearing a Shadow

With a twenty-minute delay, the Anrealage show that marked the first day of Paris Fashion Week began.

Models wearing asymmetric jackets and coats in black and white took turns walking across the rectangular stage. There were twelve models in total. The audience must have thought it was a boring show of black and white.

Halfway through the show, two models in white coats paused at the center of the stage.

The models stood back to back, with one looking forward and the other looking backward.

They didn't move a muscle.

For fifty seconds, the venue was filled with silence. Boredom began to show on the audience's faces.

The models began to walk forward and backward.

Shadows appeared on their white coat and jacket.

Aside from the part where the models' hands had blocked the light, the entire garment had turned gray. Except for the parts where the models' bodies had overlapped, everything appeared ashen. The audience could clearly see that the white hue was supposed to represent a shadow.

The venue exploded in applause.

A finger whistle resonated in the space.

I listened to it all from backstage. It is very unusual to hear applause and finger whistles during a fashion show.

I thought something great had happened. The show was only halfway through.

Models wearing an overdress with lace-like cutouts took off their dress after being exposed to intense light. The white dress underneath had changed to gray in the pattern of the cutouts.

Another applause.

In the end, a laser projector beamed UV light on a white dress.

Two minutes and twenty seconds. The two models didn't move. This time, the audience wasn't bored. There was only an increasing expectation.

The finale.

A gray patchwork pattern surfaced on the two models' dresses.

Applause and whistling. Ten models wearing black dresses walked around the stage.

Someone shouted bravo.

Some of the models were crying as they returned backstage. Staff members collapsed, out of breath.

Everyone said, "It was a great show."

I couldn't help crying.

The fifteen minutes and thirty seconds of my Paris debut ended this way.

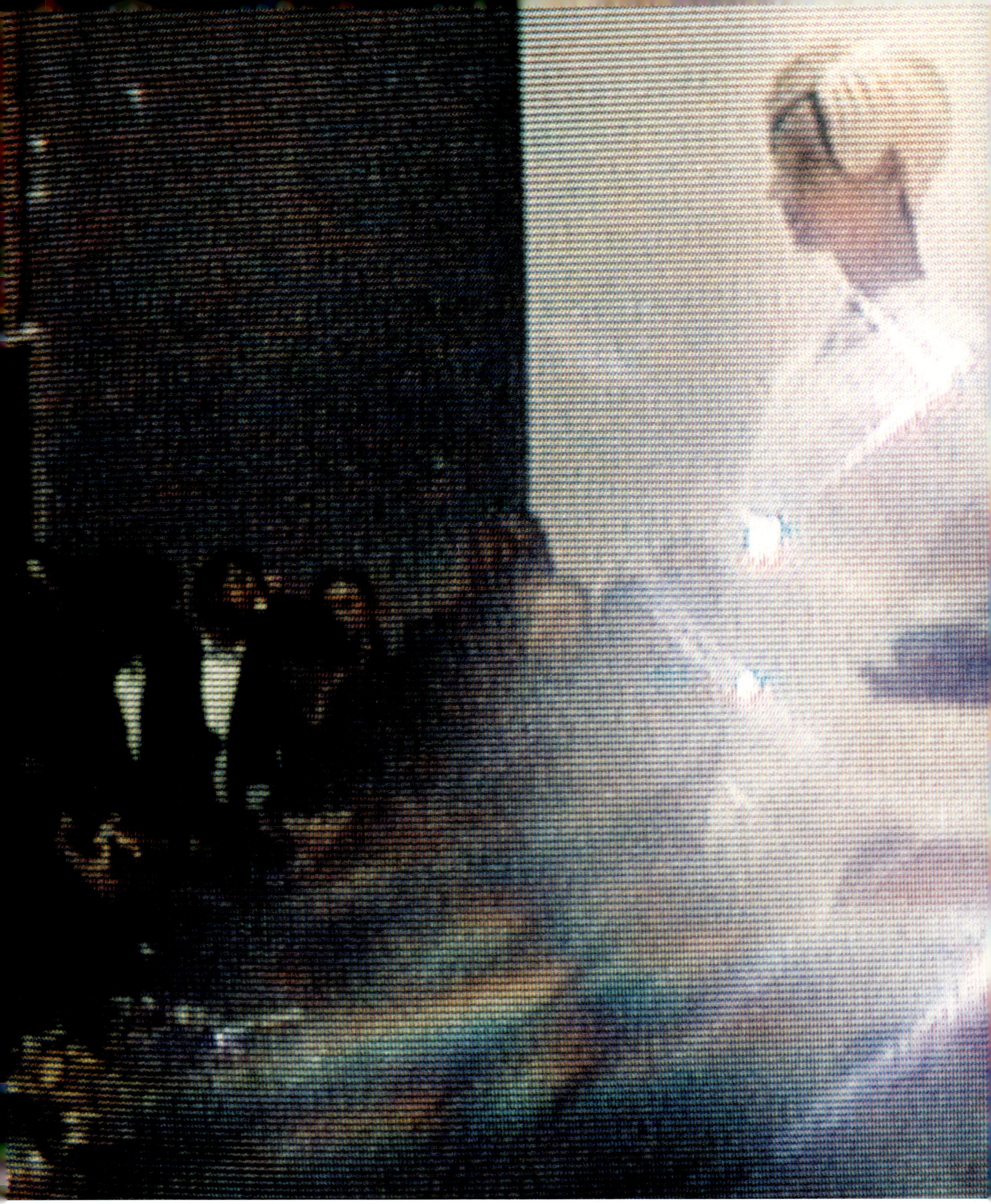

Shadow the light, light the shadow

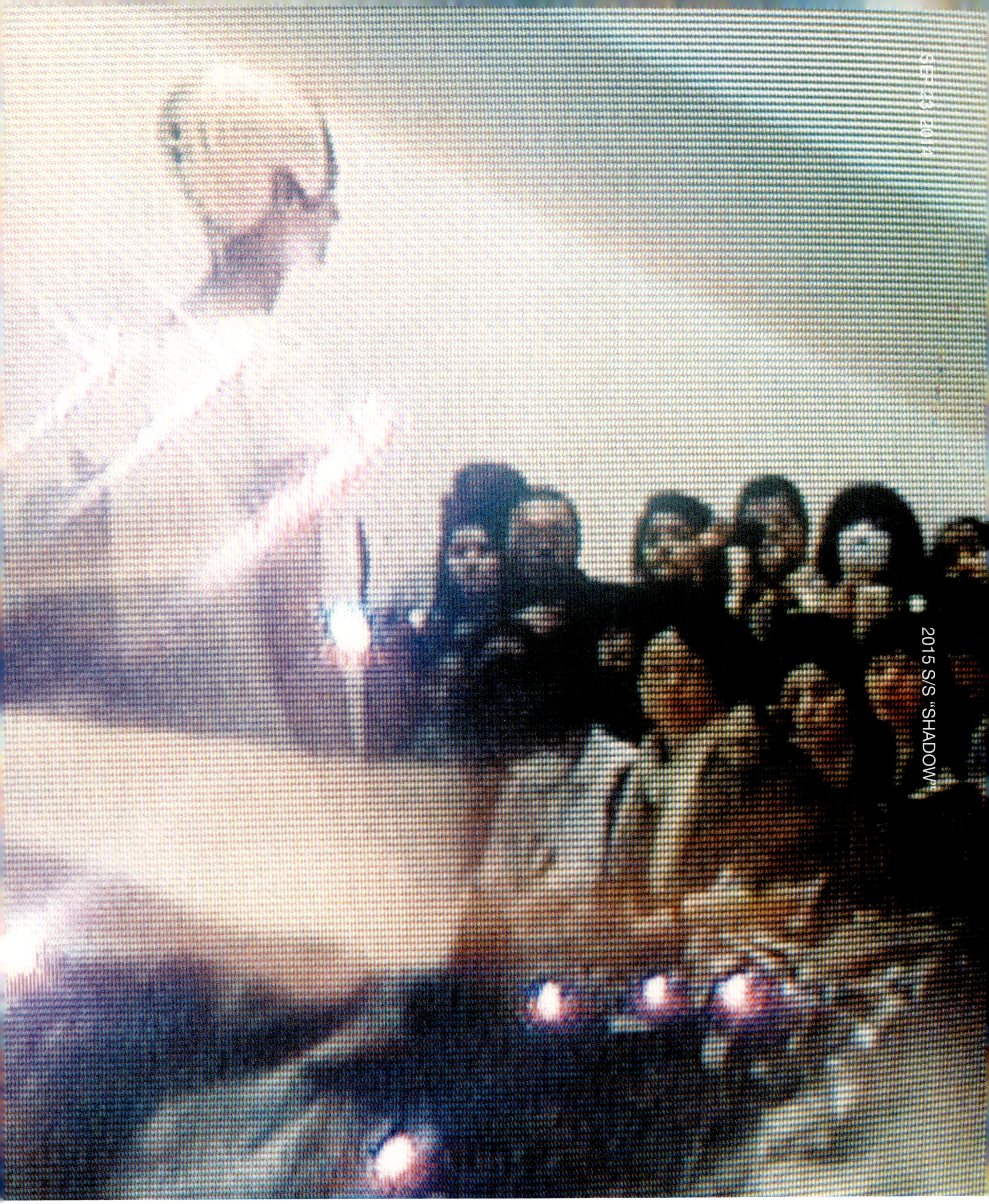
SEP 23 2014

2015 S/S "SHADOW"

light [noun] (BRIGHTNESS)

the brightness that comes from the sun, fire,
etc. and from electrical devices, and
that allows things to be seen:
a piece of equipment that produces light,
such as a lamp or a bulb

light [noun] (FLAME)

a light
something that will produce a flame and
cause burning, such as a match or a
cigarette lighter

shadow [noun] (DARKNESS)

an area of darkness, caused by light being
blocked by something

1

LIGHT / SHADOW

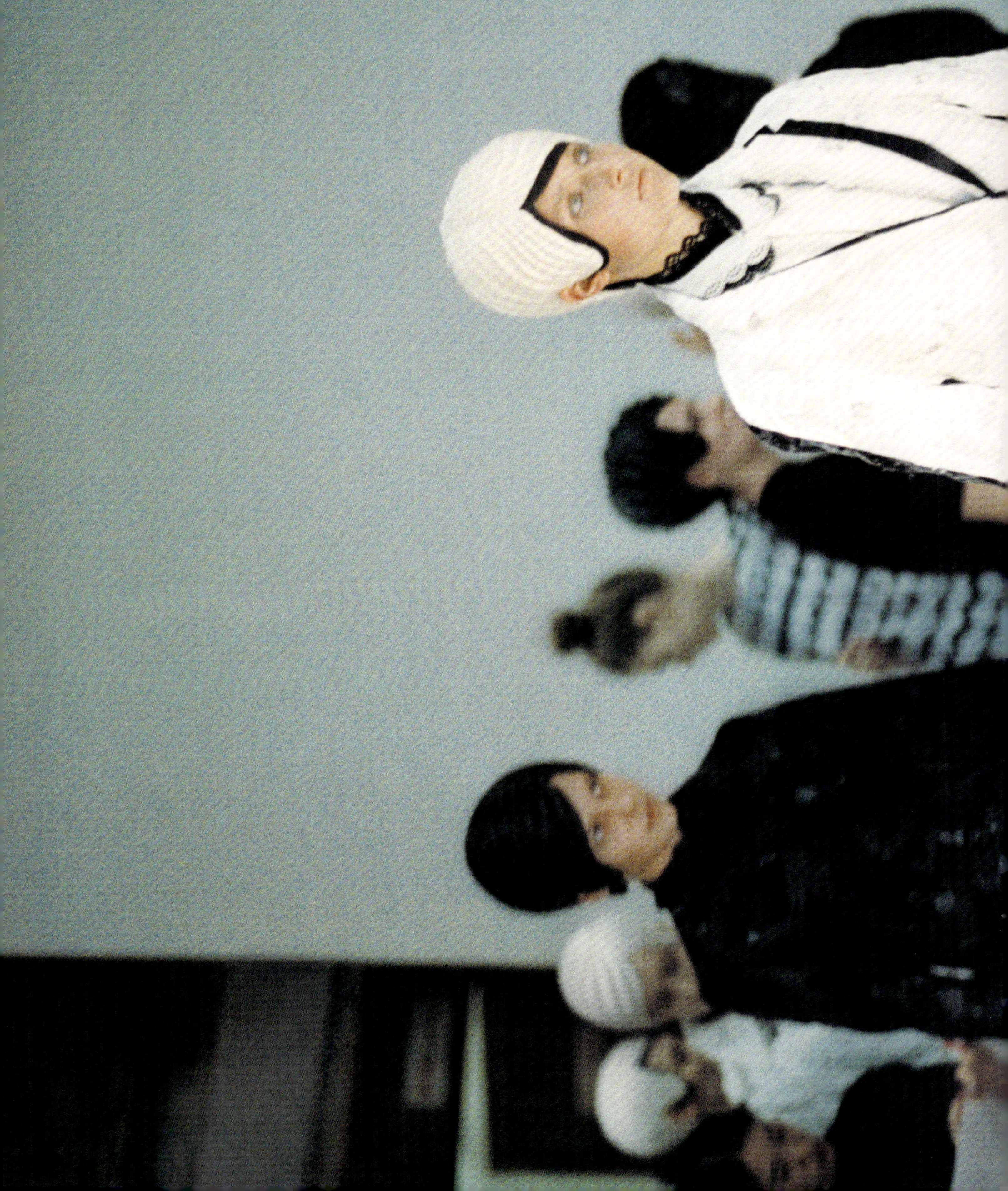

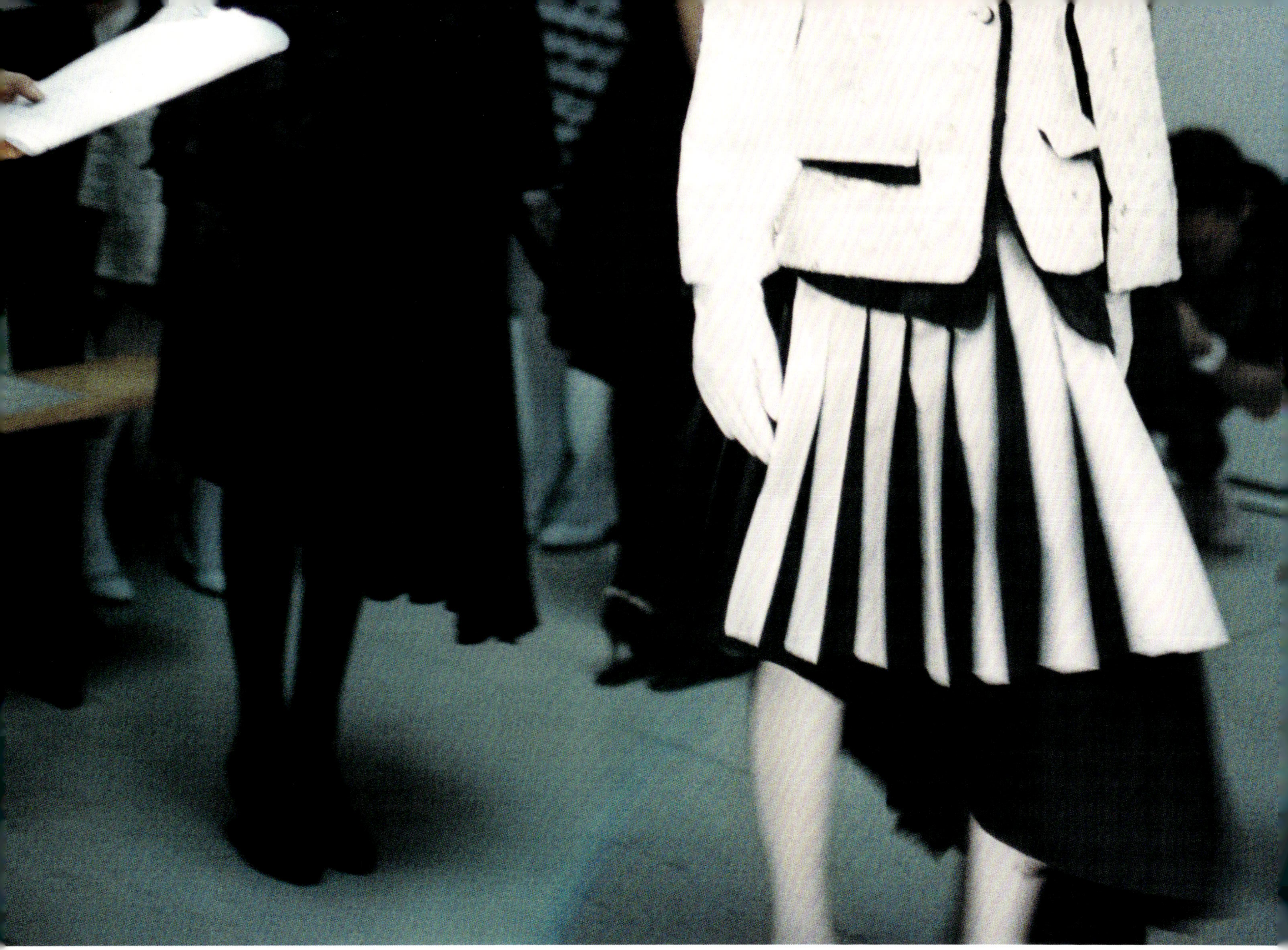

Shadows are always falling on clothes

SEP 26, 2014

2015 S/S “SHADOW”

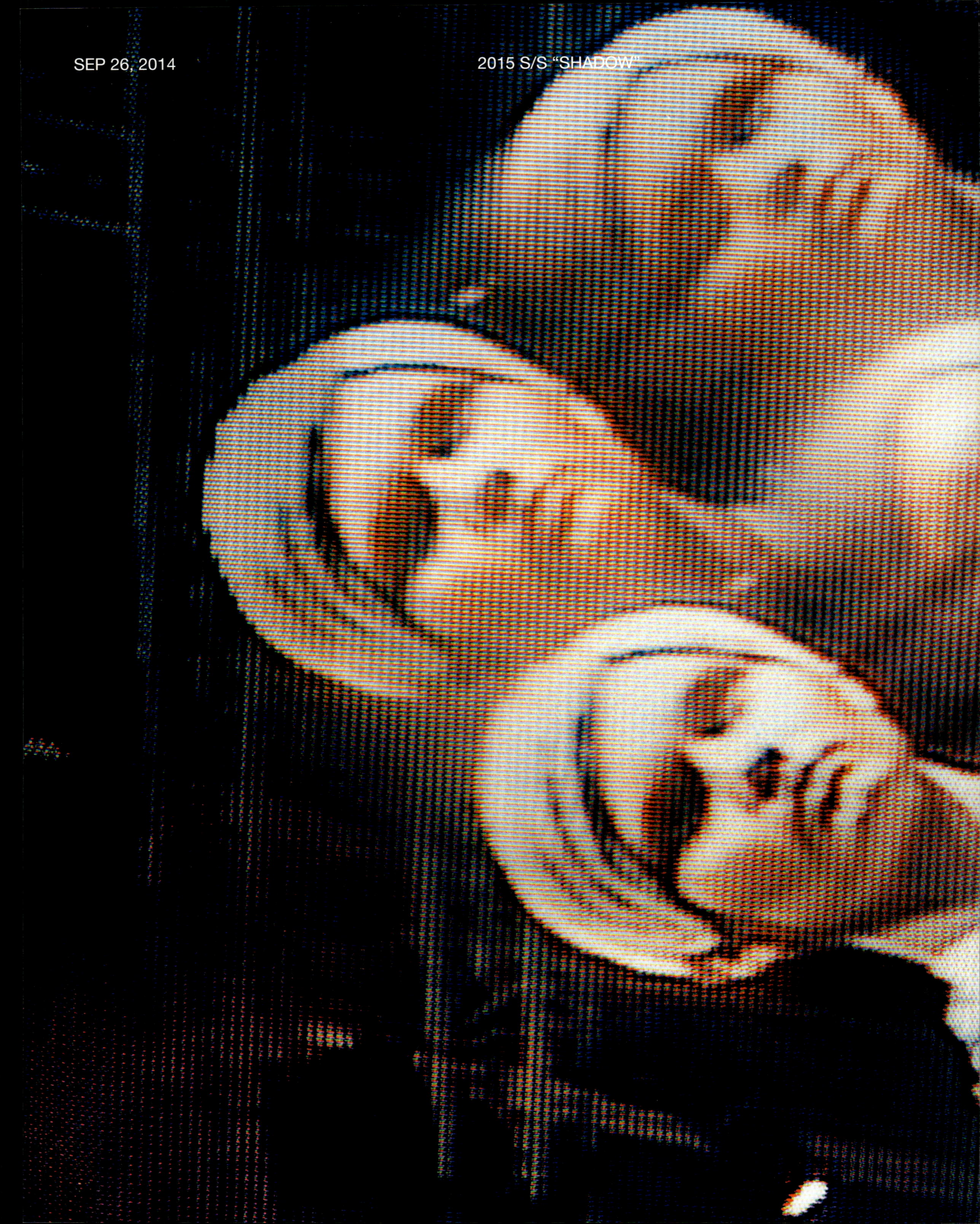

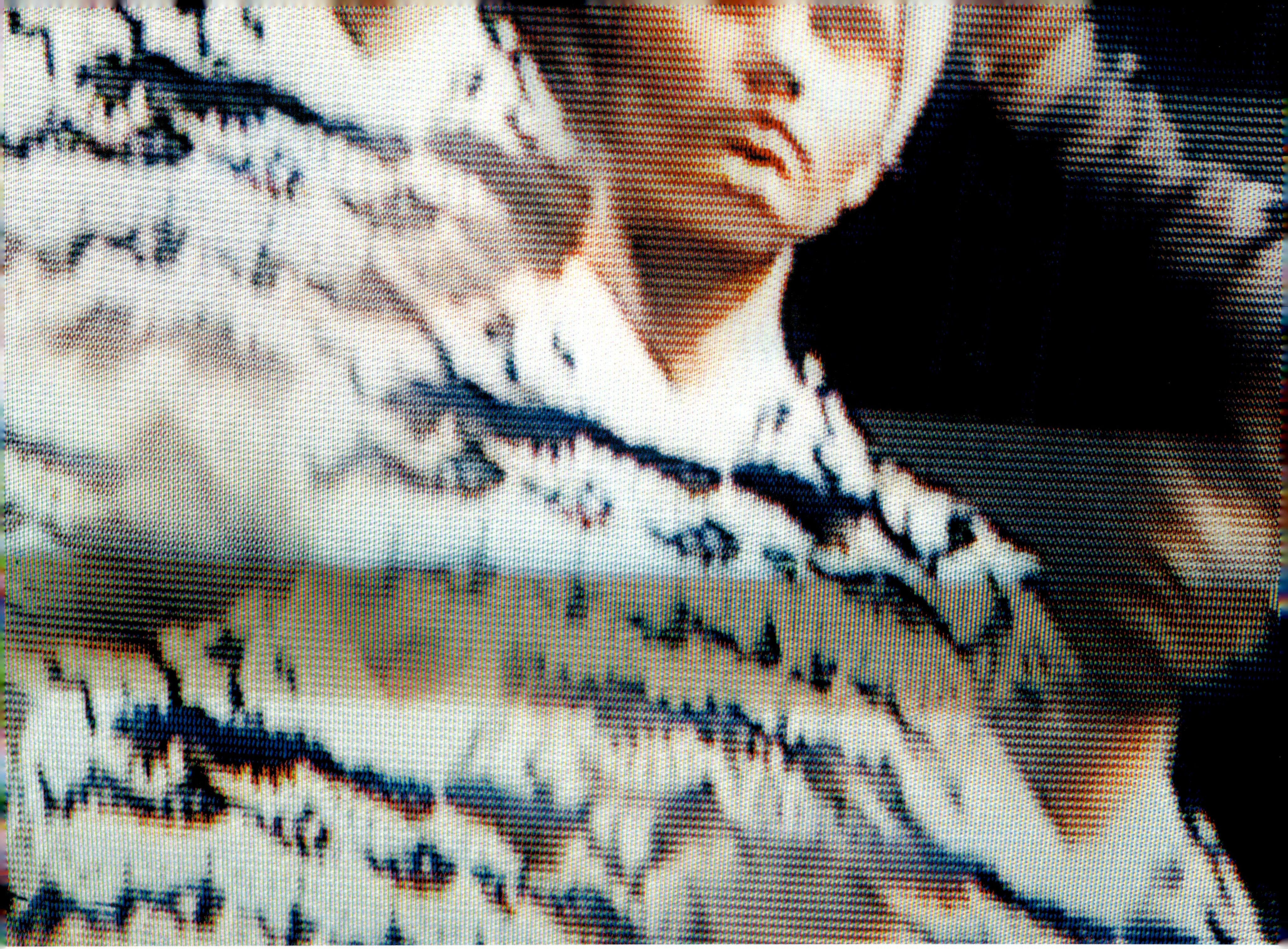

What if we could capture them?

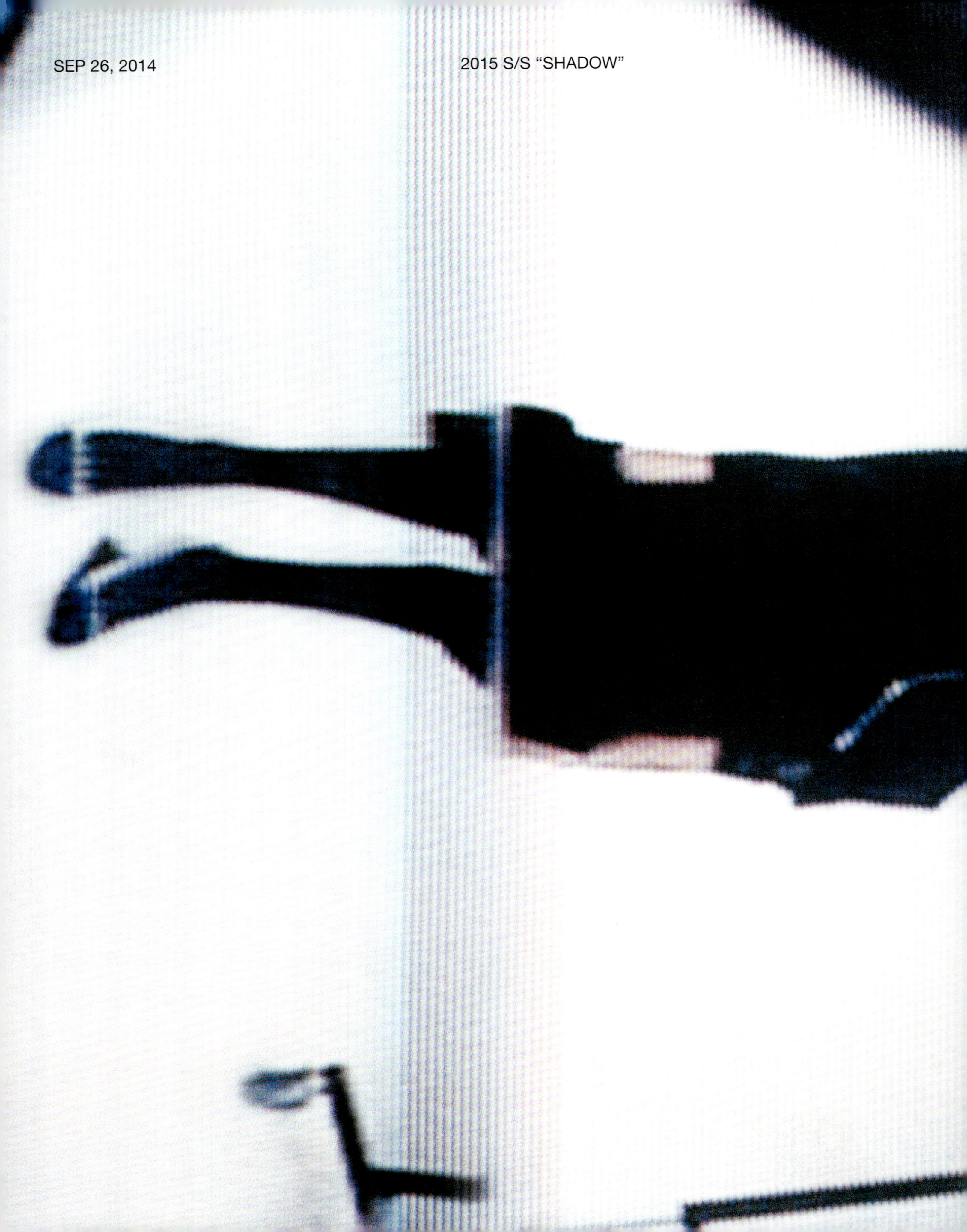

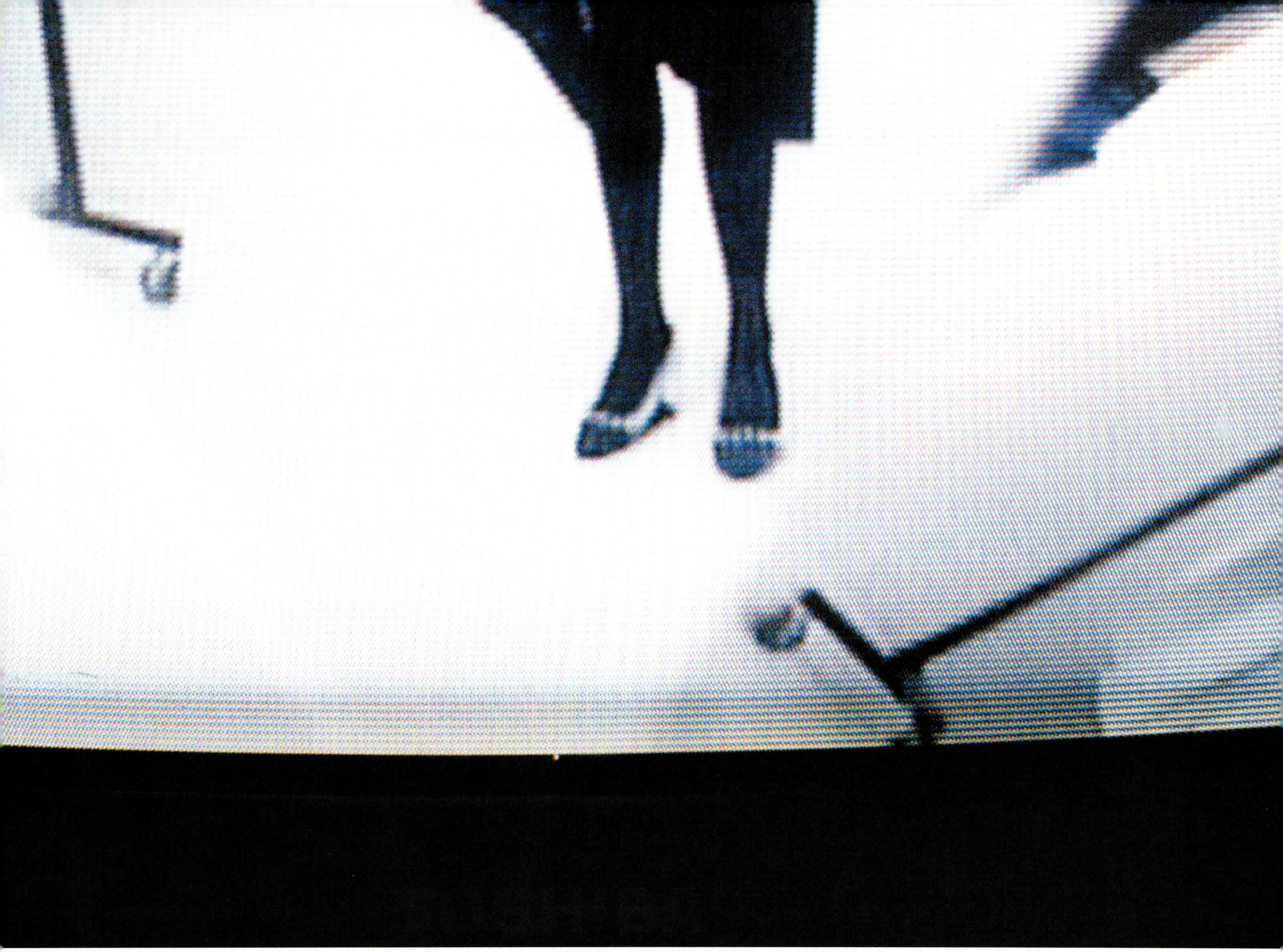

When the person next to you moves...

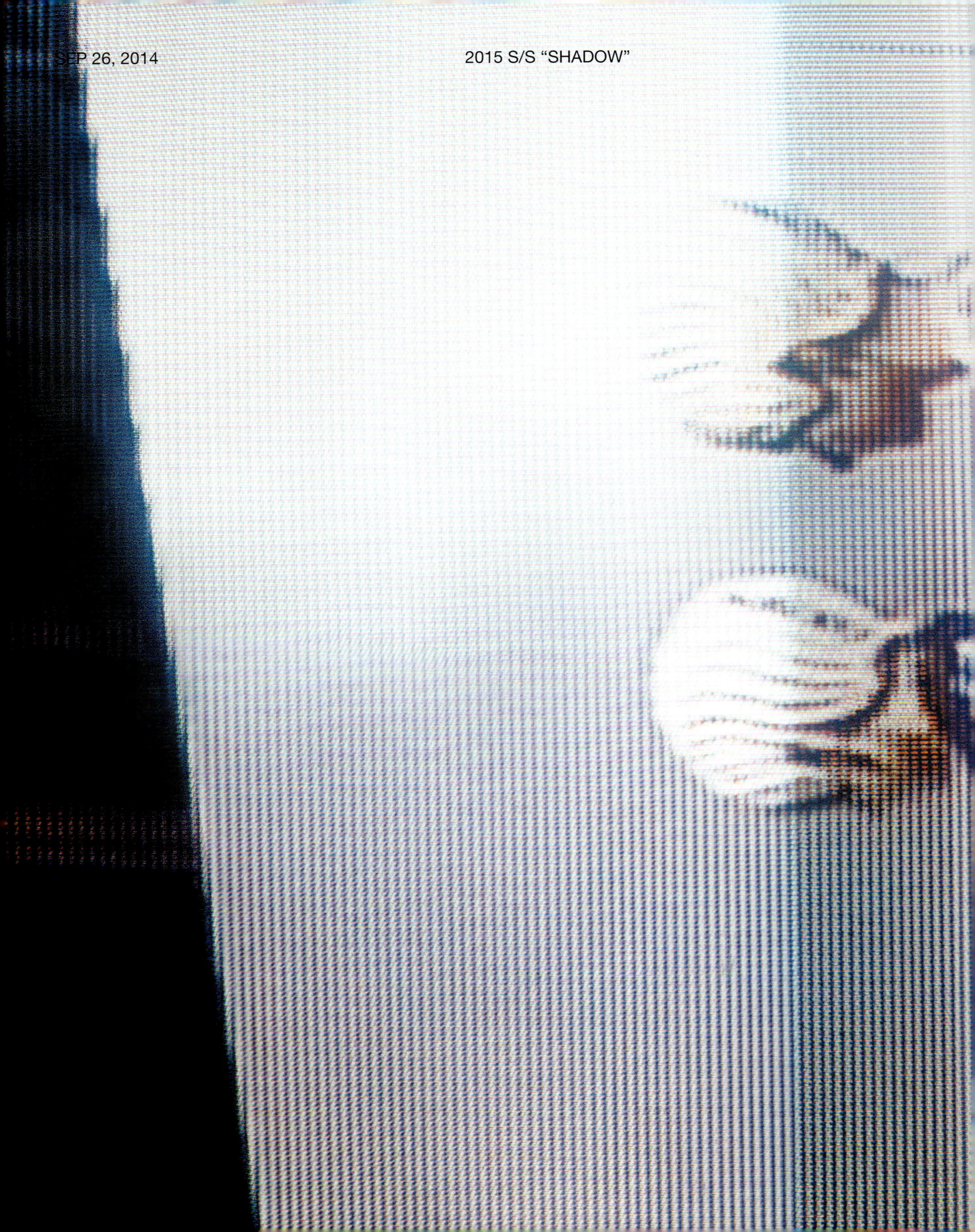

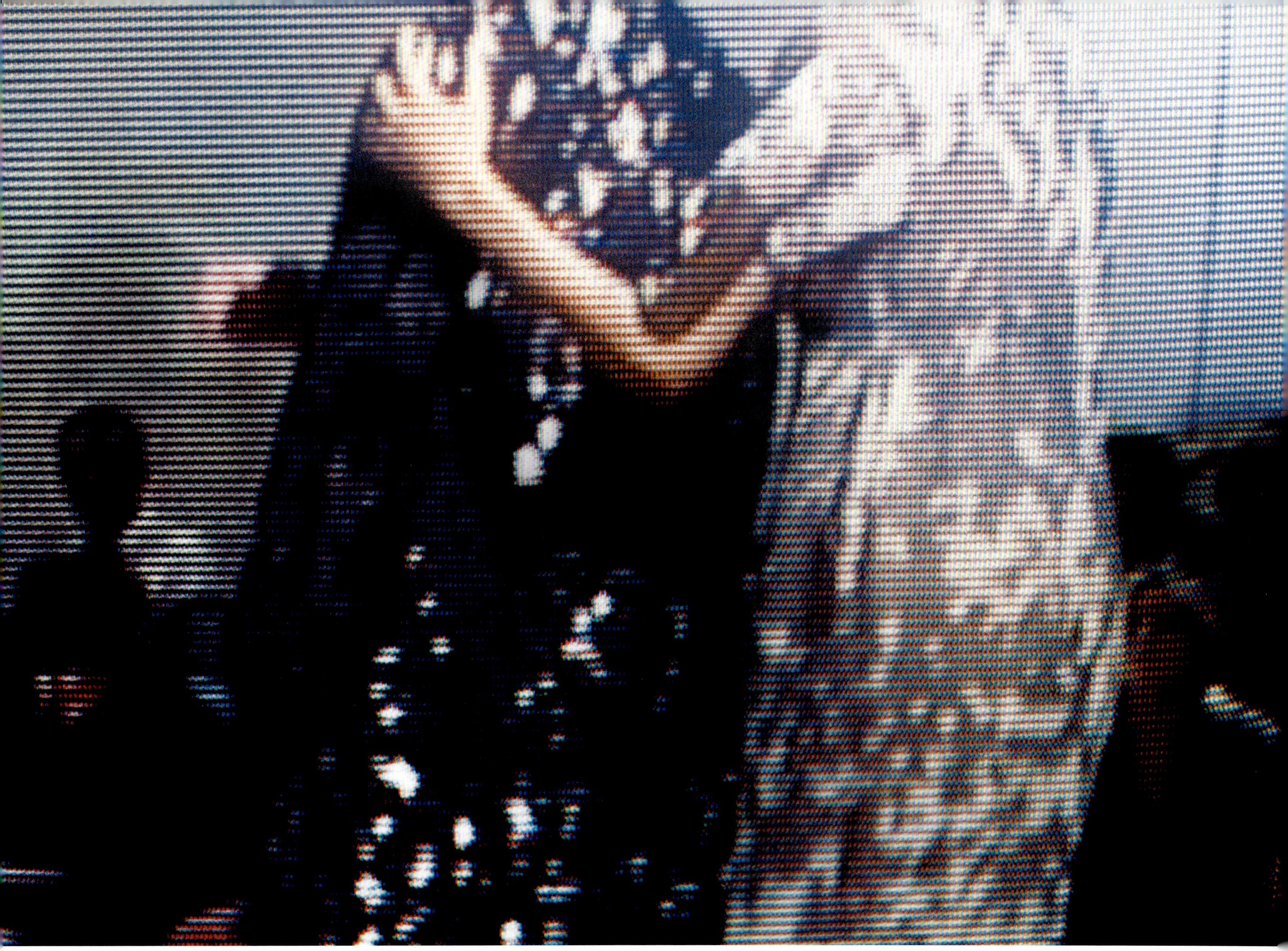

...what if just the shadow remains?

SEP 29, 2015

2016 S/S "REFLECT"

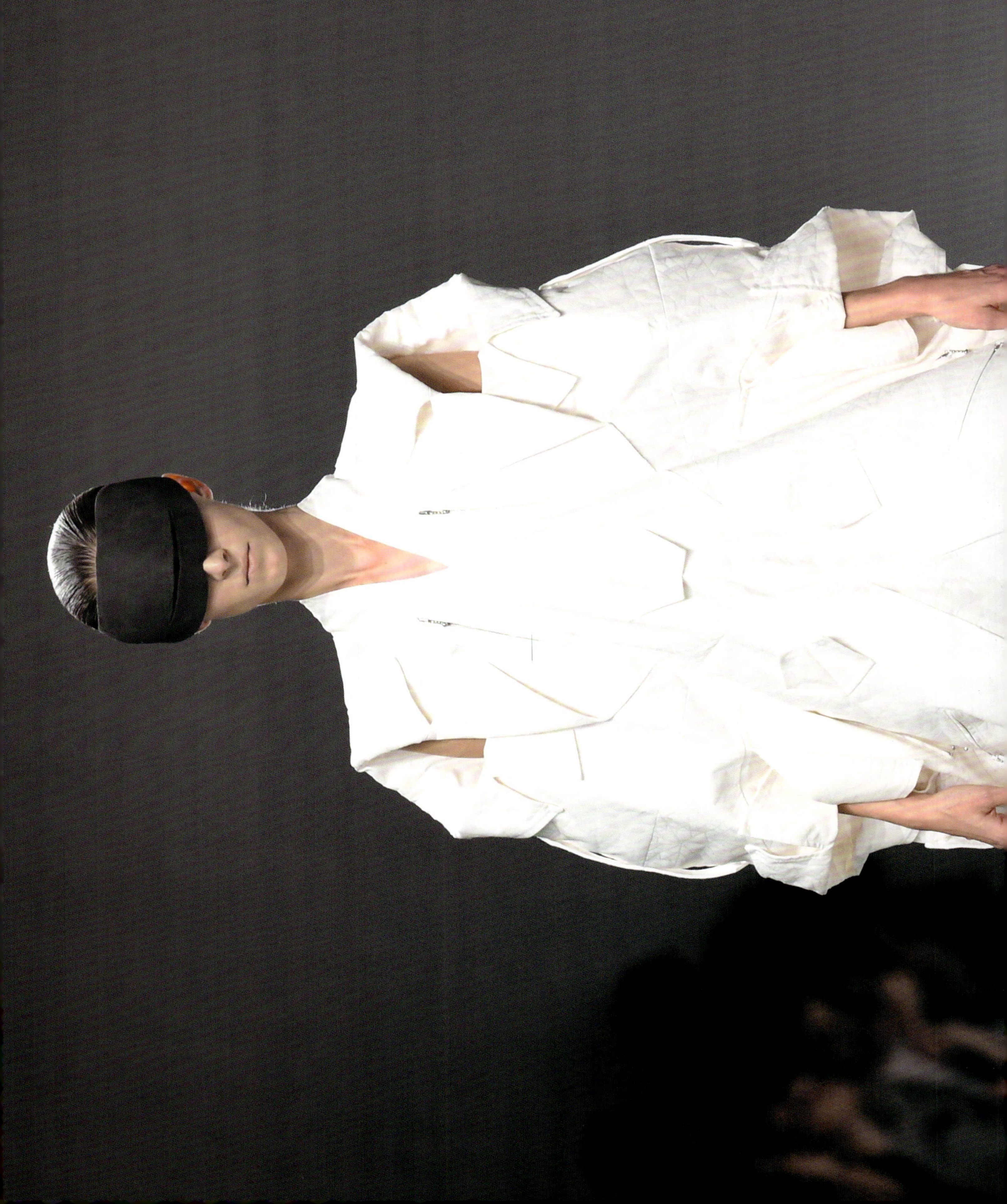

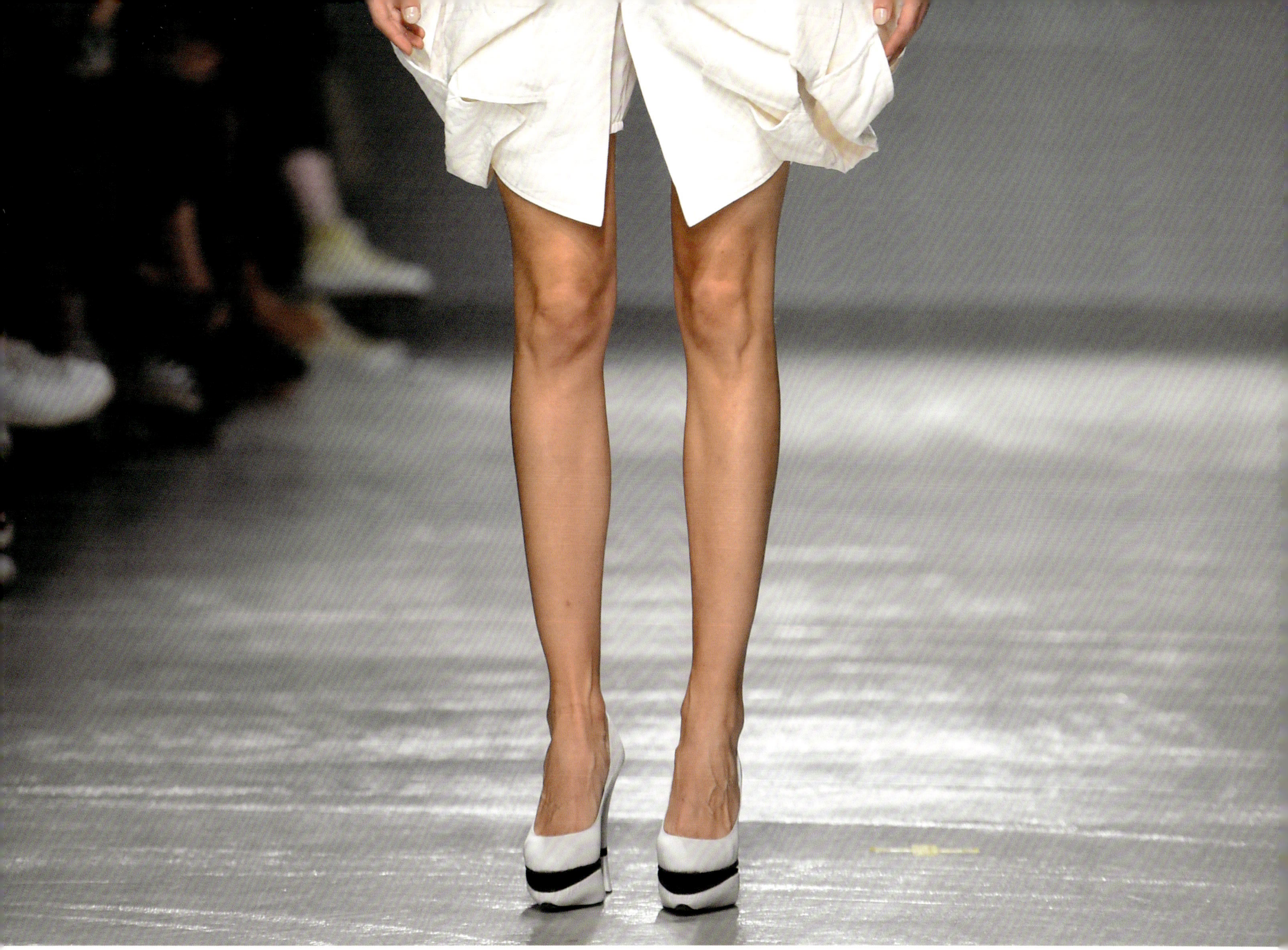

Reflect light, it gives a new light

SEP 29, 2015

2016 S/S “REFLECT”

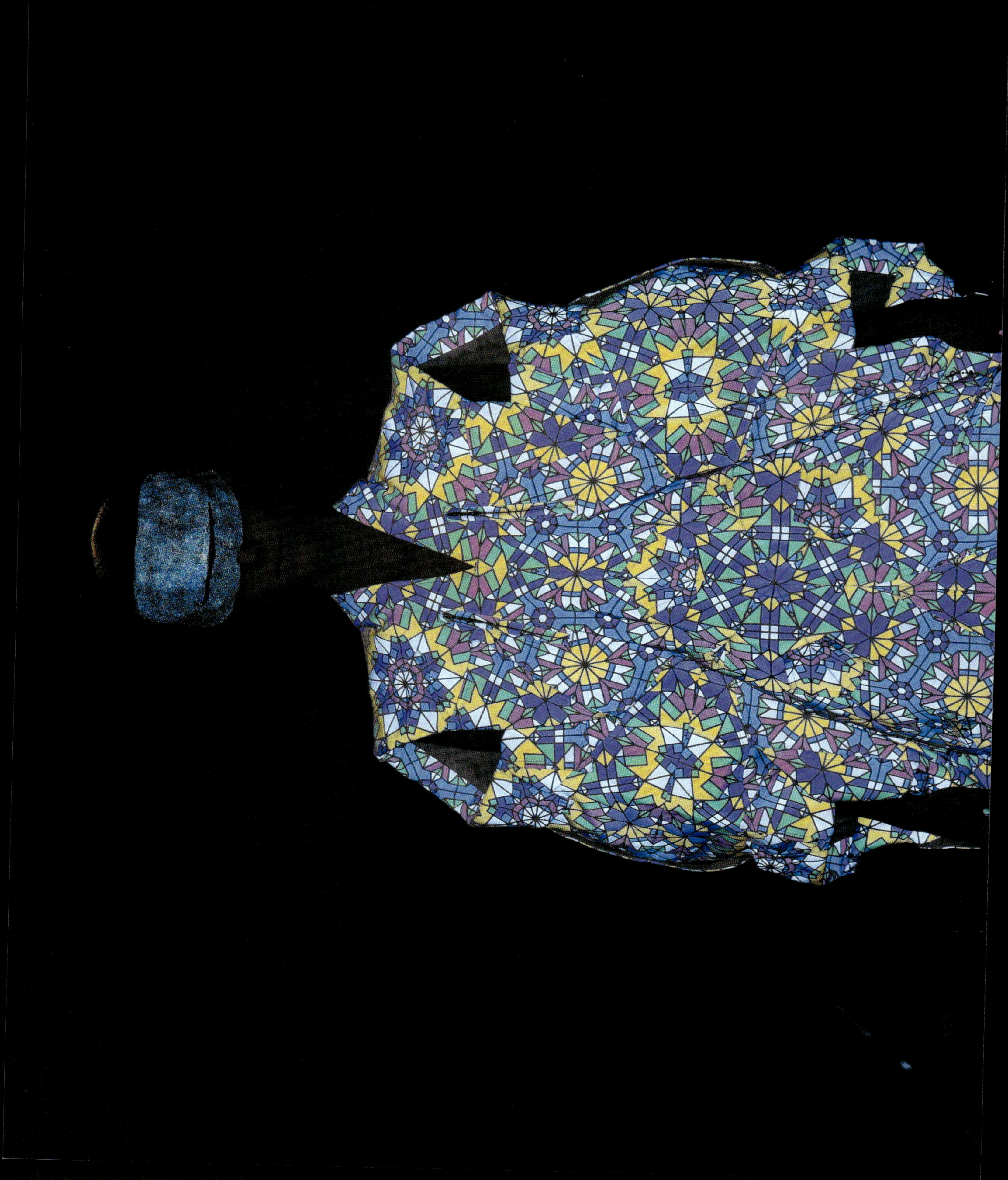

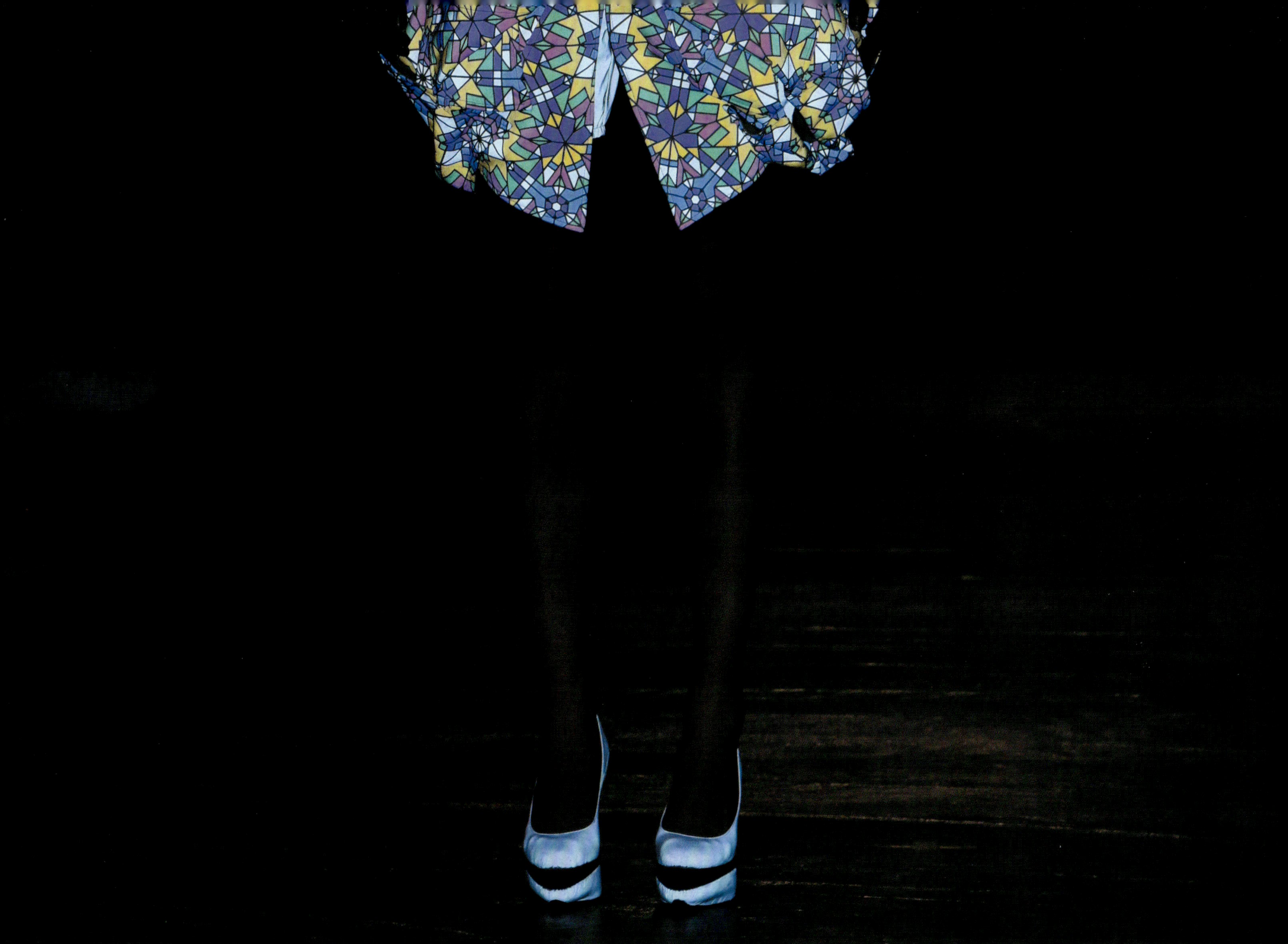

Reflect reality, and it makes a new reality

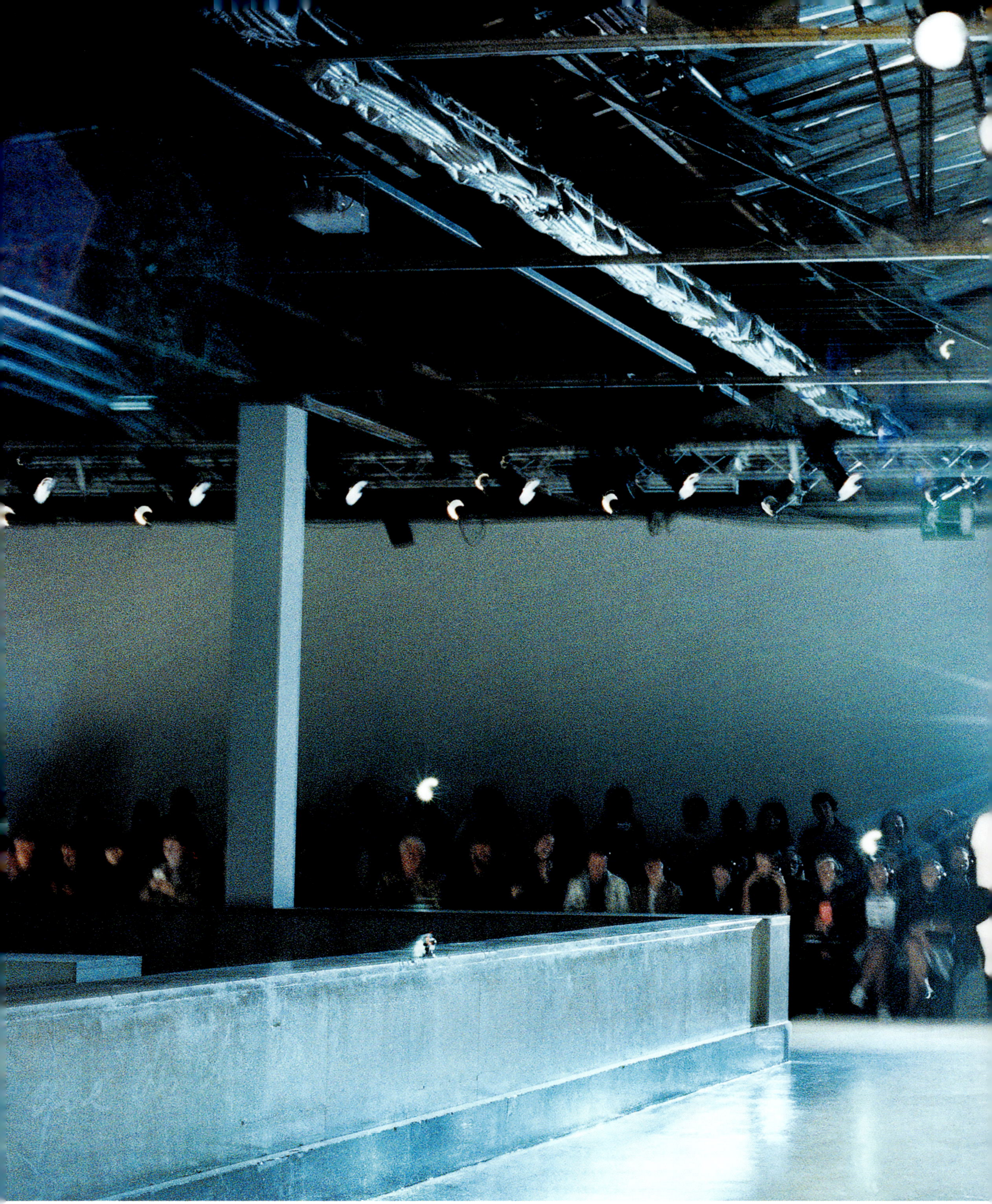

Wearing a dress with a hidden pattern r

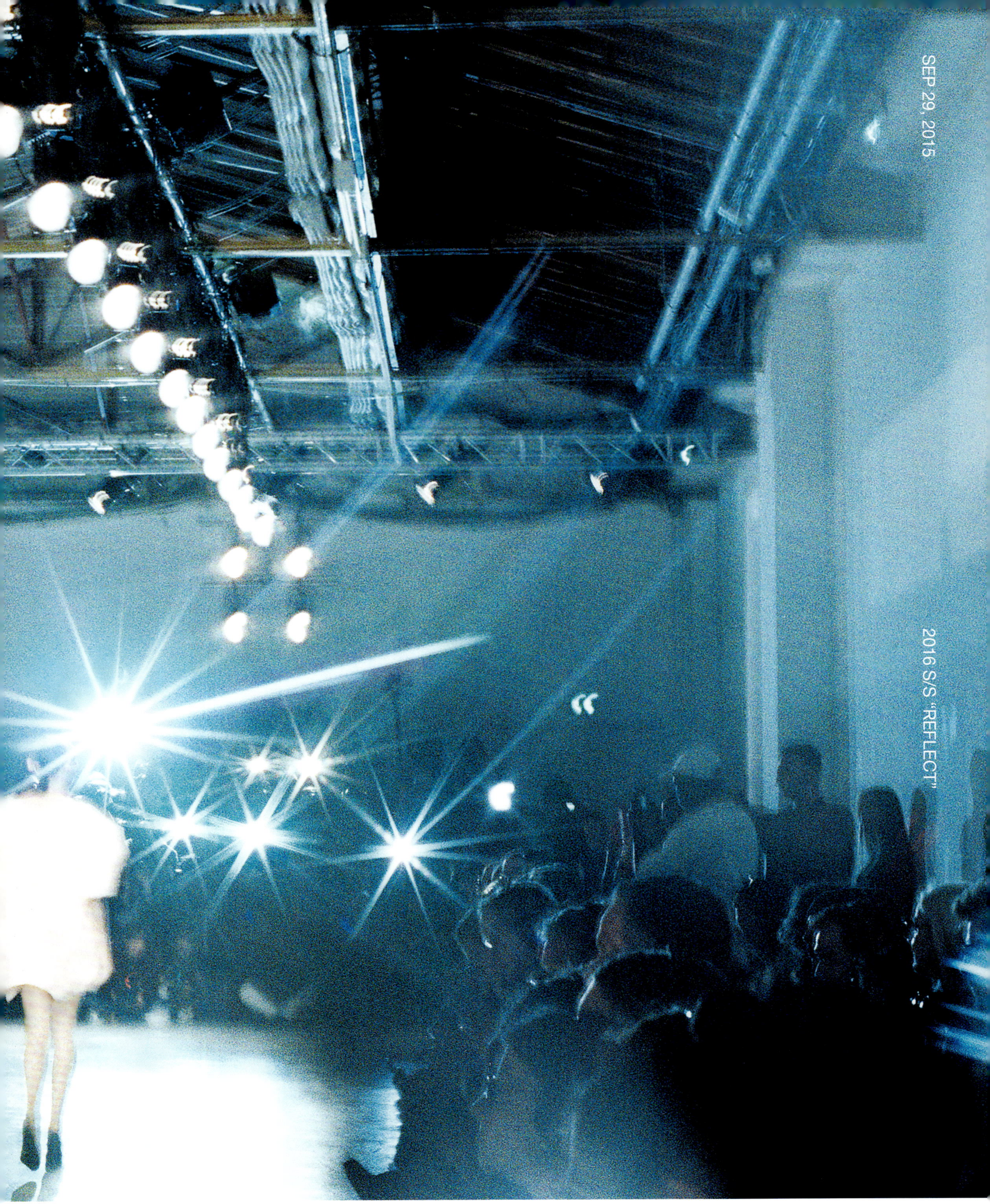

ay evoke a very different feeling

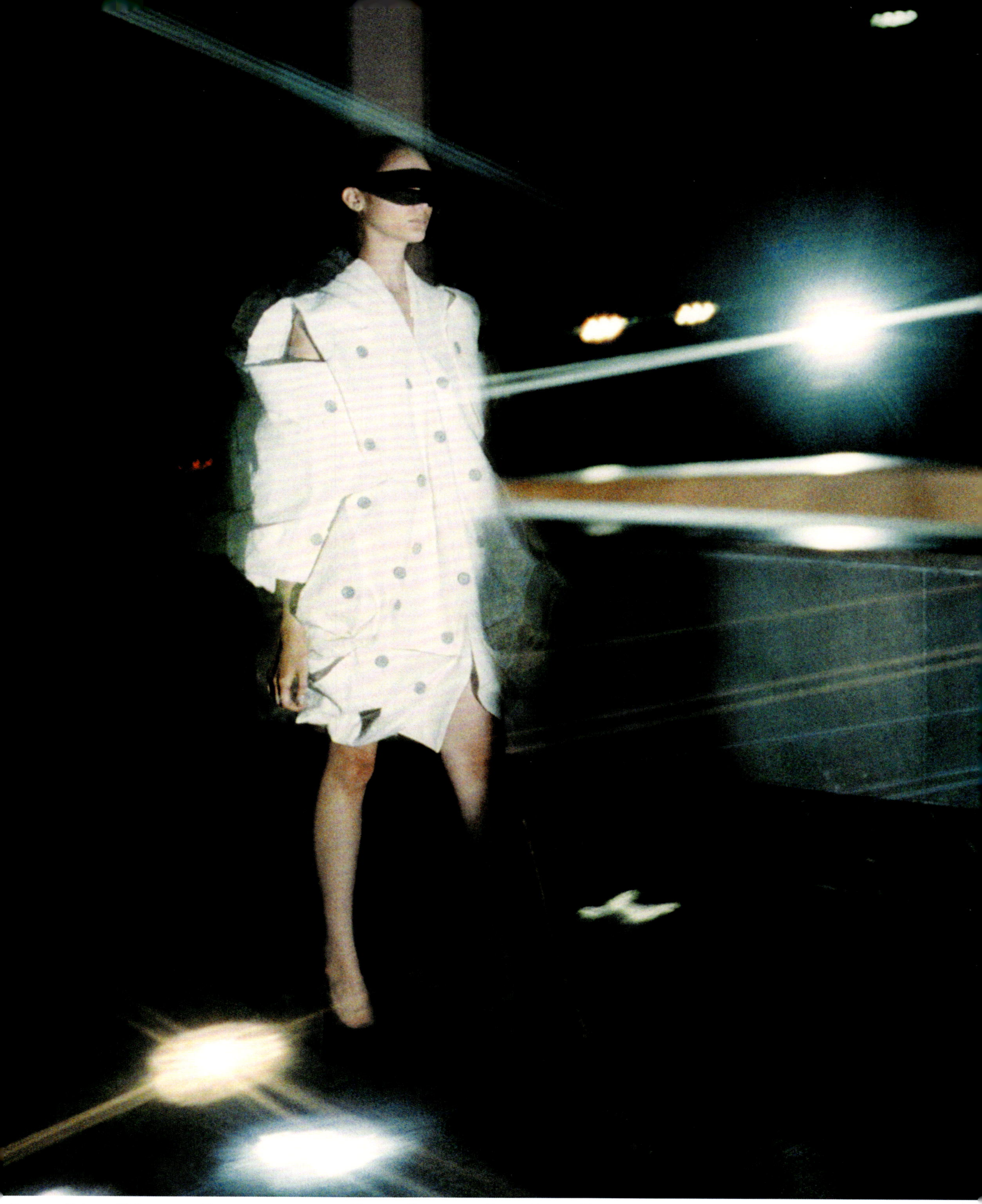

Is it flashy, or is it plain?

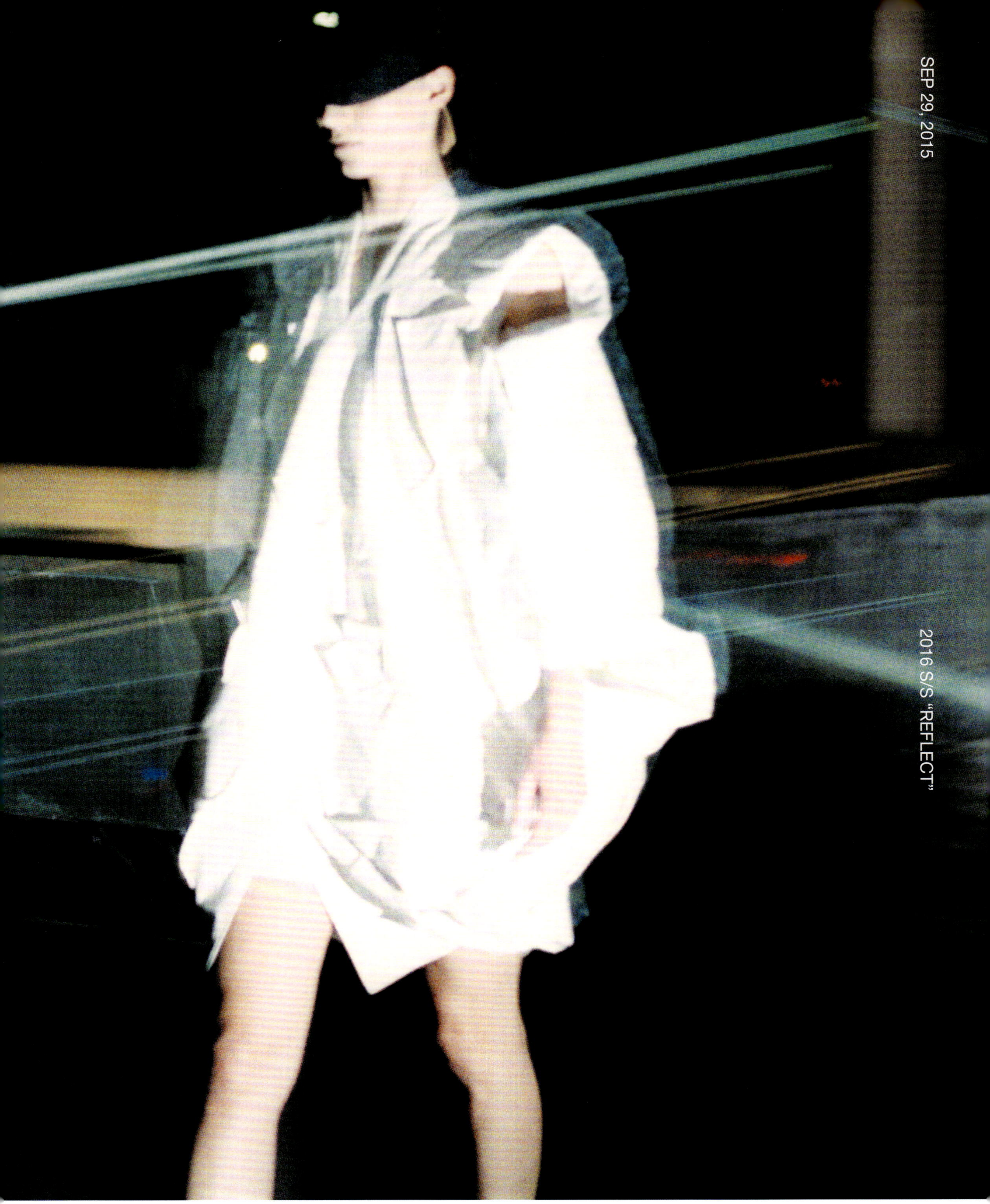

SEP 29, 2015

2016 S/S "REFLECT"

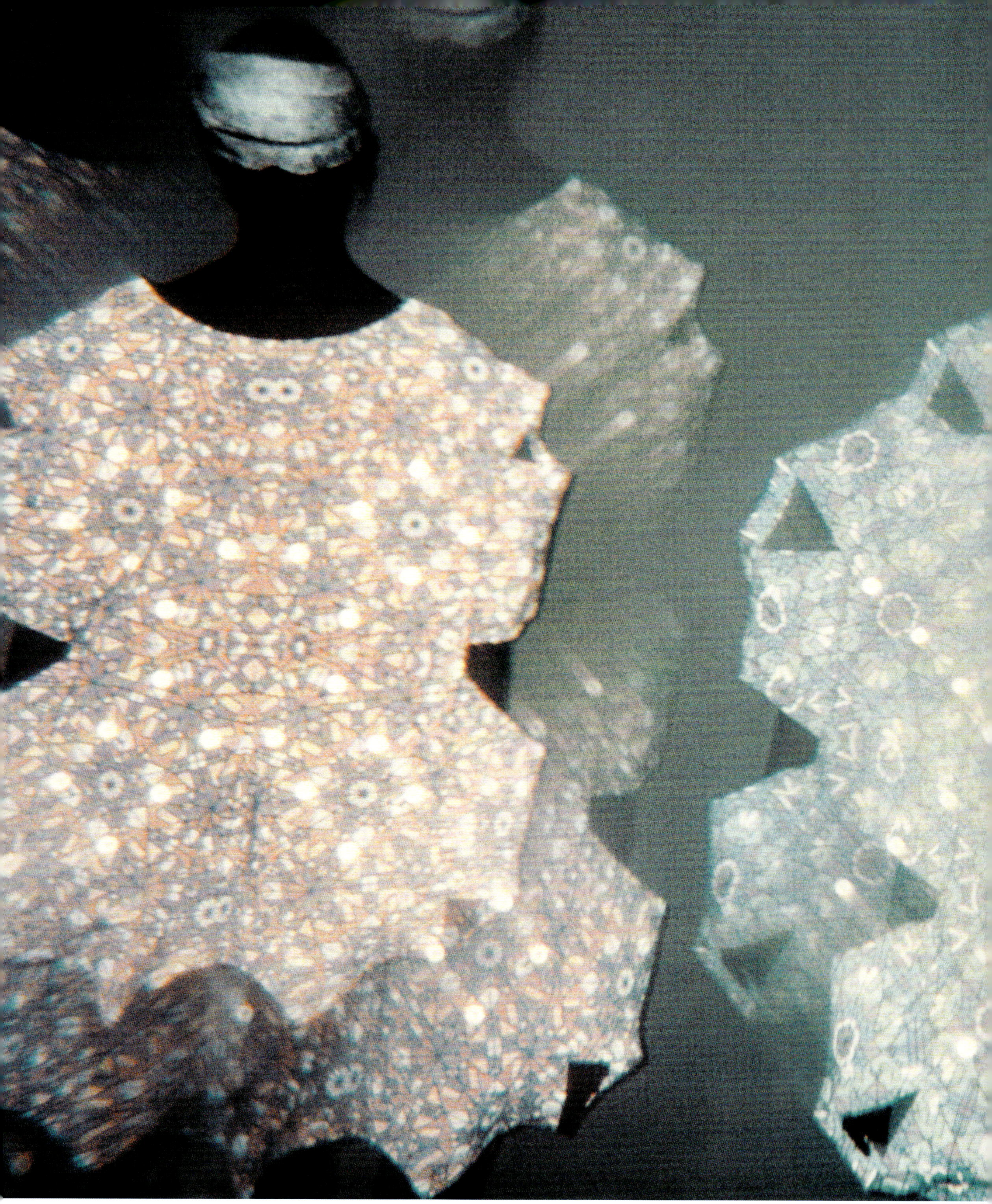

It is as if we are questioning the meanir

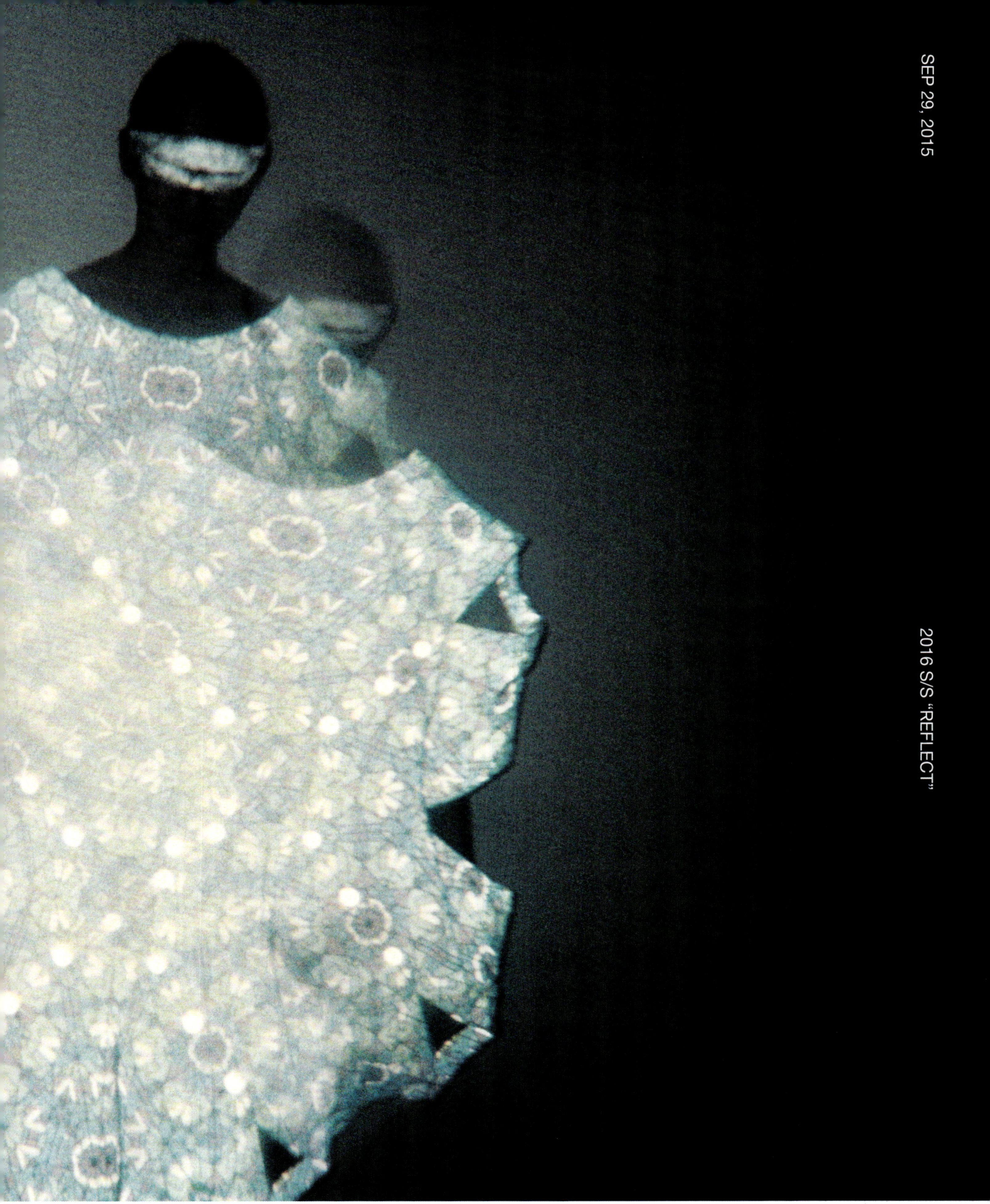

SEP 29, 2015

2016 S/S "REFLECT"

g of fashion

SEP 29, 2015 2016 S/S "REFLECT"

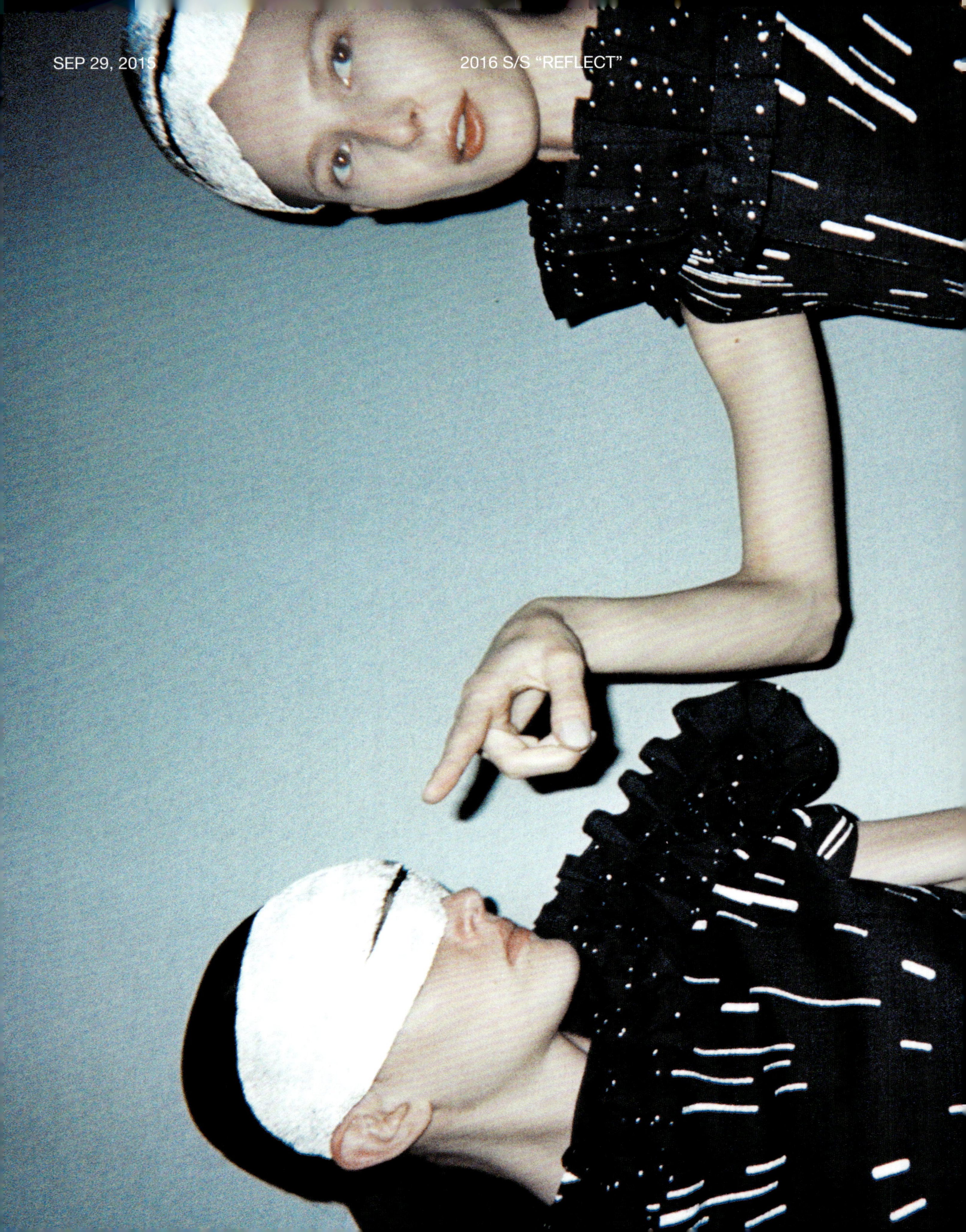

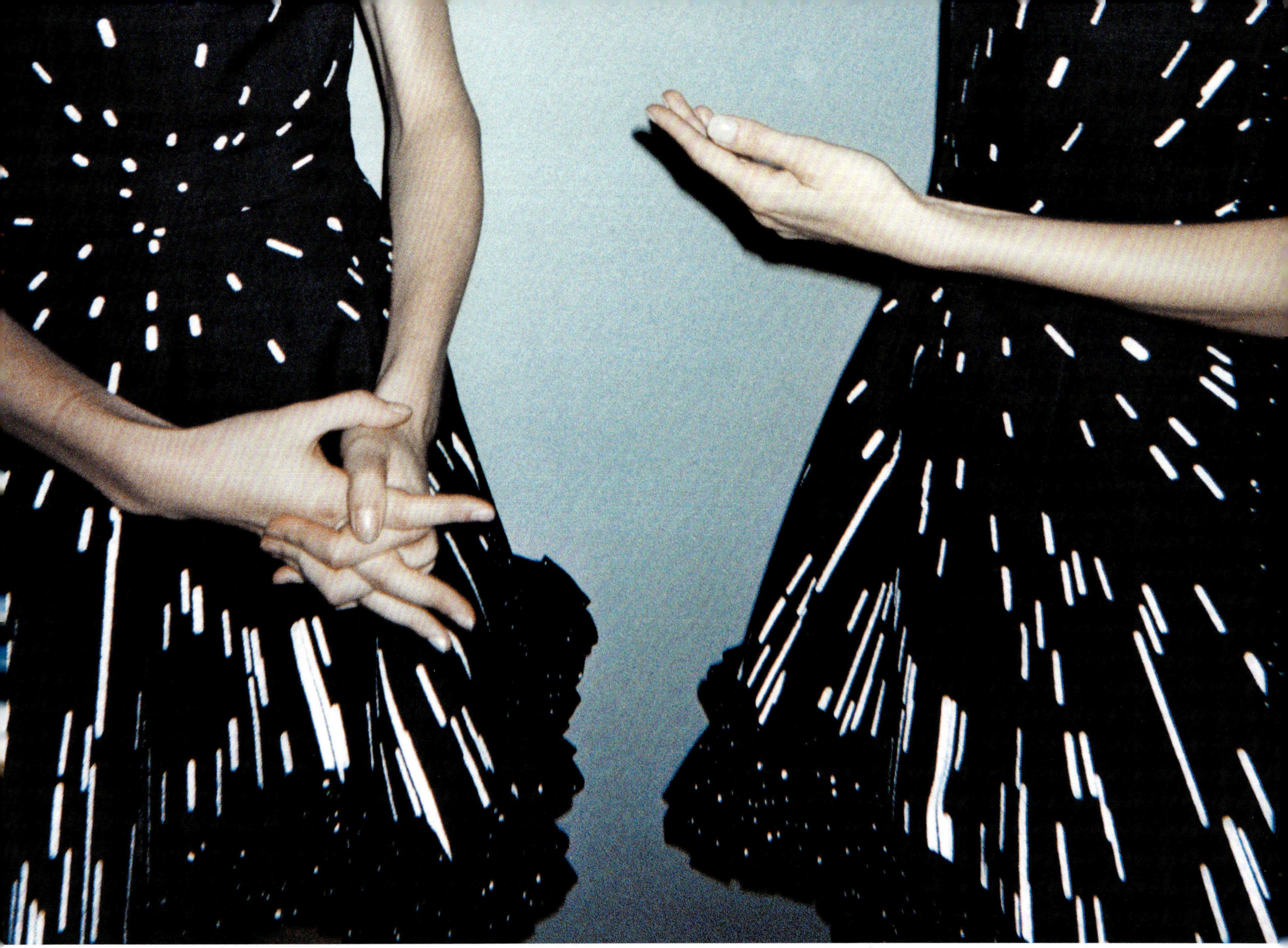

It opens a different door in daily life

Tokyo Tower

In Tatters

The day left me in tatters.
I was 25 years old, getting yelled at inside the office of the Tokyo Tower, where they told me that the police would be called.

If someone were to ask me when I had been yelled at the most, I would, without hesitation, answer November 14, 2005, the evening of my Tokyo Fashion Week show.

"There were camera flashes all over the observation deck. What if it had caused trouble for the airplanes flying above?"
"Do you even realize that you could have caused a life-or-death accident?"

Before I knew it, I was in tears.
I continued to apologize inside the office, enduring it all.
I wondered if they were going to keep yelling at me like this for the rest of my life. Just when I had resolved that I had no choice but to accept my fate, I was released.
I quickly took the elevator up to the observation deck that had doubled as a venue for my show. Regrettably, the show was already finished. The only thing I heard was the audience's applause.

I was in tatters.
The reason I was reprimanded was because I had used Tokyo Tower as a venue for my fashion show without permission. For the

employees working at Tokyo Tower, my first joint show with my *shisho* (mentor), Keisuke Kanda, was like a sneak attack. For me and Kanda-san, who was 29 years old at the time, it was a guerrilla war that we had risked our lives on. There was no way for the two sides to see eye-to-eye.

Anger

I was completely aware that I had made a mistake.
From the standpoint of the police and public security, there was no way for a guerrilla show that would attract a huge crowd would be permitted. In the end, the show had drawn an audience of over a thousand.

Kanda-san's show, which went after mine, presented what appeared to be clothes but revealed themselves to be elaborately decorated collection of lingerie.
This only added fuel to the Tokyo Tower employees' anger.

We couldn't justify what we did.
The show was set to begin at 7 p.m. for the general public, then at 9 p.m. for the members of the press and buyers. Once everything ended, Kanda-san and I were taken to the office where the employees yelled at us.

When they told us that the police would be called, we got on our knees and hands and begged for forgiveness. It was the first time I had ever kneeled in supplication. I didn't feel any pain or numbness in my legs.

We were yelled at for what felt like a very long time. The clock ticked past midnight. Like me, my mentor was also left in tatters.

I didn't feel miserable though. The audience told me one by one that the show was wonderful and amazing; this gave me a sense of accomplishment. The show had finished without any incident, and no complaints came from the general visitors to the tower. There was a part of me that felt relief.

Darkness and Light

I had assigned the first floor of Tokyo Tower as the backstage and was putting the clothes back on the rack. I was preparing to leave. I didn't want to spend another second there.

"Let me see the clothes."

A man approached us backstage. When he asked again to see the clothes, we declined. Suddenly, the man became enraged. He shattered a window in anger. Tension ran through the floor. He caught us completely off guard.

2006 S/S "BUTTER"

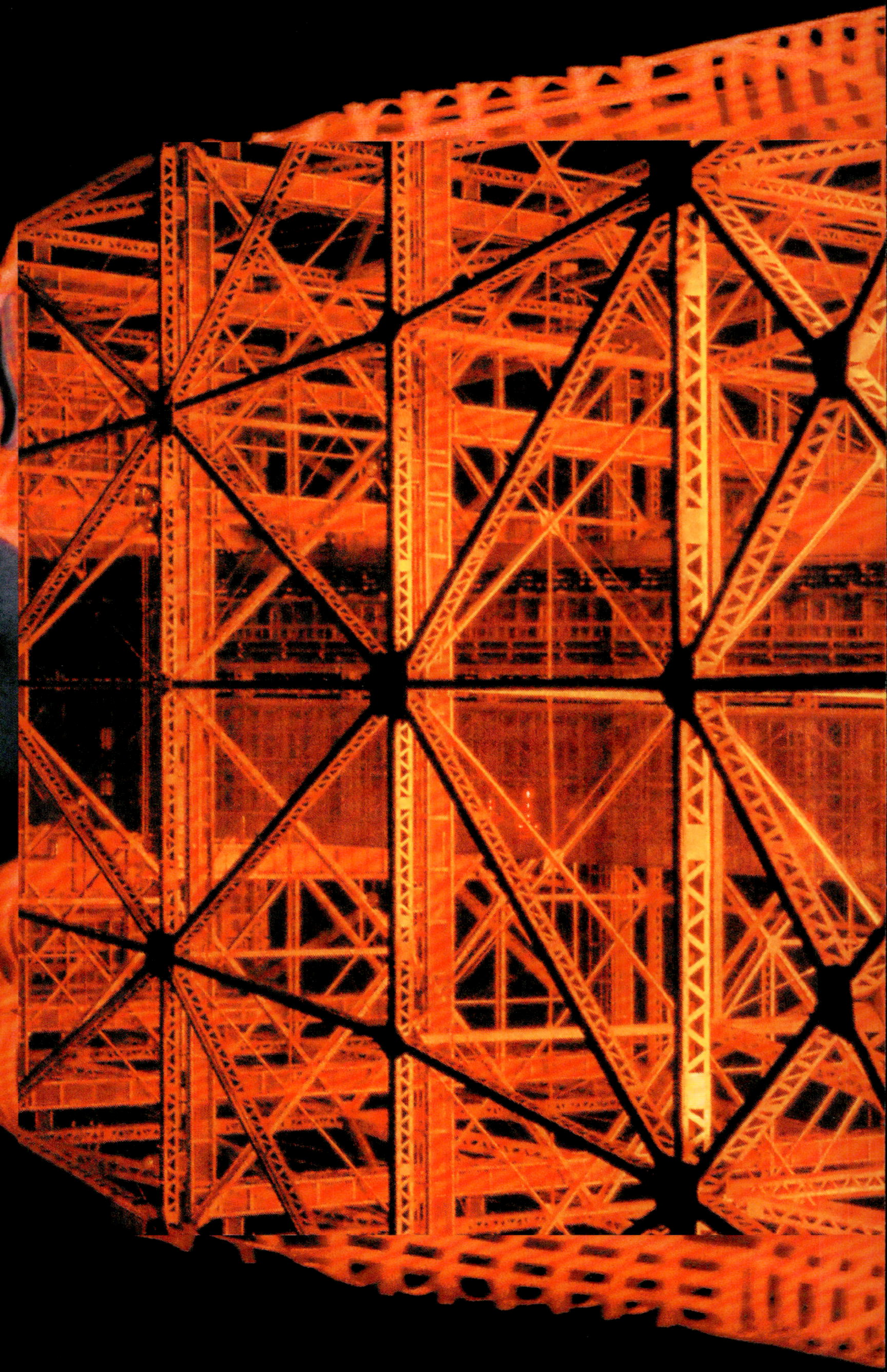

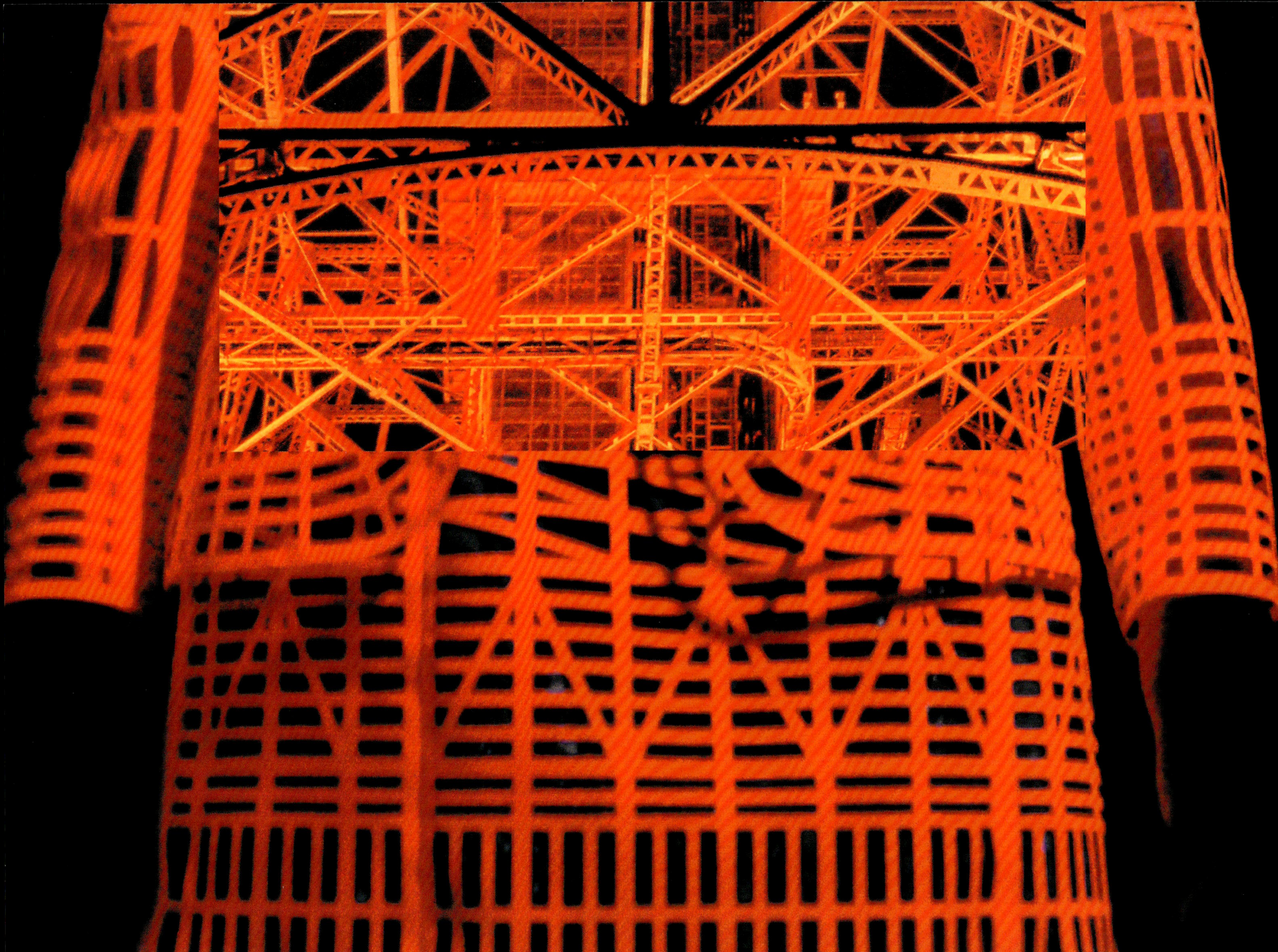

That day, which ended in tatters...

Tokyo Tower was also left in tatters that day. The unexpected turn of events made me feel defeated.

The following day, I learned that the man who had broken the window was a fashion journalist who was usually known for being a mild-mannered gentleman. He had become interested in our collection and approached us backstage, hoping to get a closer look at the clothes, when the conversation turned into an argument.

While I was being yelled at that day on the first floor, my joint show with my mentor that I had longed dreamed about had continued on the observation deck. The difference was night and day. I vacillated between despair and hope. I was able to climb to the observation deck because I was working alongside my mentor. On the ground, we came close to being defeated time and again, yet up on the observation deck that night, our fashion held their own against the glimmering view of Tokyo beneath our eyes. I will never be able to forget that day of darkness and light. We left a part of our souls on that observation deck.

A Man Climbs Up

In reality, before we executed our show, I had inquired if it would be possible to hold a fashion show on the observation deck of Tokyo Tower. I had also sent a letter asking for permission. Citing the lack of precedent, issues with the police and public security, and the possibility of disrupting the general visitors, my proposal was swiftly declined. My mentor and I felt hopeless. The two of us felt that if we did not climb to the top of the tower together, there would be no future for us.

Just when our spirits were about to break, an incident that saved us from the edge of despair jumped into our lives. The news headline read, *A Man Climbs Tokyo Tower, Drops a Heart-Emblazoned Curtain*.

The police had apprehended a man for scaling the steel pillars of Tokyo Tower and confessing his love to a woman. The incident occurred nine days after my mentor and I had gone to see a show of the punk rock band, Ging Nang Boyz. The man who climbed the tower draped a curtain with a red heart and the letters “Tomo-chan” from a height of a hundred meters.

The man’s purity and daring shocked us. His red heart symbol pierced our own hearts and moved us. The height that we were hoping to reach was much higher than a hundred meters. But we wanted to follow the man’s example. Our show invitation to the media was a collage of the newspaper articles about the man.

To make the collage, we purchased over ten different newspapers that reported on the incident, and we cut up the sentences in the articles and used them as the framework of Tokyo Tower. We then drew many hearts on the tower, since the man's heart symbol had pierced our hearts. The articles all wrote about the man with disdain. To risk one's life to communicate one's feelings—one man had managed to do it, so why couldn't we? We had seen ourselves in the man.

We thought long and hard. In order to do the show, we would have to climb to the top of Tokyo Tower. In order to do that, we needed to purchase entry tickets—entry tickets for all thousand attendees. Buying all the tickets at once would raise suspicion, so I needed to space them out.

I enclosed the entry ticket inside the invitation to the show.

On the day of the show, my mentor and I circled the observation deck over and over in order to check the models' runway route. We walked the deck dozens of times until we were satisfied. It was as if we didn't want to stop going around.

The employees at Tokyo Tower sensed something was wrong when the number of people coming into the tower suddenly increased before the show. The attendees kept on coming. An employee demanded to see the hosts of the show. Their anger was at its peak. The show was about to start.

I turned to Kanda-san and told him, "We need to protect the show, so I'll leave it in your hands. I'll go down and talk to them." In order to keep the show going, my mentor remained on the observation deck while I went down to the office on the first floor to calm down the employees. The distance in height between the office and the observation deck was 150 meters. While riding the elevator down, I imagined myself falling straight down from the observation deck, despair coursing through me.

Fighting

The idea to hold a fashion show at Tokyo Tower was mine. I got the inspiration for the idea from the Ging Nang Boyz' show at the Hibiya Open-Air Concert Hall that Kanda-san had invited me to one evening. It was the first time my mentor and I went to a show together. I was overwhelmed by the band's powerful, expressive energy and passion. I felt deep within me that the band and my mentor were united in their singular dedication to their craft. I had a premonition that the members of the Ging Nang Boyz would one day perform in a show wearing my mentor's clothes. But my mentor didn't sell the clothes he made.

After the show, we didn't feel like getting on the train. We had to walk in order to calm down. The Ging Nang Boyz and I were both engaged in self-expression, but what made us different was that they were fighting. My mentor and I continued to walk aimlessly through the city.

It was a complete coincidence. The Tokyo Tower came into view. We gravitated toward it, and before we realized we were standing at the foot of the tower. I decided to tell my mentor what I had always wanted to say: "I want us to do a show together at least once. Let's do it at the top of the Tokyo Tower!" We needed to fight, too.

By then, I had already quit my part-time job and installed myself in the fashion world by selling the clothes I made. My mentor, who was four years older than me, yearned to live in the fashion world too, but he made his way with part-time jobs instead of selling the clothes he designed. I was distressed that our mentor-mentee relationship had been reversed in terms of achievements.

My mentor had graduated from Waseda University in March 2000. I had entered my third year and sixth season of making clothes under the brand name, Anrealage. My mentor continued to say he had no intention of selling the clothes he made. To him, putting a price on something into which he had spent so much precious time and passion was like putting a price on his soul. That's why he couldn't sell them. I insisted that clothes should have a price tag and be properly distributed in the market. That was the first and last time I had ever argued against my mentor.

I knew I could not be the only one who wanted to wear the clothes my mentor made. I wanted to see people wearing his designs. Above all, I wanted him to live in the fashion world with me, putting a price tag on his clothes and selling them.

My fashion show at Tokyo Tower was a turning point. That day was the day my mentor and I began living inside the fashion world. If we didn't climb up the Tokyo Tower together, we would not have seen the same view. We completed the show together, fighting alongside each other. We might not have been able to make a breakthrough in the world of fashion. And yet, the next day, my mentor affixed a price tag on his creation. I was able to purchase my mentor's clothes for the first time and wear them.

We did make a breakthrough in our world. That day, which ended in tatters, was the beginning of everything.

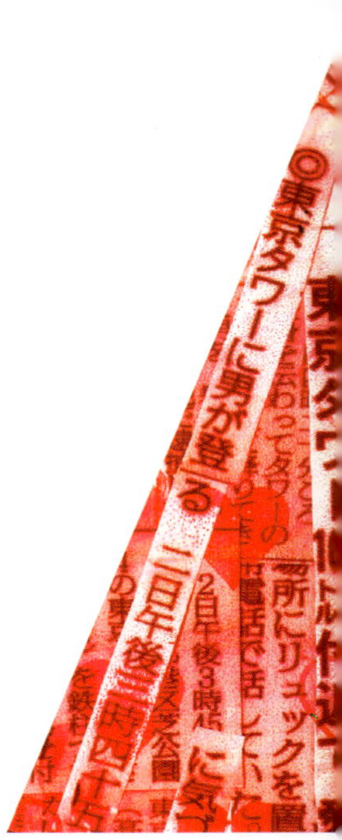

神田恵介

2006年春

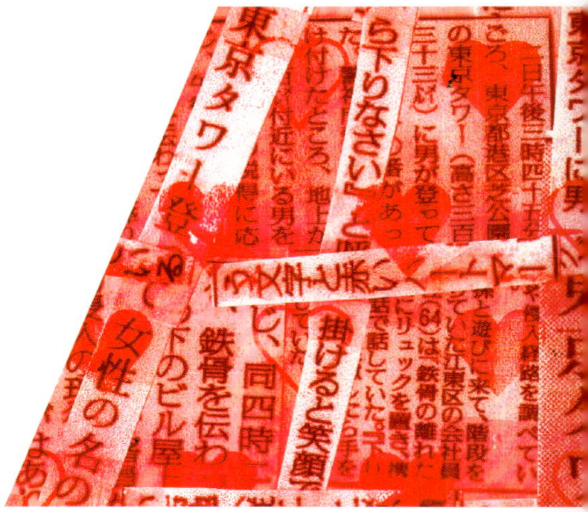

日時　2005
19:00
21:00

会場　東京タ

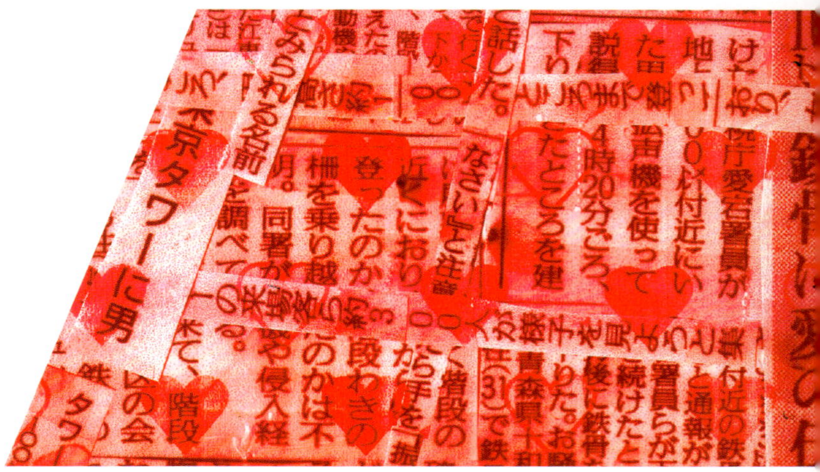

...was the beginning of everything

NOV 9, 2005

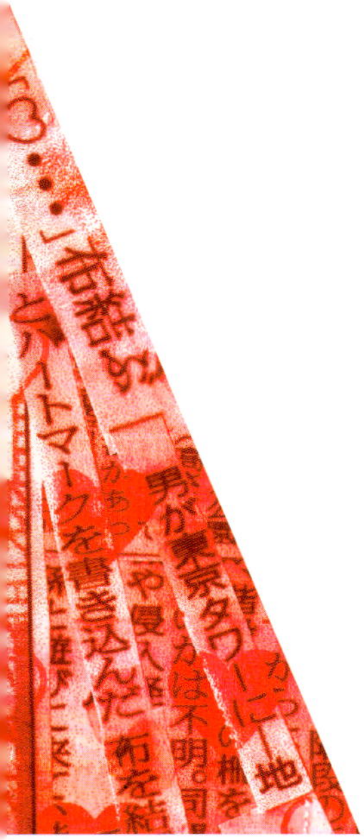

ANREALAGE

コレクション

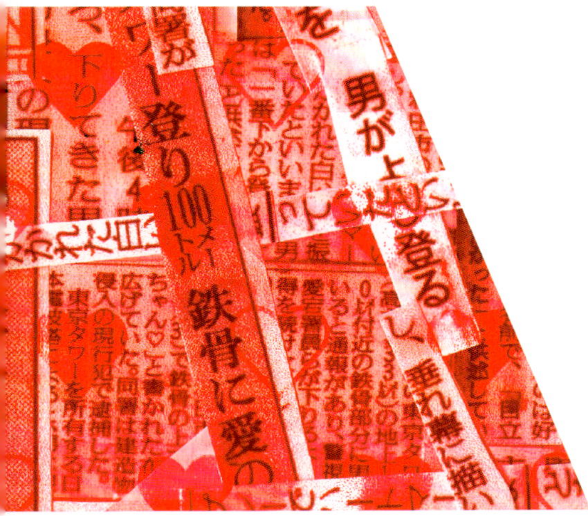

2006 S/S "BUTTER"

1月14日（月）
（一般）
（プレス／バイヤー）

一大展望台1F

God [noun]

in certain religions, the being that made the universe and controls it

oh my God! [informal]

used to emphasize how surprised, angry, shocked, etc. you are

thank God [informal]

something you say when you are happy because something bad did not happen

a spirit, especially a male one, that people pray to

detail [noun]

a piece of information about something

2

GOD IS IN THE DETAILS

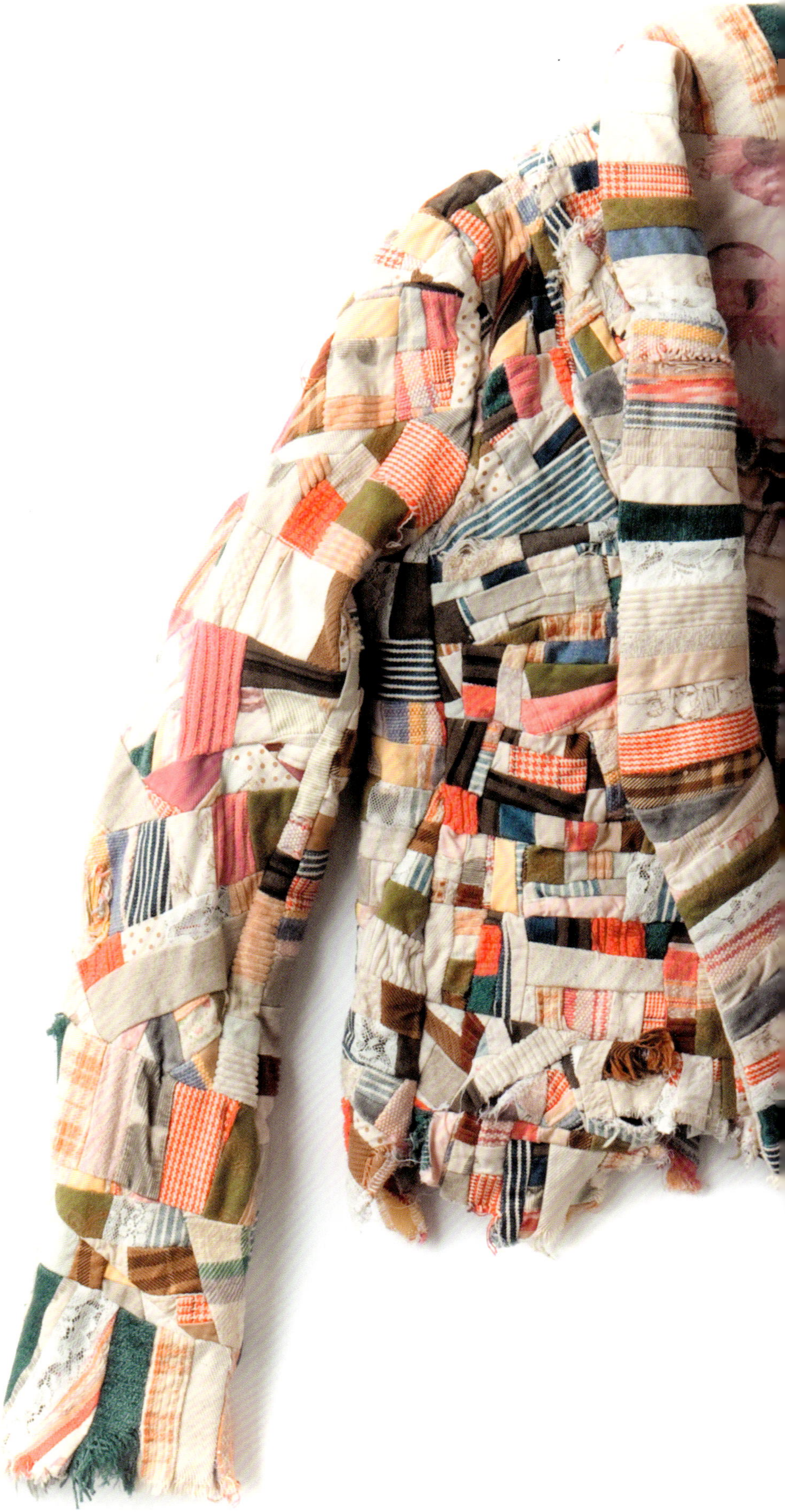

To exceed limits and boundaries, both i

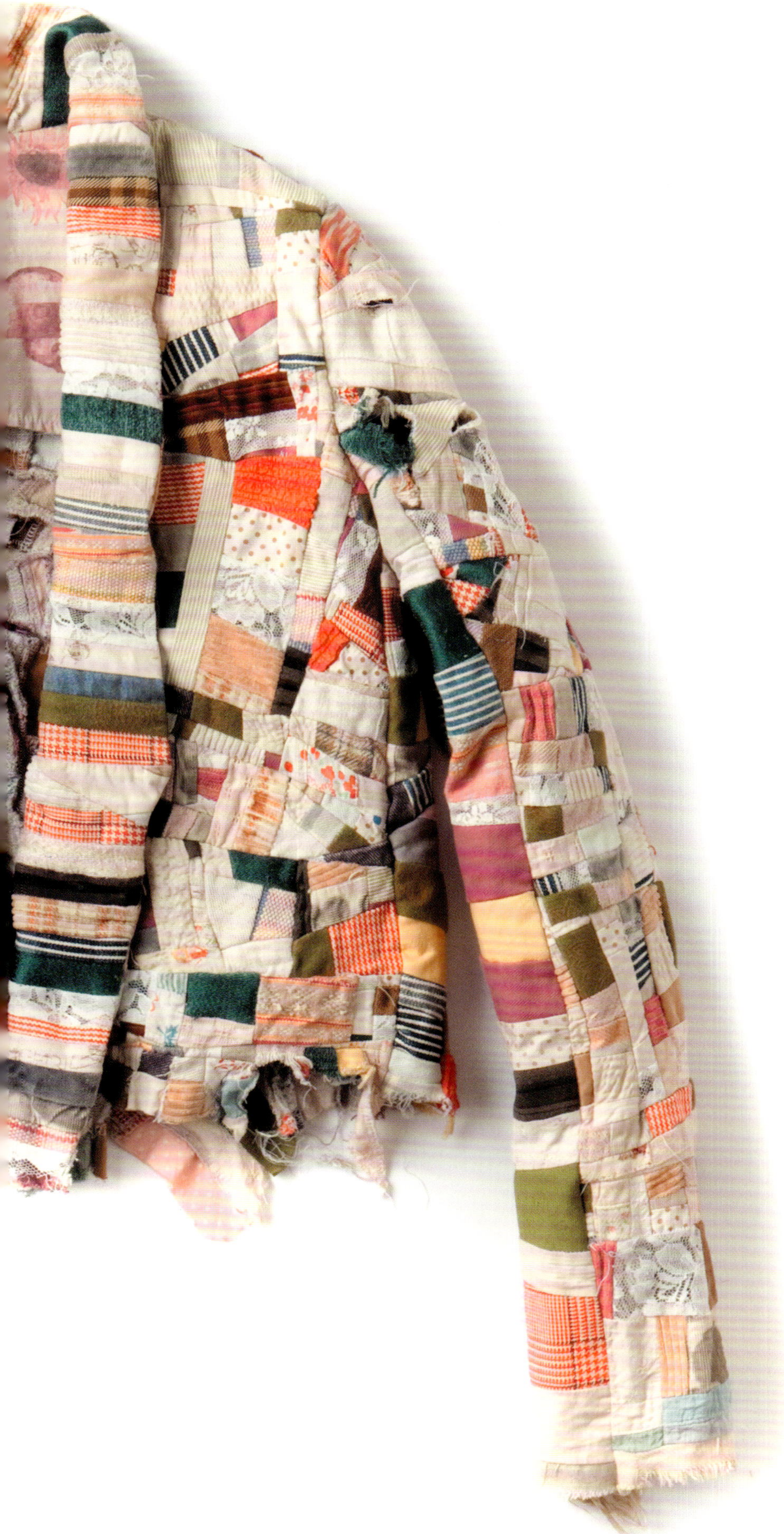

APR 26, 2005

2005 A/W "SUZUME NO NAMIDA"

designing, and how I spend time

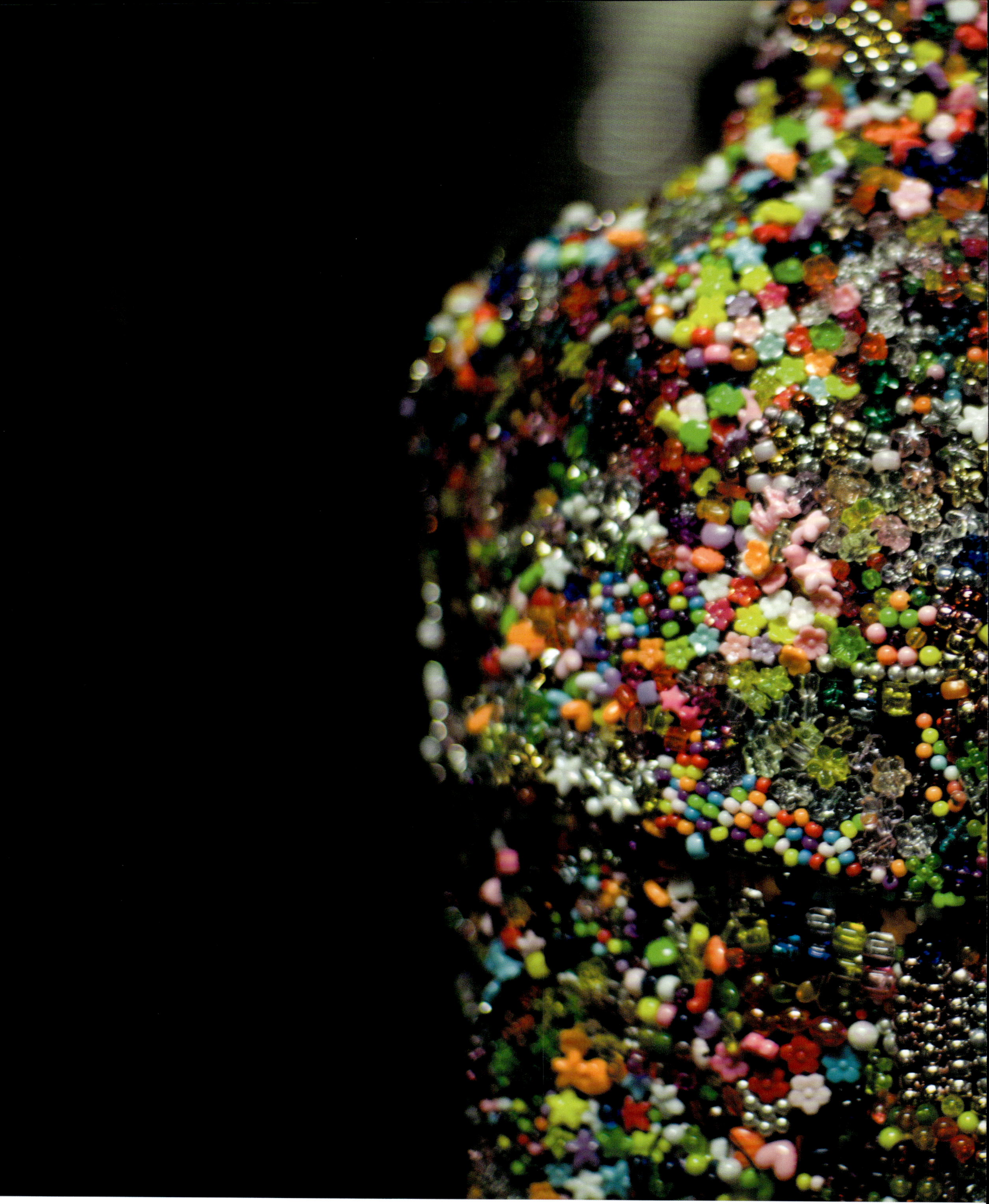

The god of fashion does exist, that is or

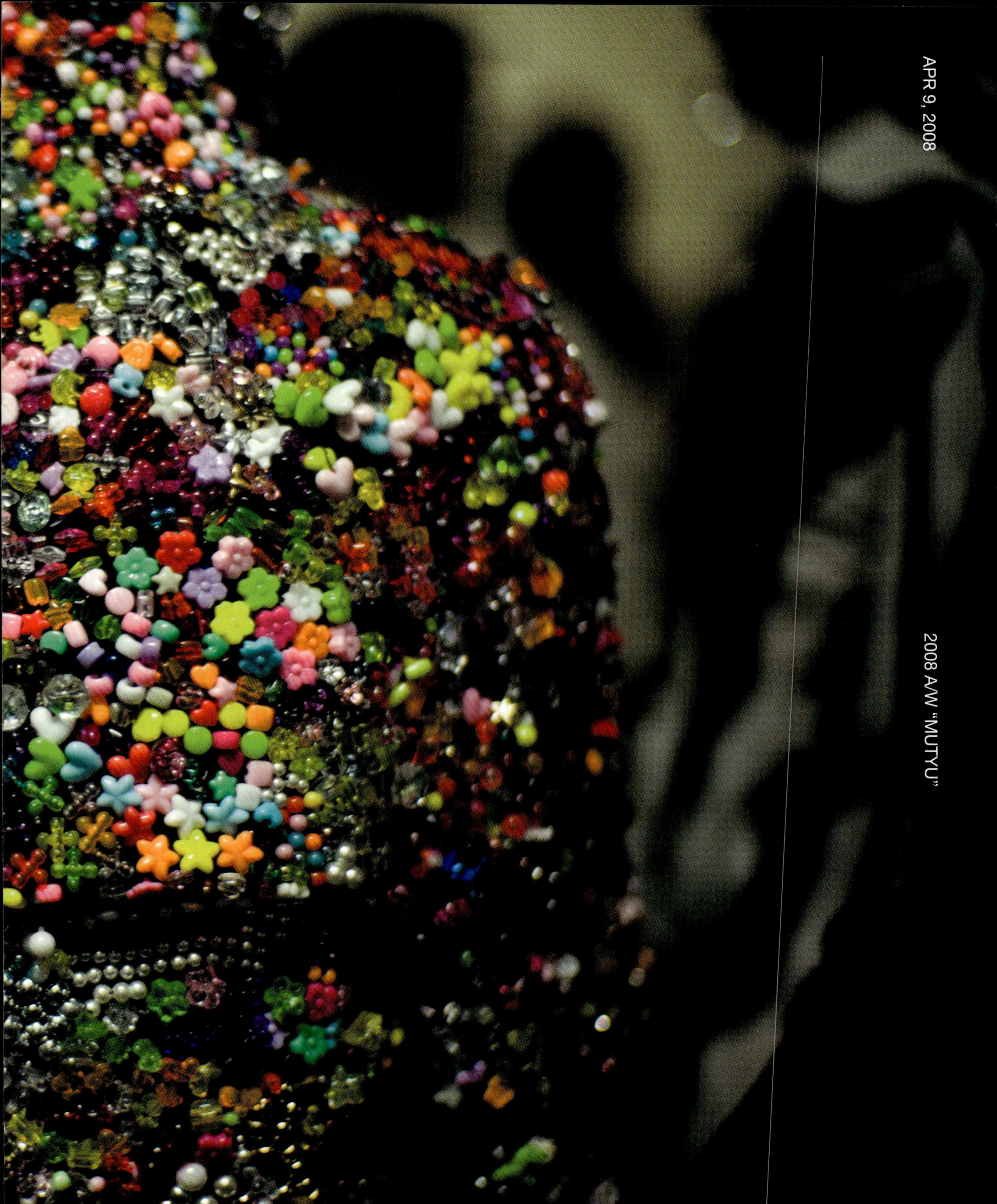

APR 9, 2008

2008 A/W “MUTYU”

e thing I am 100% sure of

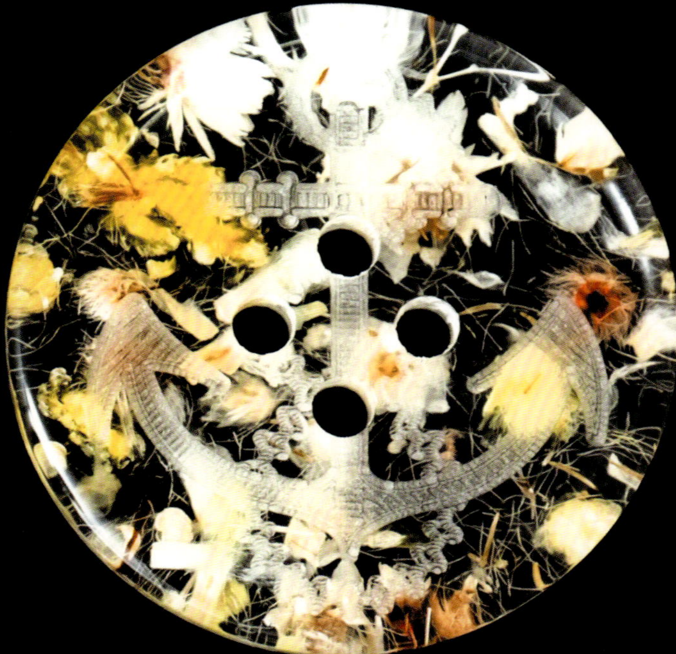

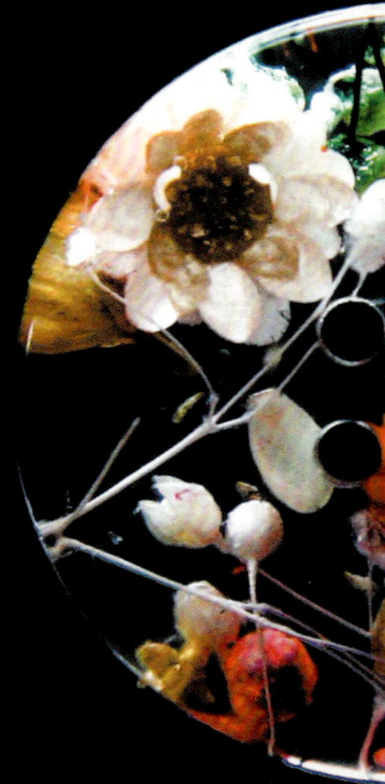

The divine resides in the mind that takes

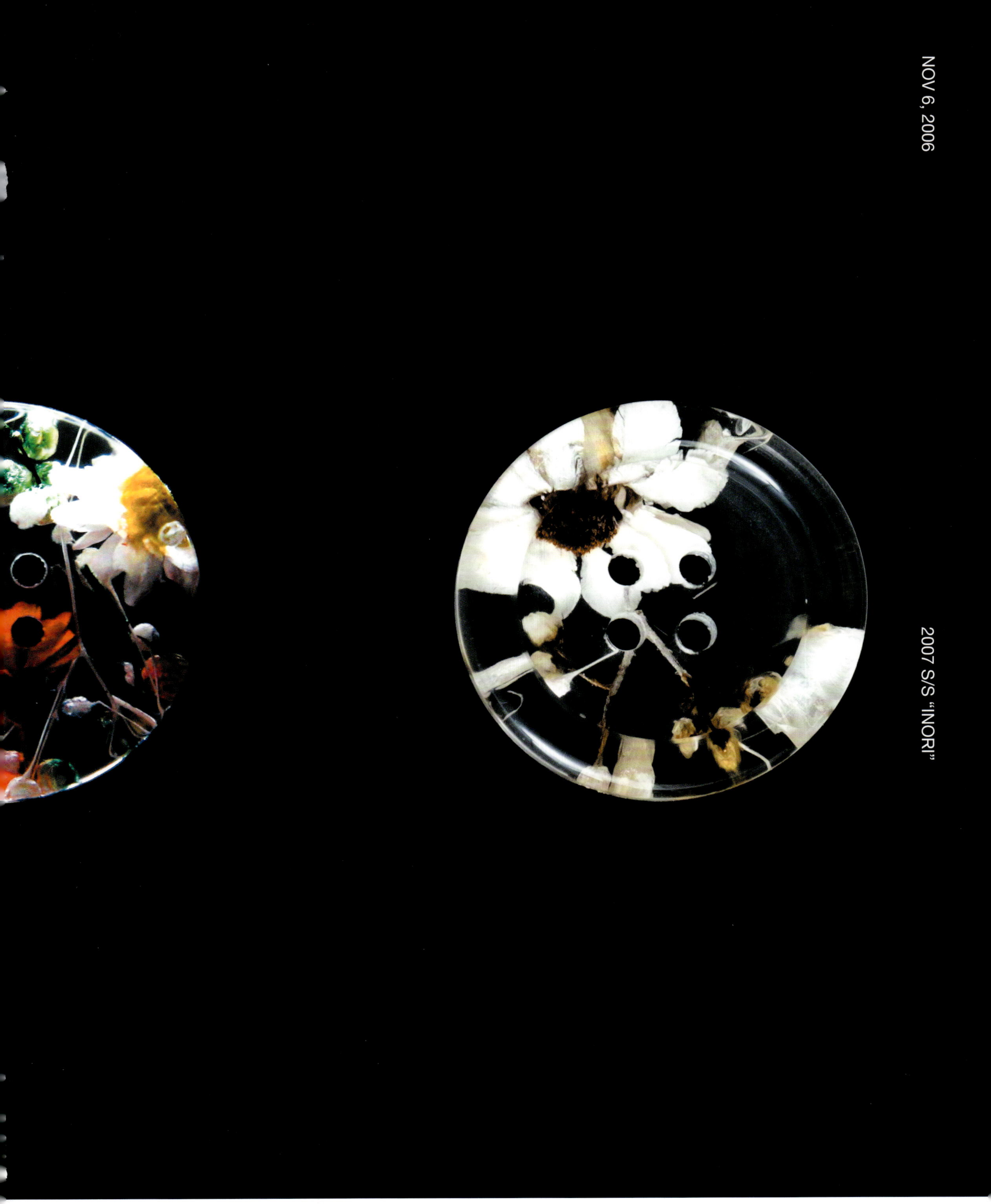

NOV 6, 2006

2007 S/S "INORI"

in the smallest details

NOV 6, 2006

2007 S/S "INORI"

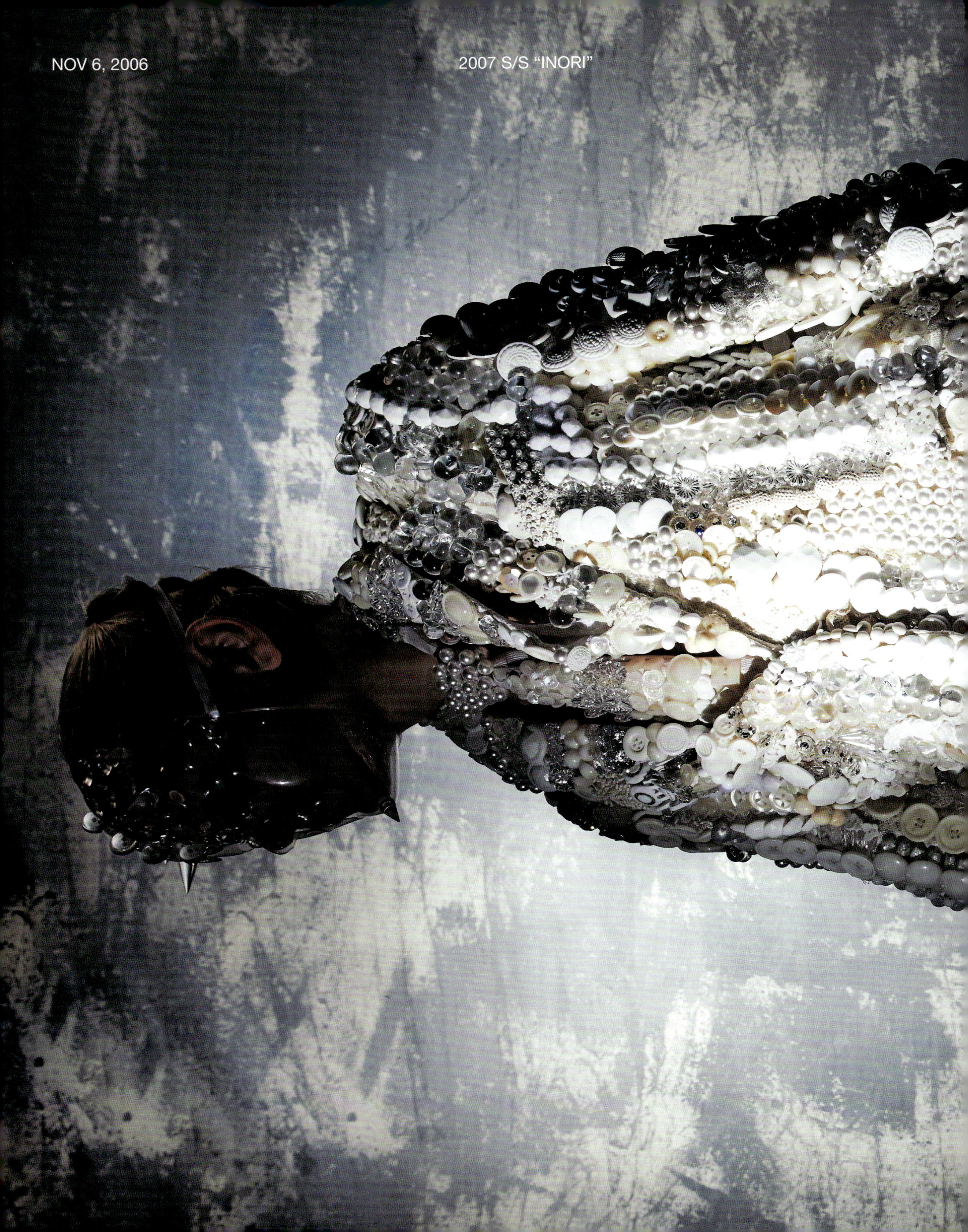

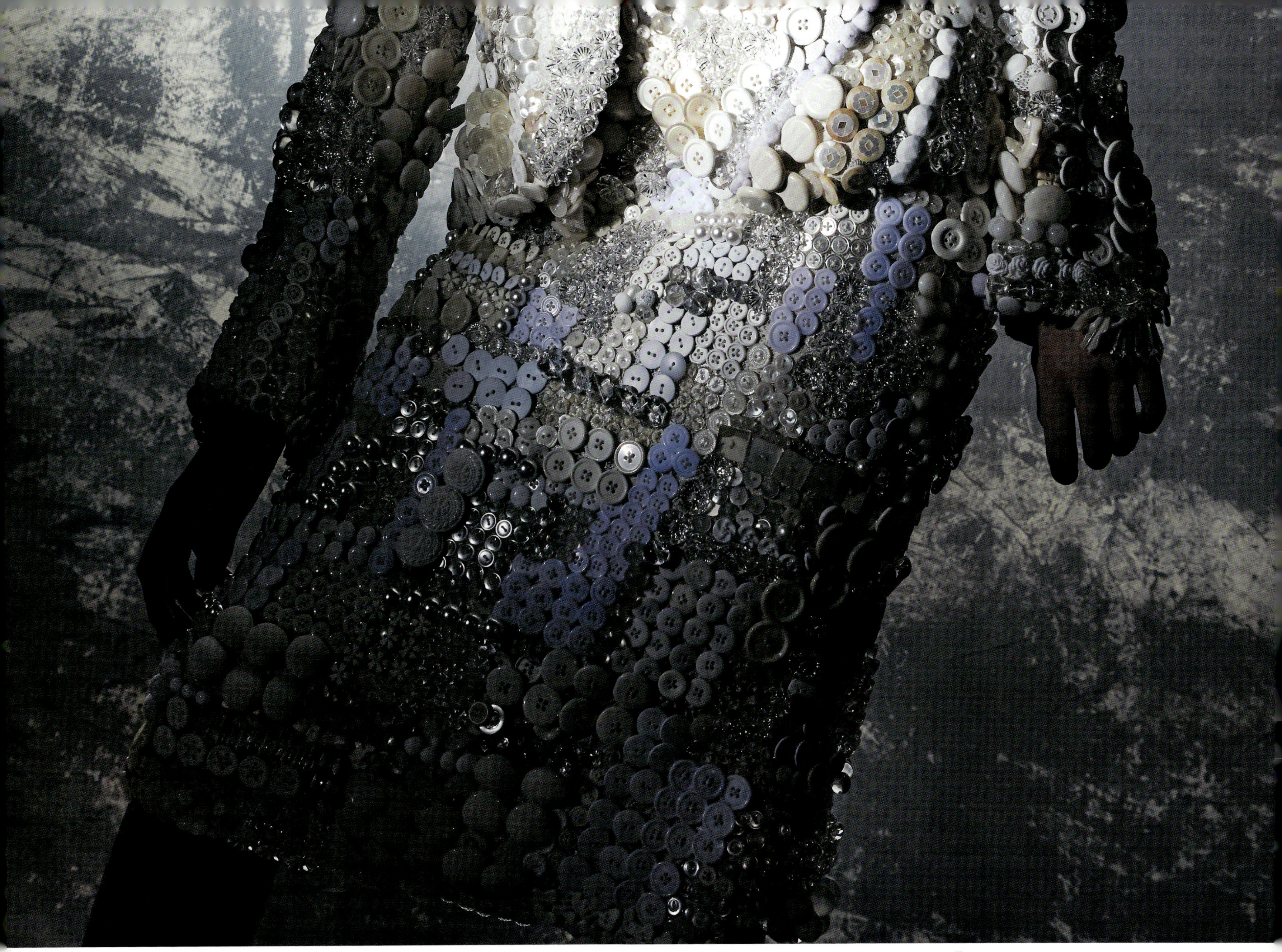

To pray that the unreal changes to real

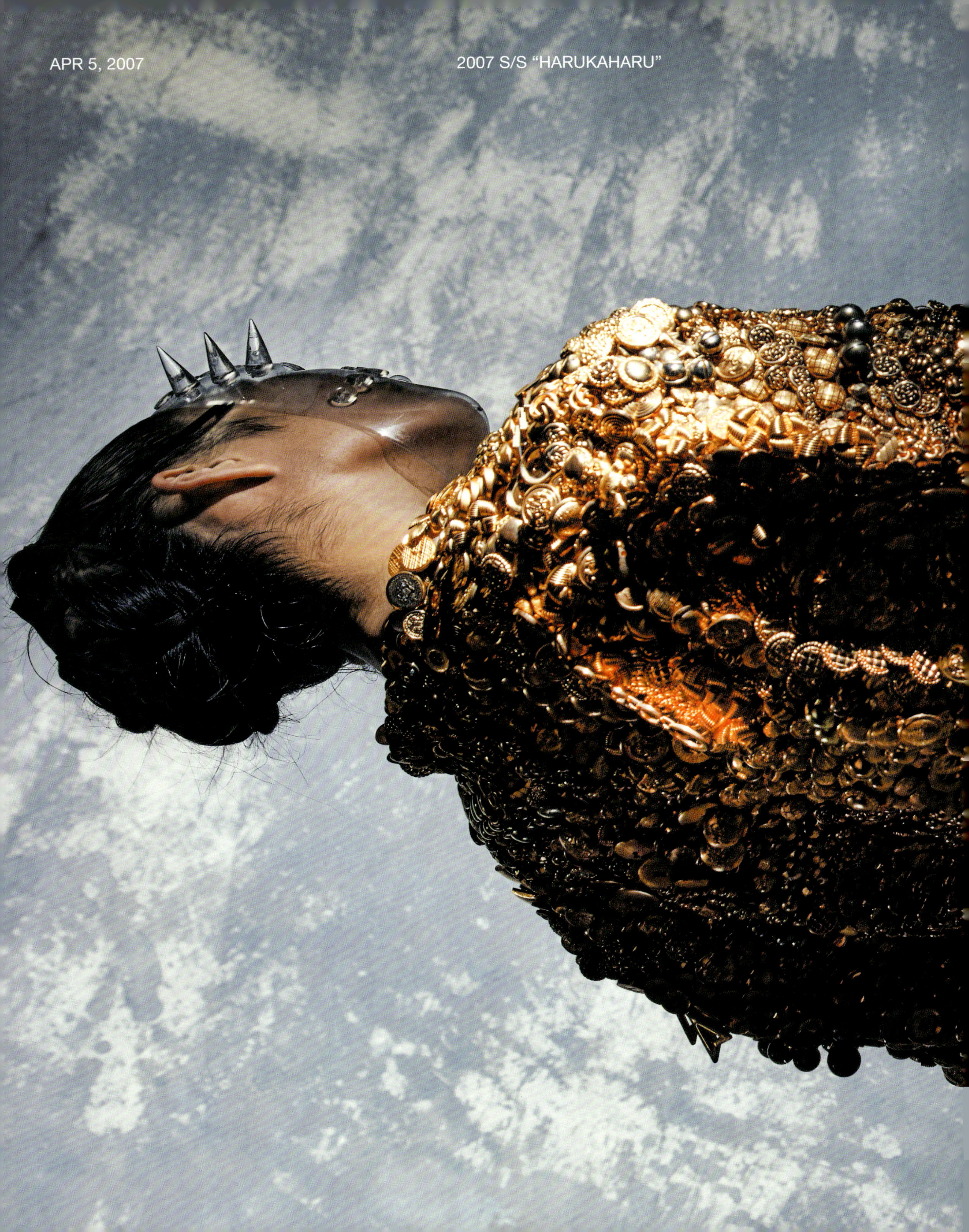

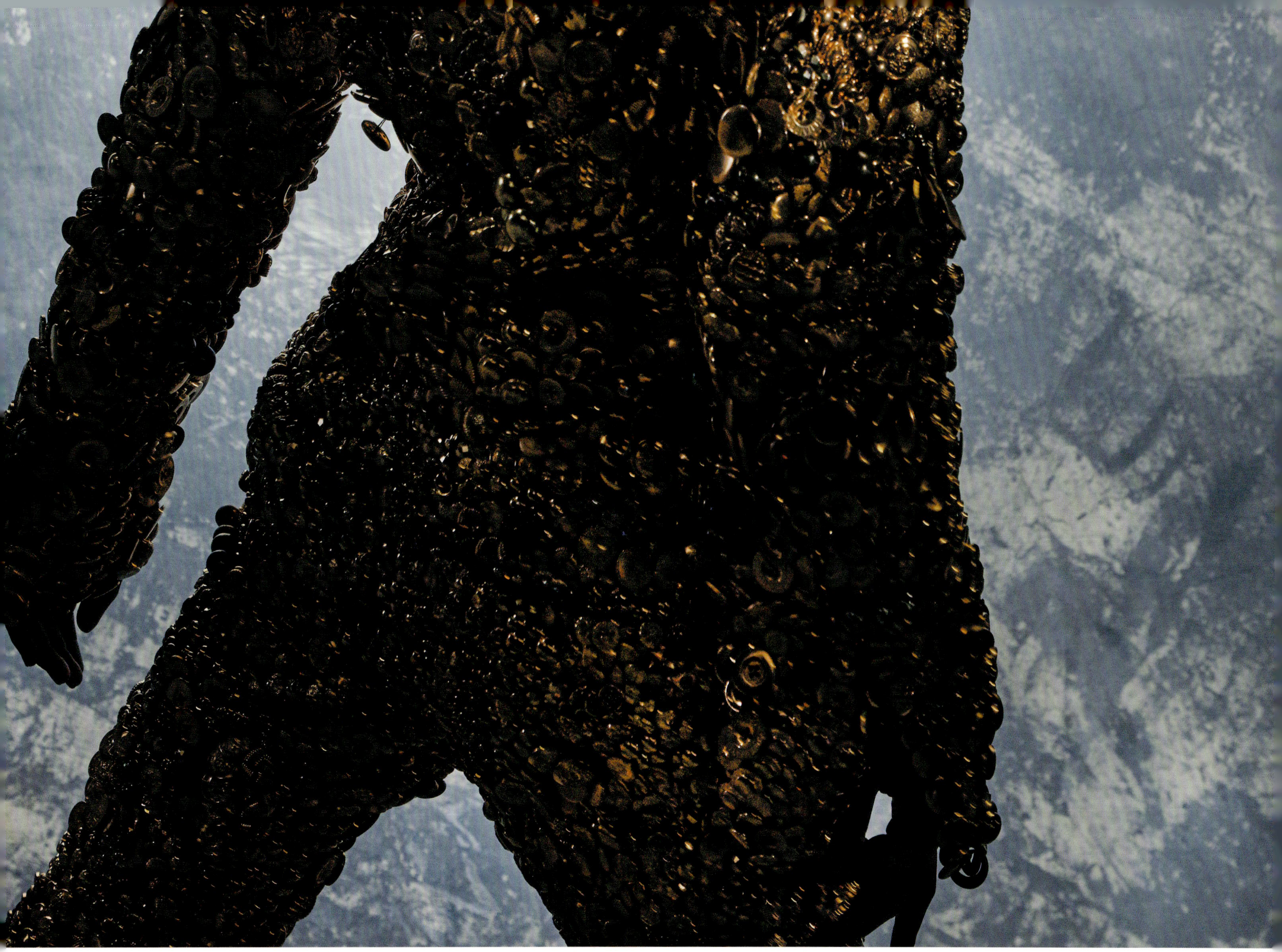

To hope to change real to unreal

shape [noun]

the physical form of something made by the line around its outer edge

shape [verb]

to make something become a particular shape

3

SHAPE

Shape

Shirt

I was staring at the shirt all day long.
Day after day, from morning to night.

I was observing the shirt.
I was thinking about the shirt.
A week passed.

You must not touch the shirt—that was the assignment I had given myself. This was so that I could think thoroughly about the shirt. I wanted to distance myself from "handwork," which had been so important to Anrealage. That's why I couldn't touch the shirt.

I thought I was done for now with the "world of patchwork," which required mindboggling amount of labor by hand to make something unlike any other. I had declared that I was parting ways from the method of "making additions on top of additions."

And yet, I wasn't done with it.

A fashion journalist wrote: "What makes Anrealage interesting is that it holds within a ray of hope in a decadent world. Is communicating the allure of clothes with the sheer number and volume of adornments the brand's true aim? In any case, 'God is in the details' are words that should never be declared so loudly."

Additions on Top of Additions

I knew all of this too well.
Whether affixing more than ten-thousand beads or combining thousands of fabric fragments together, there is a limit to working by hand. In reality, we couldn't speed up our production even when we worked with our hands all day. We had to cut back on sleeping in order to fulfill the orders. The method of making clothes through "additions on top of additions," which required a staggering amount of time to accumulate the quantity of adornments needed, was about to collapse.

Let's stop working with my hands.
Let's think instead of working with my hands. Let's observe so that I can think.

I had a three-month grace period before the next 2009 S/S Collection. I continued to look at the shirt in order to think. Even after a week, however, no idea came to mind. I had an overwhelming urge to touch the shirt. But I stopped myself. I didn't want to return to how I was before. I wanted to move forward.

Then I realized something.

Working with my hands and thinking were equally important. Spending a huge amount of time working with my hands or thinking was in essence the same thing.

Dress Form and Human

One by one, questions popped into my mind.
Why are collars on shirts triangular?
Why do shirt sleeves have a gap?
Why are shirt sleeves curved?

I also started to ponder the dress forms, which are shaped like human torsos and used for draping shirts.

Why are shirts meant for human beings always fitted on the dress form?

A well-balanced dress form can make anything look beautiful. But are people shaped like dress forms? Of the 7.7 billion people in the world, how many have the exact same figure as the standard size? I've always made clothes to fit a size 7 (Small) or 9 (Medium) dress form. Hadn't I always assumed that clothes that fit a dress form would also fit a person?

I realized then that the standard way of making clothes was nonsensical and even violent.

Generally, torsos are presented in odd numbers, from 5 to 21. There are no even sizes, as if those sizes do not exist. In truth, there is an infinite variety of body types. Our bodies come in a continuing array of different sizes, each with its own boundary. Instead of clothes fitting the body, our bodies are made to fit the clothes. In the world of fashion, people are forced to confirm to things, rather than things confirming to people.

A Cloth and a Rock

I prefer fashion that continues, instead of fashion that is chiseled to fit a moment in time. No, that's what I *should have* preferred. I used to think that the ordinary and the extraordinary continued one after the other, and so did life and death. The name Anrealage was supposed to represent this idea. So what happened? It seemed I had deviated too far from my initial stance.

When my mother was young, she attended a technical fashion school. Her first assignment in class was to wrap an irregularly shaped rock with a piece of cloth. I immediately picked up a rock and observed it closely.

The cloth is flat, but the rock is three-dimensional. Dialectically speaking, the two are in conflict with each other. Our three-dimensional bodies stand at the polar opposite of clothes, which are flat. What is a three-dimensional object that is farthest from a flat surface? The answer—a sphere—provided me with a hint for my next collection. An electron that spins around a nucleus was a sphere, and so was the celestial body.

The most fundamental shape in the world—from the micro to the macro realm—is the sphere. Could I wrap a sphere with cloth and make it into clothes?

The Meiji Jingu Stadium was close to my atelier. I went for a walk there and decided to watch a baseball game. Suddenly, the baseball piqued my interest. I immediately purchased the baseball, made of leather. Next, I acquired a basketball, a soccer ball, then a volleyball. I even got a beach ball. What surprised me when I took the balls apart was that depending on its type, the way the layer of skin created the shape of the sphere was different. A vast variety. The baseball, for instance, was structured out of two layers of skin that covered its core.

Unfitting

A small hint begets a larger hint. I love oranges. Peeling an orange, I realized the similarity between patternmaking—used when designing clothes—and peeling an orange. What's inside the skin of an orange was like the human body. When I drew a line across the skin of an orange with a knife, it took on the shape of a shirt. The skin of an orange can be peeled in any shape.

I had found my answer.

So long as there were four holes, a person can wear anything. As long as there were holes for the head and arms and the hem, any cloth can become a piece of clothing. Making clothes that fit a sphere perfectly shows that the traditional way of making clothes is nonsensical and violent; it brings out the "distortion," "gap," and "strain" that exist within ourselves.

Even if we had spherical bodies, we could still wear clothes so long as it had four holes. If I could make clothes that a sphere could wear, then I could design clothes that a triangular pyramid could wear. The reason I fixated on the sphere, the triangular pyramid, and the cube was because ○, △, and □ comprised the foundation of shapes and the simplest of symbols.

This was how the 2009 S/S Collection, *○△□*, came to be. I presented clothes that imagined the human bodies in the shape of a sphere with a 60-cm diameter, a triangular pyramid with a 75-cm side, and a cube with a 45-cm side. The buttons were made to suit the right angles of a cube, whereas the elbows conformed to the shape of the triangular pyramid. When the shirt and trench coat were taken off the cube and worn by a person, they made new shapes. The shirt on the sphere, when worn by a person, warped in the front and created drapes on the back. The trench coat on the cube made a cape-like silhouette.

Just as "ordinary" clothes with nonsensical and violent aspects can appear beautiful at times, the "extraordinary" clothes suited for ○△□ shapes can also look beautiful. And they do look beautiful. The clothes that I had thought so much about turned out to be so simple. The excessively adorned clothes, received with such harsh words from the fashion journalist, made a complete turnaround.

I could not have changed if I did not take the time to stare at the shirt for a week straight. I would not have been able to take on a new series that fundamentally remade the shape of clothes. After *○△□* came the 2009-2010 A/W collection, *凹凸*; and the 2010-2011 A/W collection, *Wideshortslimlong*. All of them attempted to shake up the preconceived notions around the shapes of clothes.

The same fashion journalist I mentioned before later wrote, "The work can be described as a new frontier. The design powerfully conveys the designer's devotion to creation." I had changed. The clothes with just four holes turned the norm on its head. I was genuinely happy that there was someone out there who could confirm this.

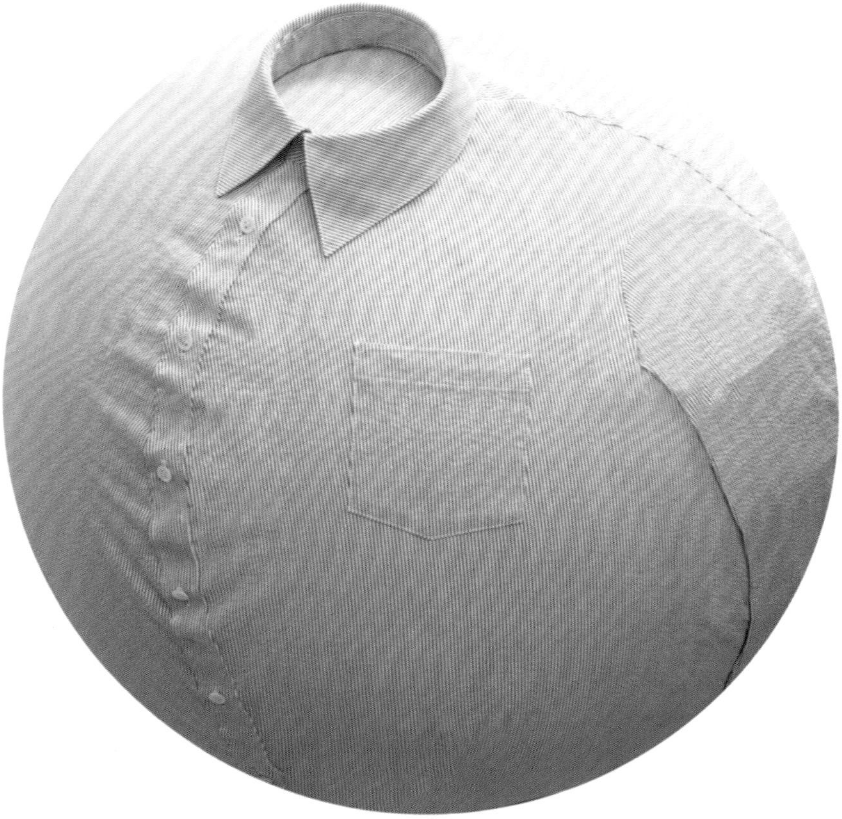

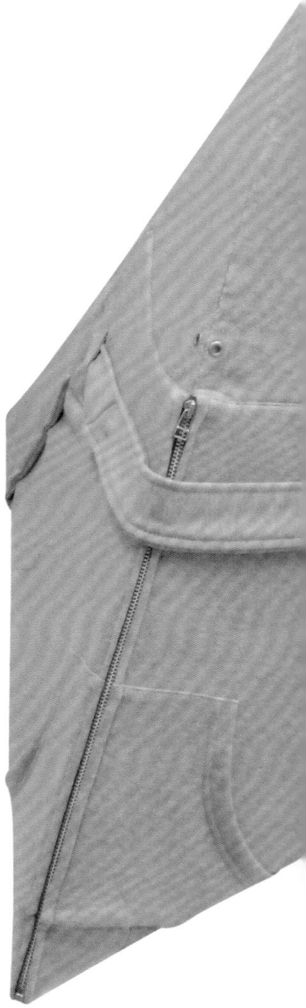

Do people come closer to clothes, or de

OCT 27, 2008

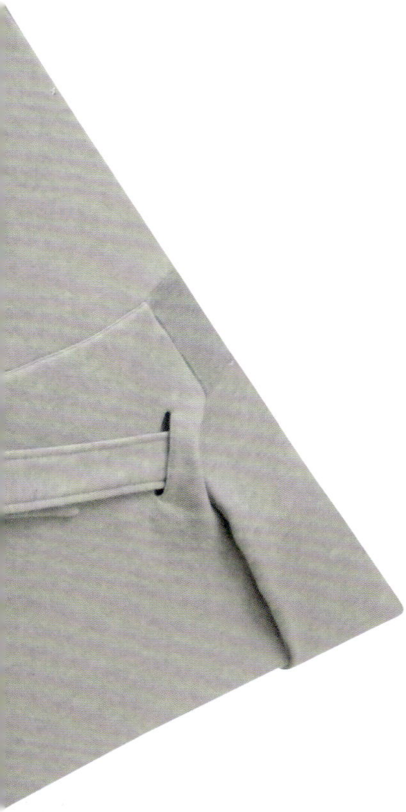

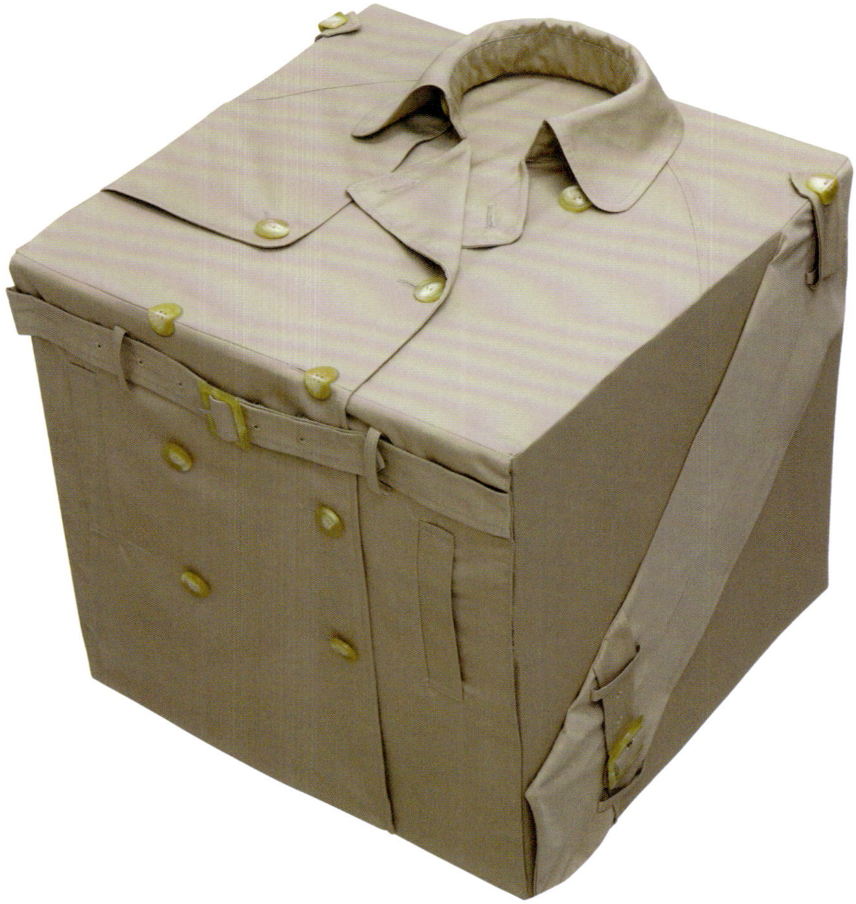

2009 S/S "○△□"

clothes come closer to people?

OCT 27, 2008

2009 S/S "○△□"

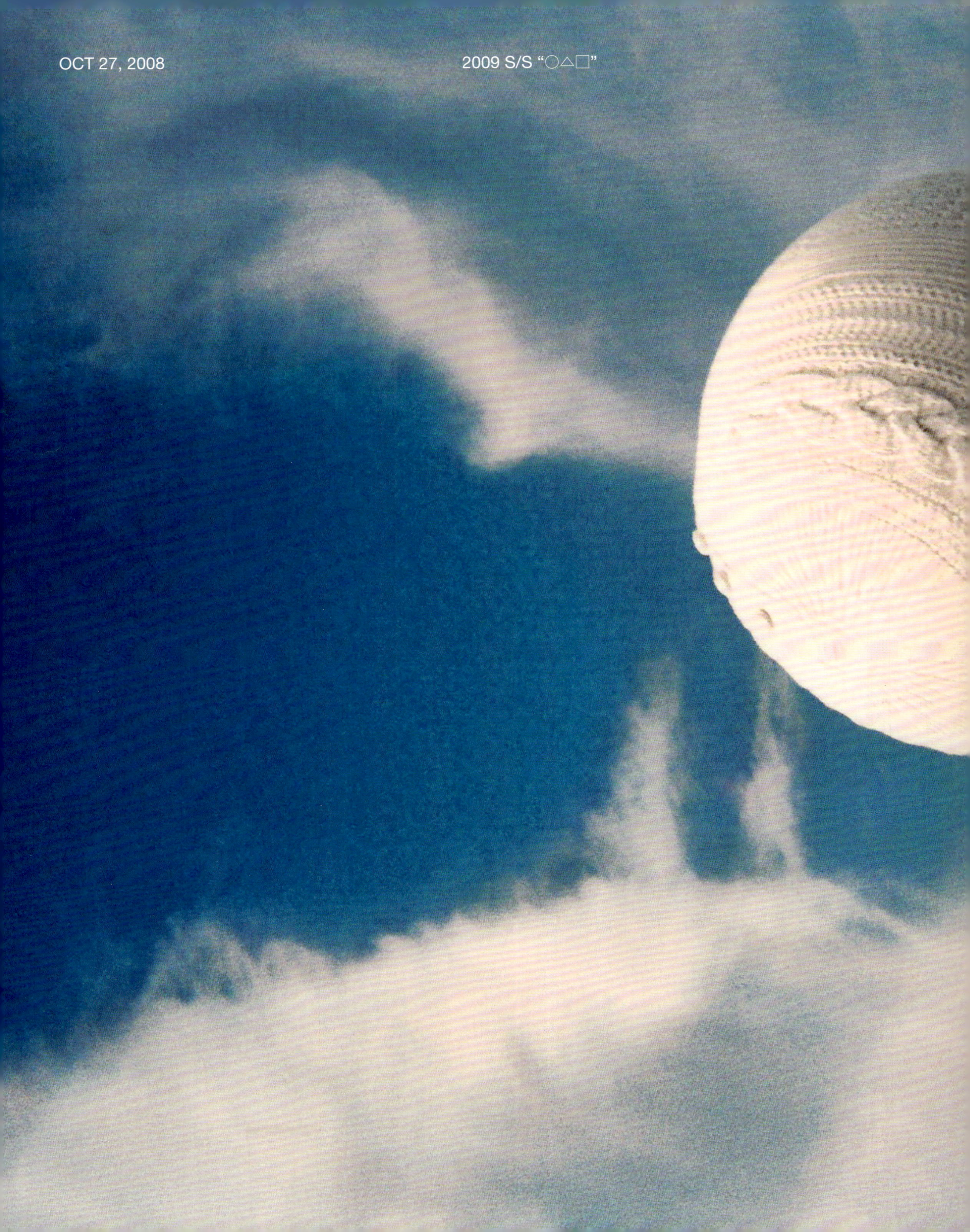

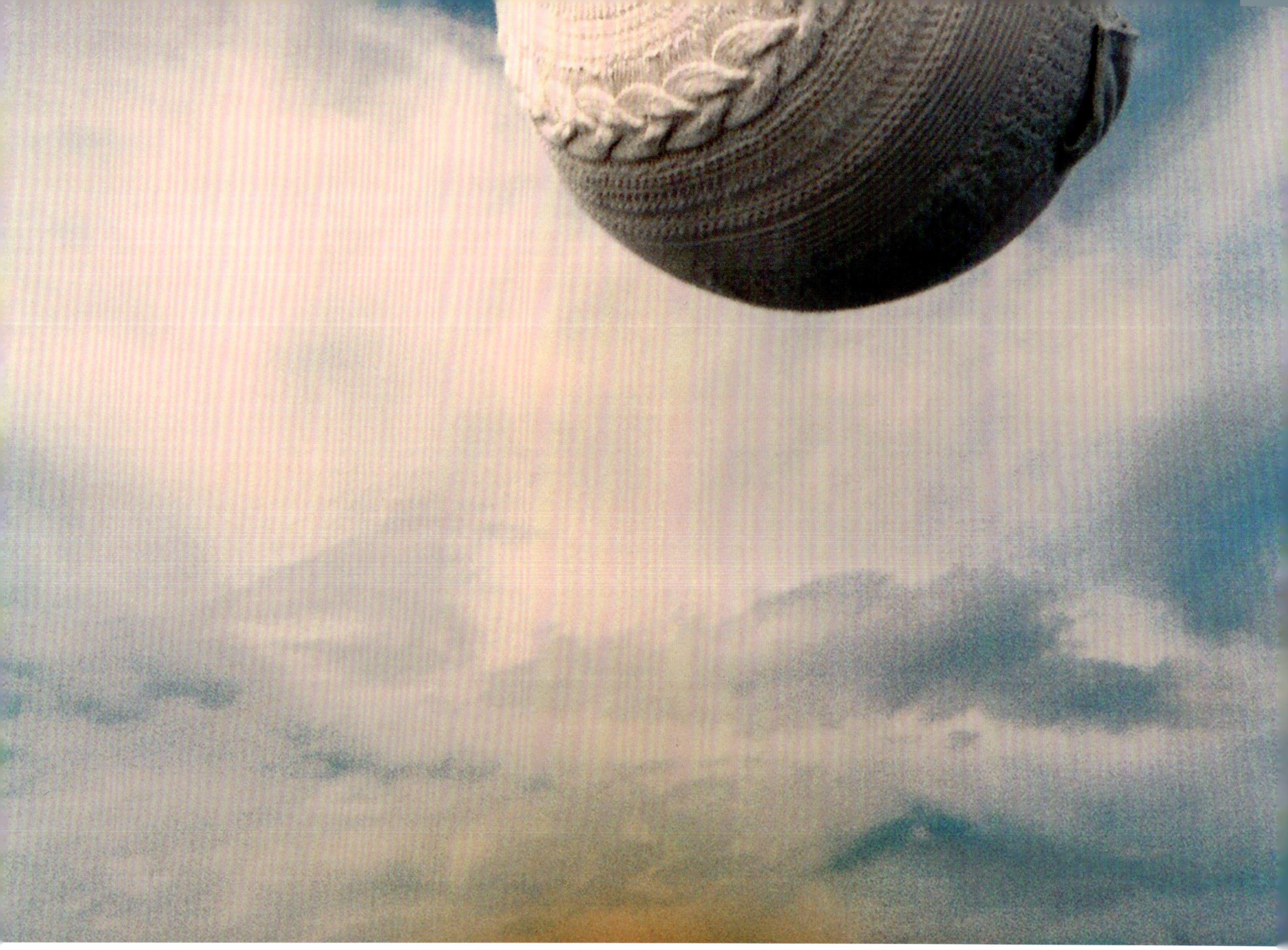

To interrogate the body, the ruler of clothes

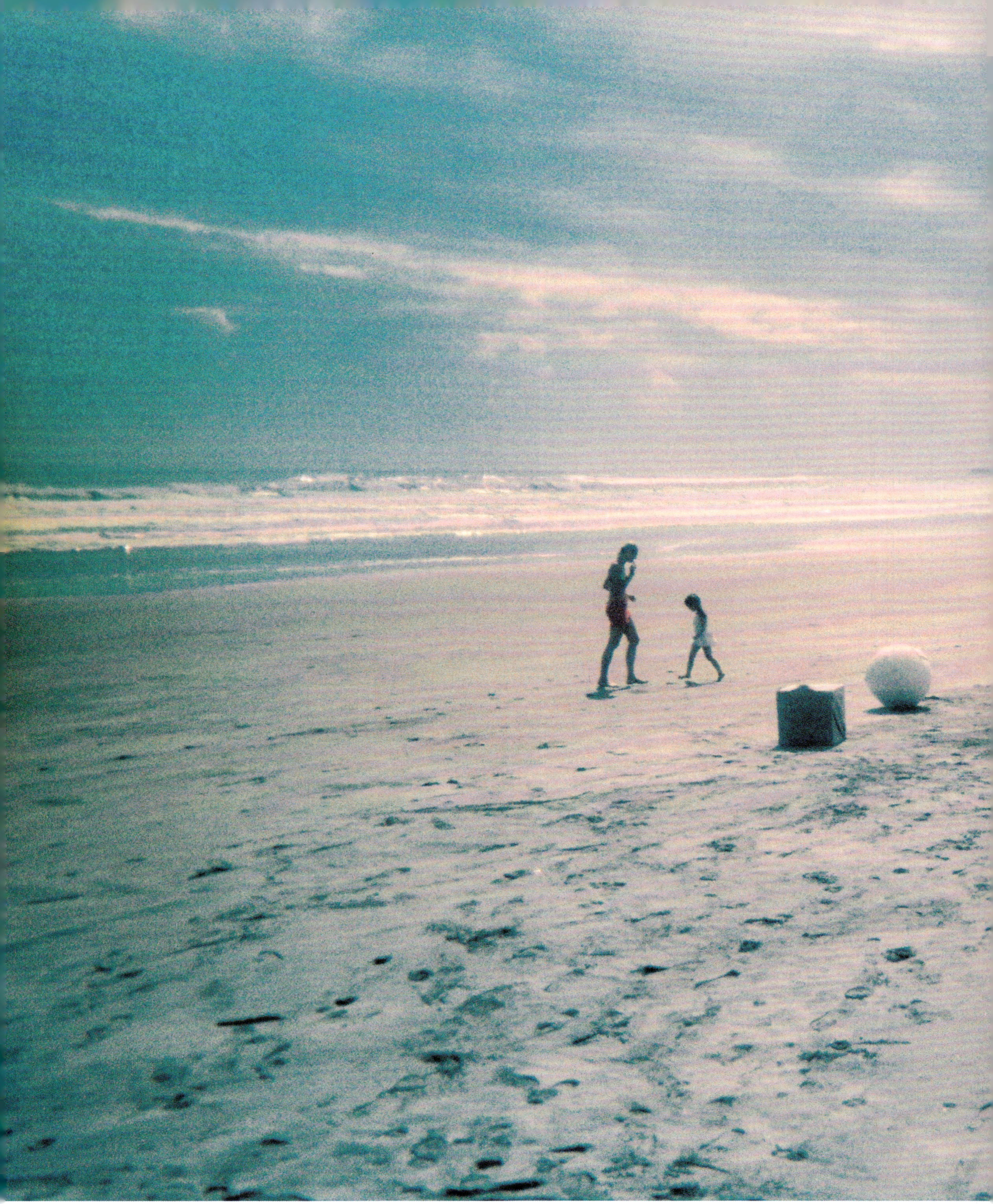

The conventional way of making clothes

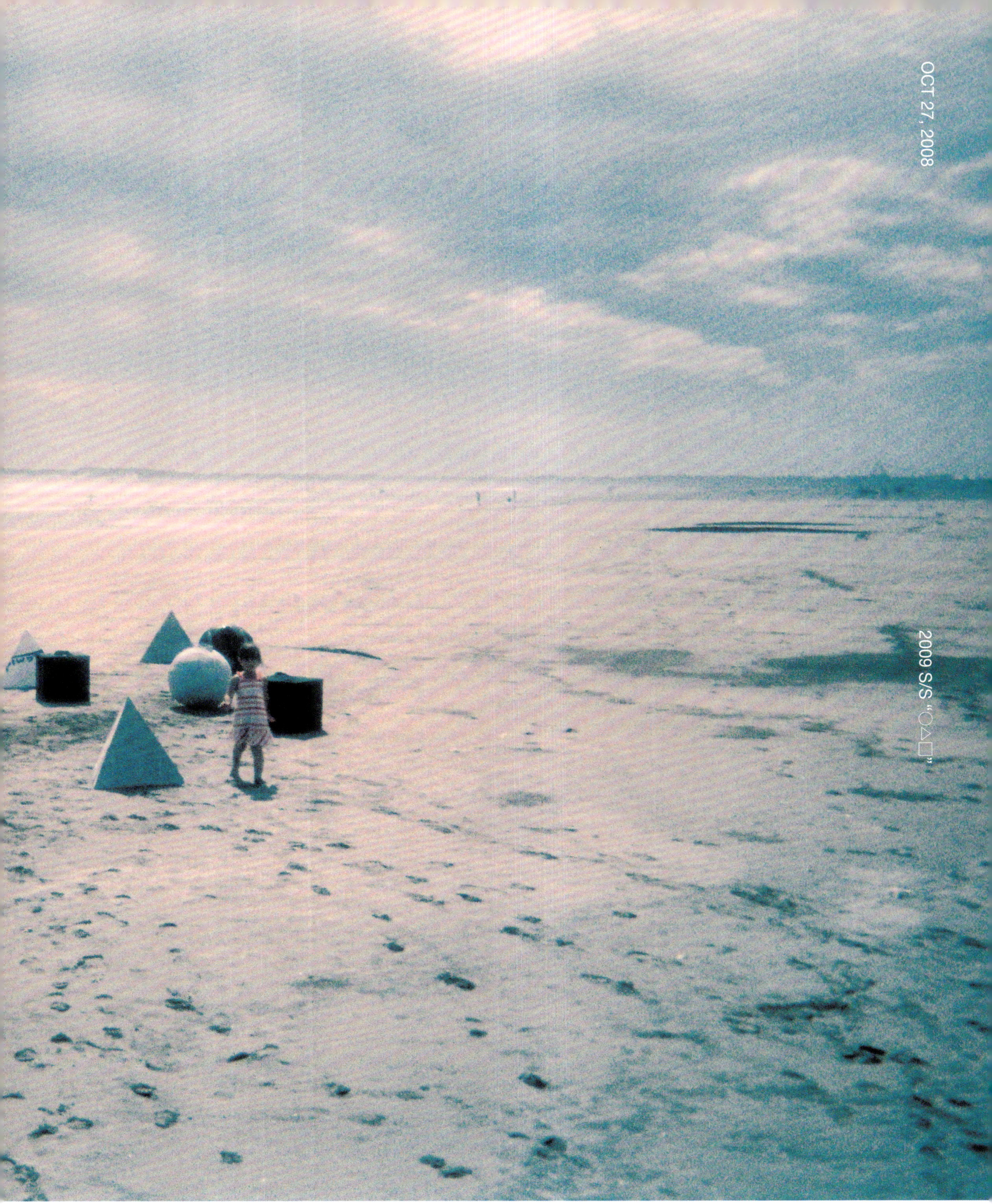

was nonsensical and even violent

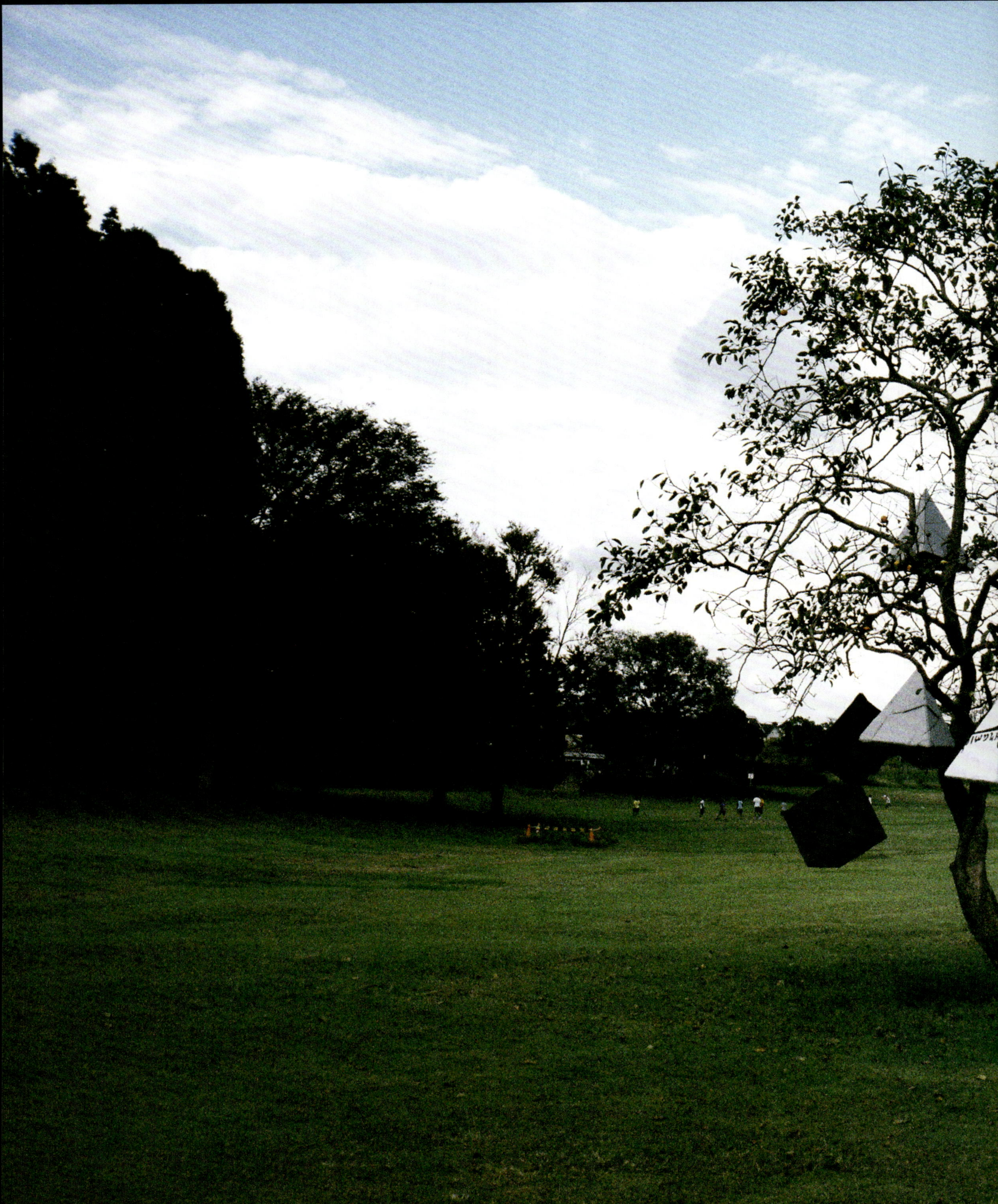

Instead of clothes fitting the body, our b

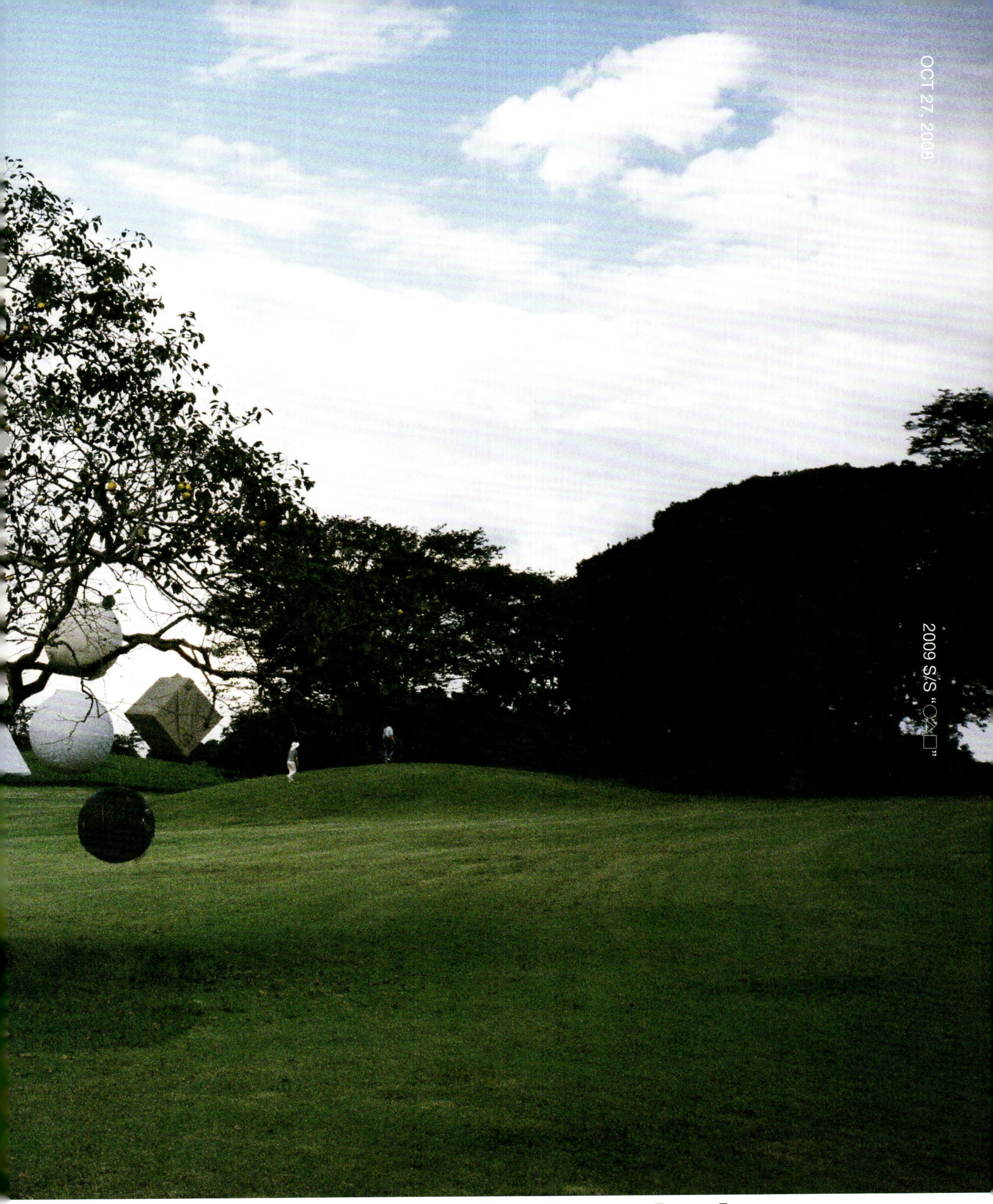

odies are made to fit the clothes

OCT 27, 2008

2009 S/S "○△□"

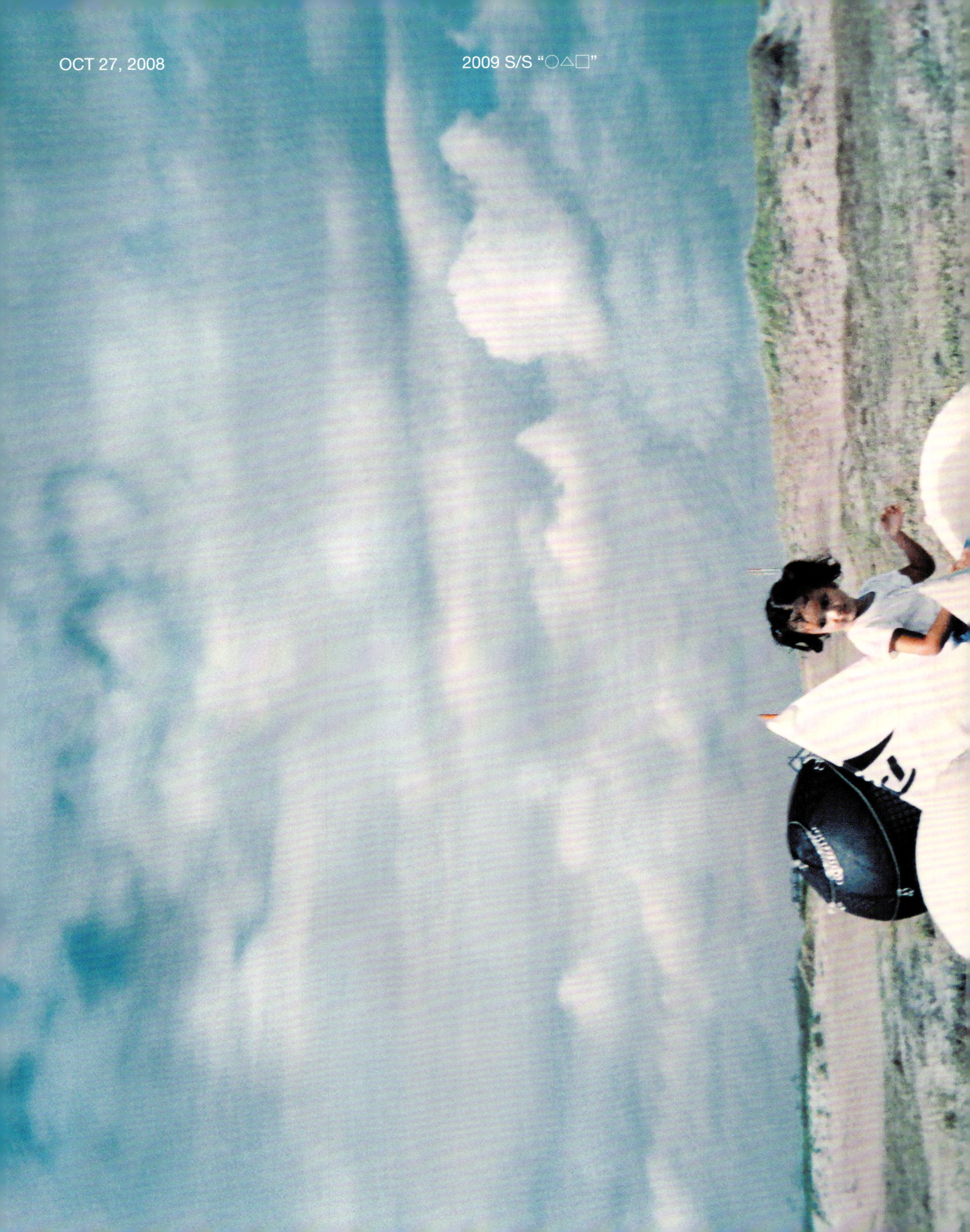

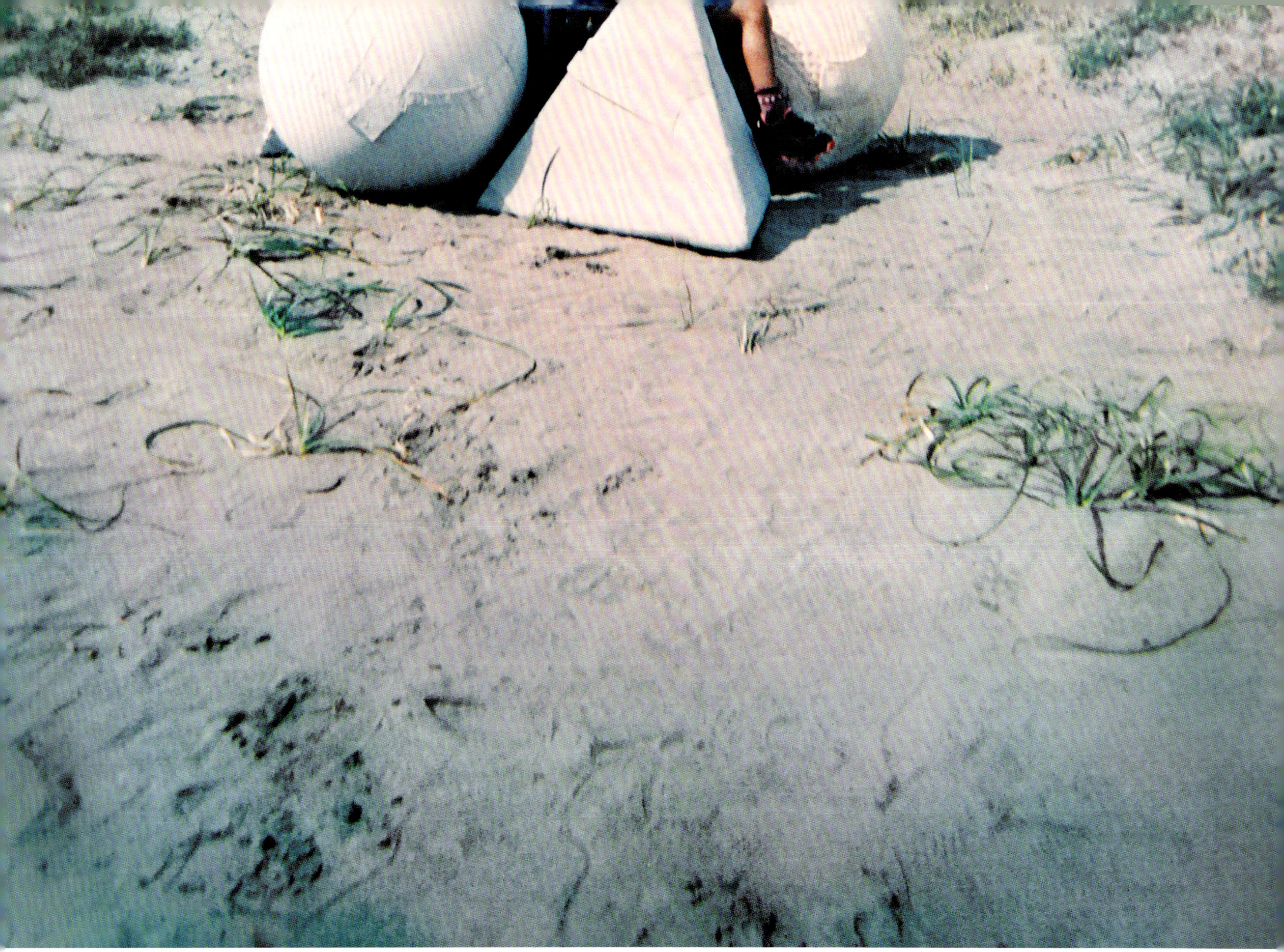

Anything with four holes can be clothing

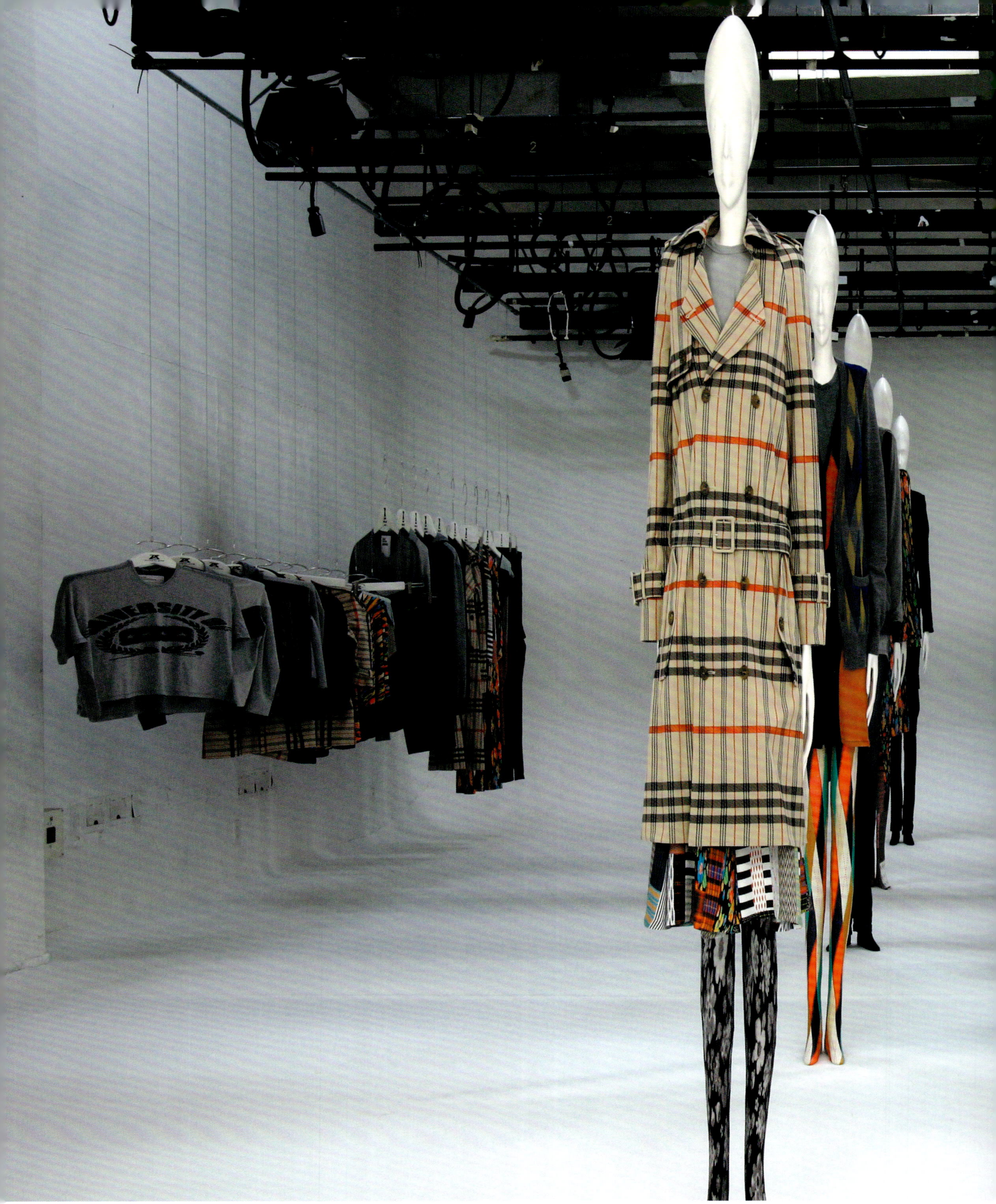

Clothing that would not suit anyone...

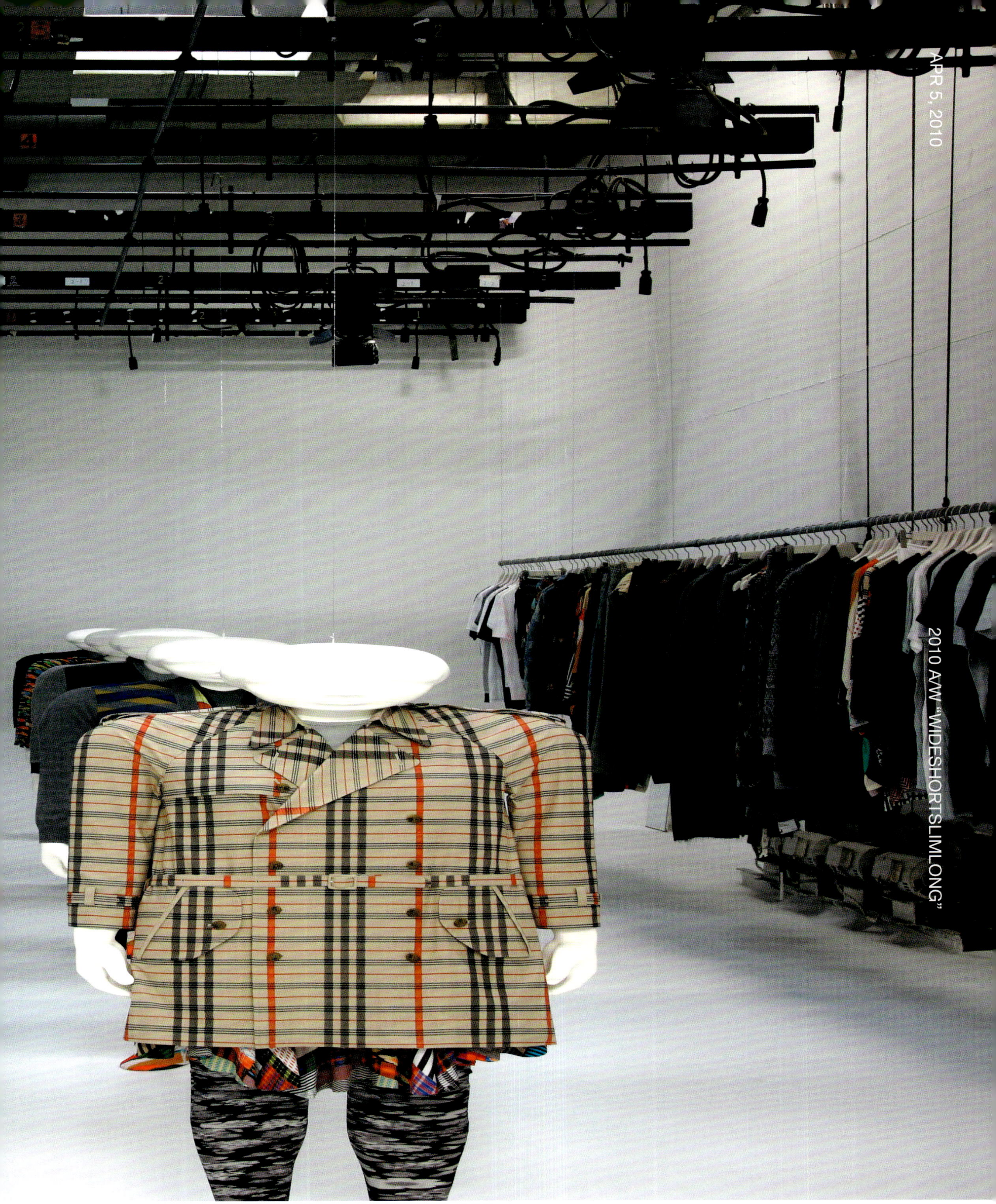
APR 5, 2010

2010 A/W "WIDESHORTSLIMLONG"

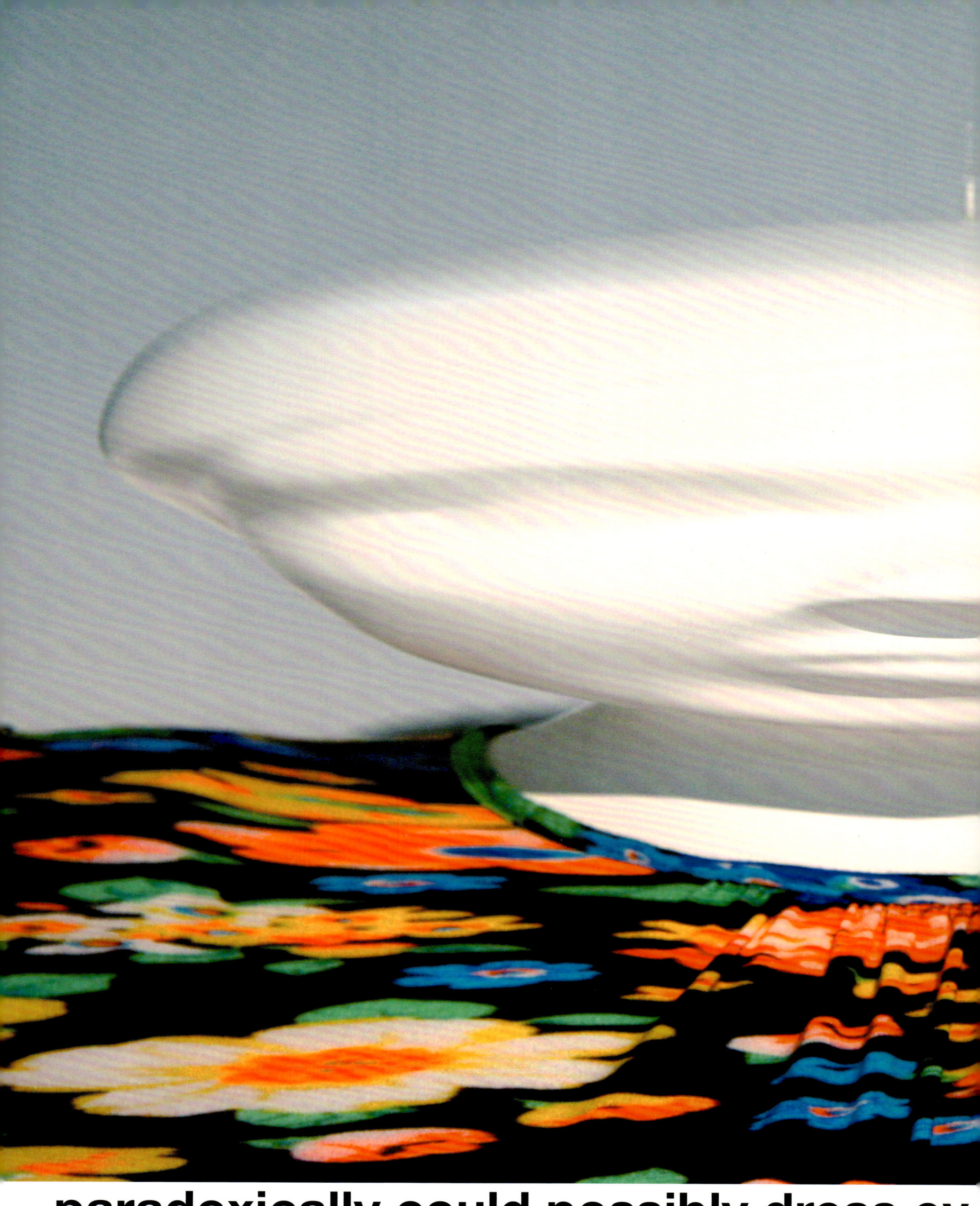

...paradoxically could possibly dress ev

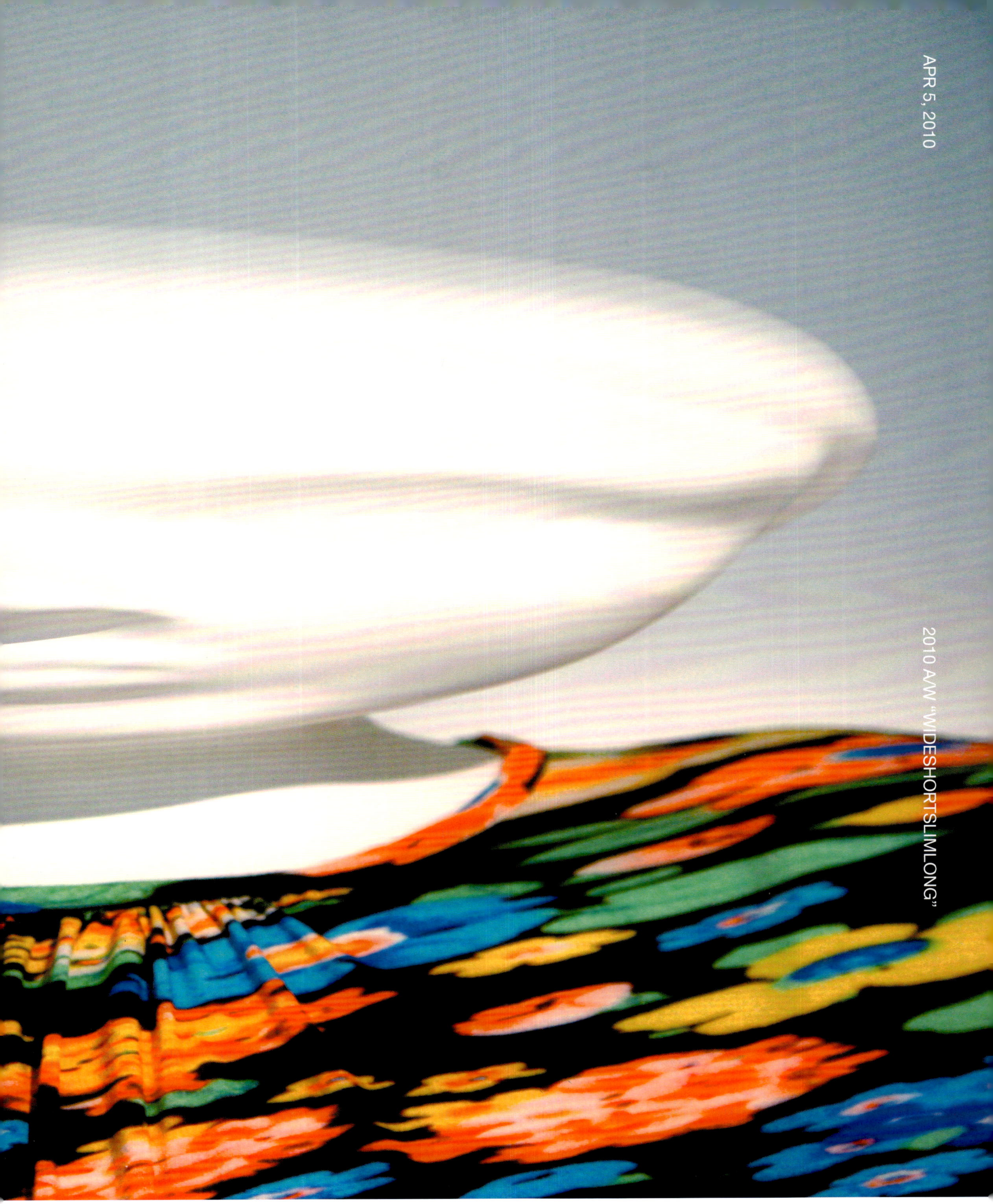

ryone

color [noun]

red, blue, green, yellow, etc.

color [verb]

to make something a particular color

4

COLOR

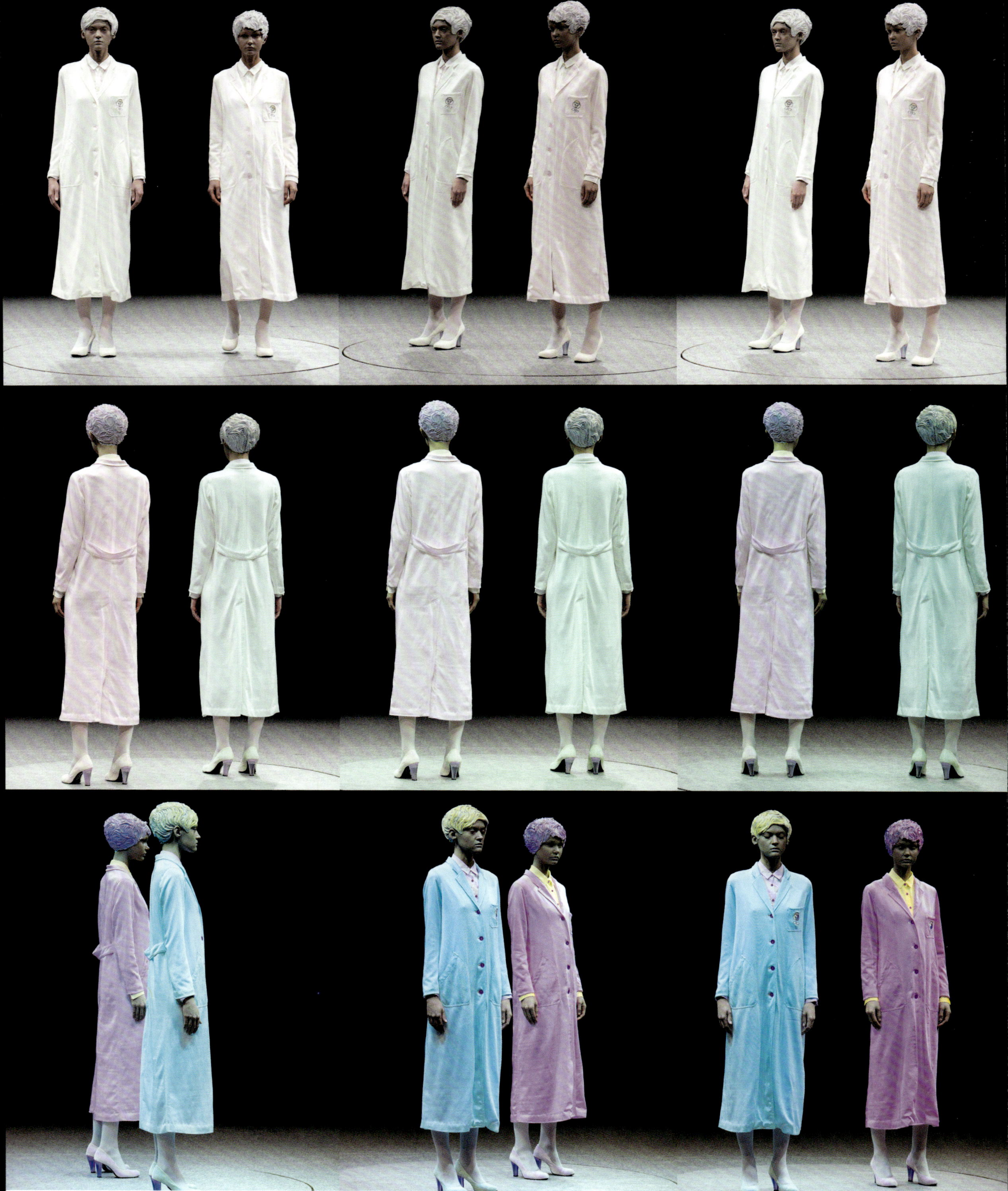

Wear the color, take off the color

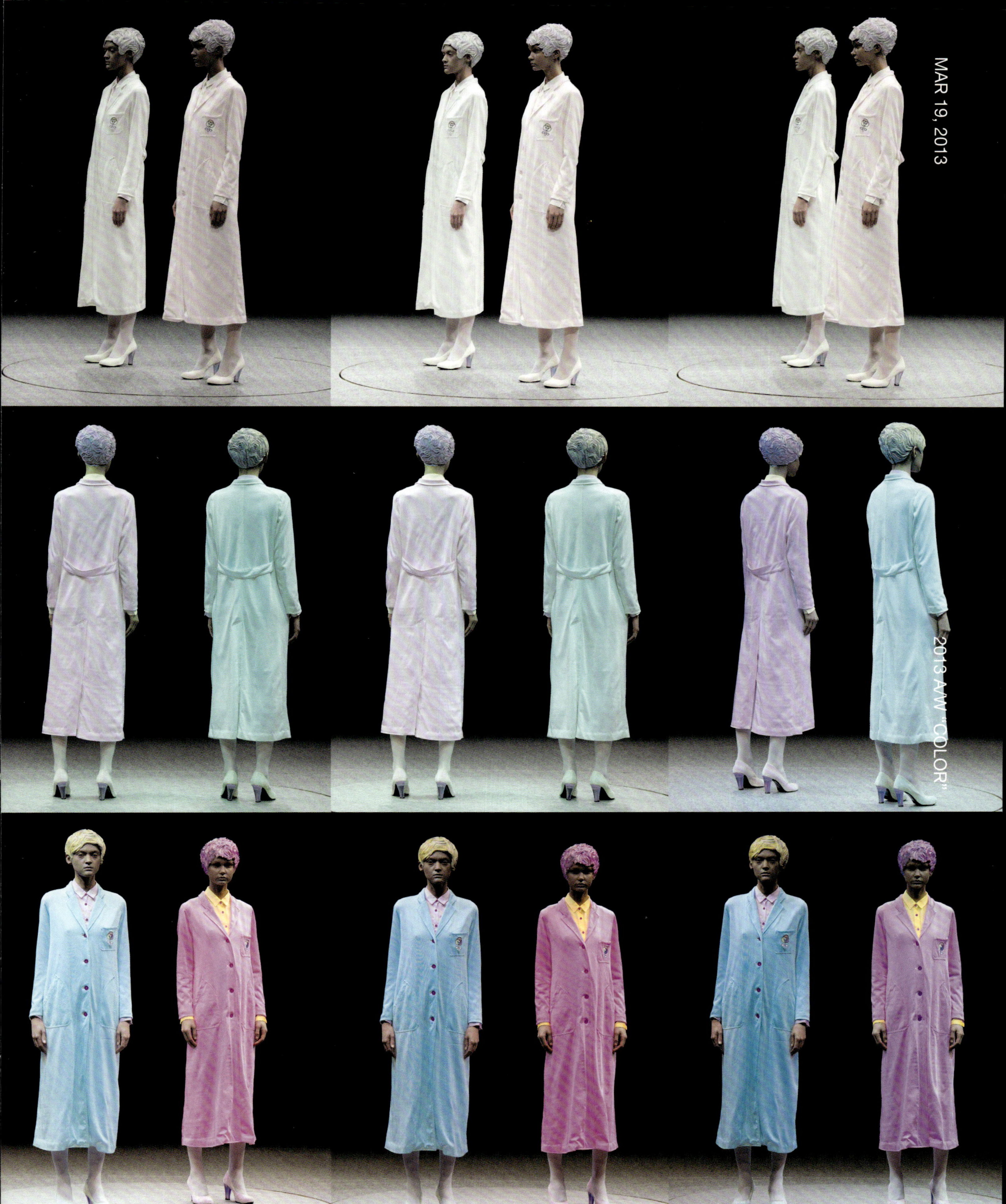

MAR 19, 2013

2013 A/W "COLOR"

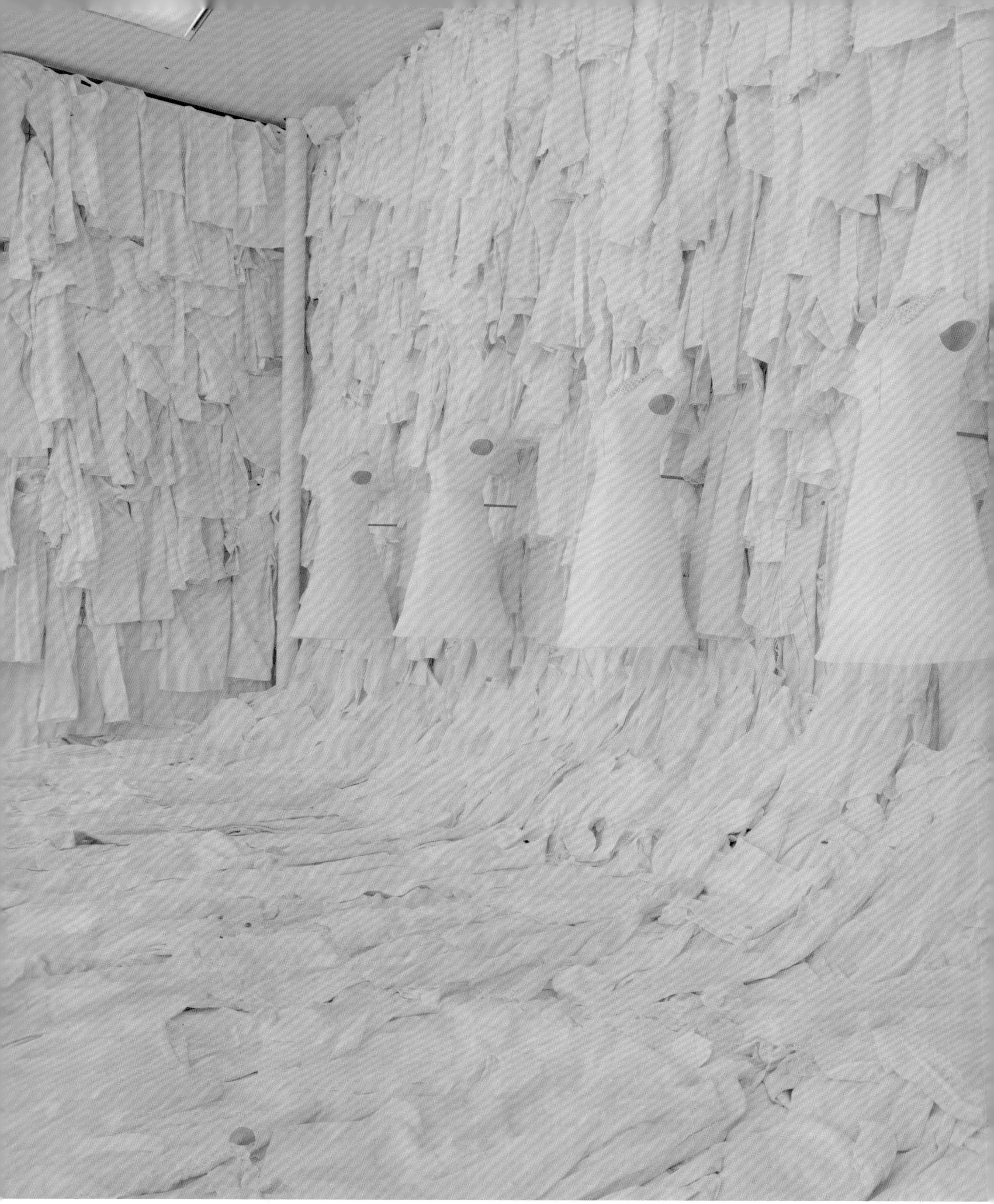

The whirlwind of fashion renders everyt

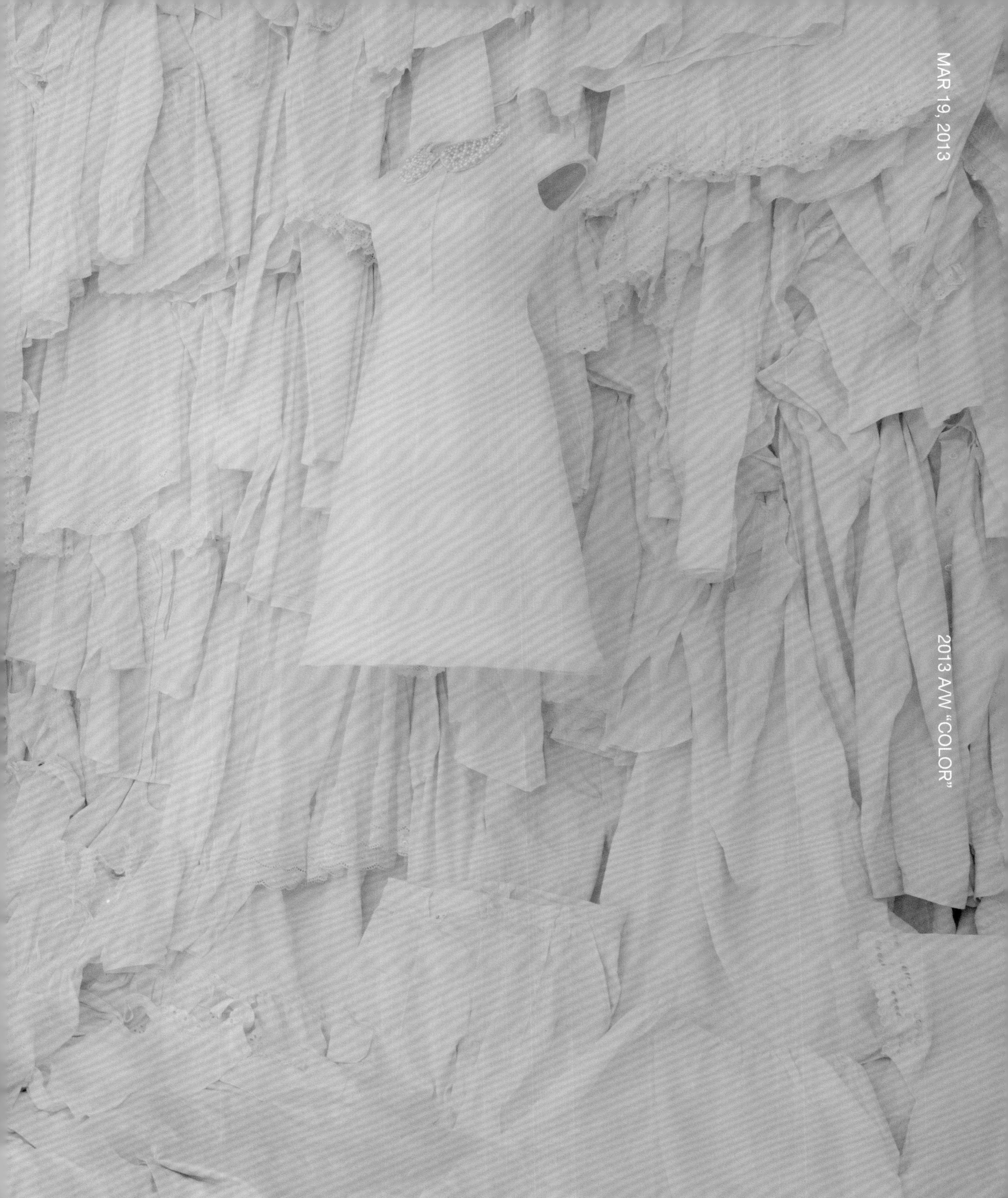

MAR 19, 2013

2013 A/W "COLOR"

ning obsolete...

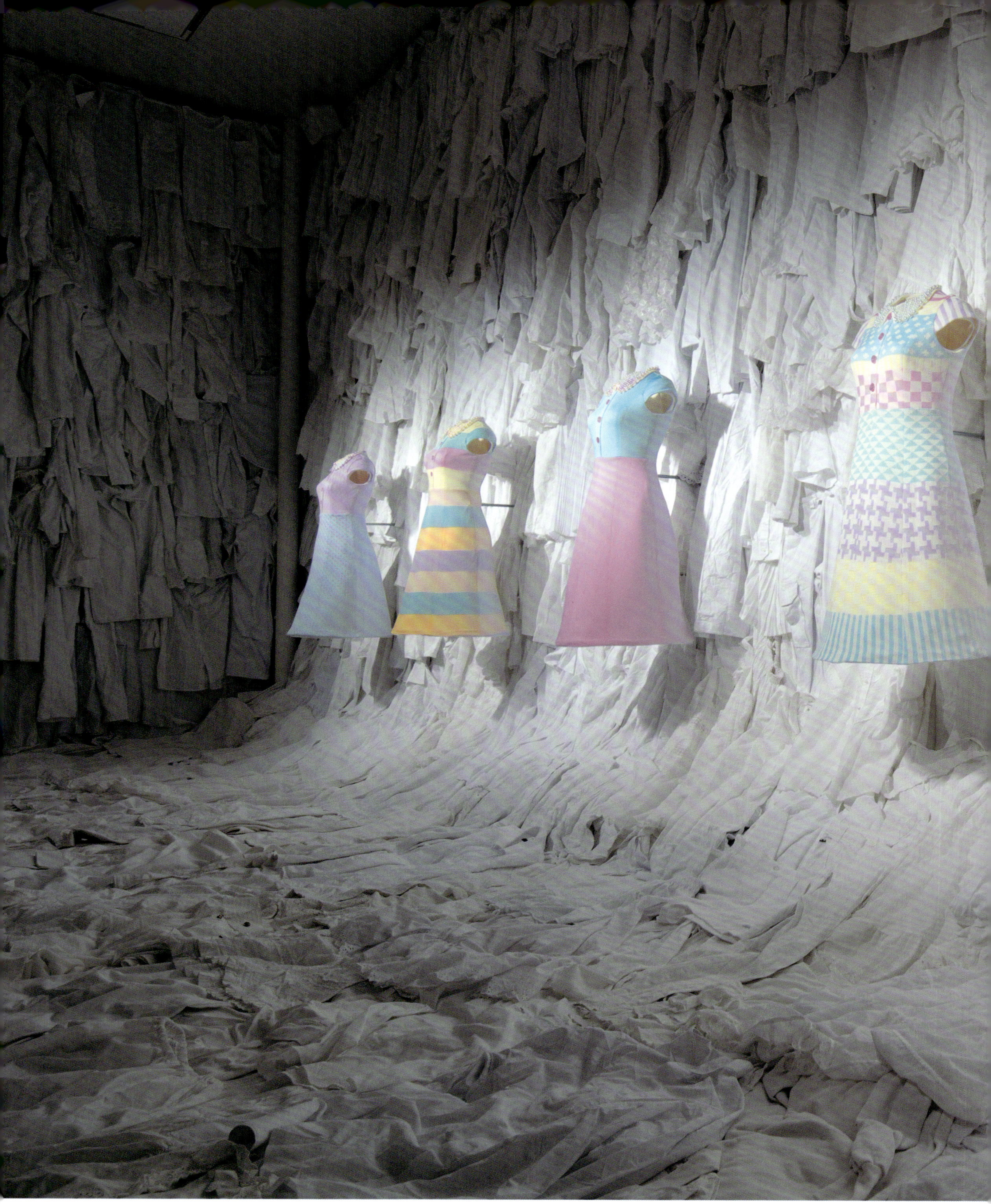

...even colors, in half a year

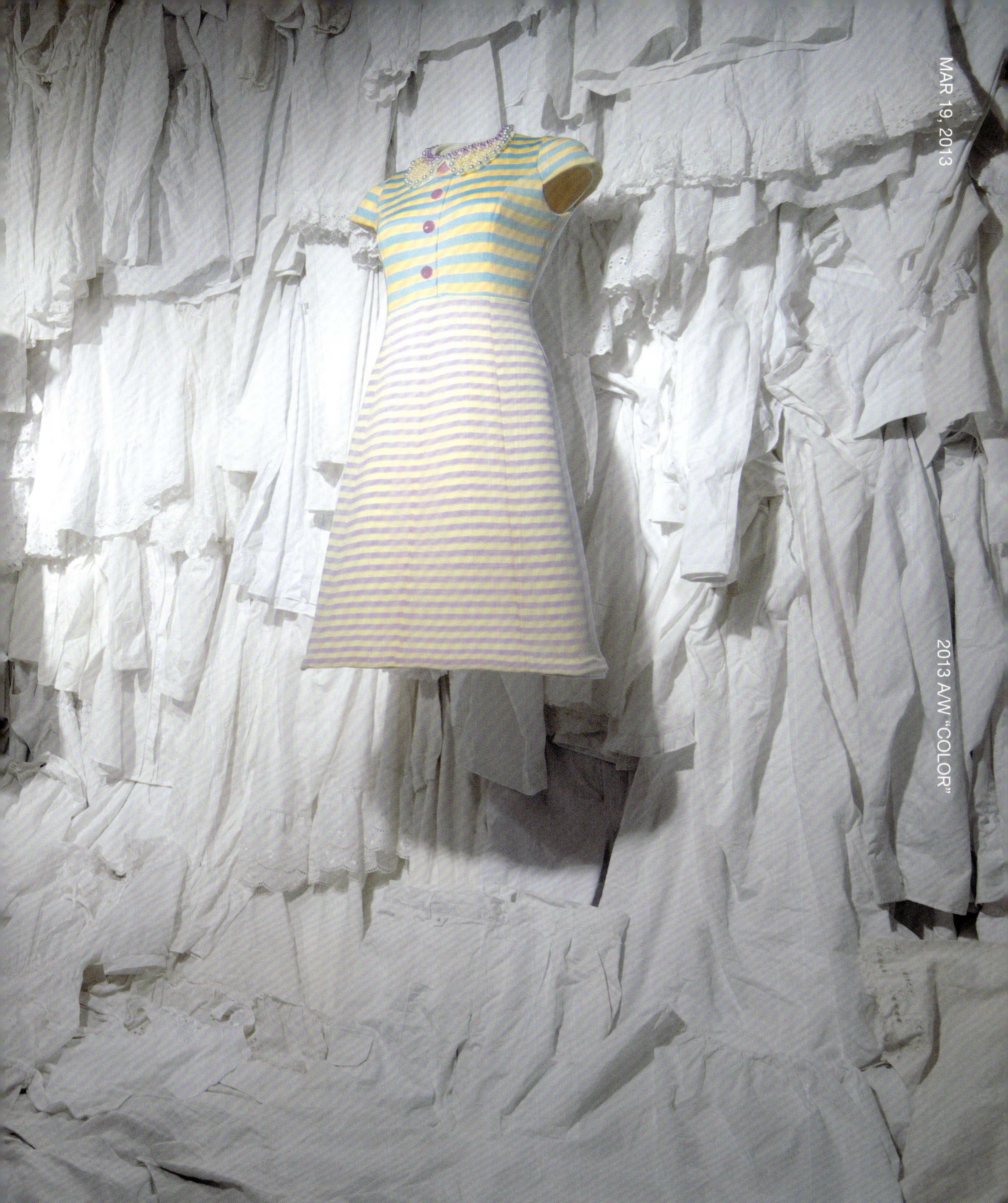

MAR 19, 2013

2013 A/W "COLOR"

Even though there’s no such thing as a

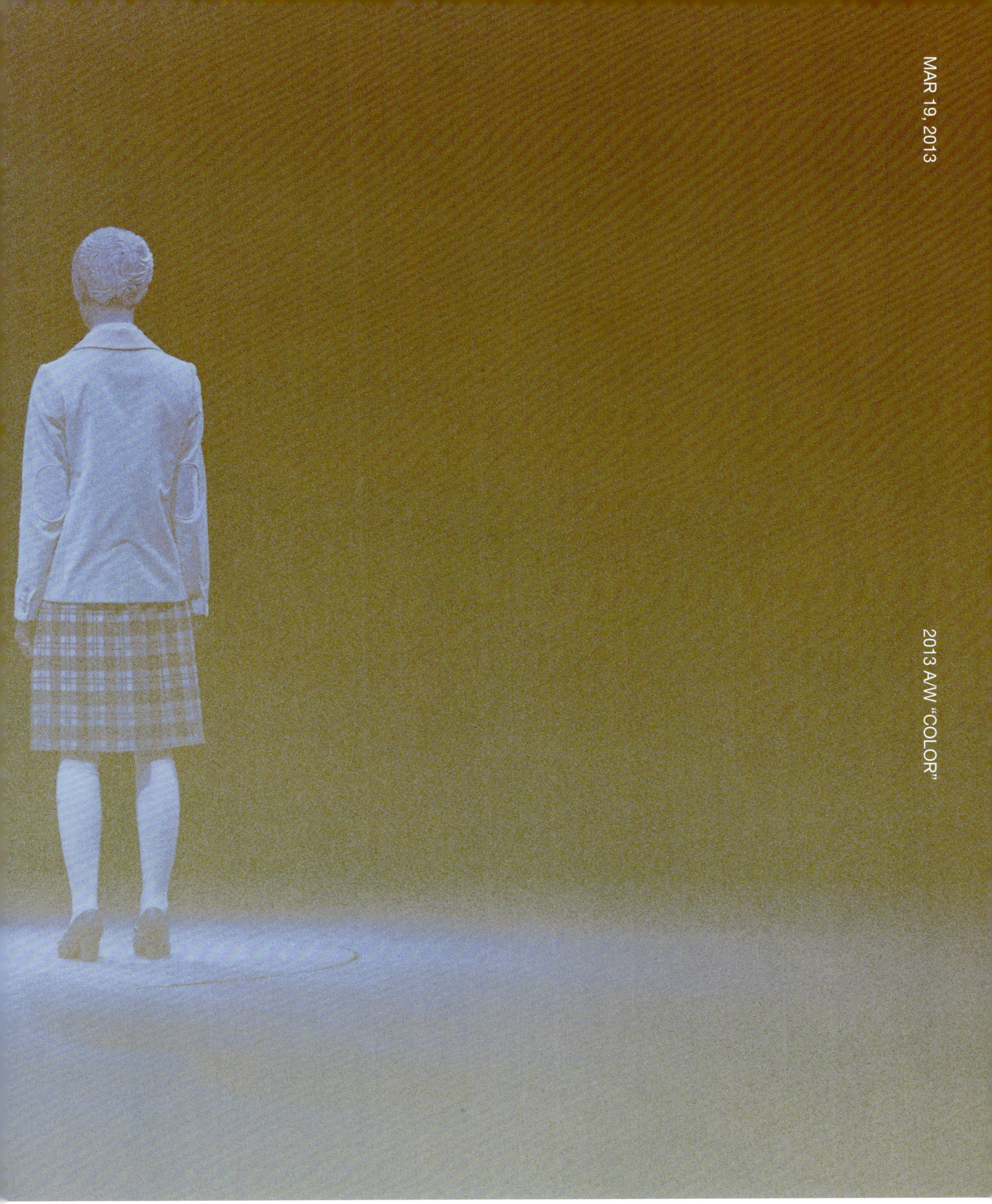

ew or old color

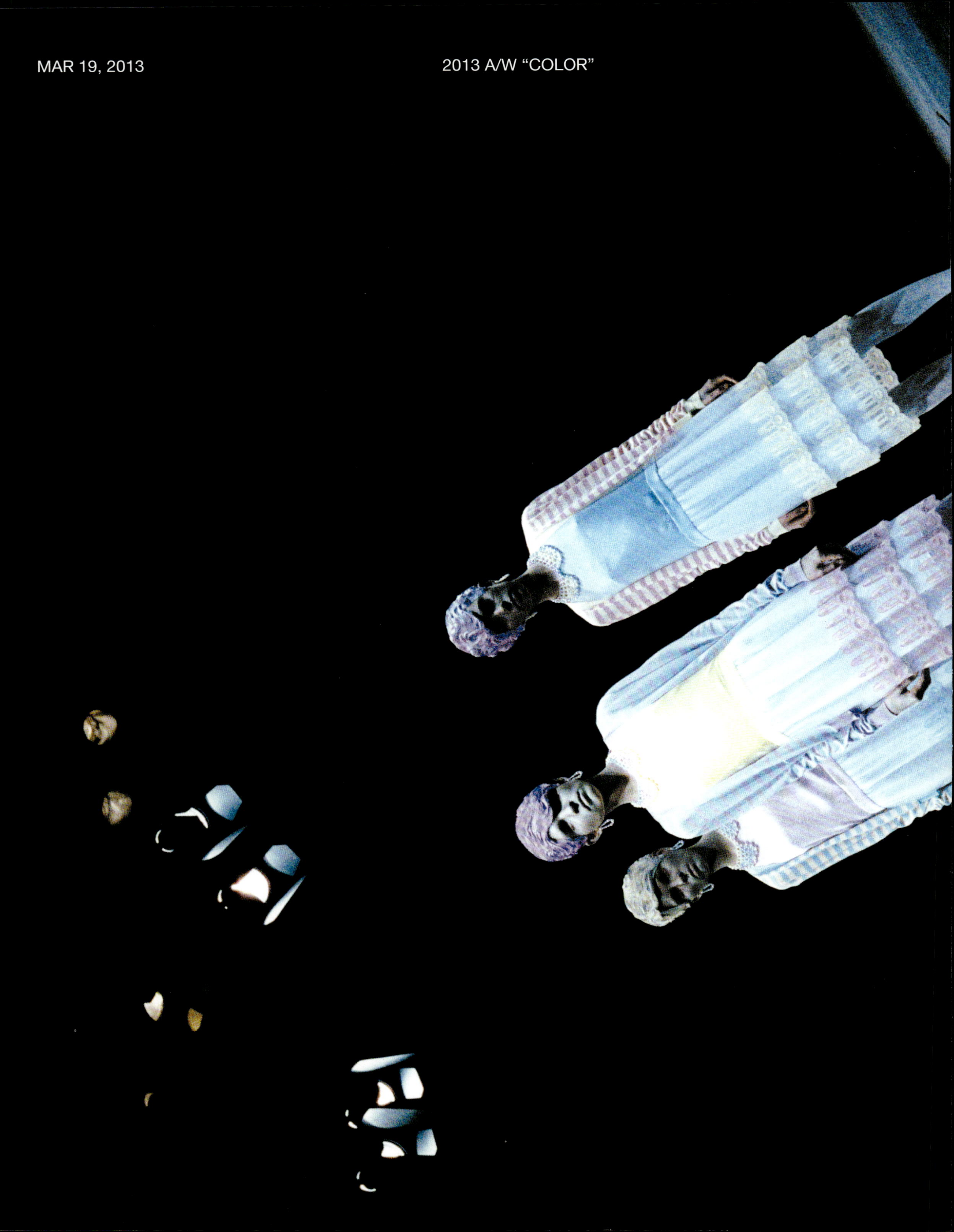

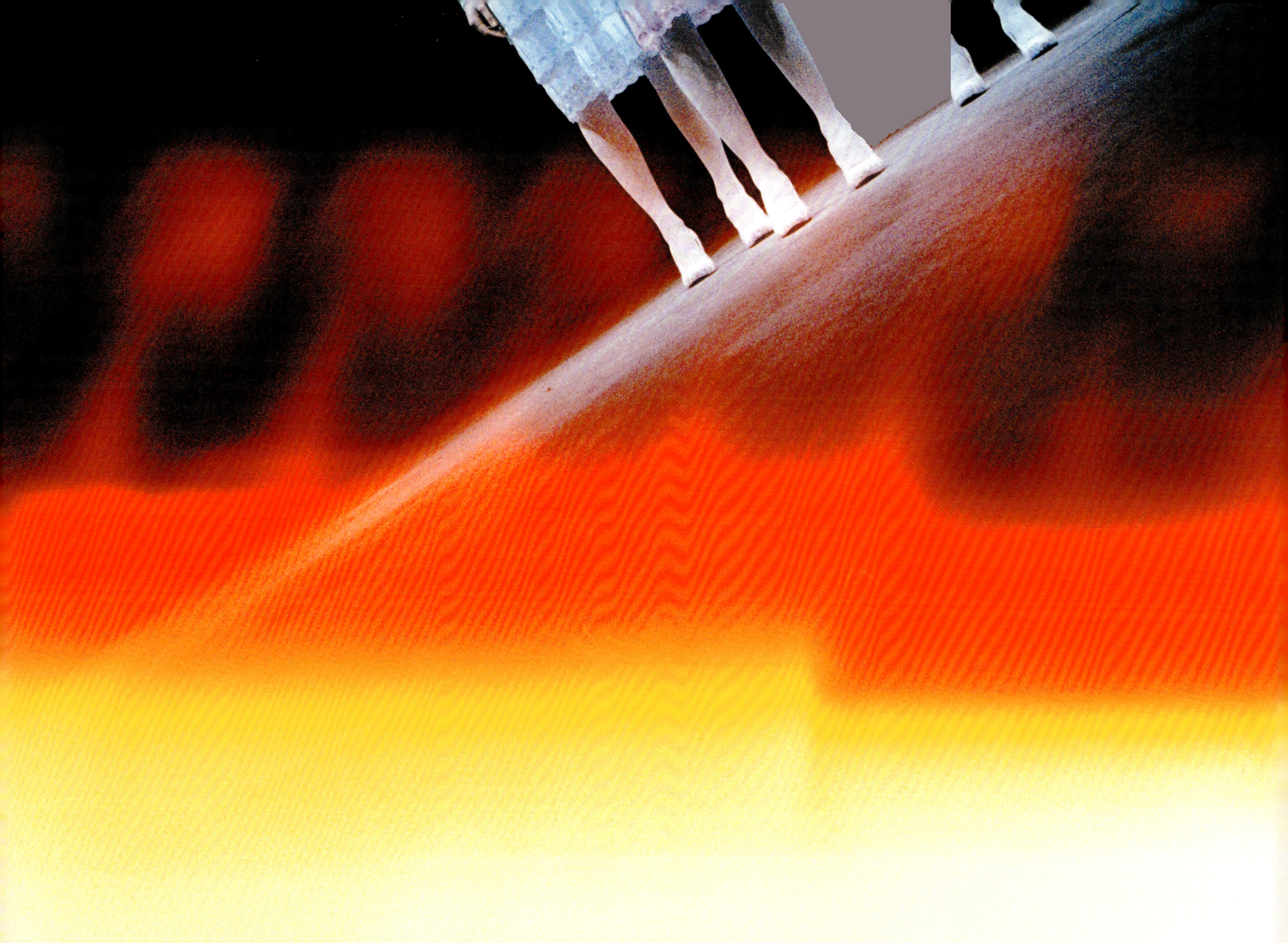

I don’t think of technology as a technology

Technology is something that will event

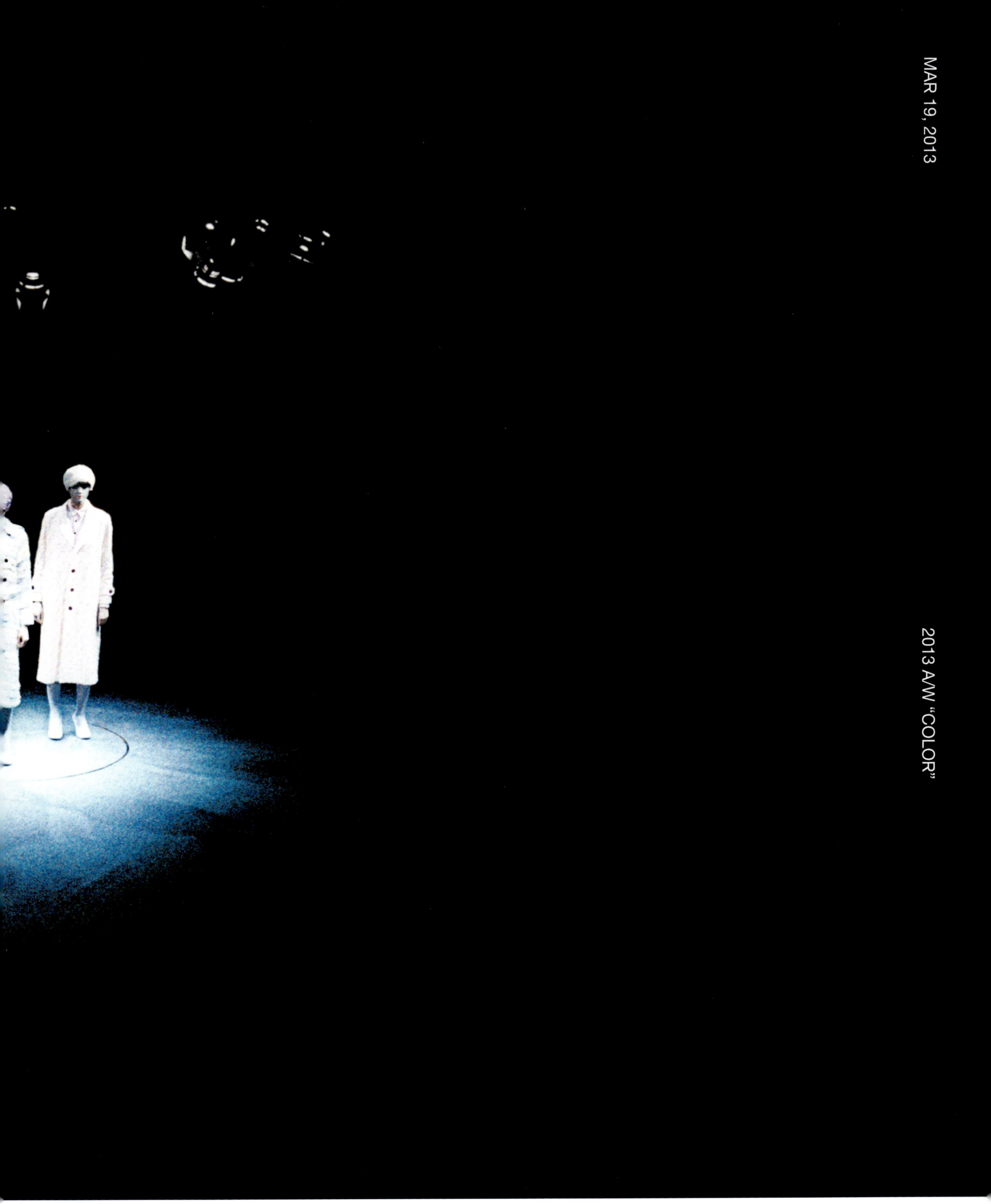

ually become part of our daily lives

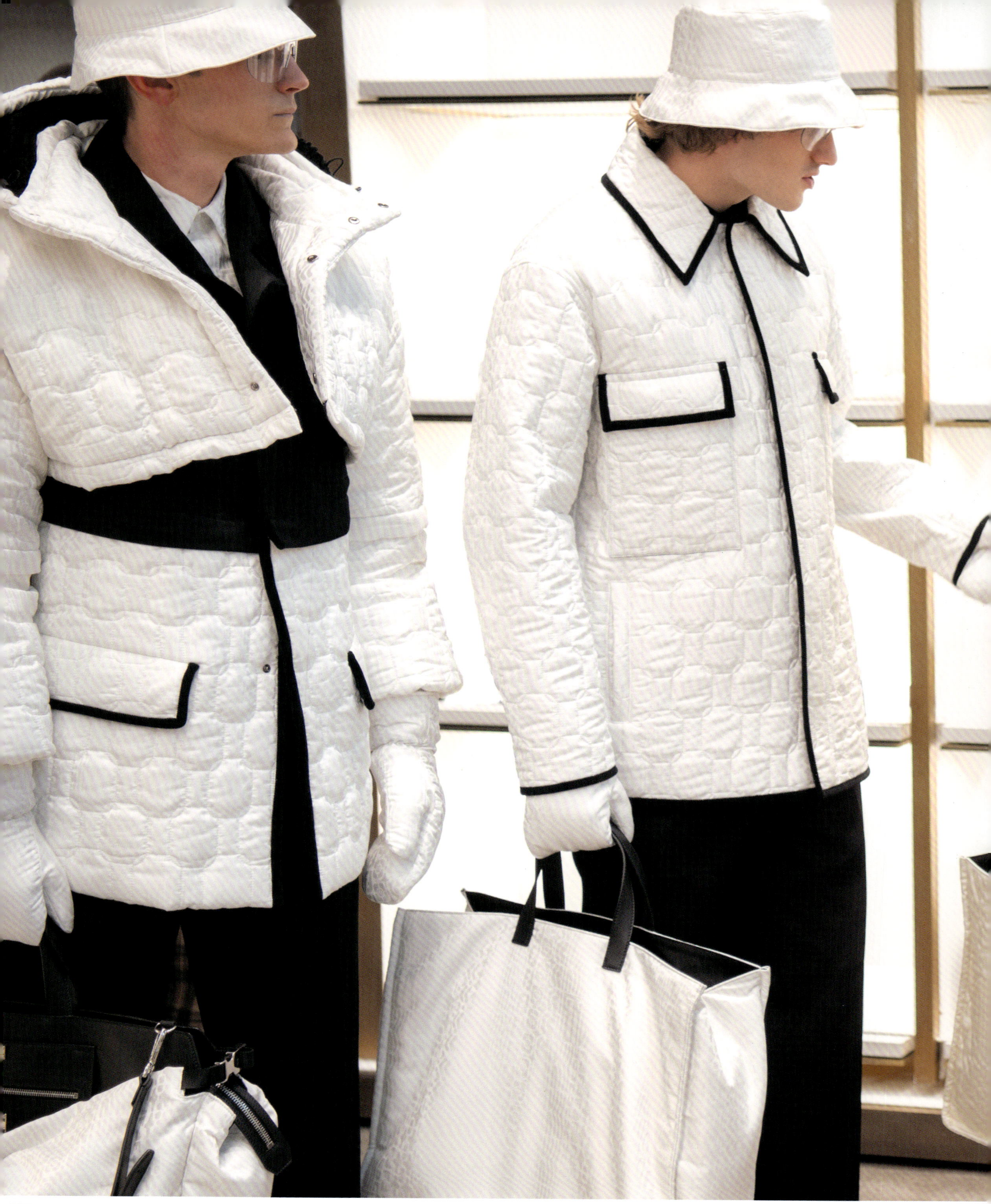

The essence of fashion is not just the d

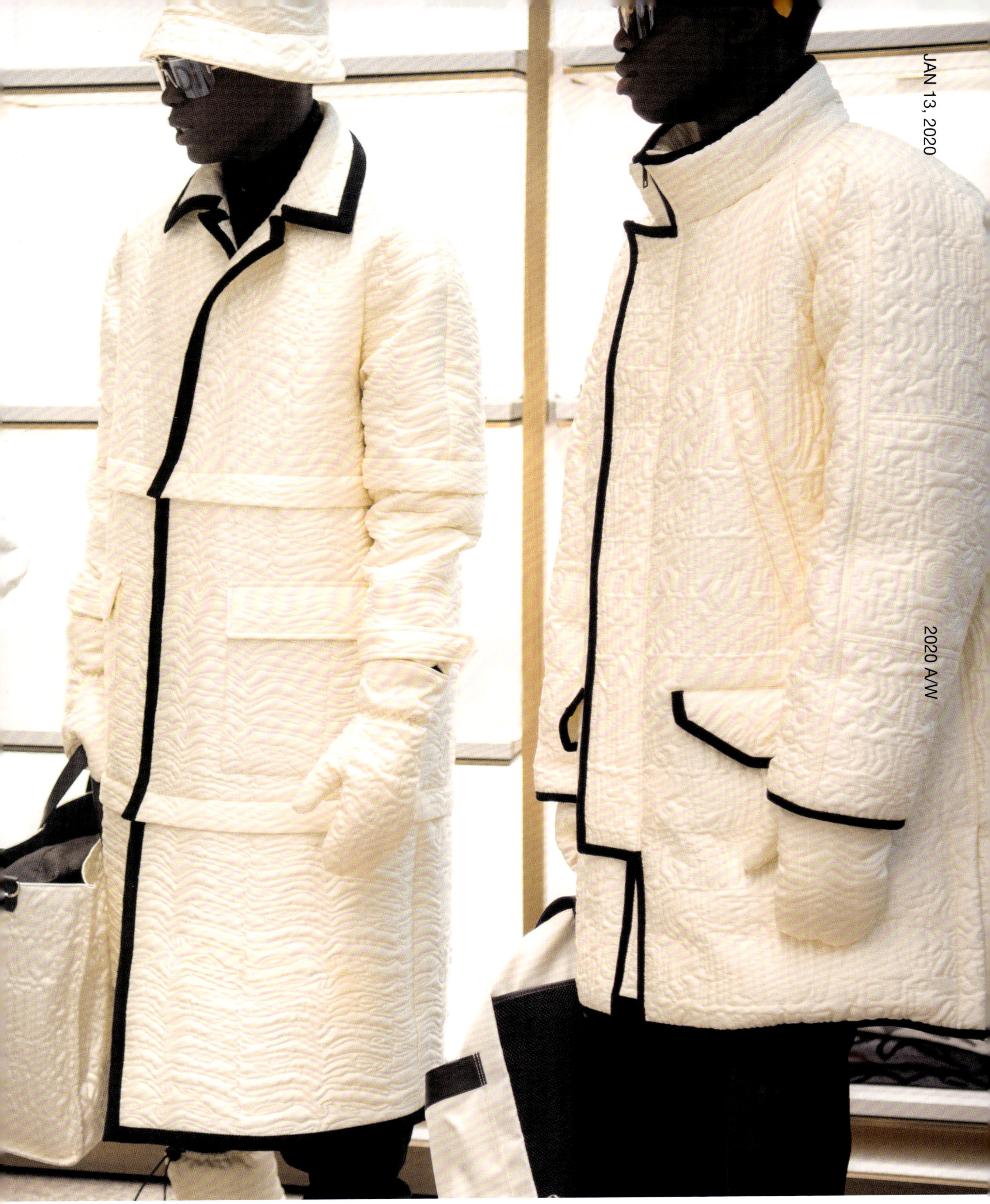

JAN 13, 2020

2020 A/W

esign and style itself...

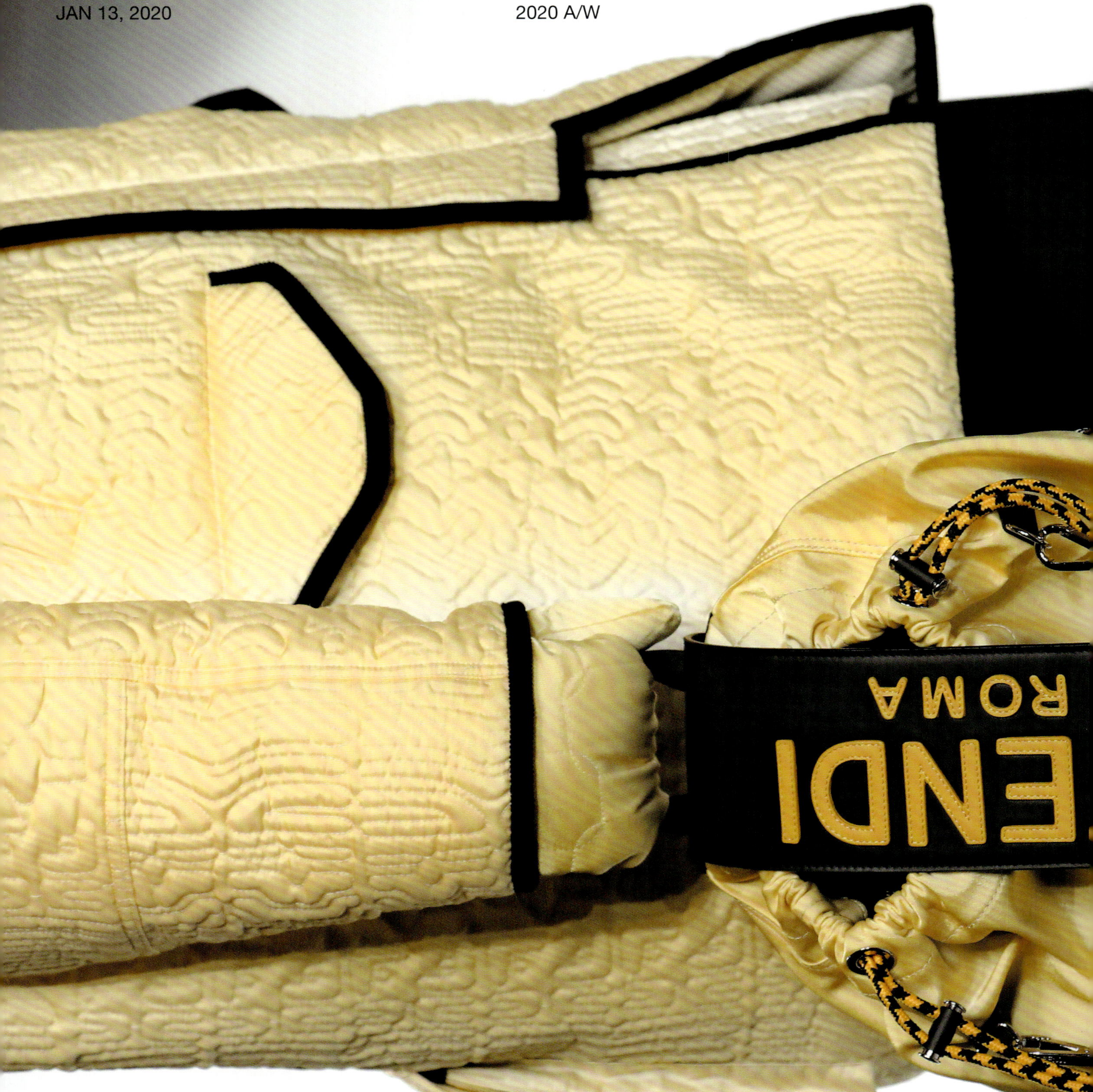
ROMA

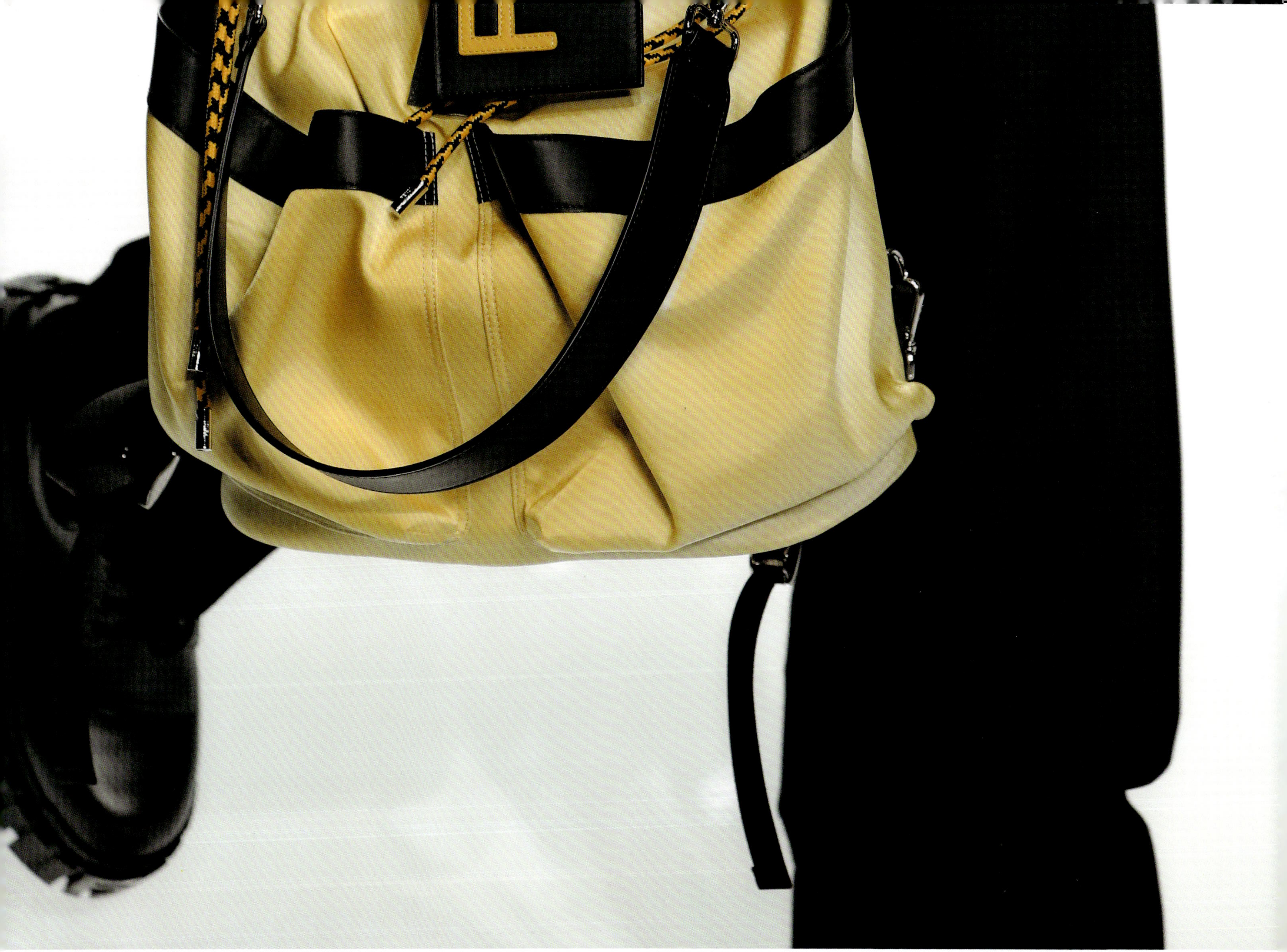

...but also what creative events are happening there

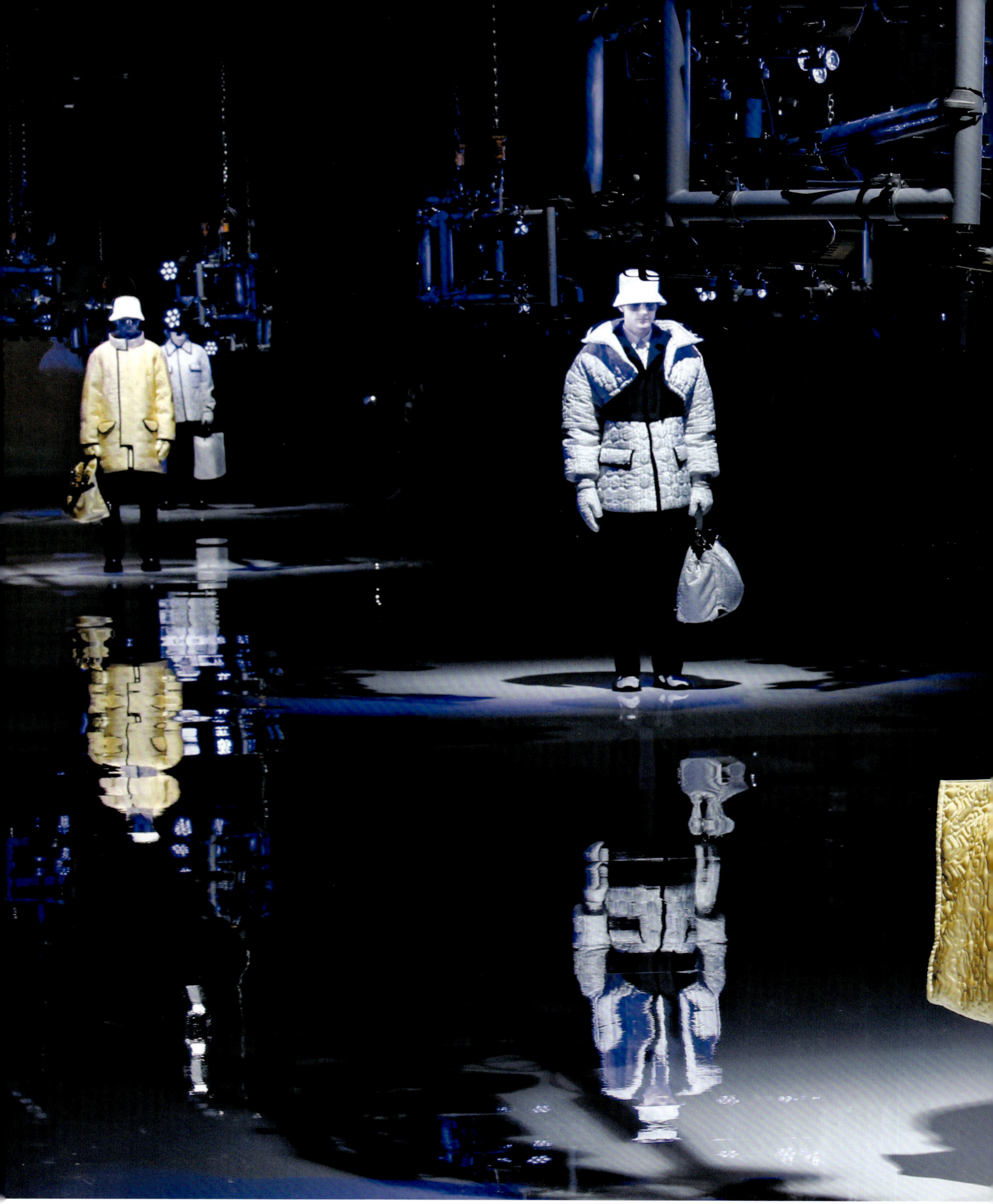

I hope to be inside of fashion, but at the

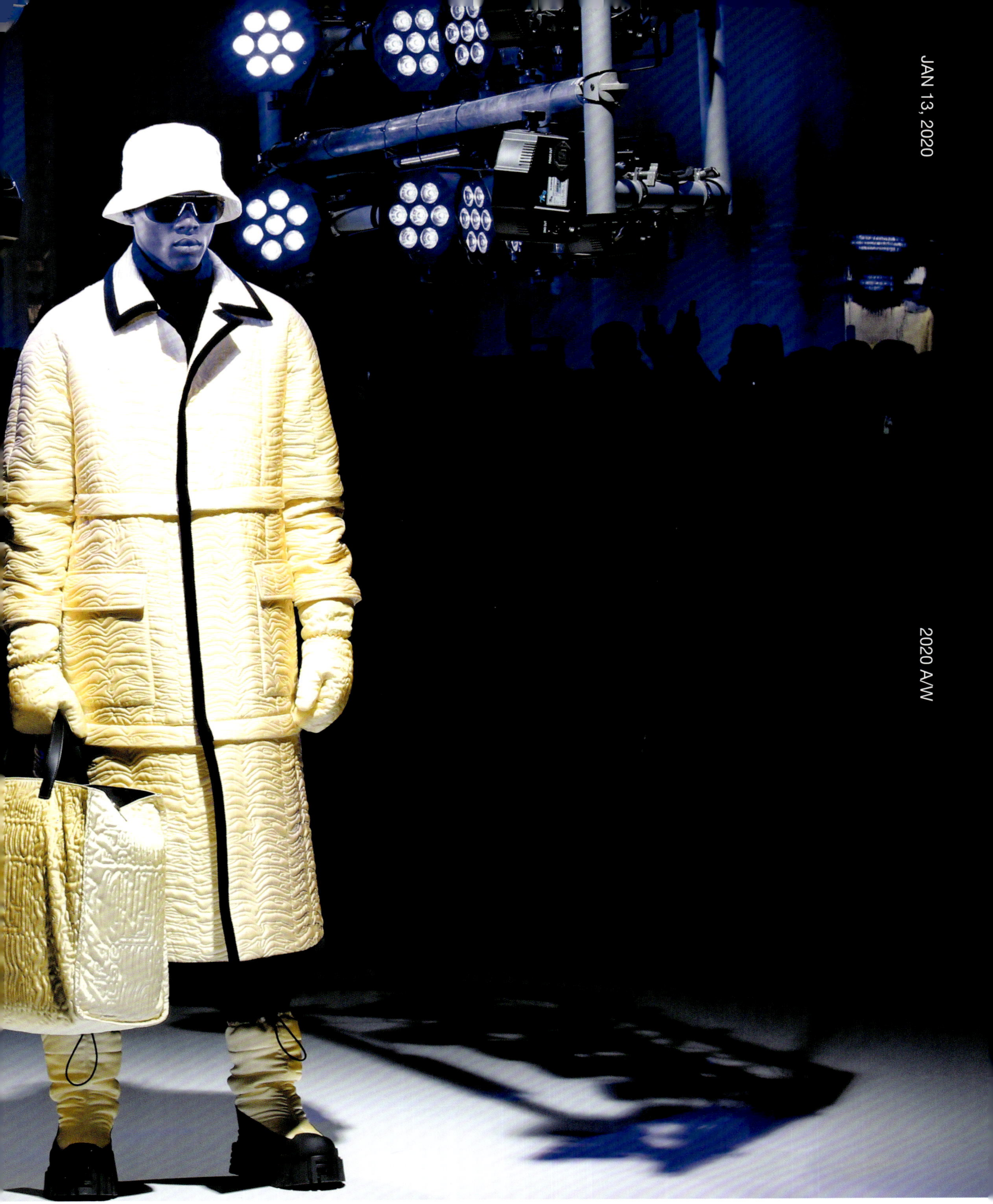

JAN 13, 2020

2020 A/W

same time, be completely outside of it

intangible [adjective]

impossible to touch, to describe exactly, or to give an exact value

intangible [noun]

something that exists but that cannot be touched, exactly described, or given an exact value

5

INTANGIBLE

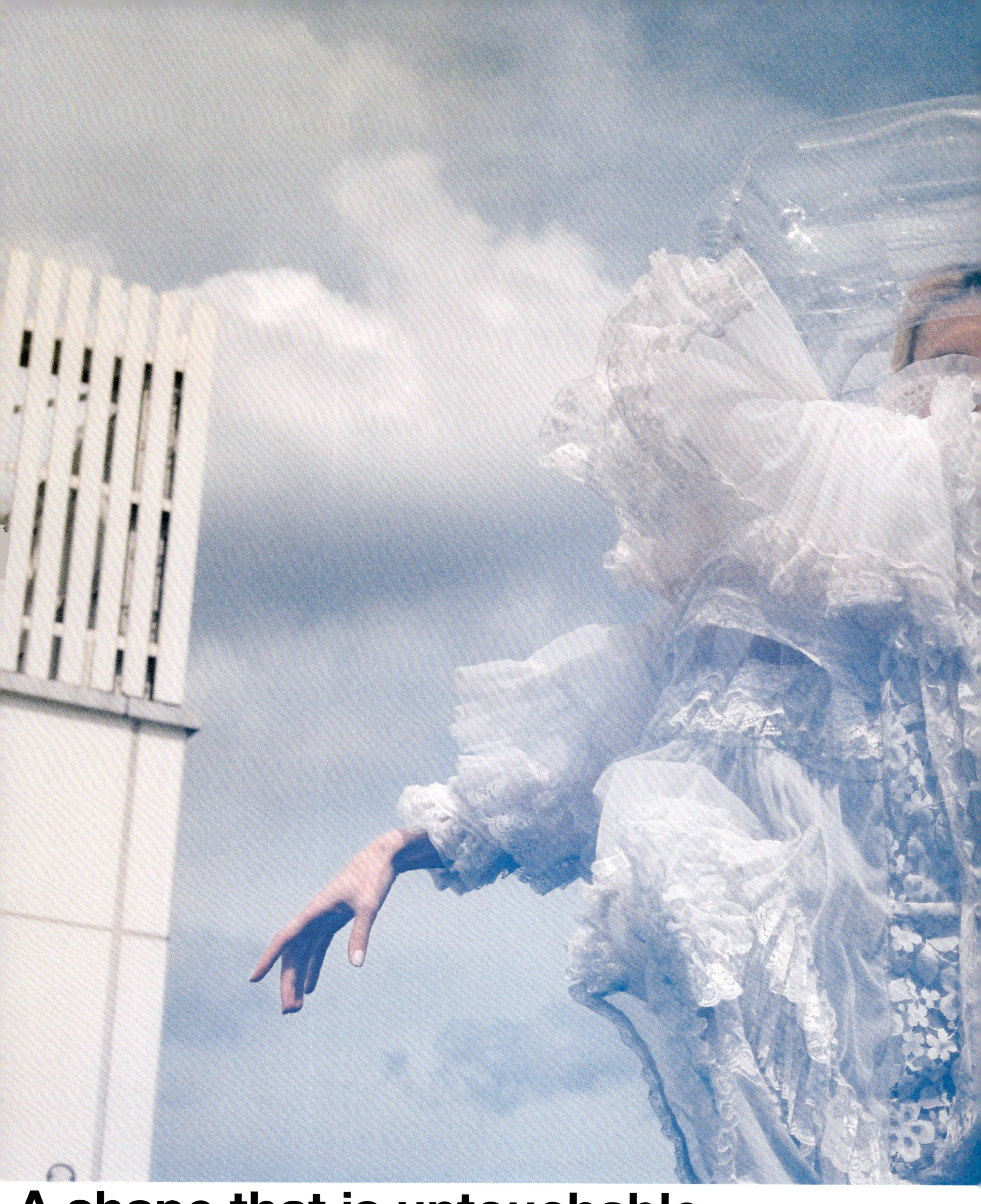

A shape that is untouchable

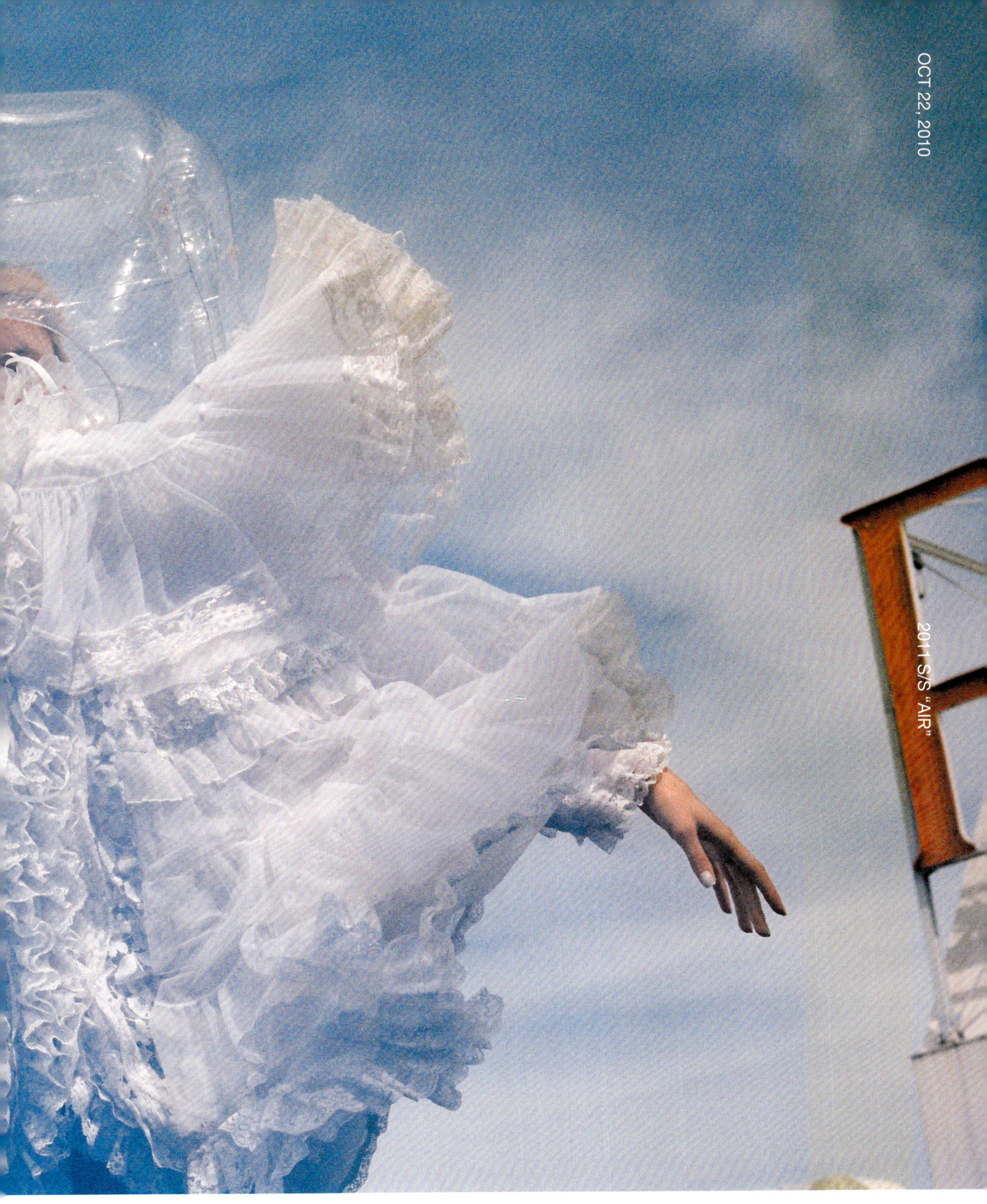

OCT 22, 2010

2011 S/S "AIR"

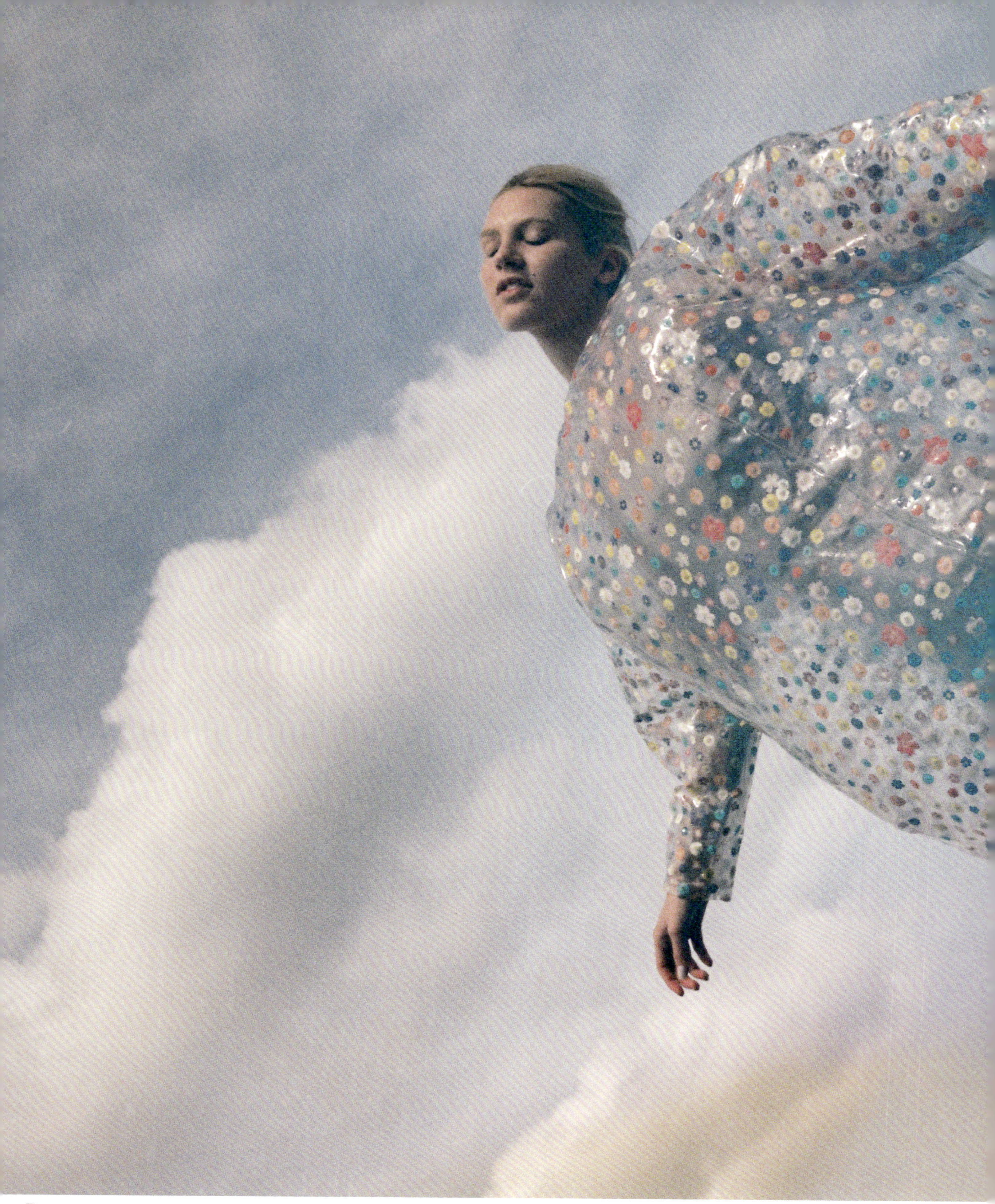

An attempt of trying to feel it

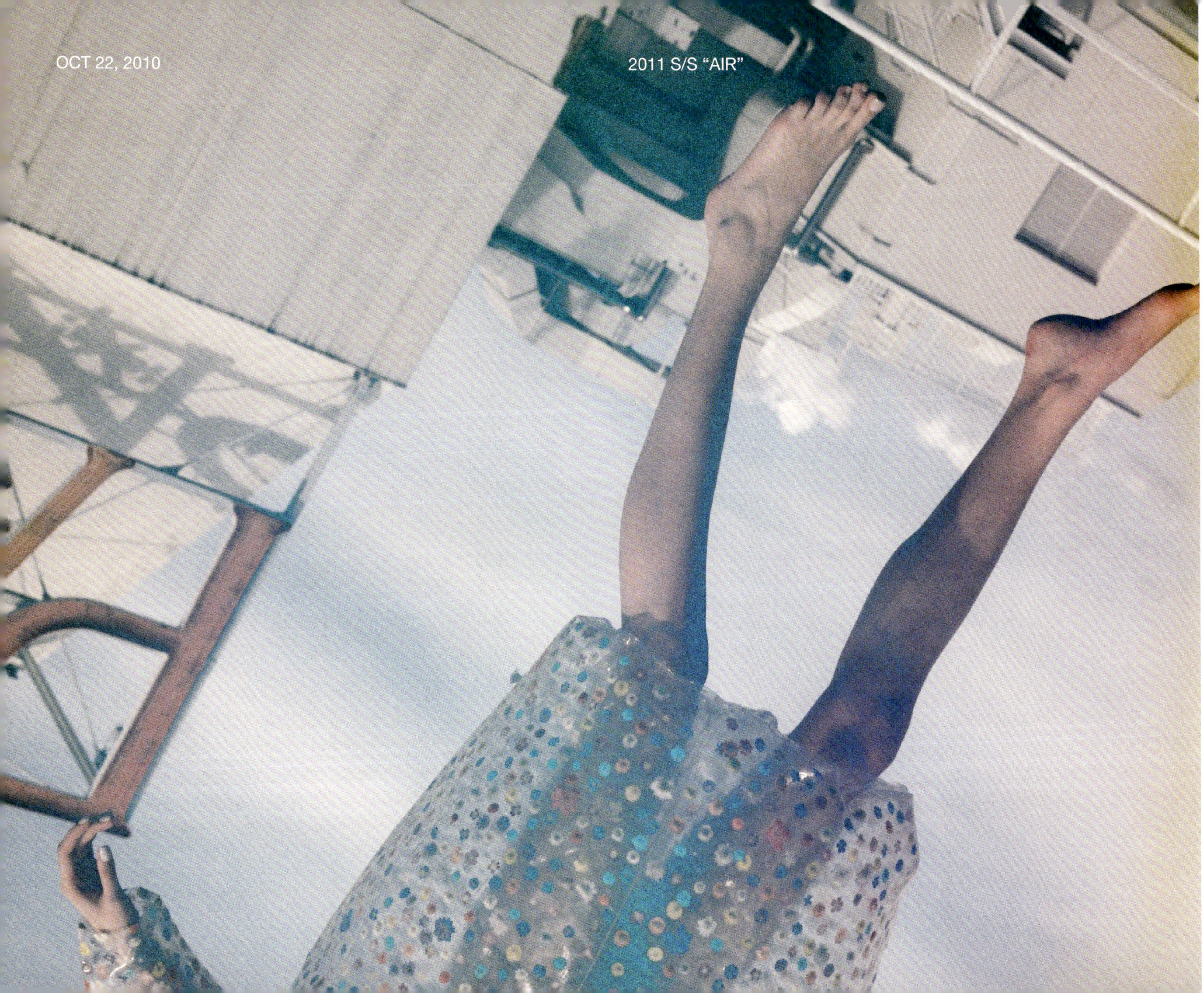
OCT 22, 2010
2011 S/S "AIR"

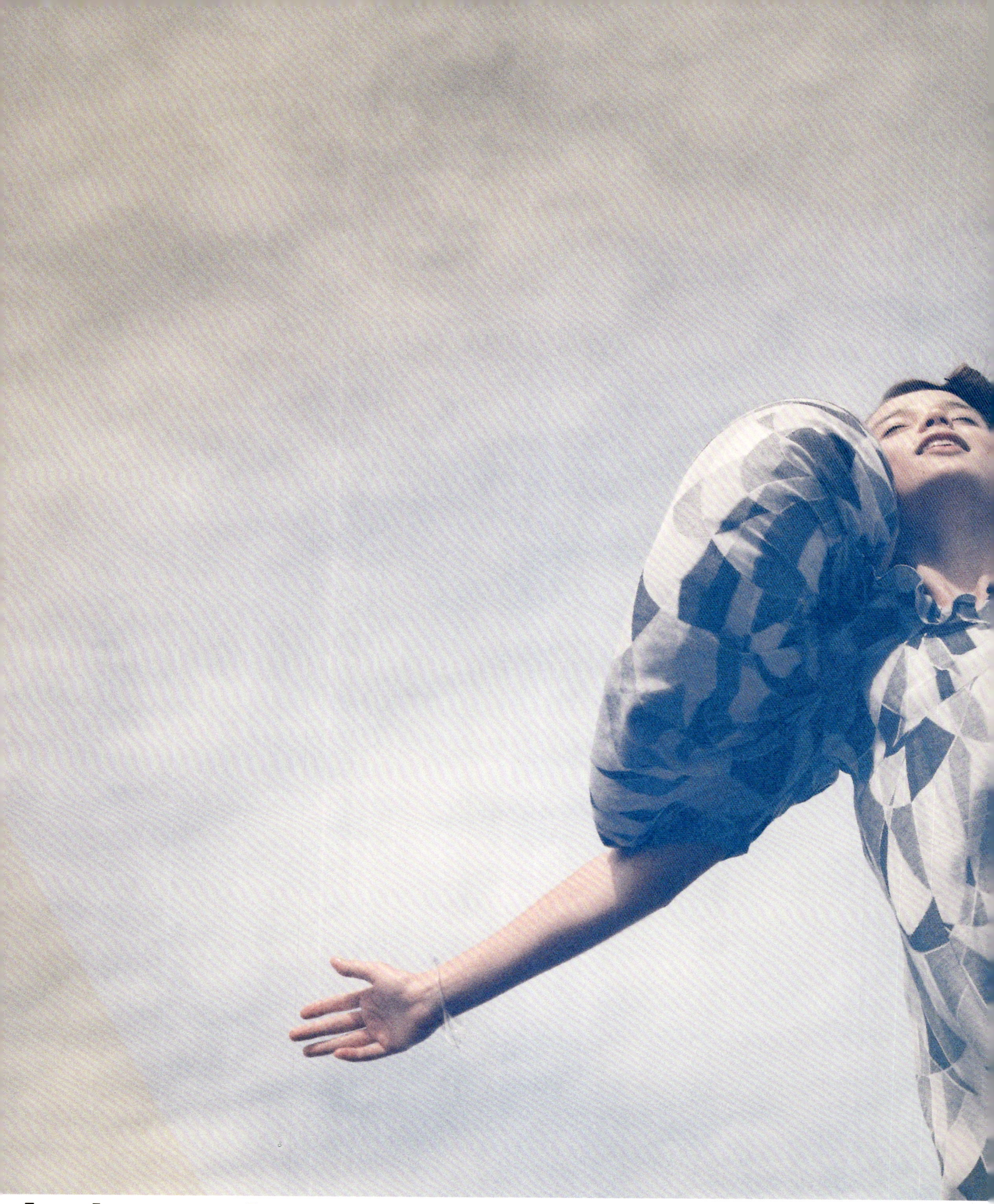

A shape that is invisible

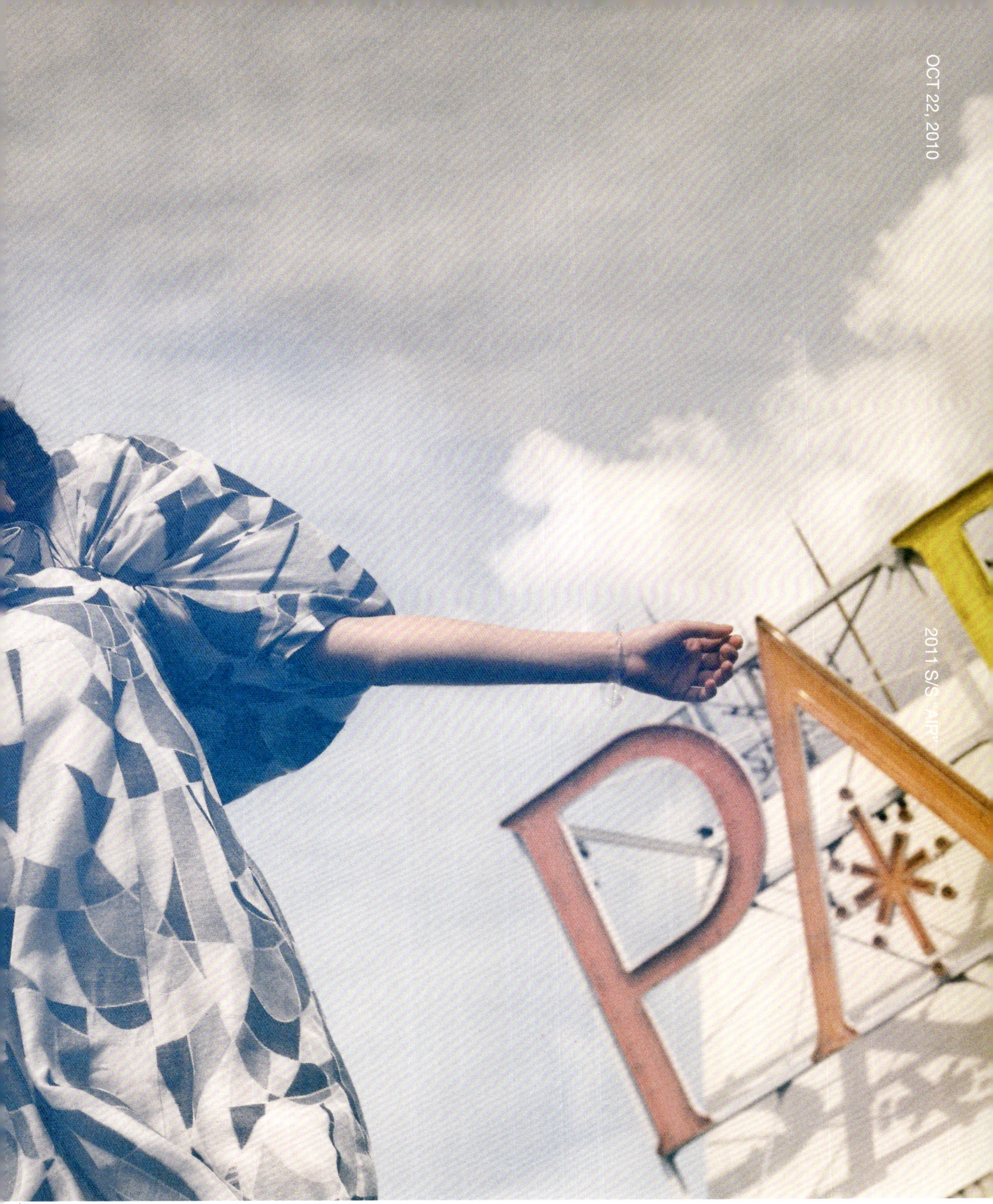

OCT 22, 2010

2011 S/S "AIR"

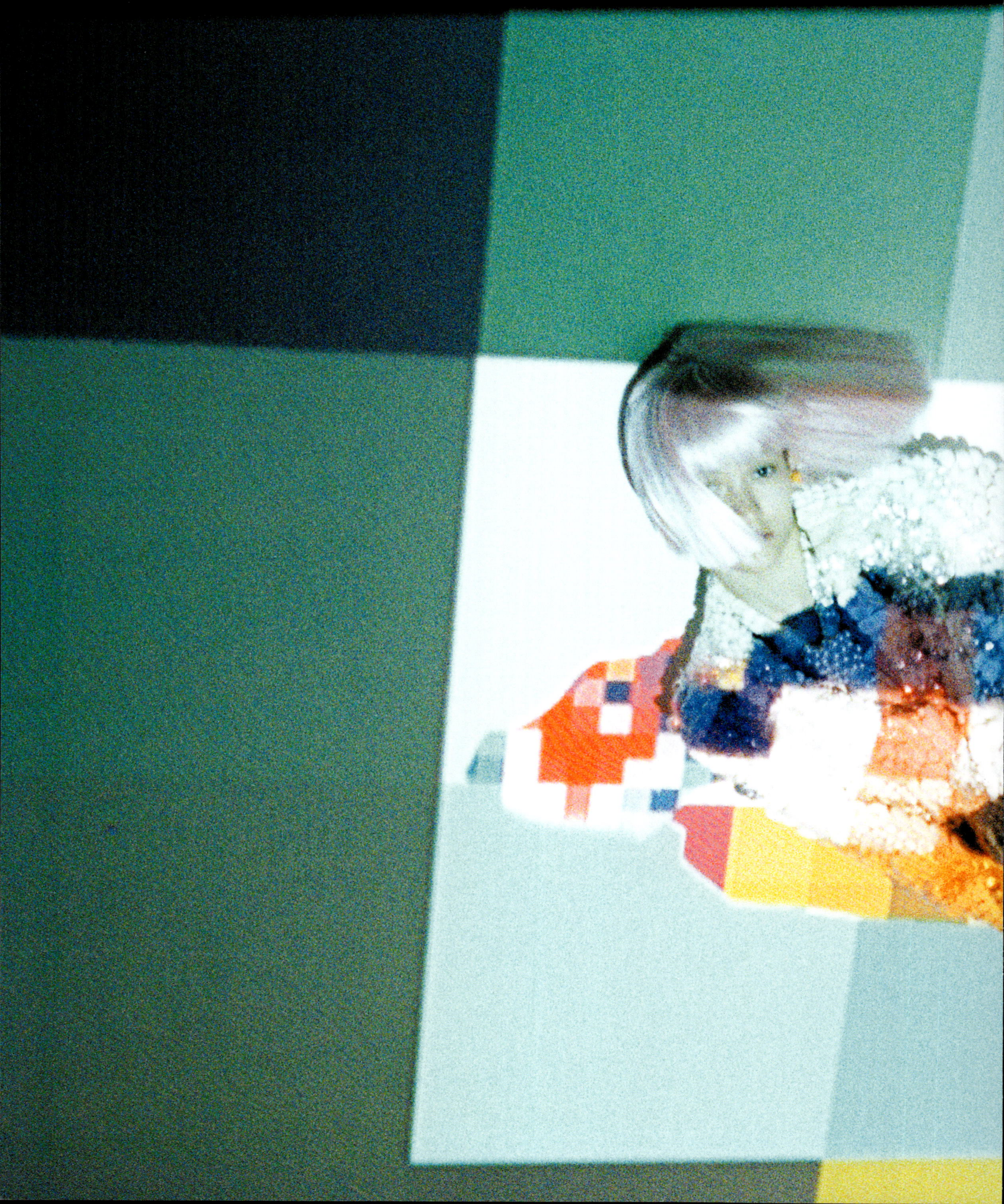

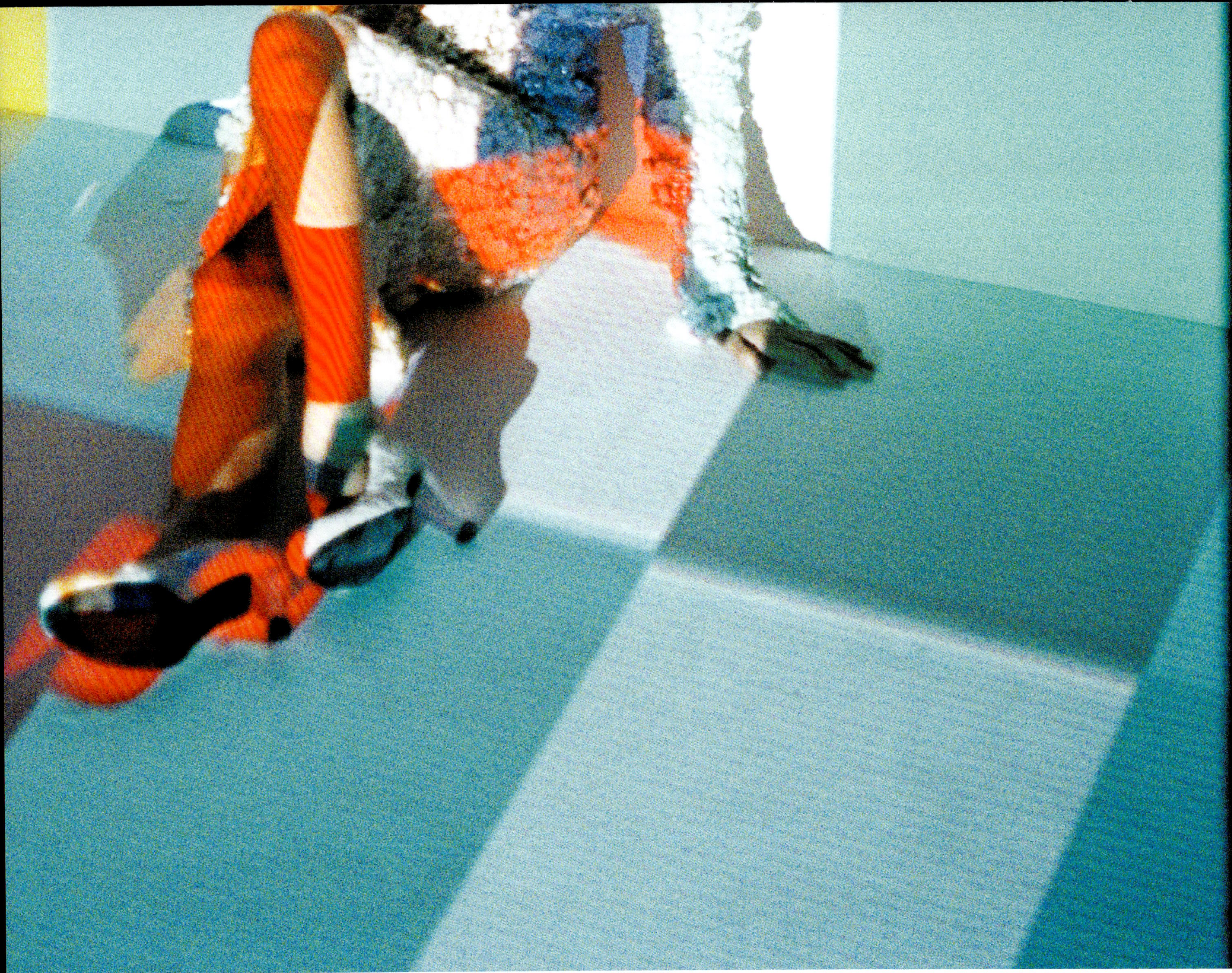

An attempt at trying to see it

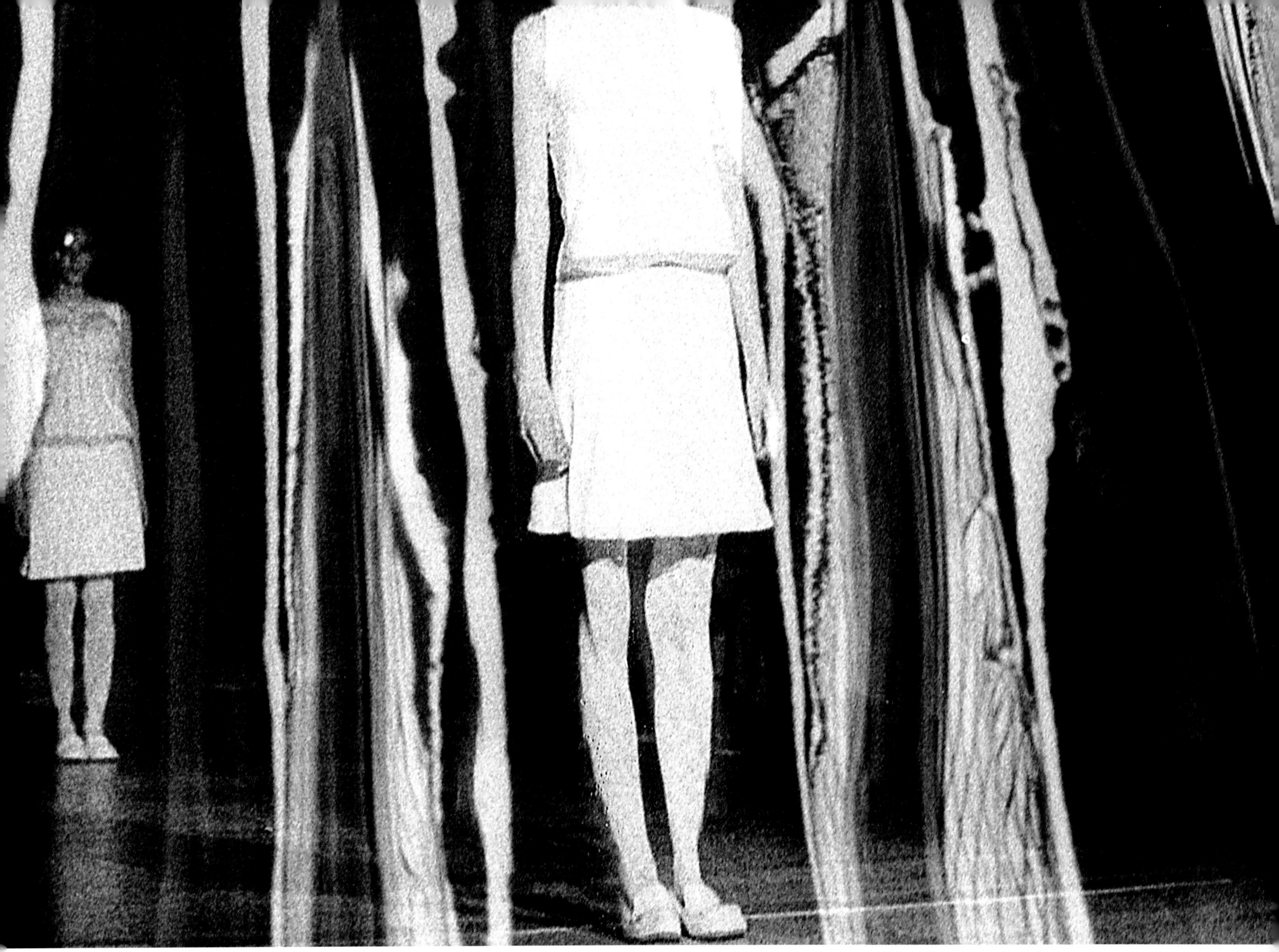

There are also shapes in the intangible things

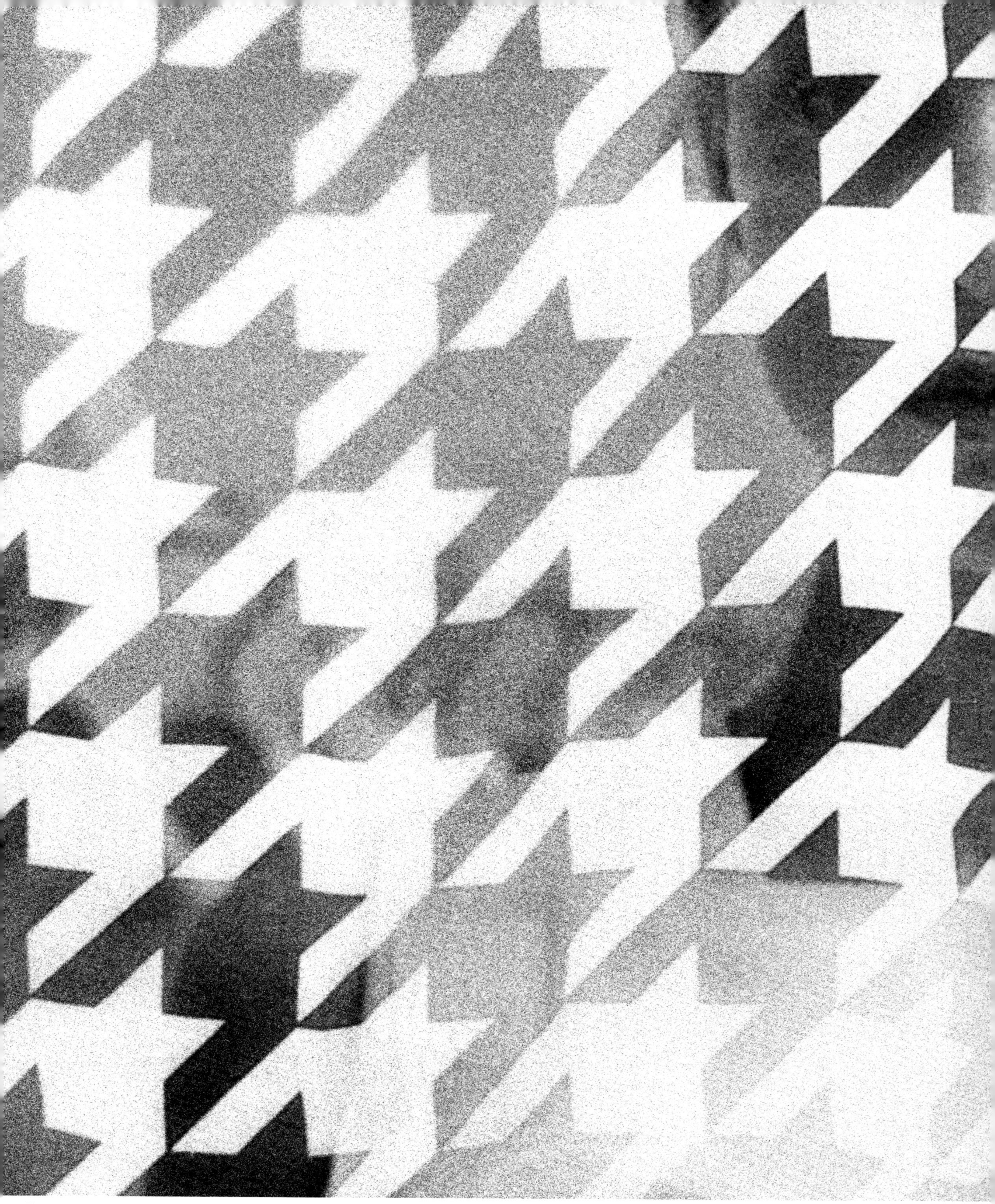

An attempt of trying to shape it

OCT 22, 2011

2012 S/S “SHELL”

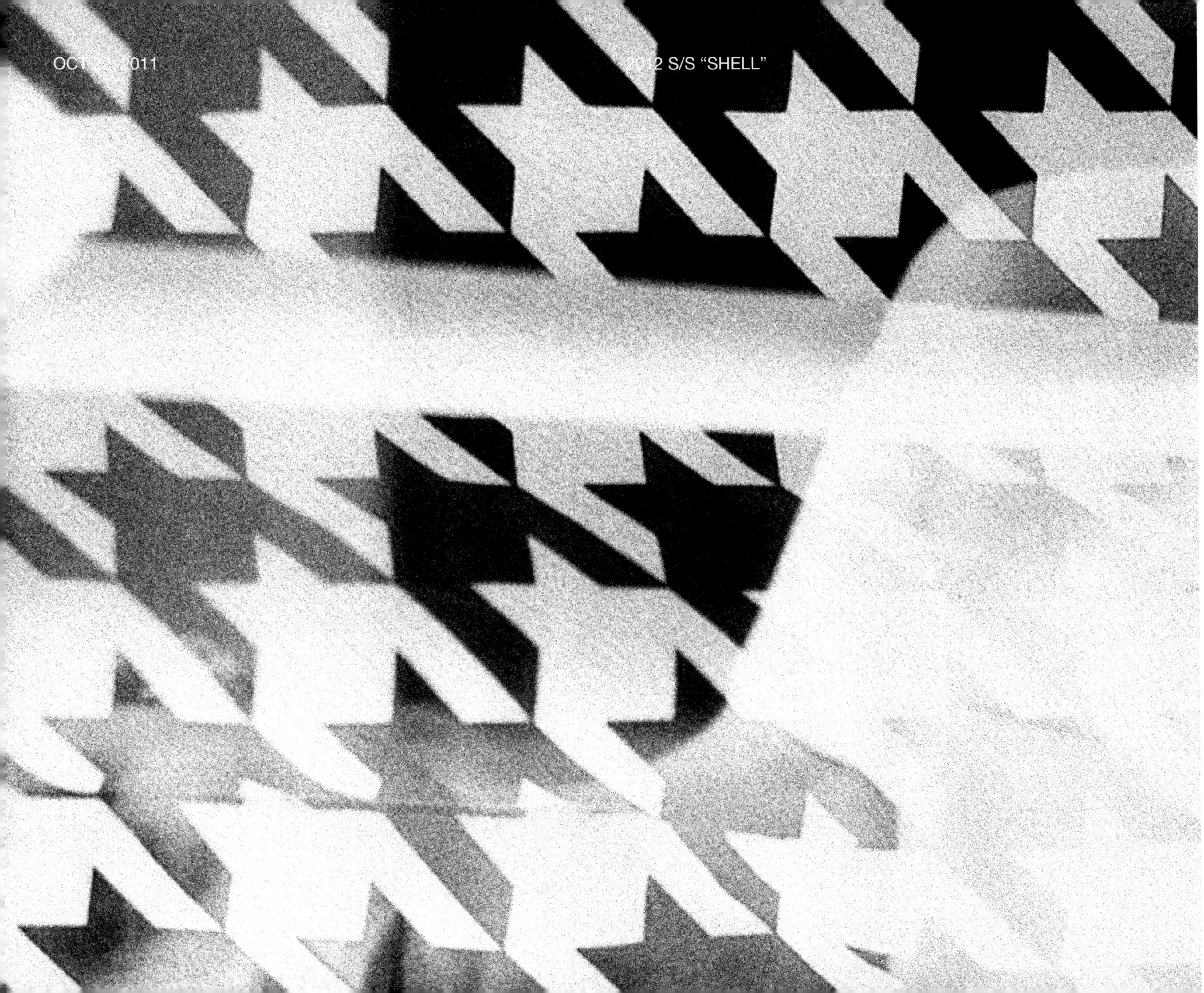

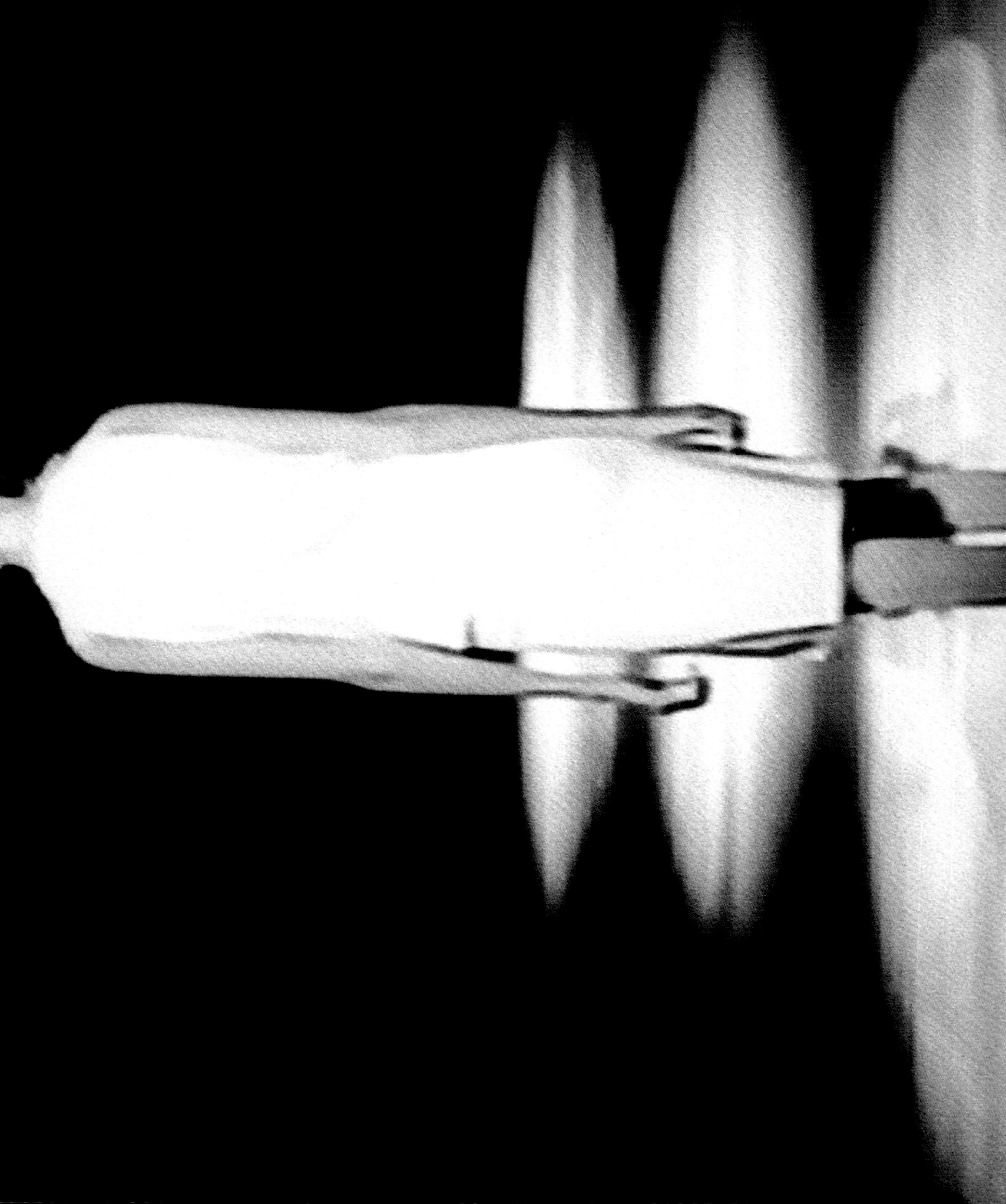

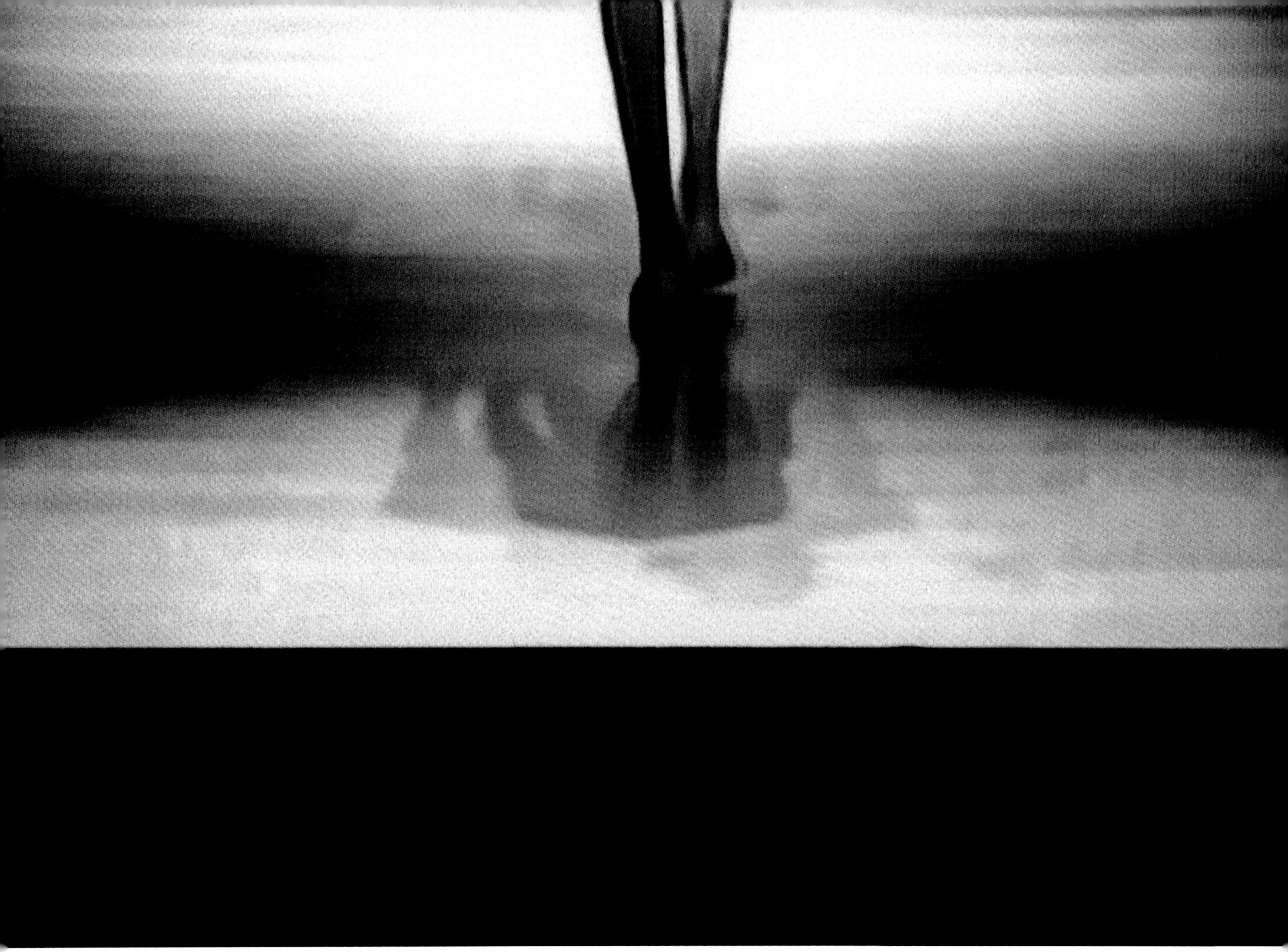

In fashion, the right choices are the ones that...

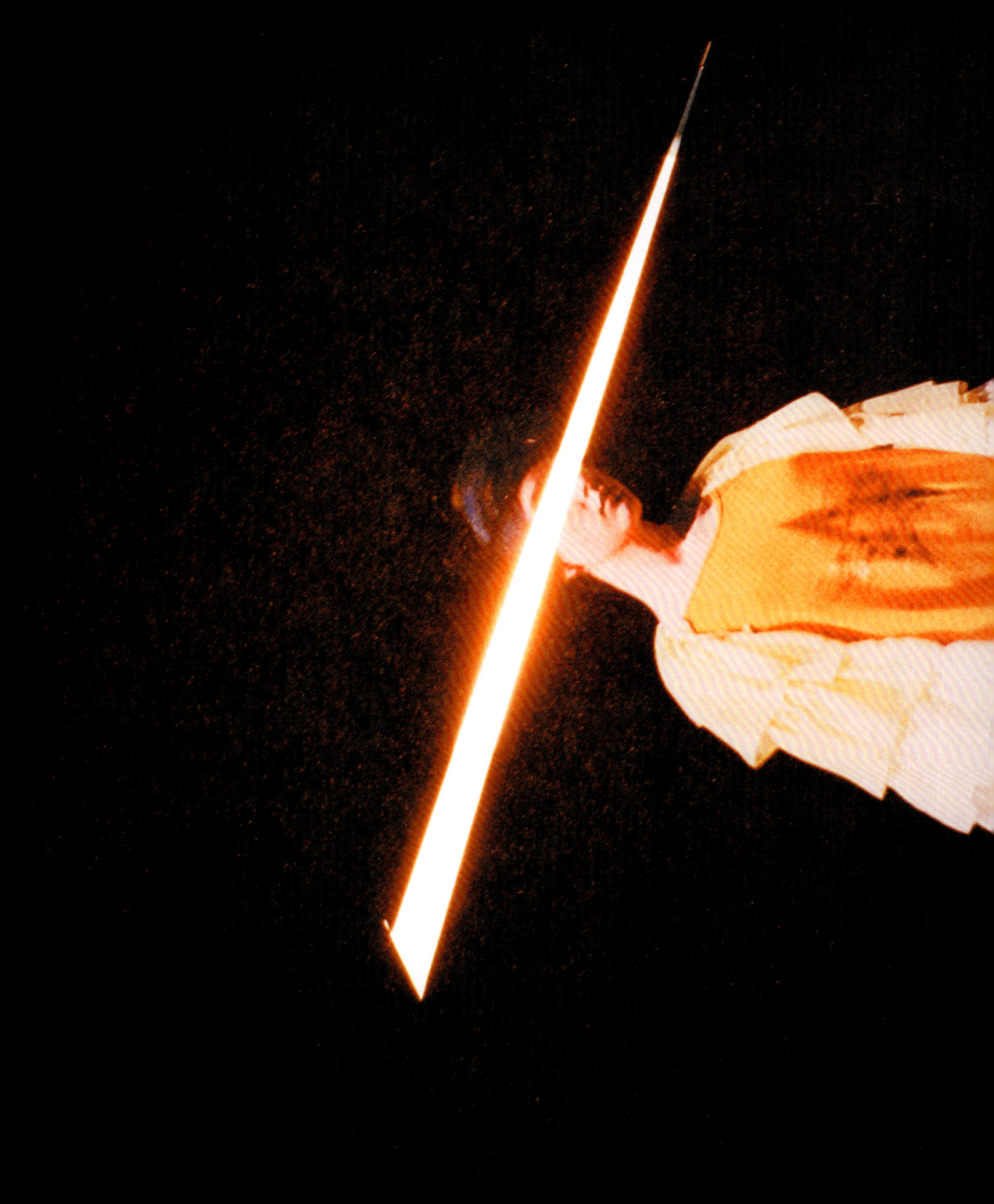

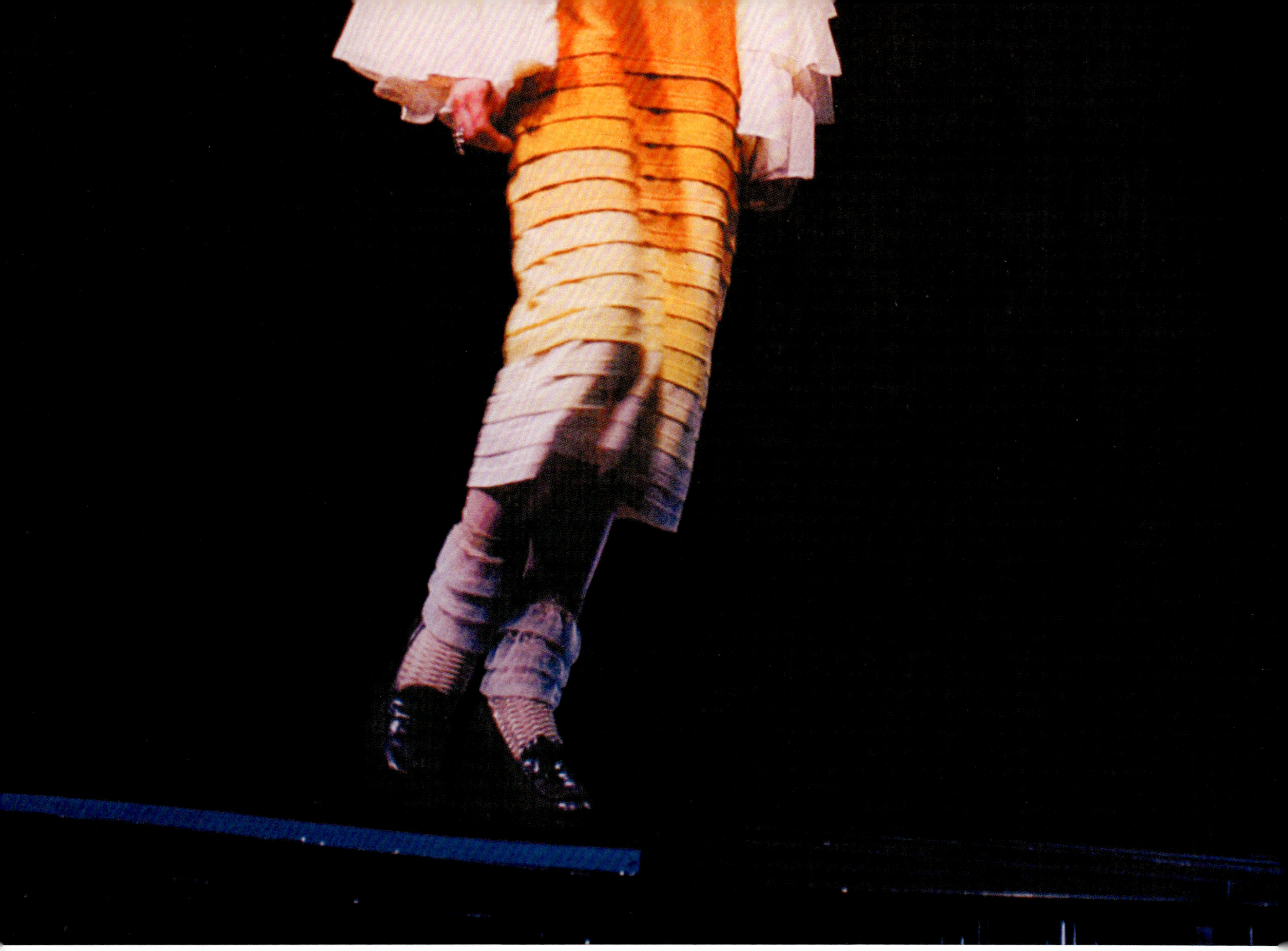

...fit that era or that moment

But in a moment, exactly the opposite c

hoice might be right

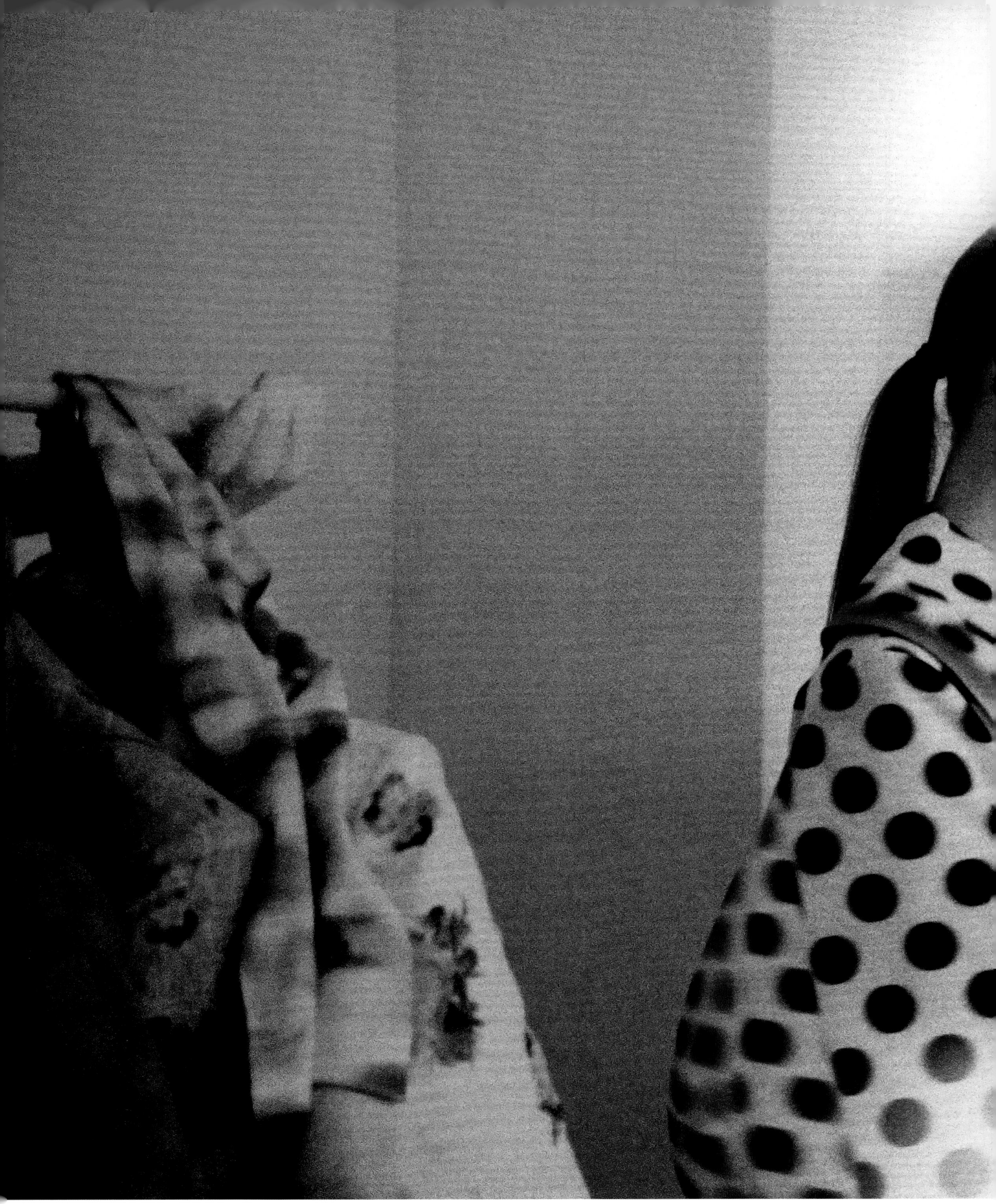

In fact they may both be right or both b

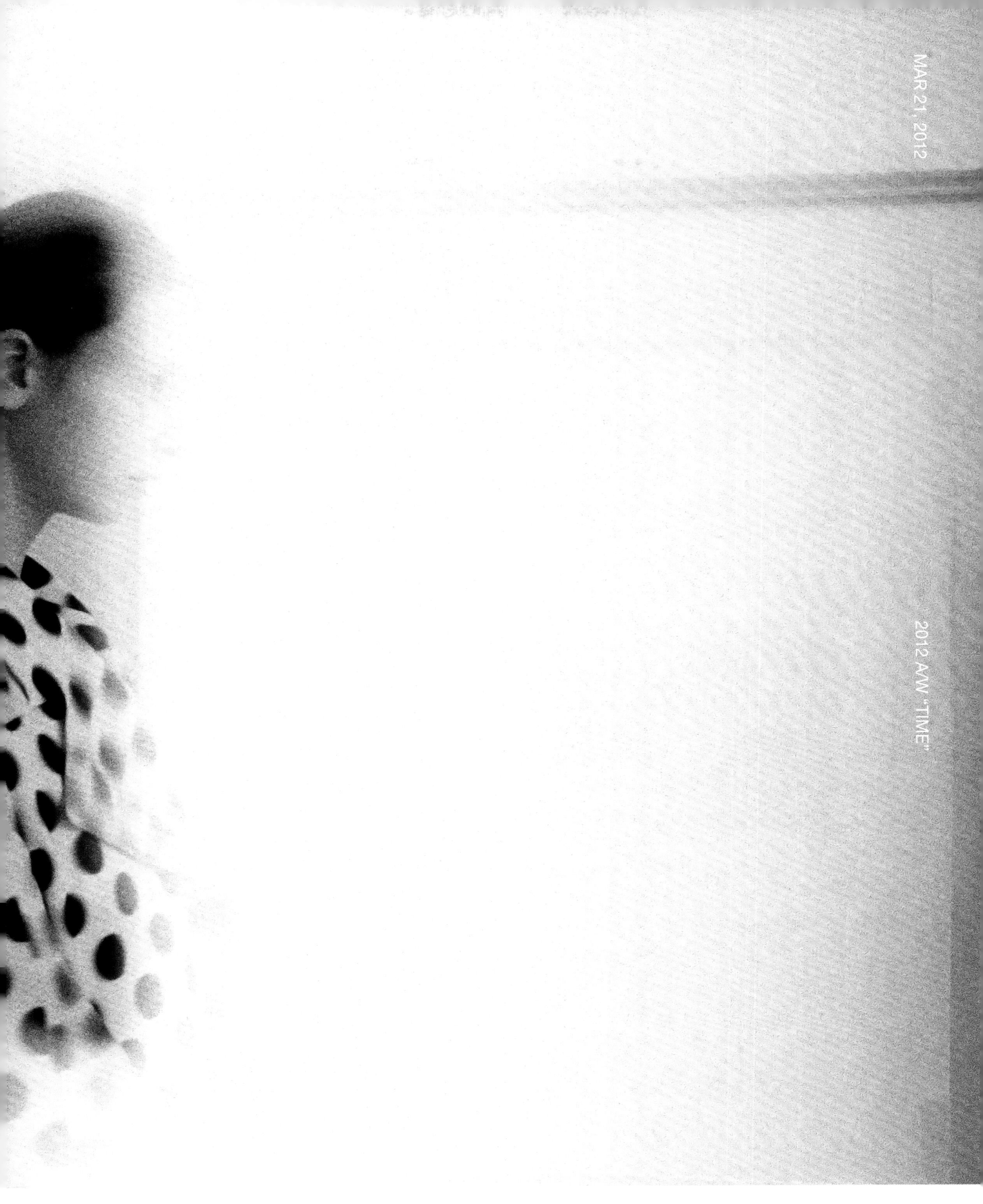

wrong

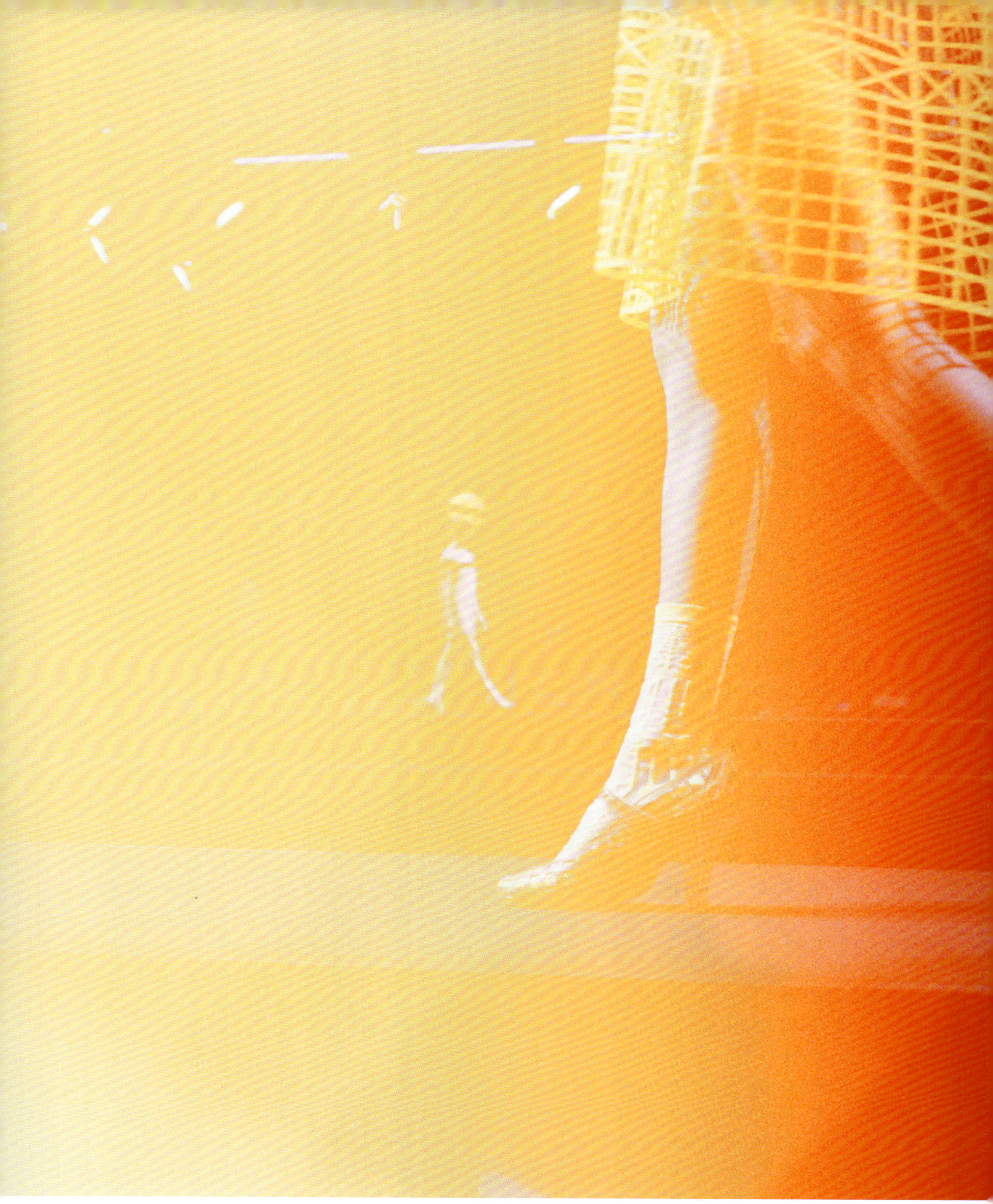

But the one certainty is that...

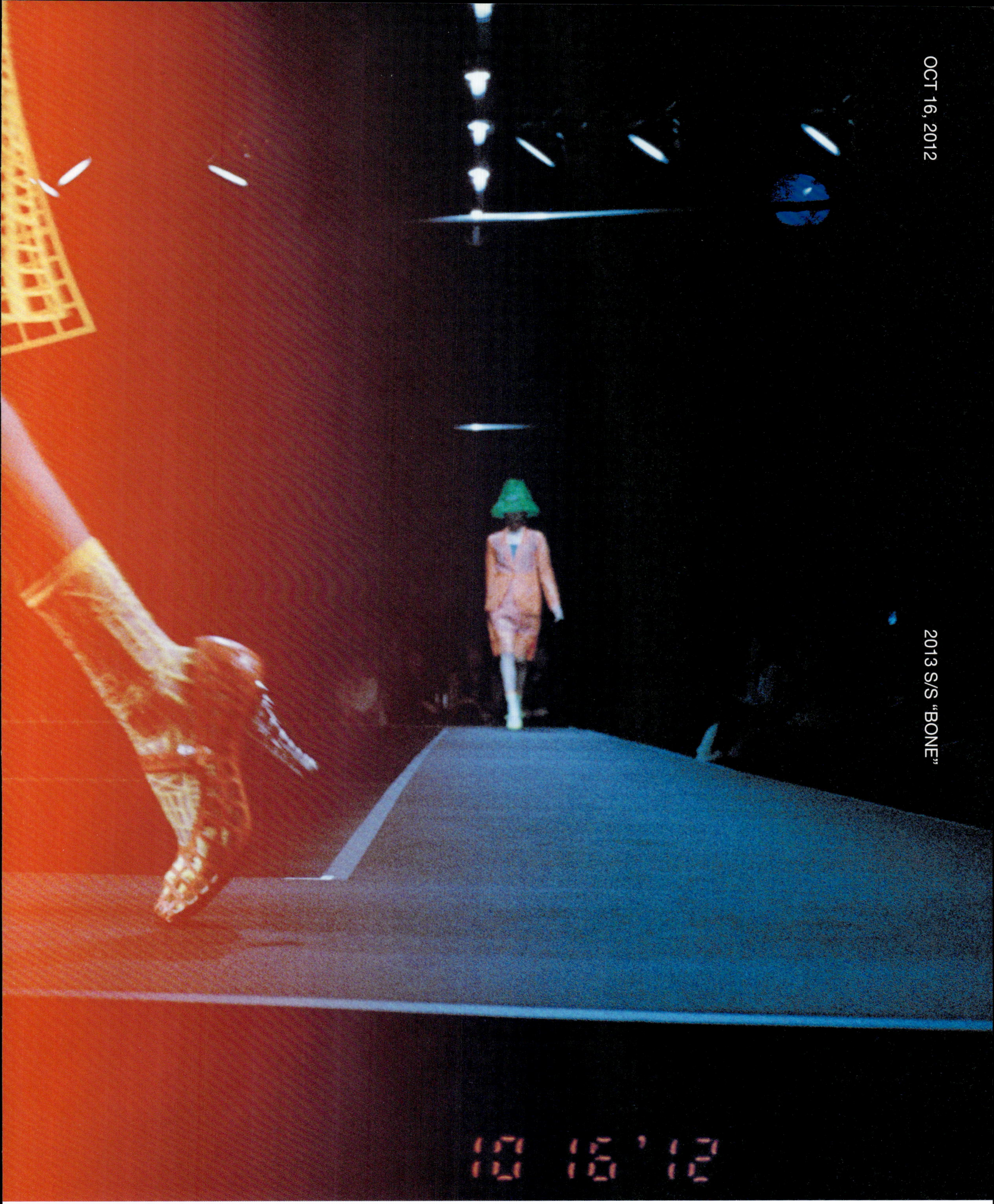

OCT 16, 2012

2013 S/S "BONE"

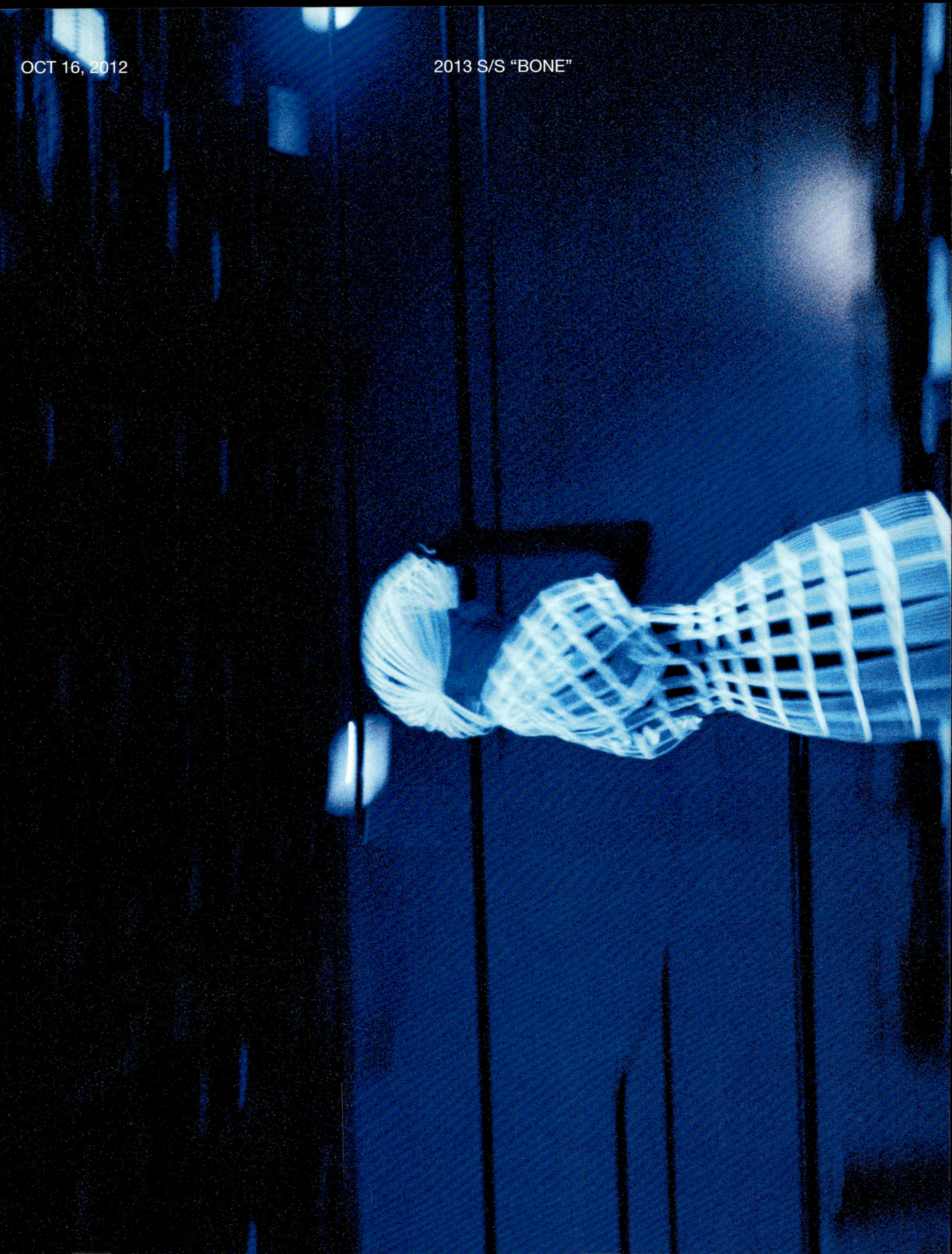

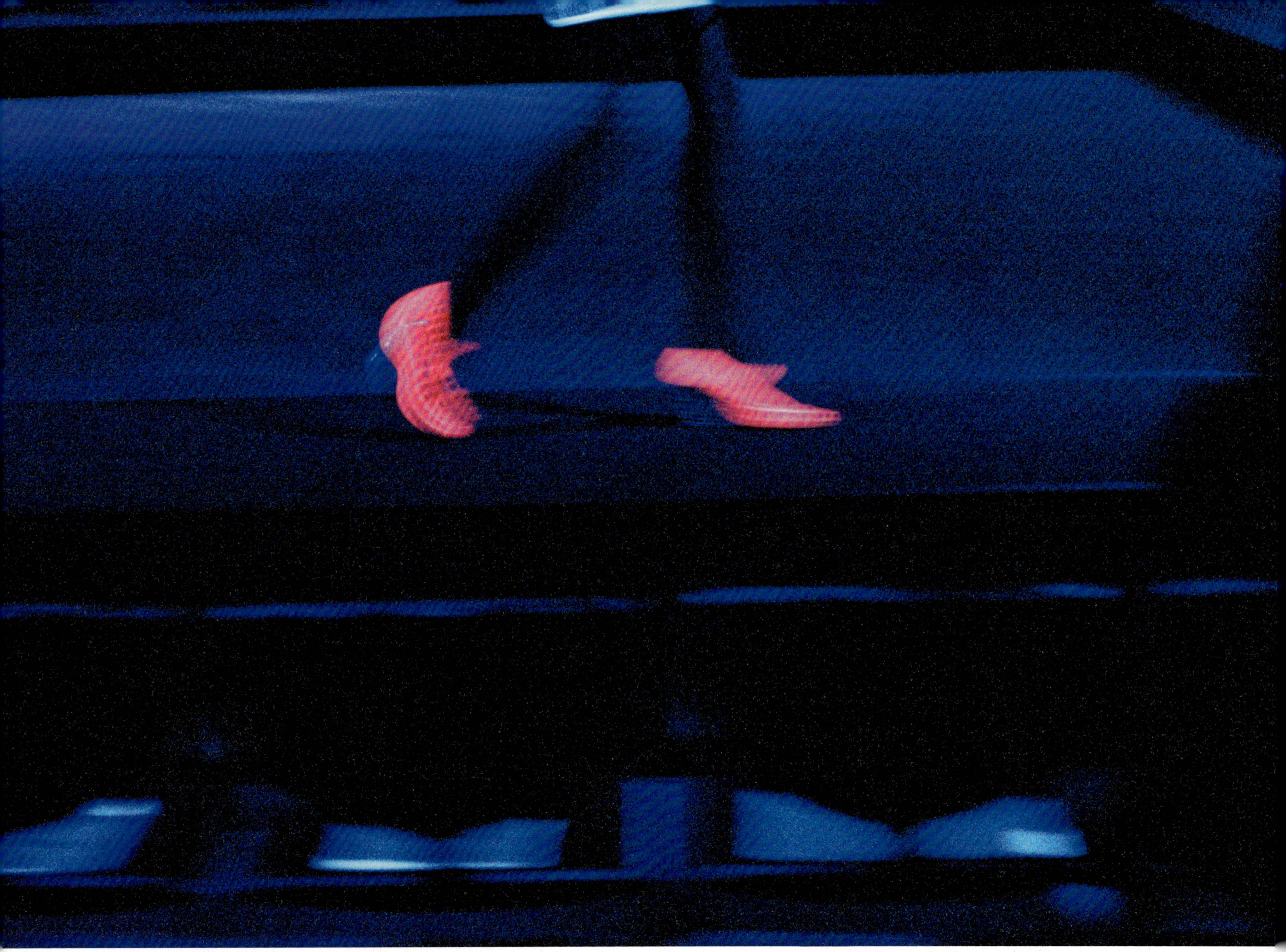

...everything changes, the new replaces the old

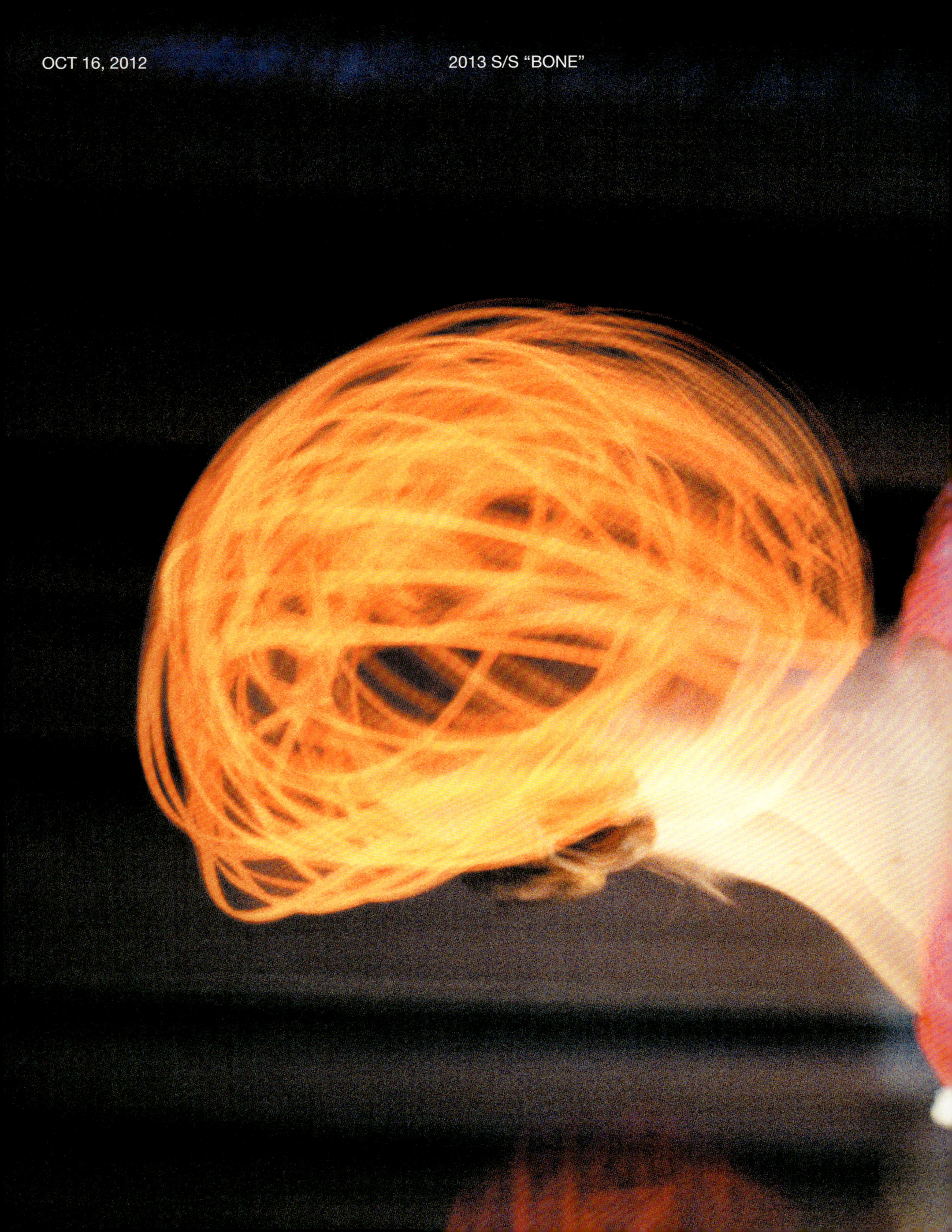

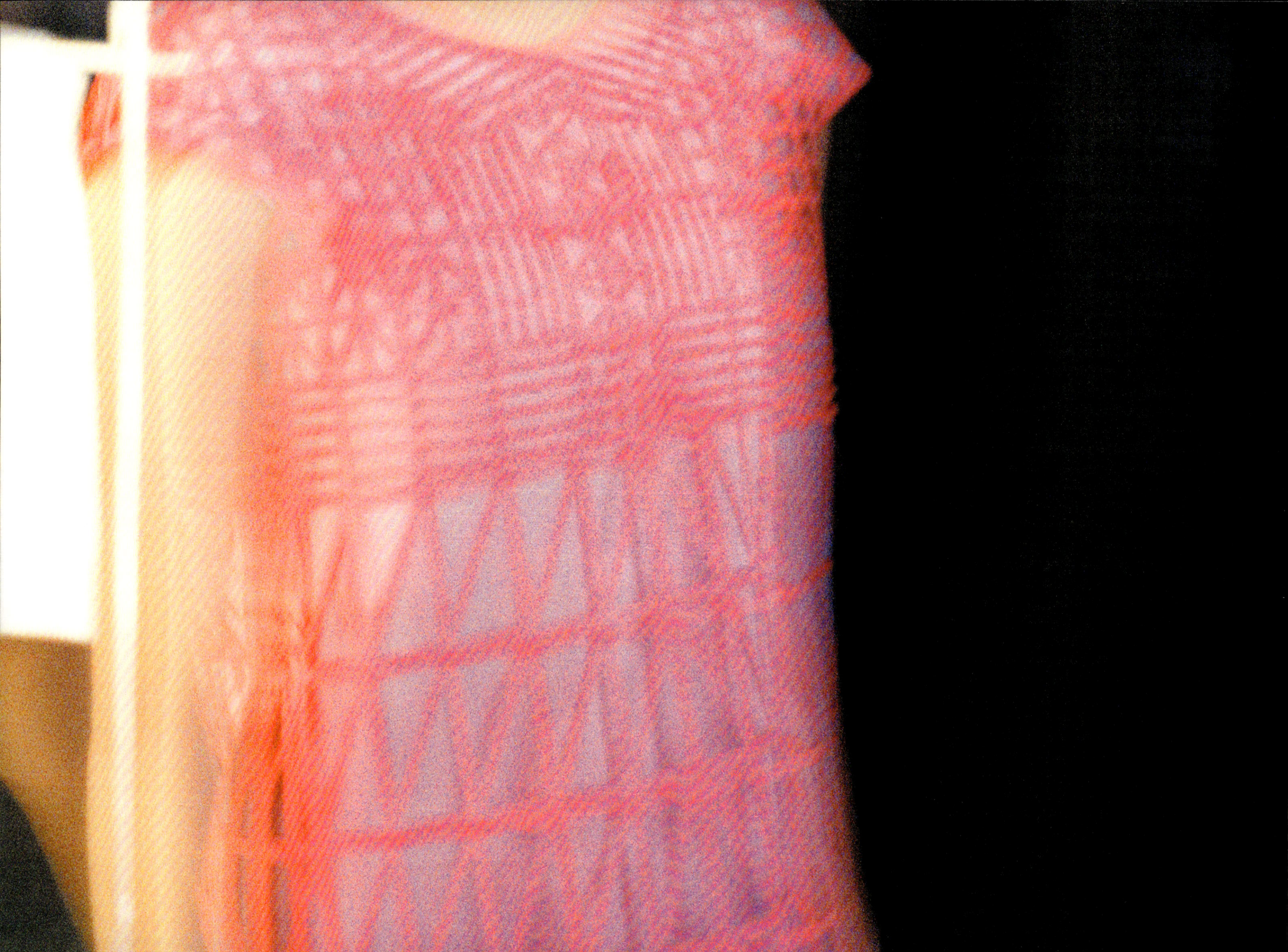

The lack of certainty is what fashion is all about

perspective [noun]

the way you think about something

6

PERSPECTIVE

A and Z

The Beginning is the End

The logo of Anrealage superimposes the letters A and Z, a simple design that uses the first and last letters of the English alphabet.

A and Z are shapes that are familiar to everyone. But no matter where I looked in the world, I couldn't find a design that superimposed the two.

The first time I created a logo was in April 2006, for the Fall/Winter 2006-07 collection, *Canon*. After I launched Anrealage in March 2002, I didn't think about creating a logo for a while. I had always thought that logos can communicate a brand at a glance, but they can also take away any interest in the details behind the brand. As someone who wholeheartedly believes that "God is in the details," representing a brand with a mere symbol was tantamount to disobeying God. I believed that no symbol could ever express Anrealage.

Once Anrealage's core values had solidified into "A REAL, UNREAL, and AGE," "*sukoshi fushigi* (slightly strange)," and "God is in the details," my perspective also changed. I began to think that if I was going to create a logo, then it had to have a shape that everyone could understand, and a design that was simple, universal, and absolute. I created the logo with my good friend from college, Masaya Muto [*], while we were planning the collection *Canon*.

Canon refers to a standard or golden rule.

Turning Alphabets into Clothes

In my collection *Canon*, I presented the 26 letters of the alphabet as "the great symbols that move the world," and designed clothes in their shapes.

I thought about the different names of clothes. For example, a T-shirt, which everyone wears on a daily basis, derives its name from the shape of the letter T. I thought that the other letters in the alphabet could also be incorporated into clothes somehow. I set out to make clothes for the other 25 letters.

The "A-shirt" was a modified top shaped like the letter A. The "B-bag" was shaped like a B. For the "C-pants," I made a silhouette where the legs curved back to form the letter C. The silhouettes of the "G-pants" and "P-coat (pea coat)" also reflected the shapes of their respective letters. The collection *Canon* followed the shapes of the alphabet rather than the human body. All 25 letters of the alphabet, from A to Y, were made into clothes. The only one I couldn't make into clothes was the last letter, Z.

With only 26 letters, anything in the world can be expressed. The letters may seem small, but they contain infinite possibilities. Muto and I were drawn to the letters A and Z, which represent the beginning and the end of the alphabet. We wrote down the sequence of letters from A to Z over and over again. A, B, C... X, Y, Z, A... The letters A and Z appear far apart, but in reality, they are both a part of a sequence. When this sequence of letters is repeated, the world of the 26 letters continues ad infinitum. Z is not an end but a beginning. If the alphabet were to form an arc, then Z and A would stand next to each other. The line that connected the dots finally turned into a circle in our minds.

A time for a beginning, a time for an end. The times that I had thought stood in conflict with each other turned out to have no boundaries between them at all. A and Z overlapped in time.

The letter Z, which we ultimately couldn't incorporate into our clothes, inspired our brand logo. An end had turned into a beginning. In contrast to the English canon, which consists of the 26 letters of the alphabet, the canon of Anrealage was consolidated into 25 letters since the letters A and Z overlapped to create the logo.

A logo that unites opposites became our canon.

Communal Living

I remember my encounter with Muto vividly.

My first class at the School of Social Sciences at Waseda University took place in a large classroom. In a room packed with first-year students, I happened to sit next to Muto, who was engrossed in his Game Boy. He didn't even look up once while I diligently took notes. After class, Muto suddenly approached me and asked, "Can I borrow your notebook?"

It didn't take long for my initial dislike of Muto to develop into a sense of affinity. Muto's home was in Chigasaki City, Kanagawa Prefecture, and it took him nearly two hours to commute to school each way. My commute was about half that time. Since Muto would often miss the last train, he started to stay over at my house, and before long we were spending every morning, day, and night together. I often told Muto about my passion for fashion. He told me he was interested in graphic design.

Muto also began to eat with my parents, and they accepted him favorably. The mood at home shifted, however, with the changing of the seasons and the beginning of summer break. One day, my father asked me awkwardly, "Do you know how long Muto-kun is staying?" I couldn't answer. It had already been three months since Muto had settled into our home.

"Muto, there's nothing I can do," I said, announcing the end of our shared life at my parents' house. Muto, my first good friend I made in university, moved out of my house.

I felt sorry for my parents, but also for Muto.

Soon, both of us rented different apartments near campus and started living alone. The distance between our apartments was thirty seconds on foot. Muto's apartment was a four-and-a-half tatami room (approximately 7.29 square meters) and had no bath. Every day, he visited my apartment to take a bath and paid a hundred yen for it. Although I lived alone, Muto remained by my side all the way to graduation.

In August 1999, during my first year at university, I bought a sewing machine so that I could start making clothes in earnest. At the same time, Muto bought an iMac computer so that he could begin studying graphic design. Since then, the two of us have always complemented each other. I was on the path of fashion design, which was a struggle against the three-dimensional, and Muto was on the path of graphic design, which was a struggle against the two-dimensional. At times, we were rivals, and at other times, we were comrades cheering each other on. The intersection of our paths led to the creation of the Anrealage logo.

Our logo is both two-dimensional and three-dimensional. It is designed so that the letters A and Z, drawn on a plane, overlap.

* Masaya Muto is a graphic designer. Since the launch of the brand, he has handled the graphic design for Anrealage.

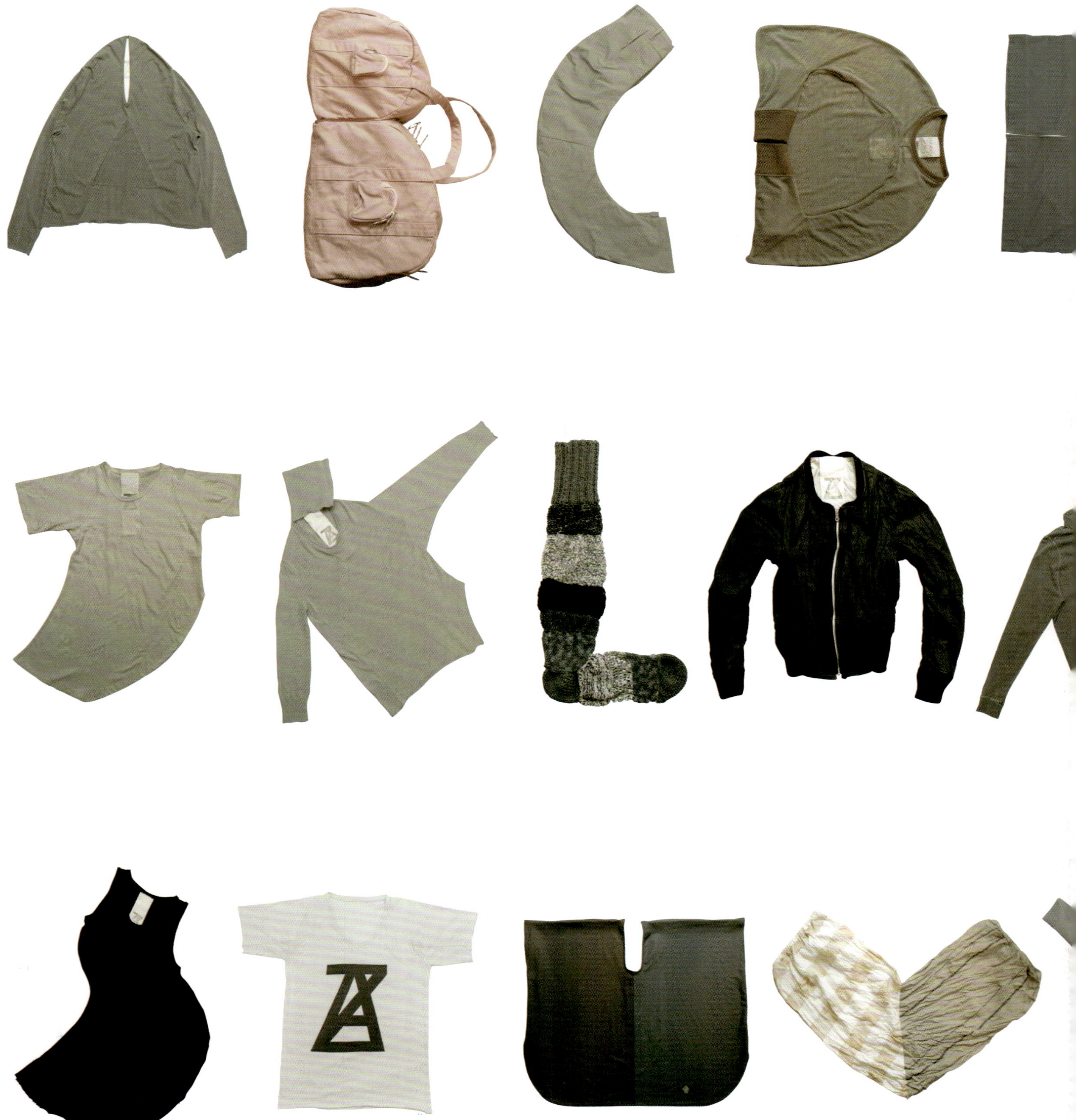

26 letters that set the world into motion

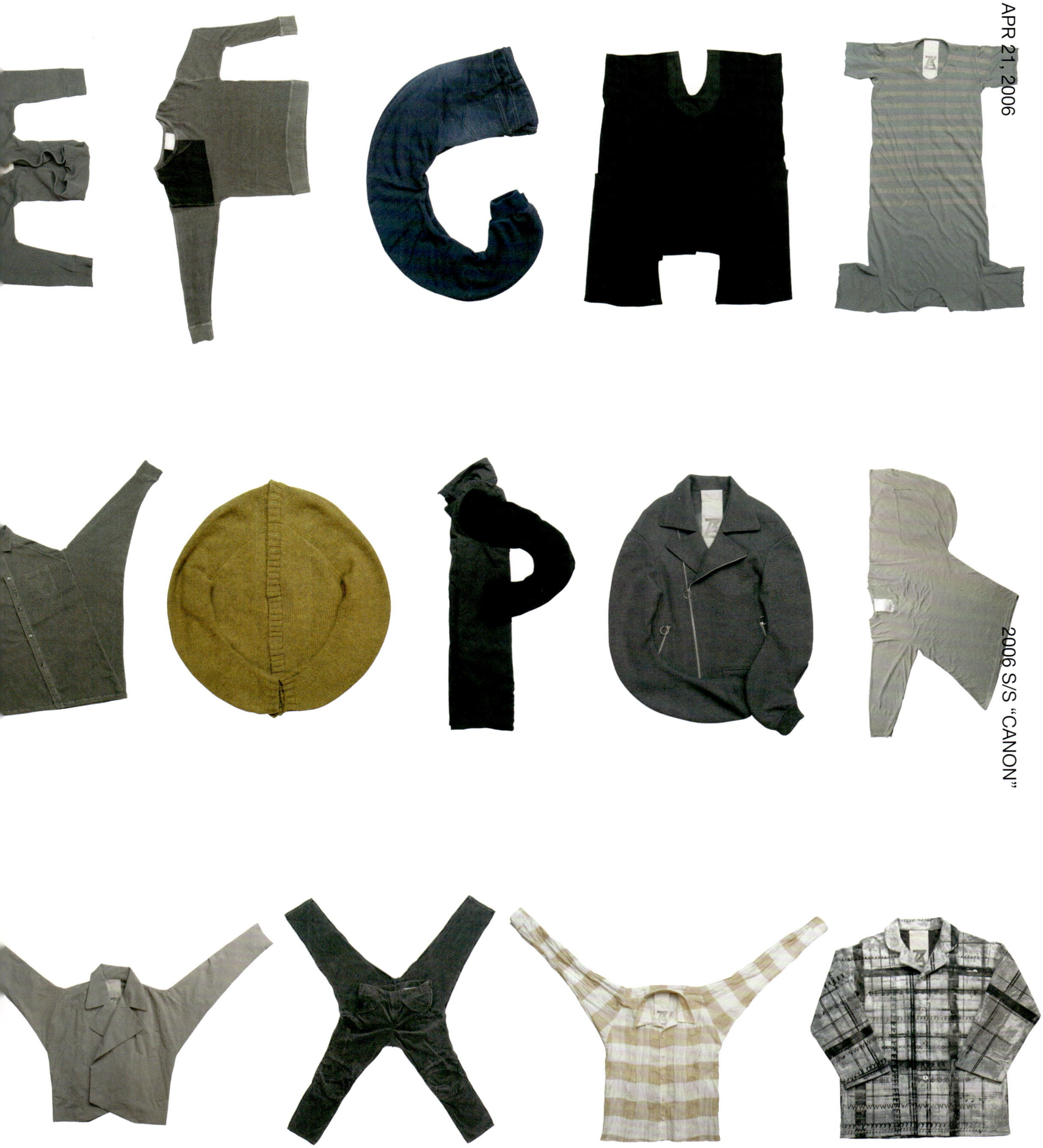

APR 21, 2006

2006 S/S "CANON"

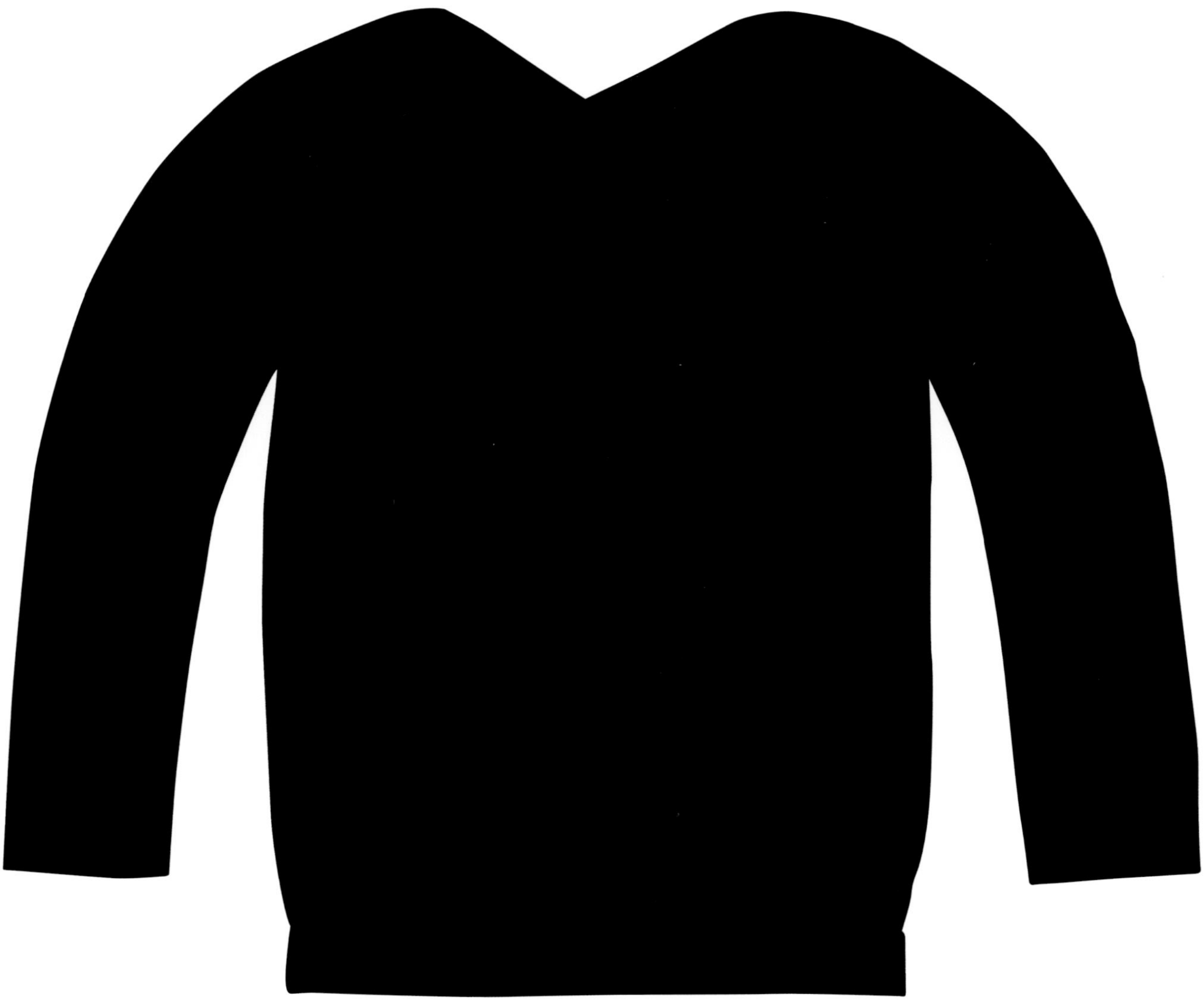

Light and shadow won’t always match

OCT 26, 2009

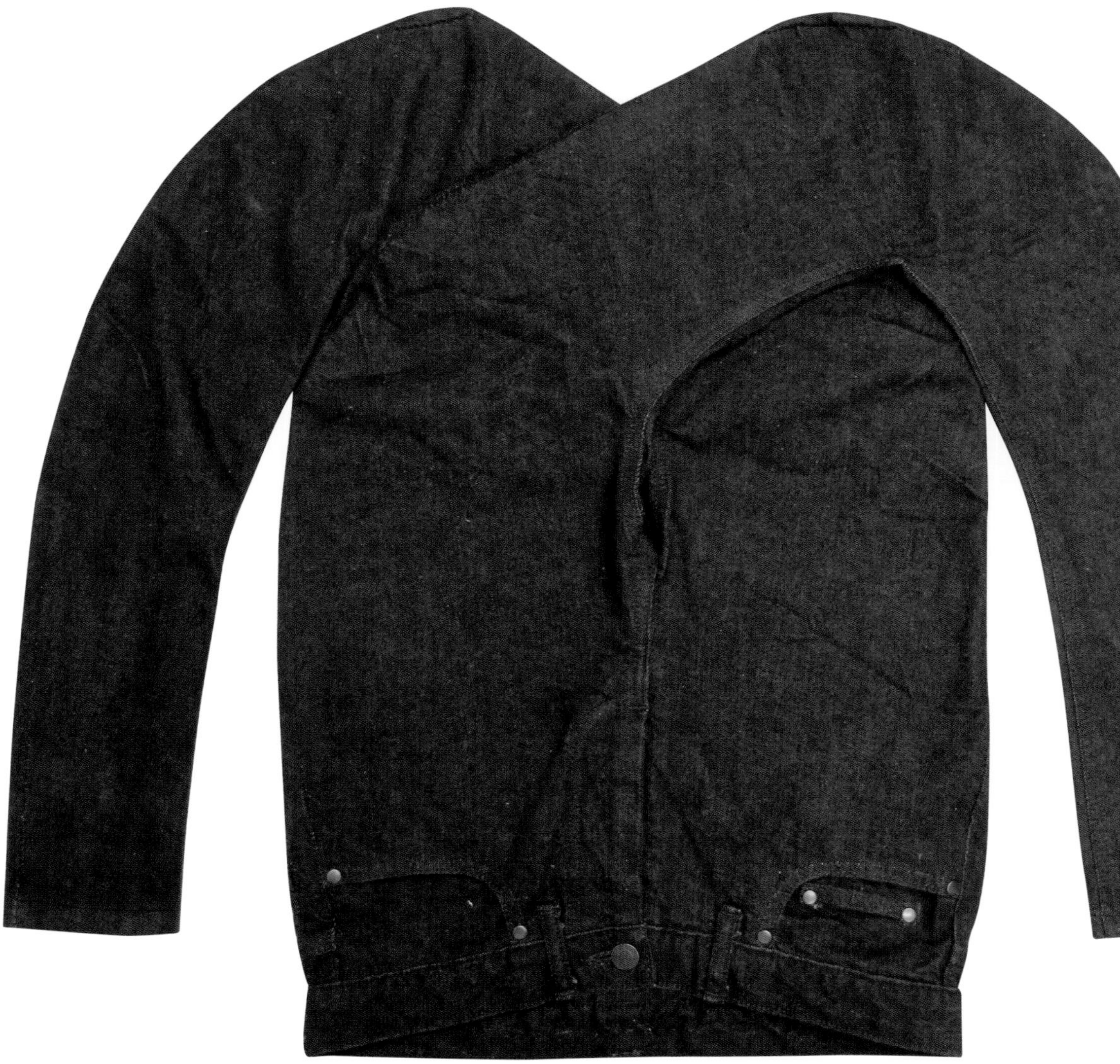

2010 S/S "SILHOUETTE"

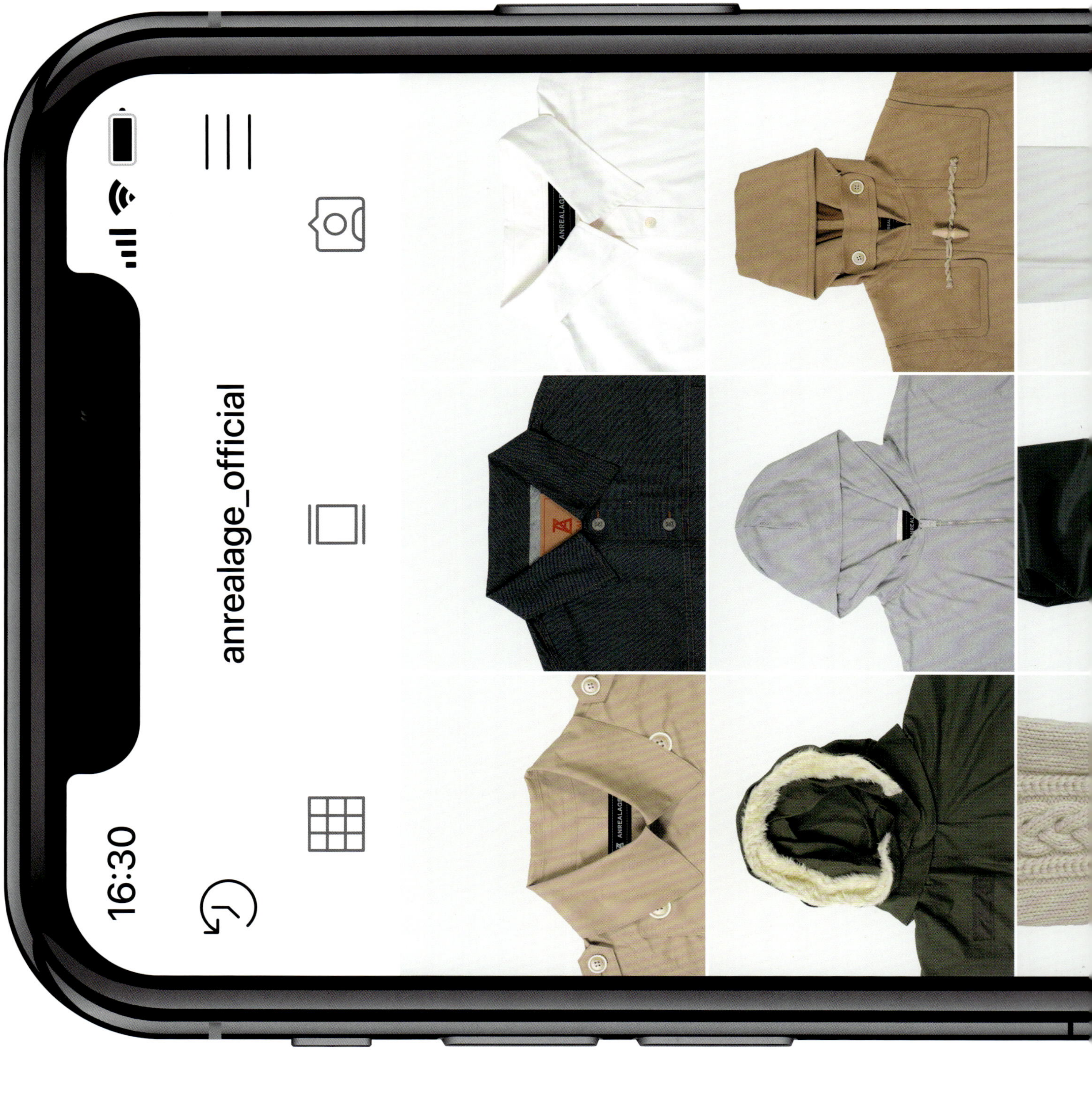
16:30
anrealage_official

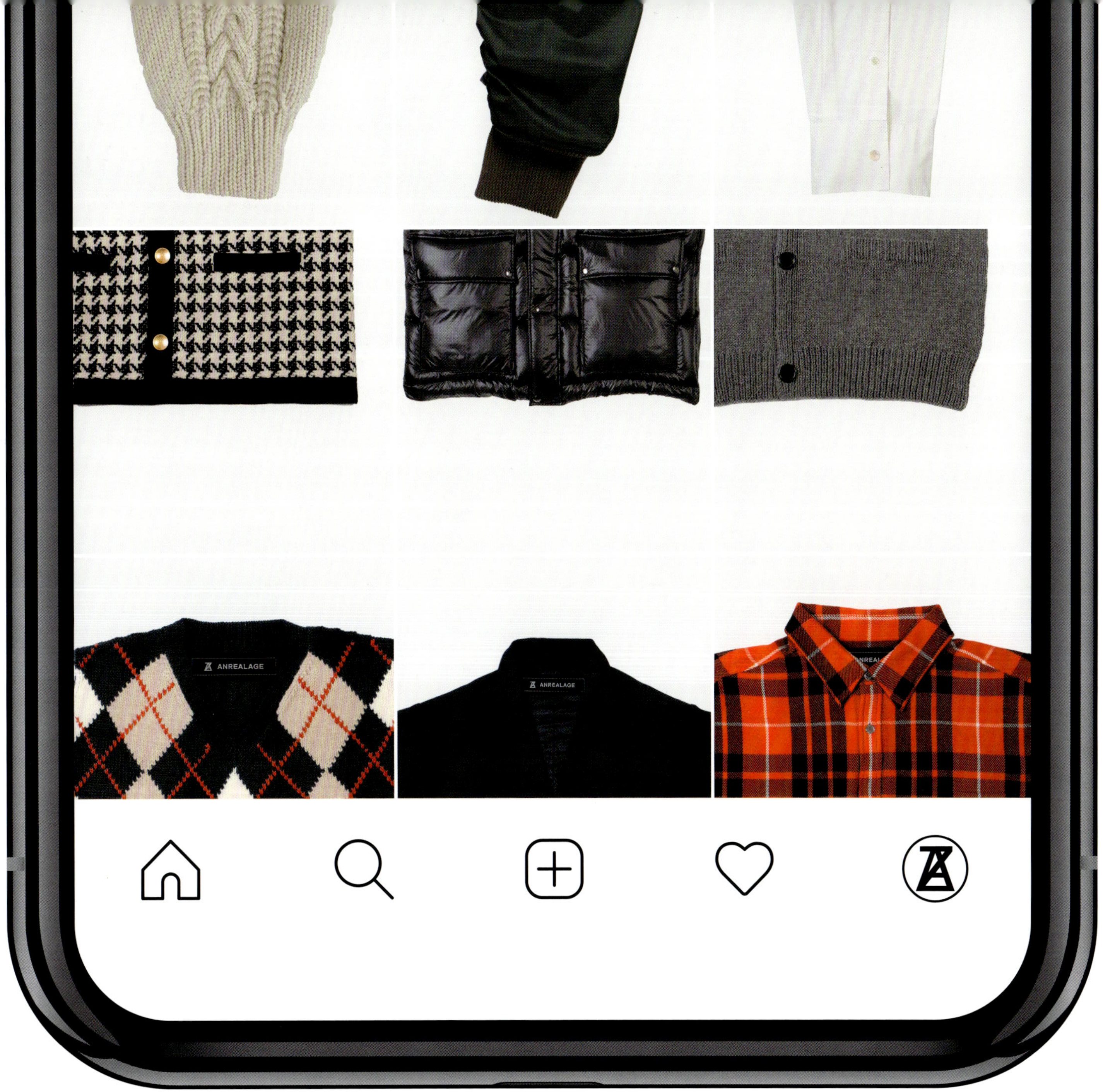

Clothes that can’t be understood on the screen

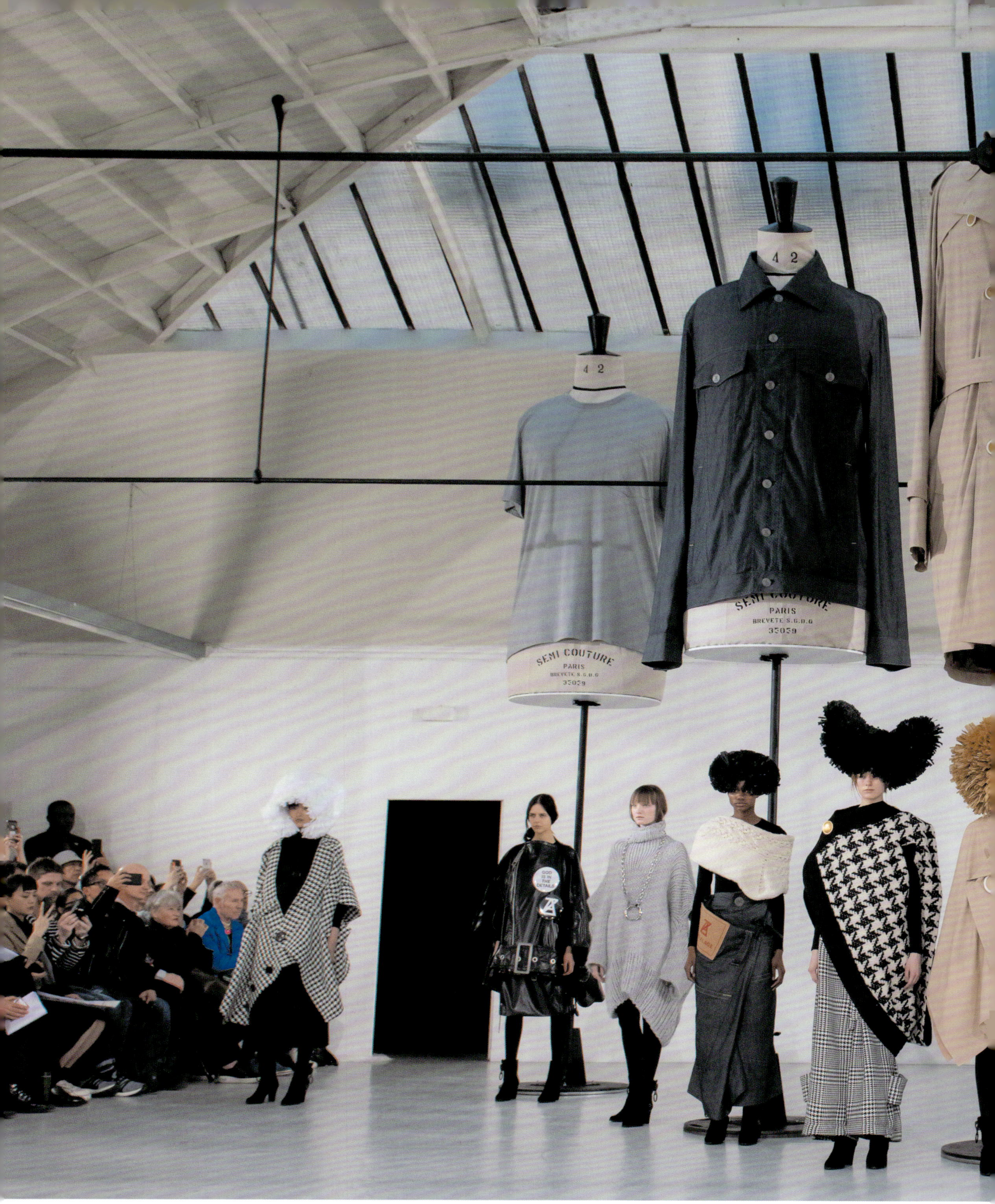

To go beyond the screen, to see what e

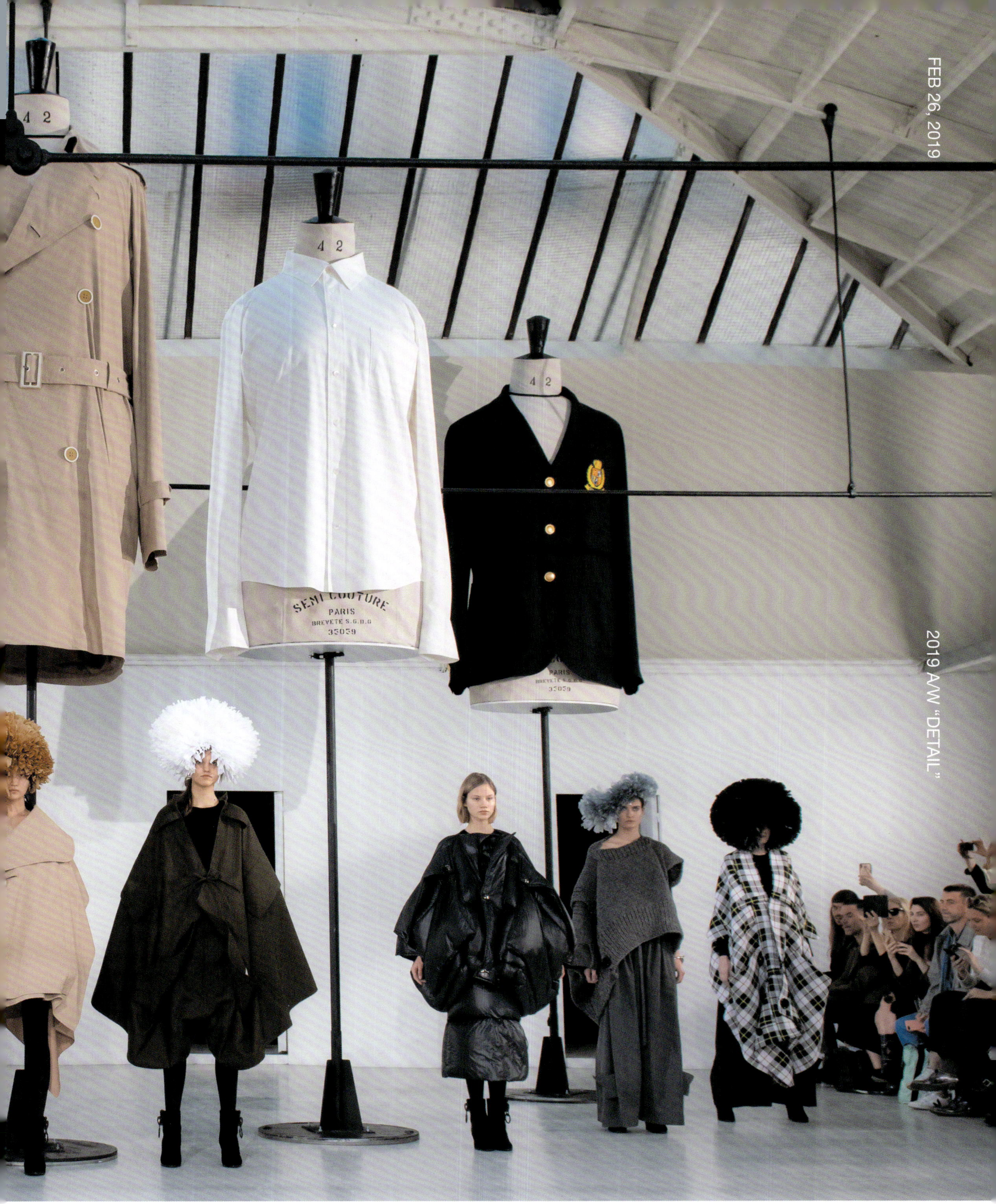

FEB 26, 2019

2019 A/W "DETAIL"

ists behind the screen

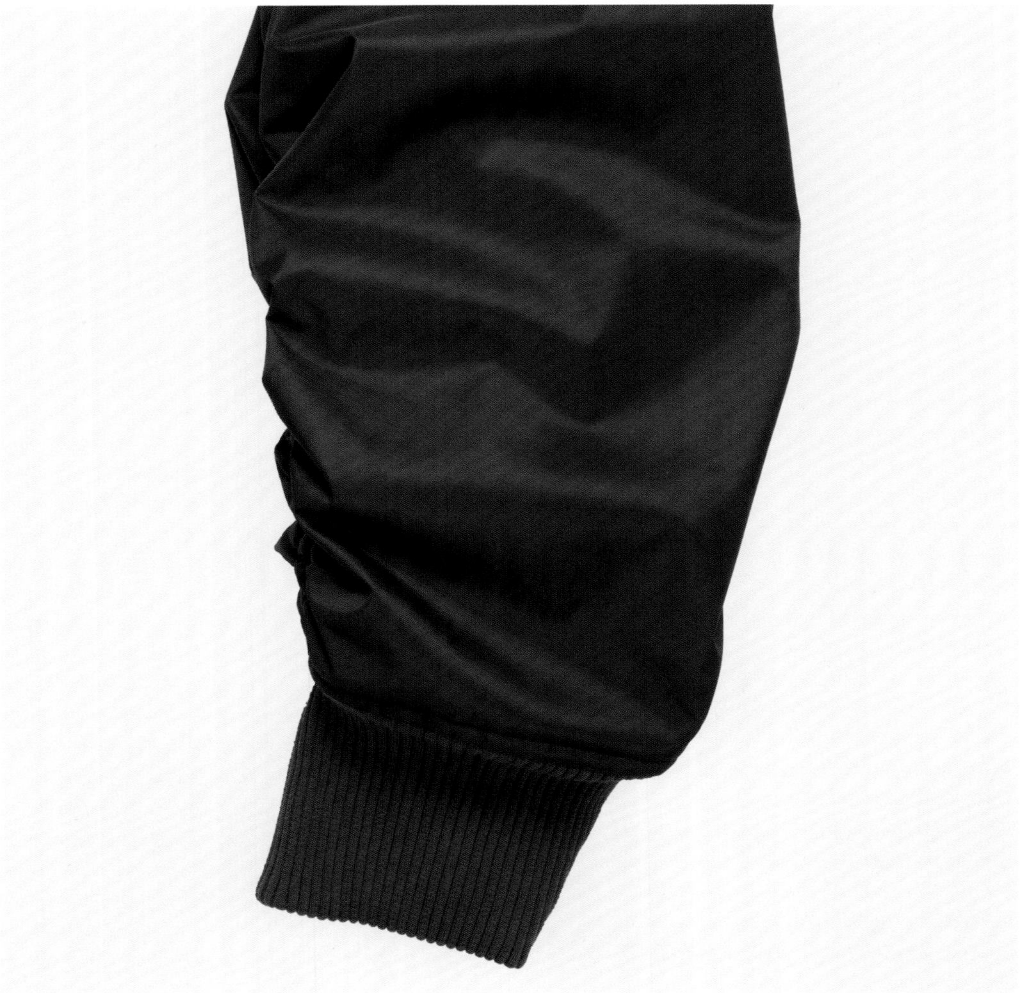

The gap between the virtual and reality

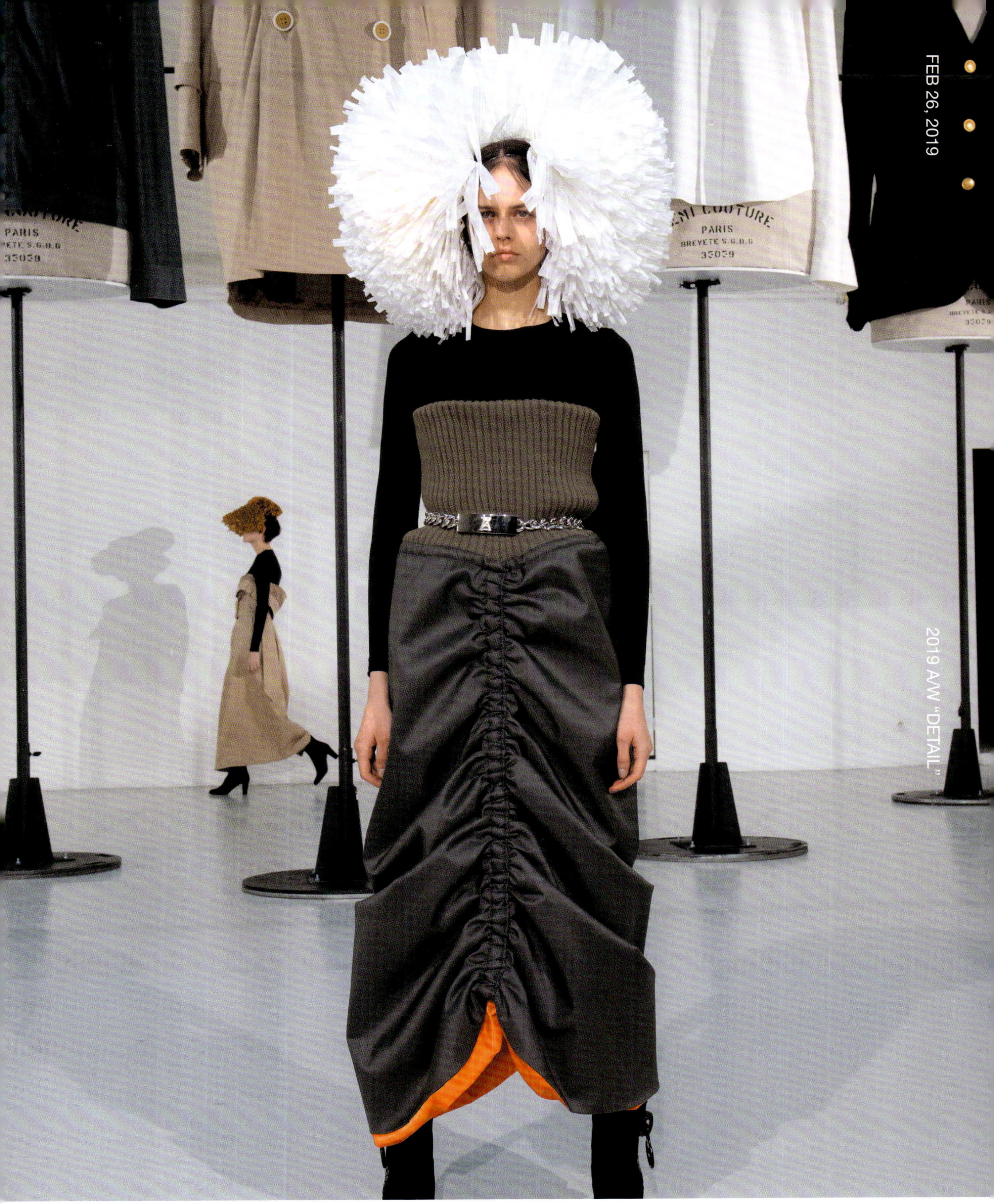

FEB 26, 2019

2019 A/W "DETAIL"

can actually be a gift

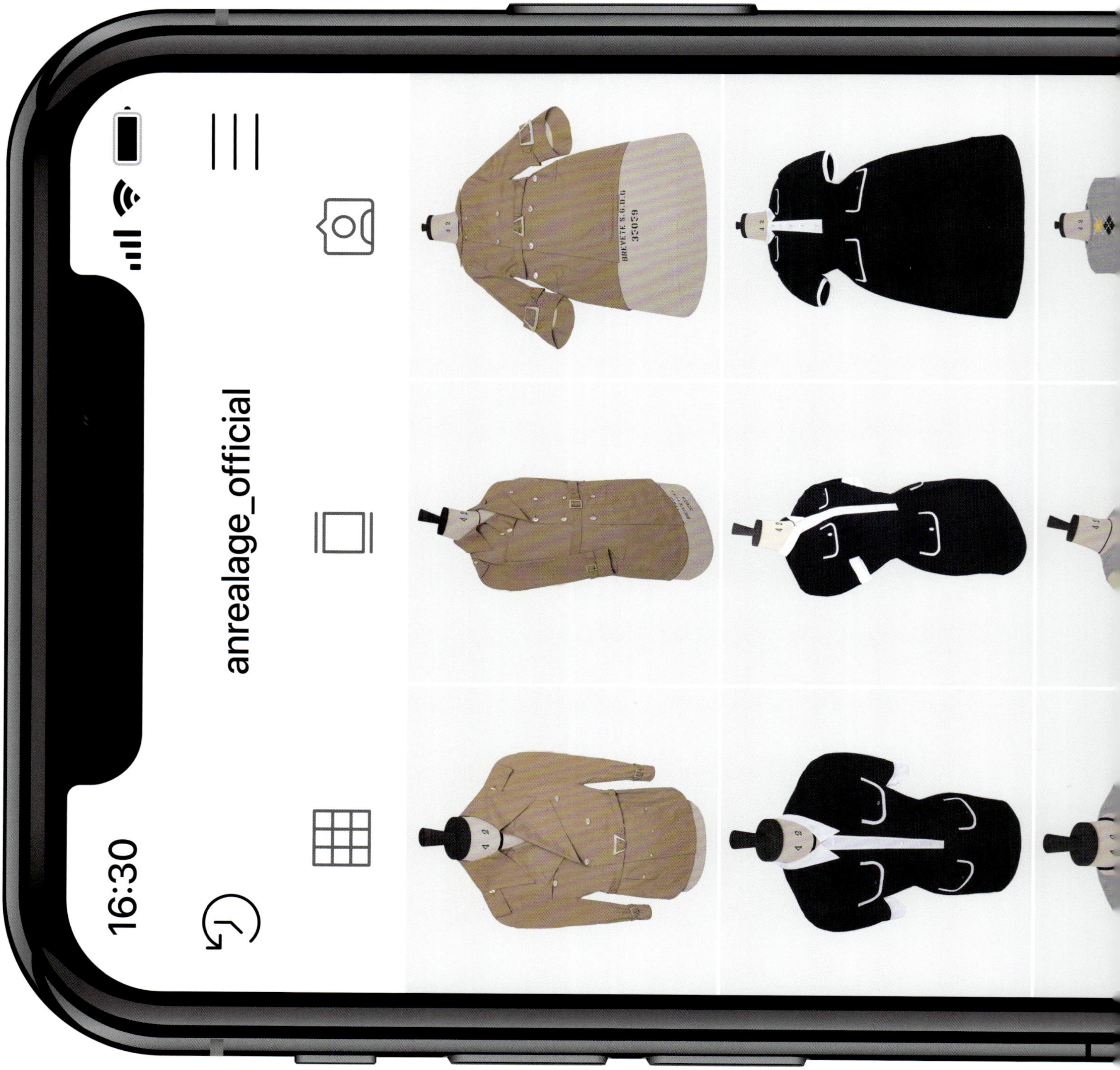
16:30
anrealage_official

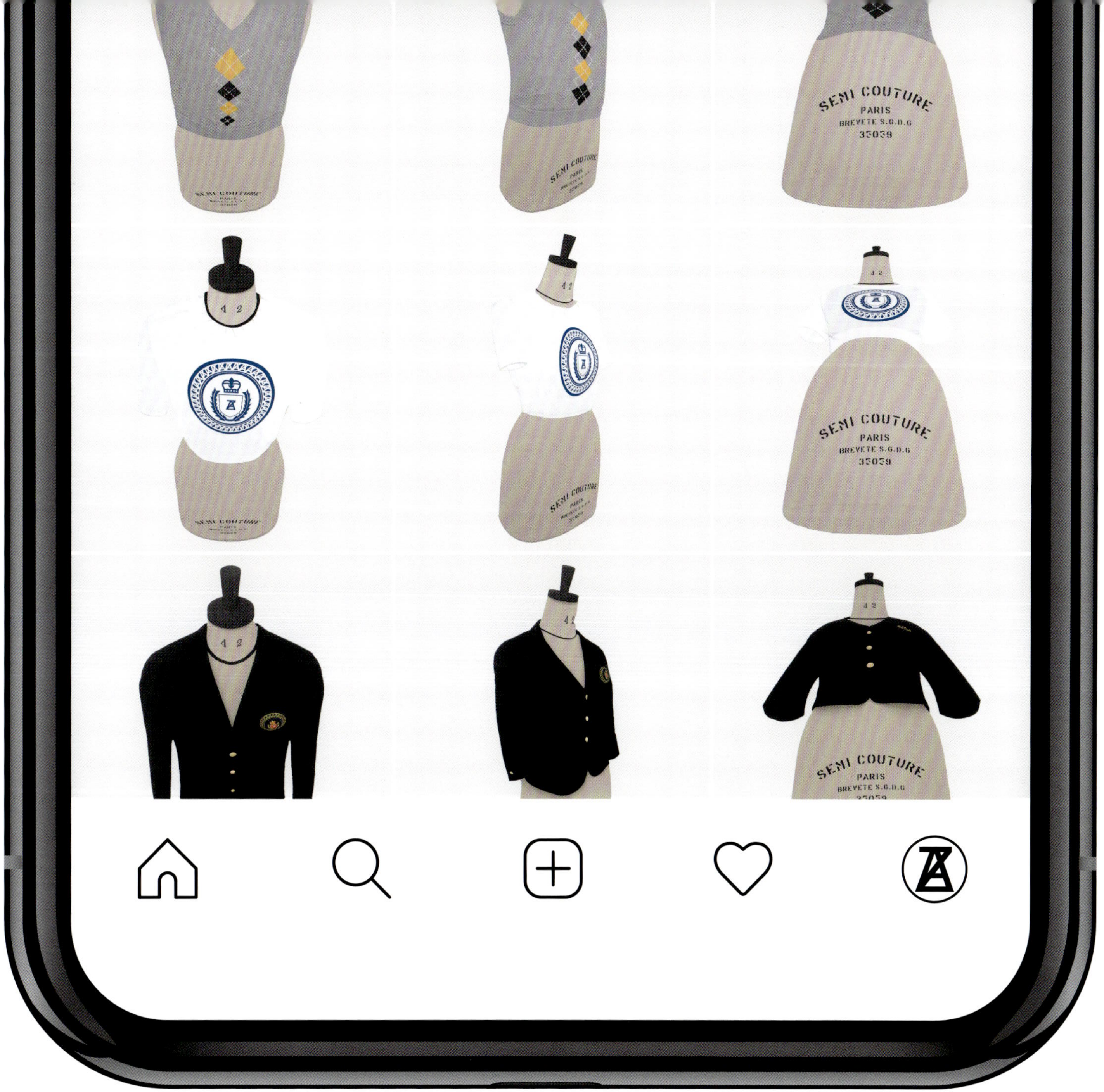

From which angle do you look at the clothes?

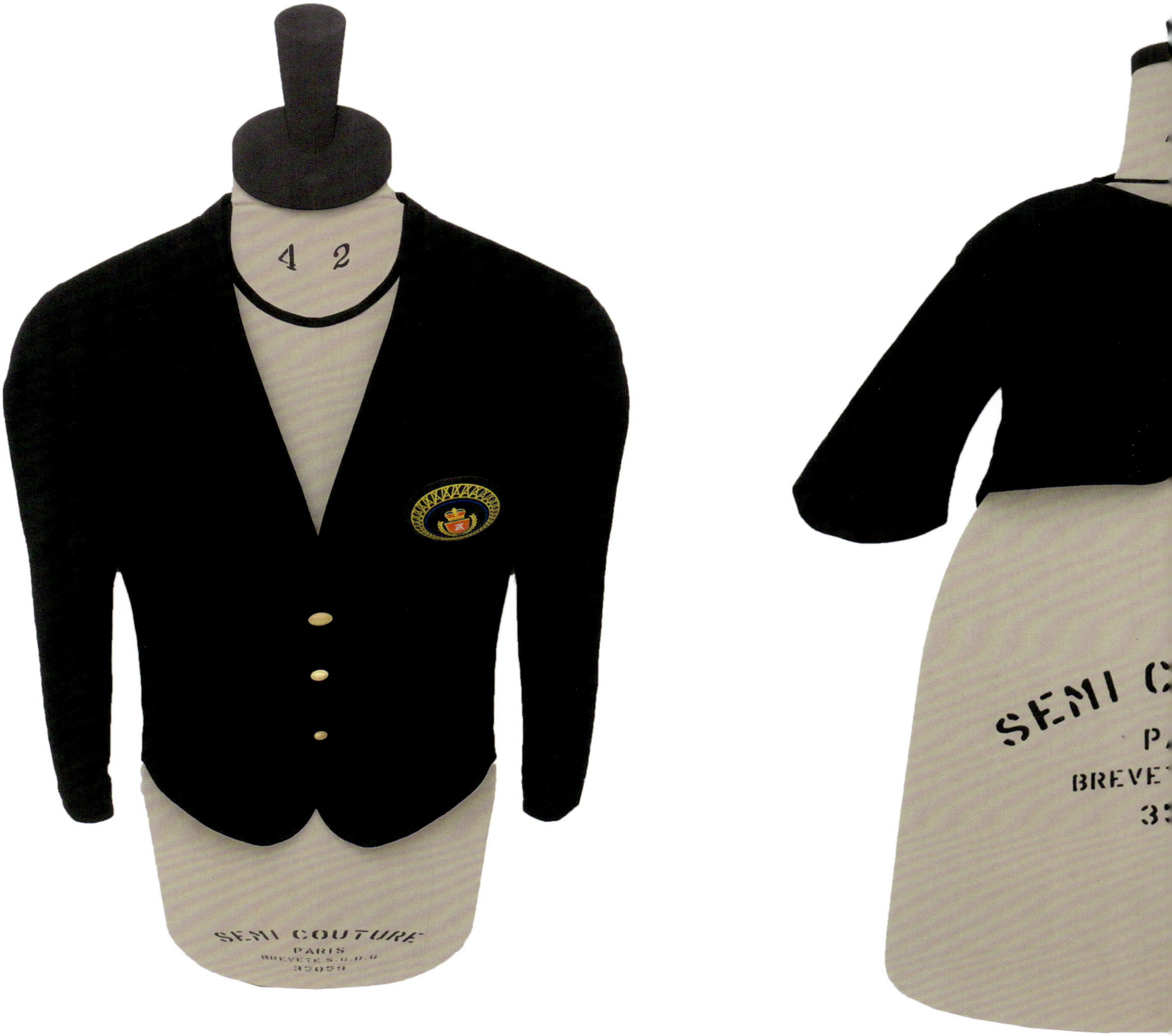

Shape the angle, shape the form

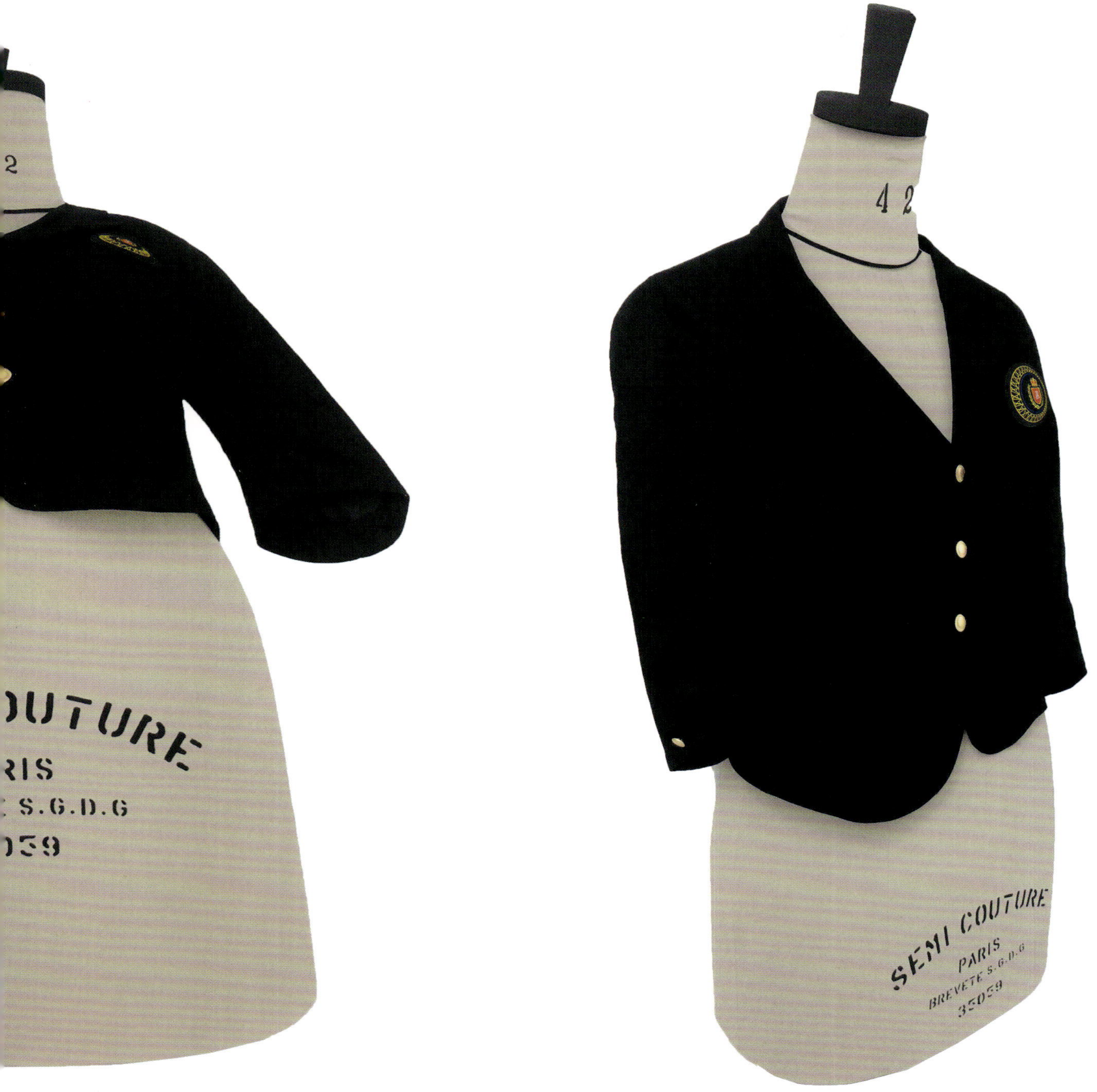

SEP 24, 2019

2020 S/S "ANGLE"

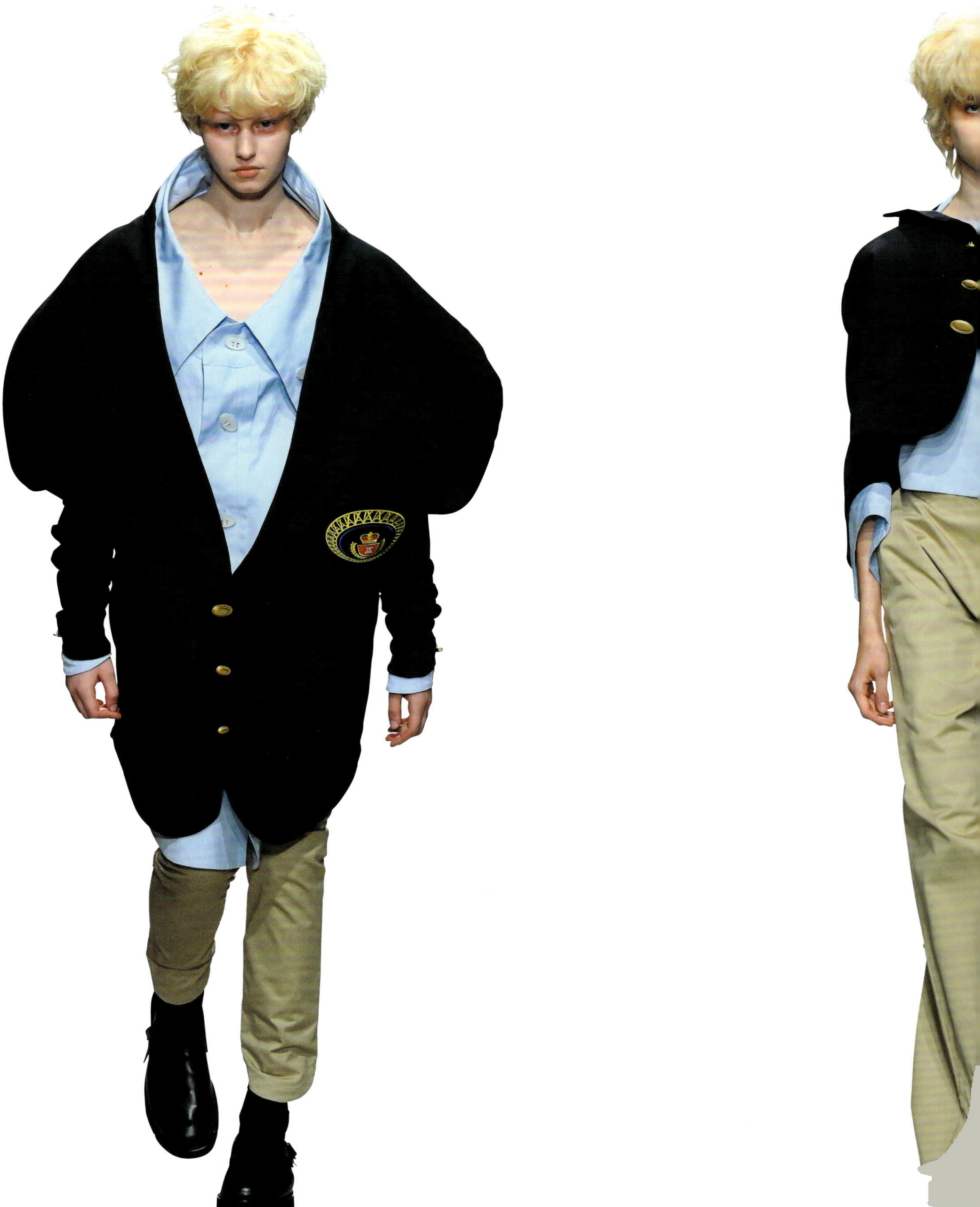

When your perspective changes, the sh

SEP 24, 2019

2020 S/S "ANGLE"

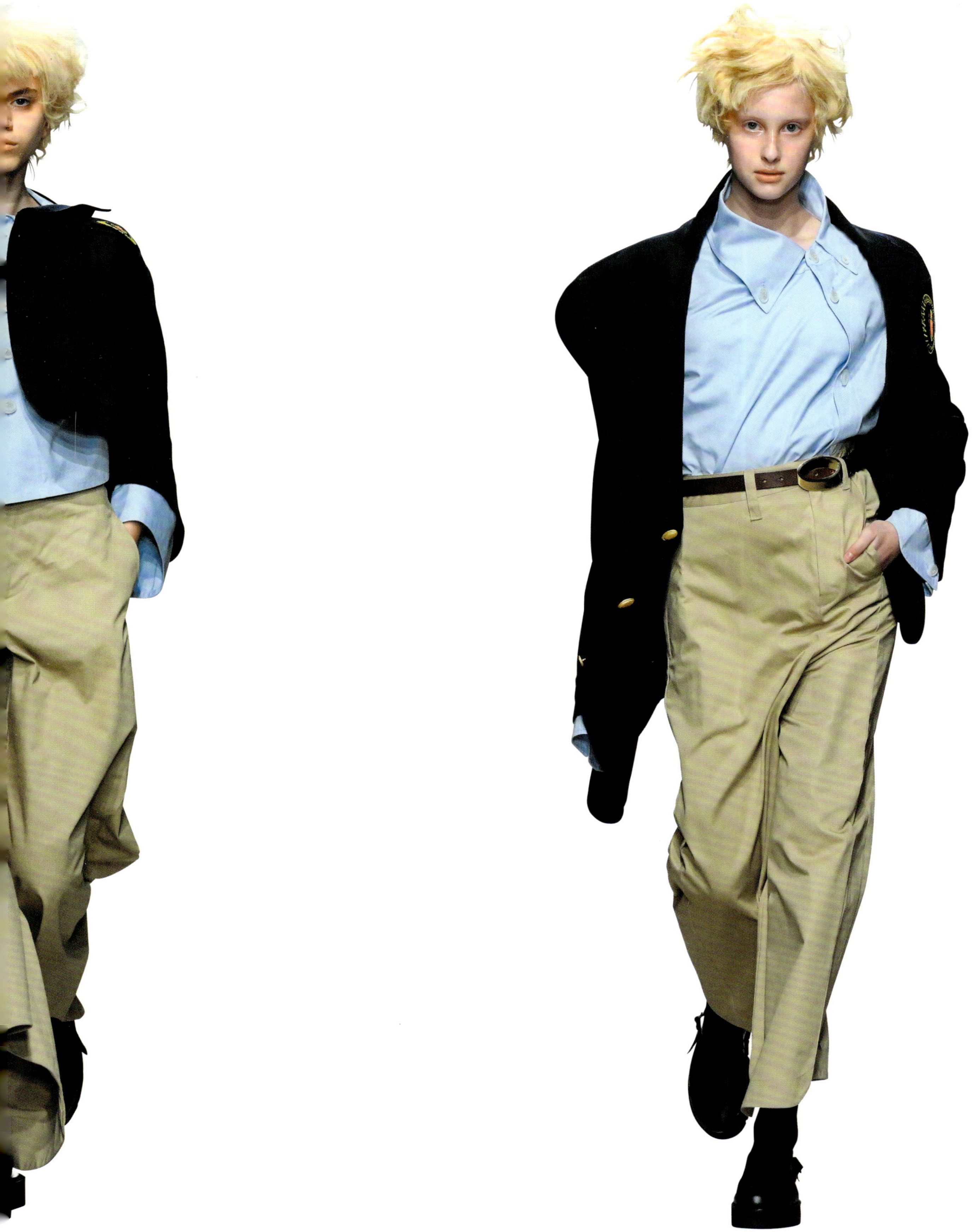

ape changes

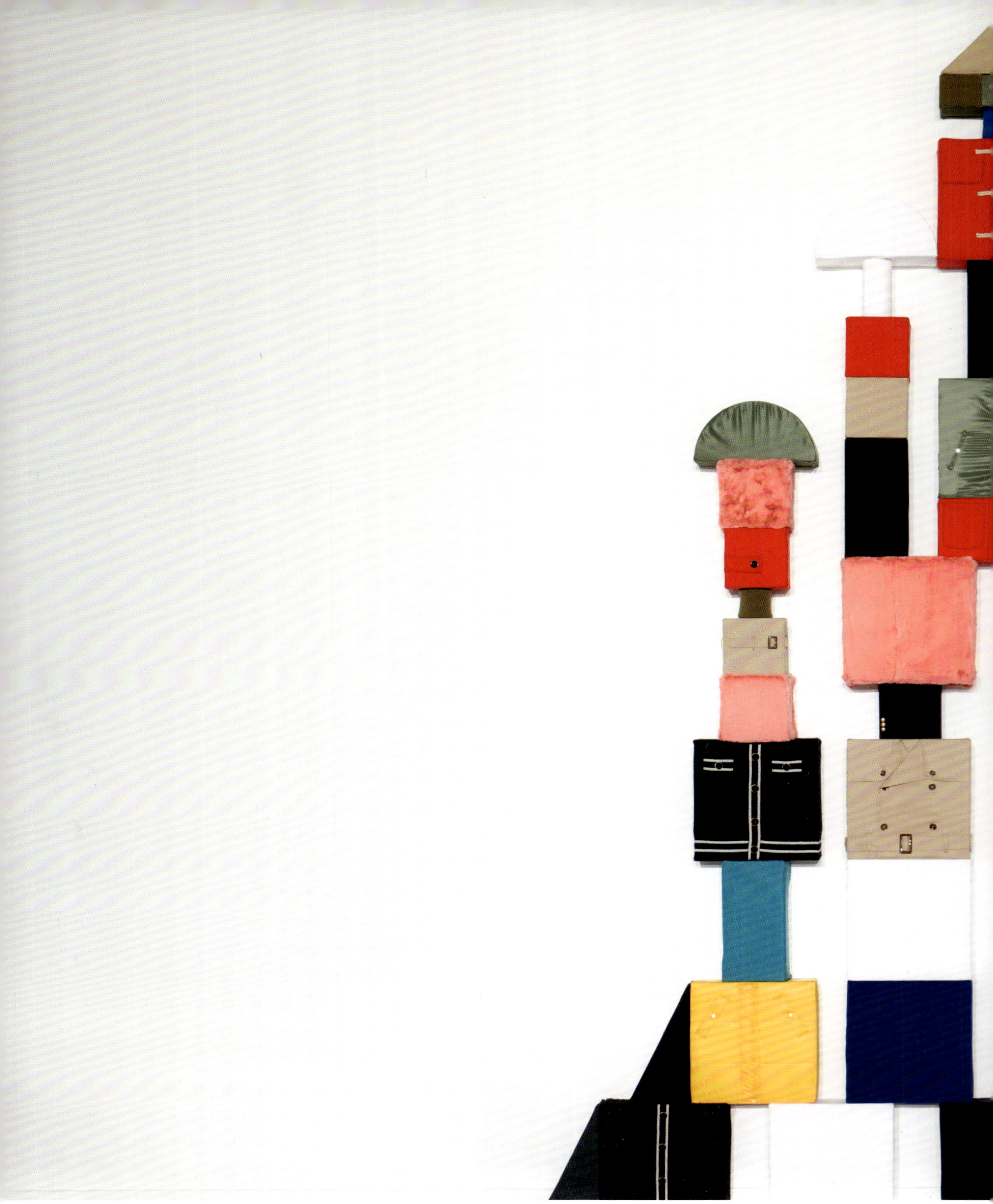

Build and break, build and rebuild

FEB 25, 2020

2020 A/W “BLOCK”

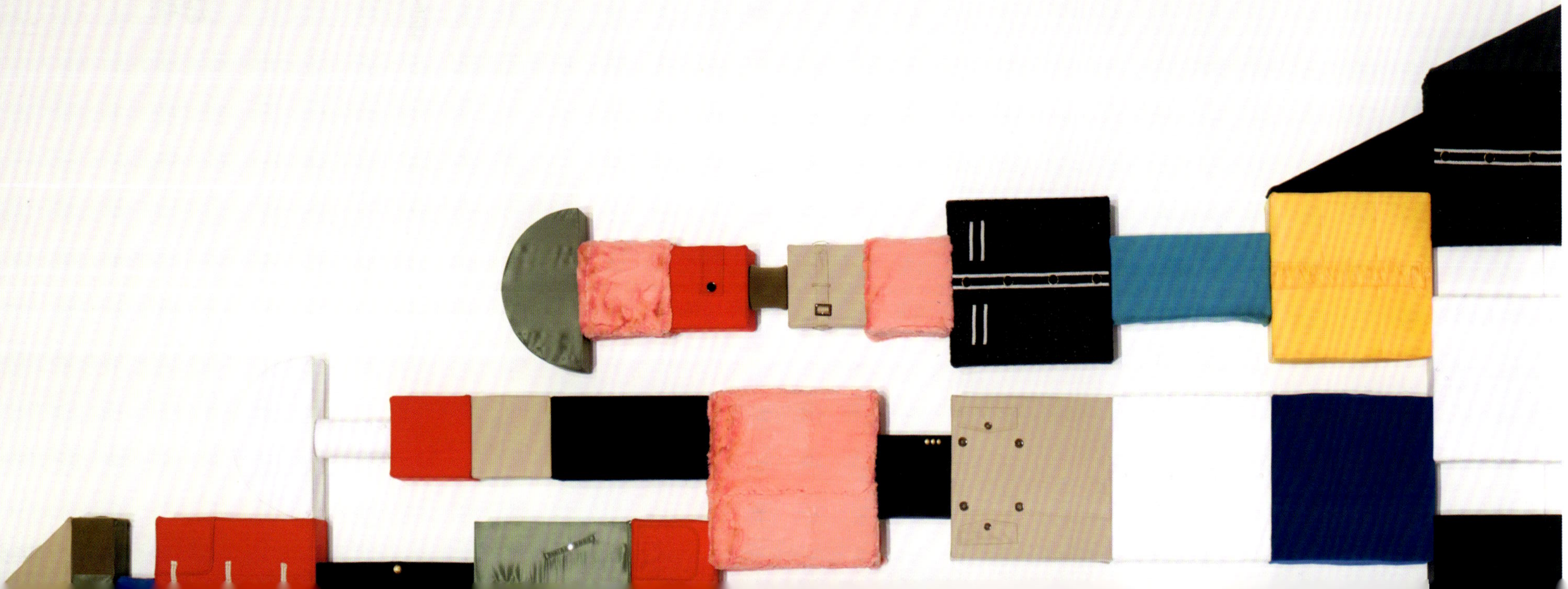

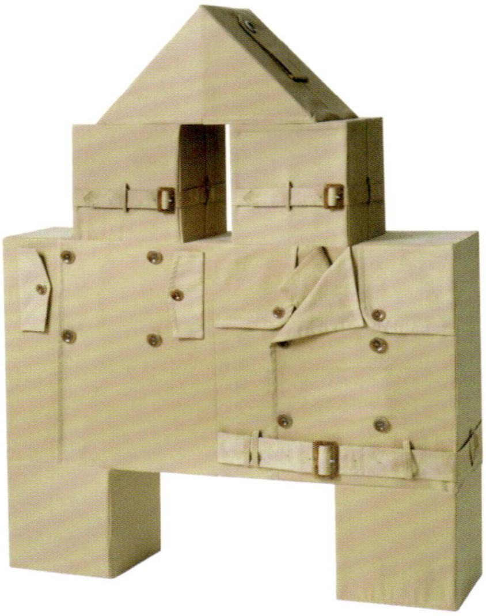
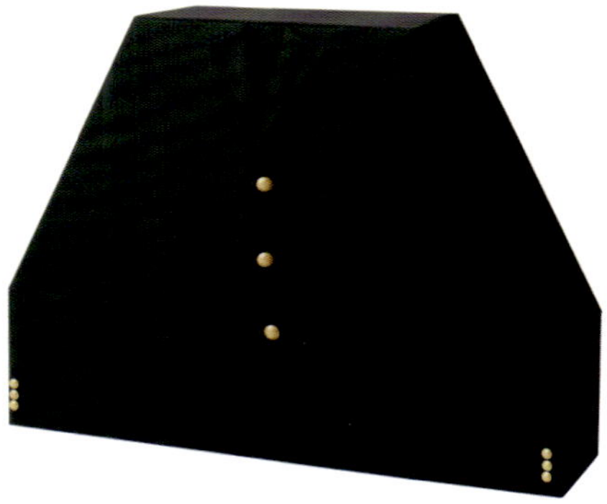
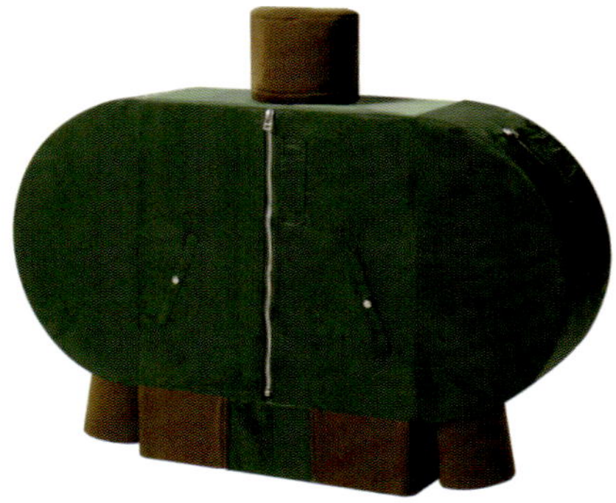
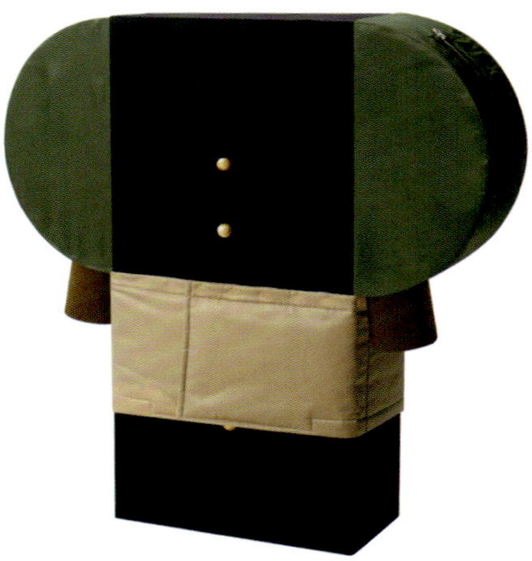
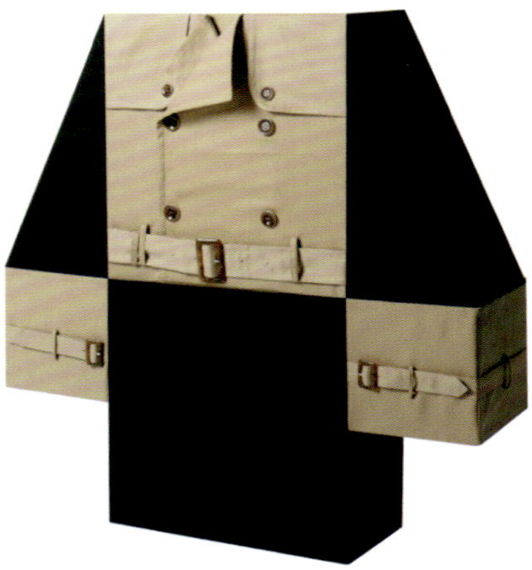
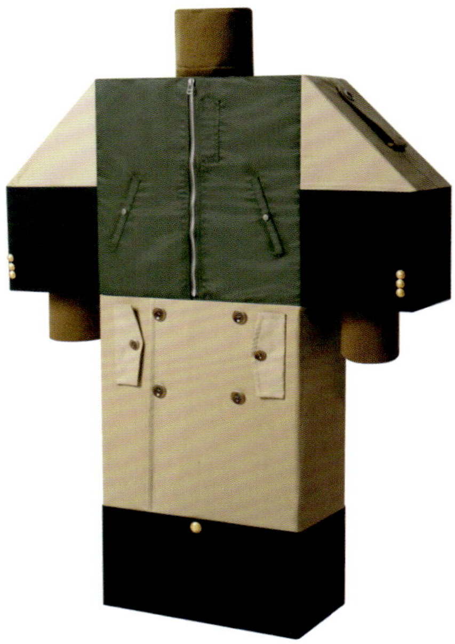

The act of recombining over and over le

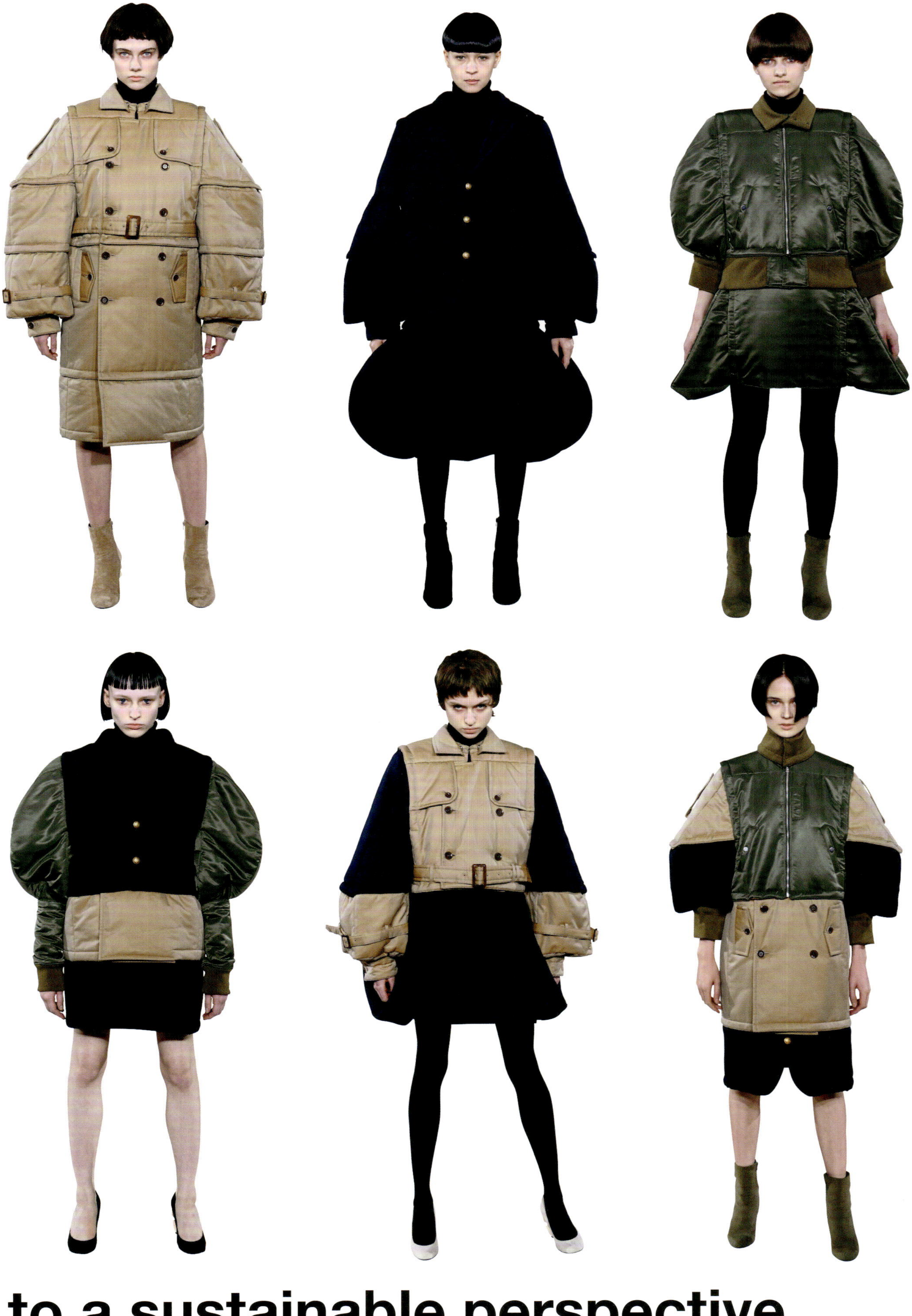

FEB 25, 2020

2020 A/W "BLOCK"

ads to a sustainable perspective

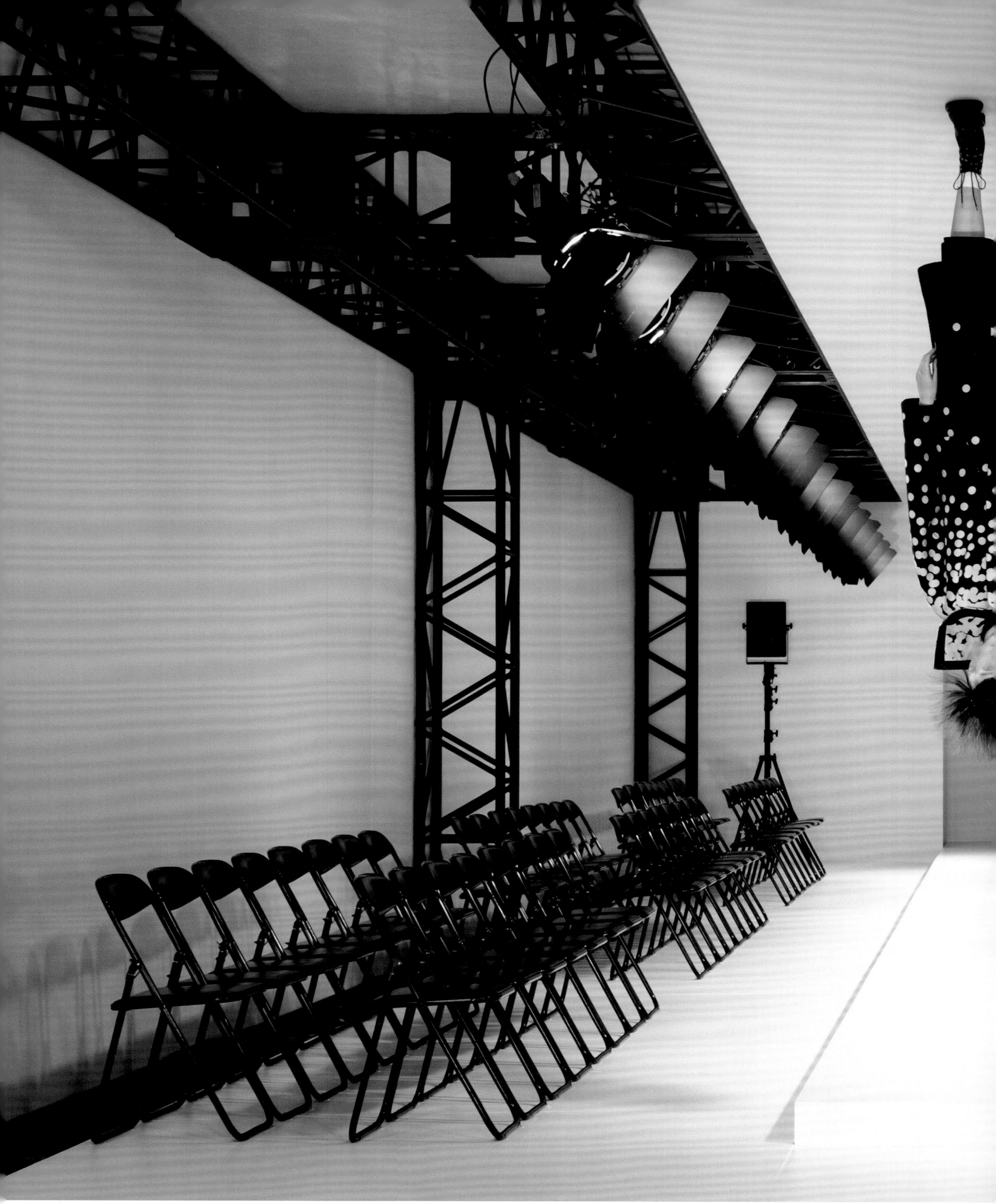

Life lived through digital screens has nc

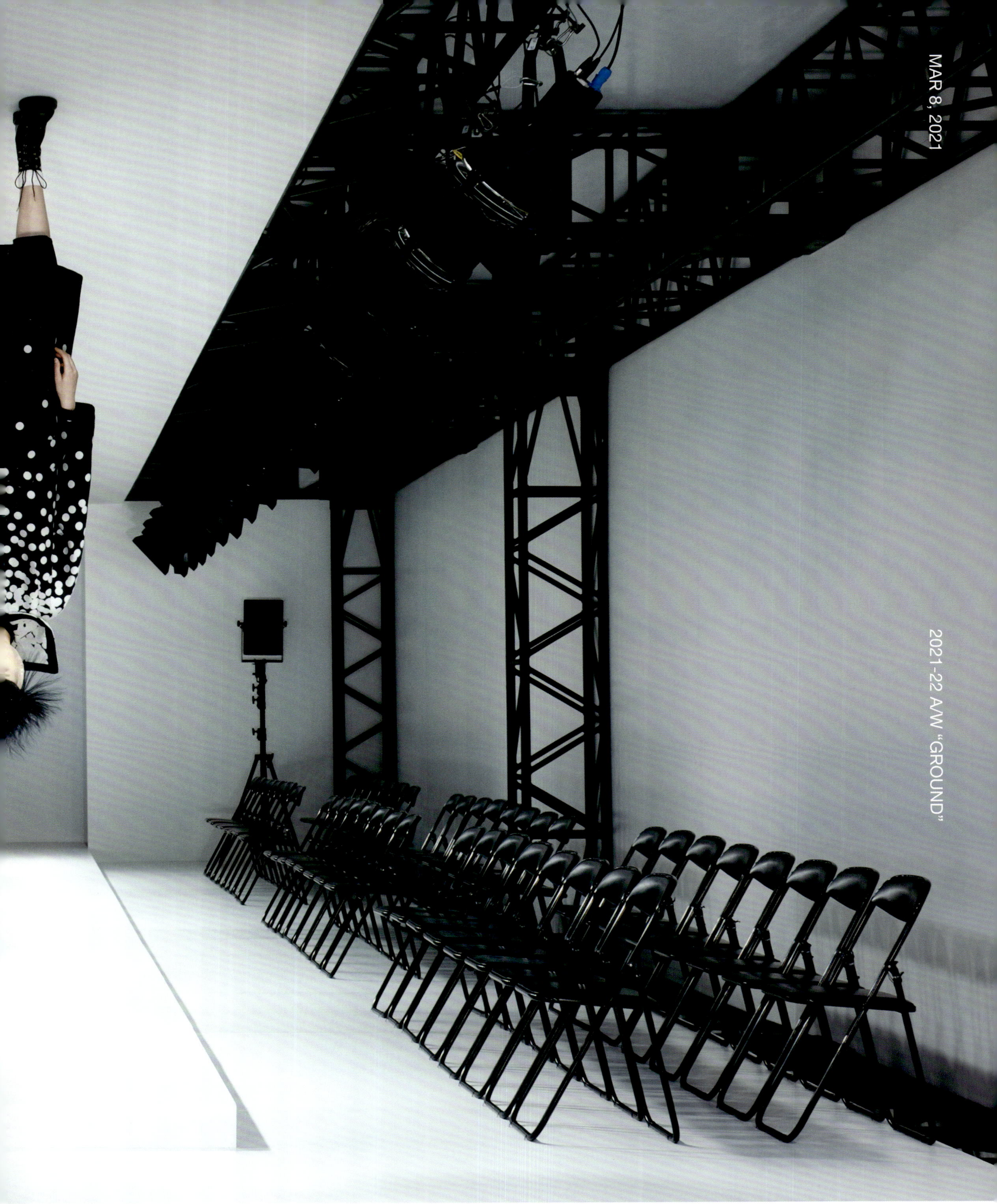

top or bottom

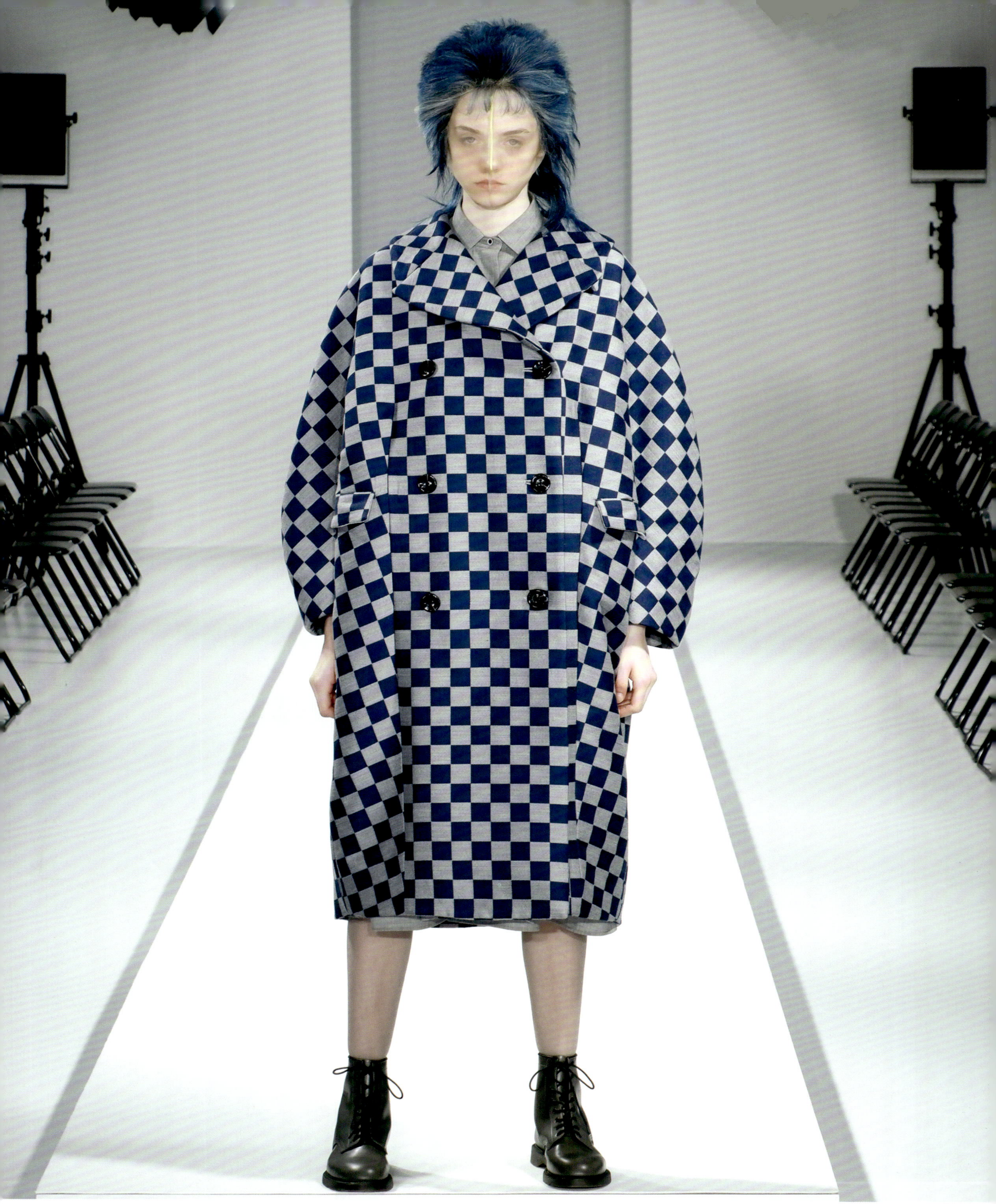

Gravity and mass are flipped and everyt

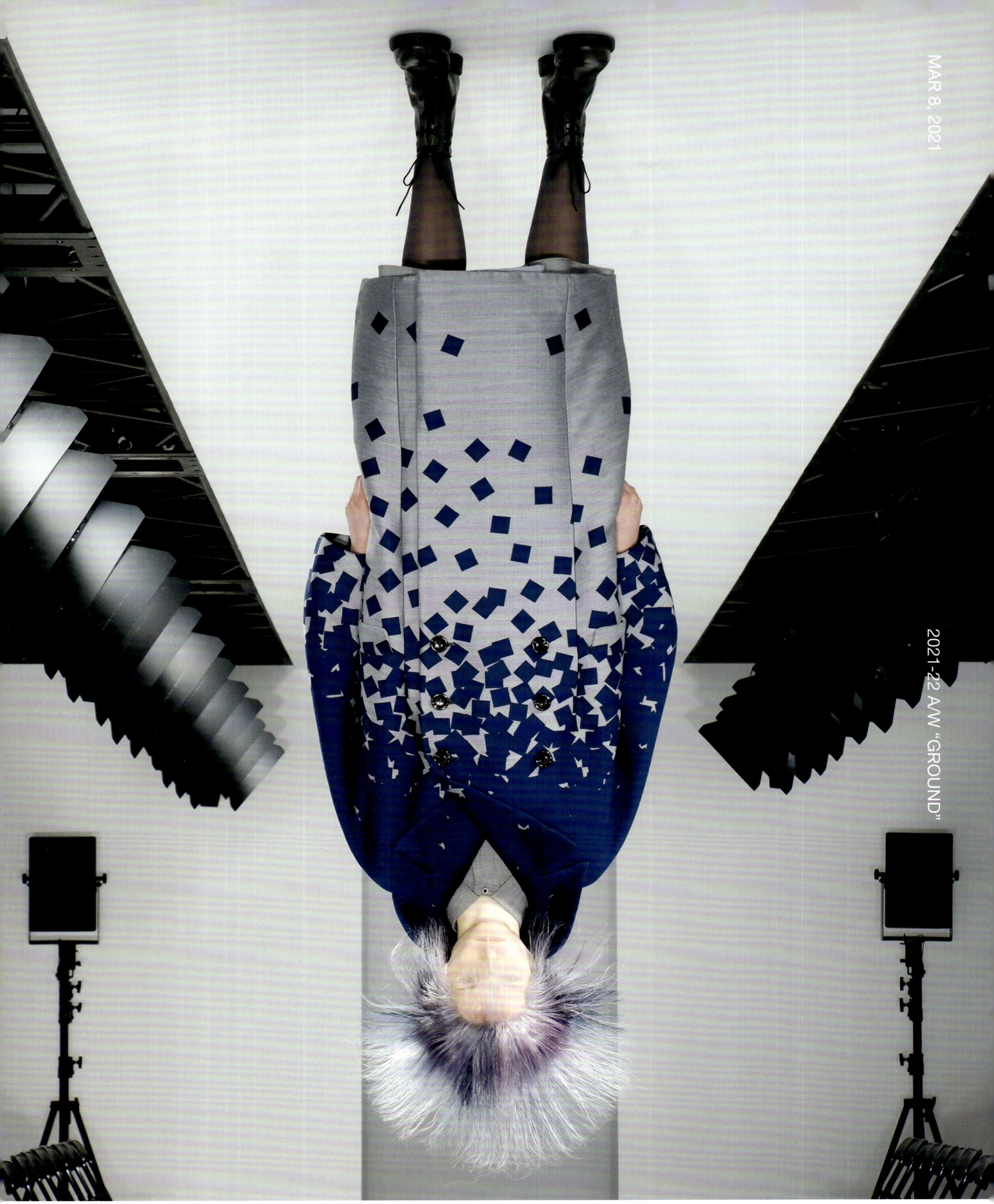

hing floats upwards

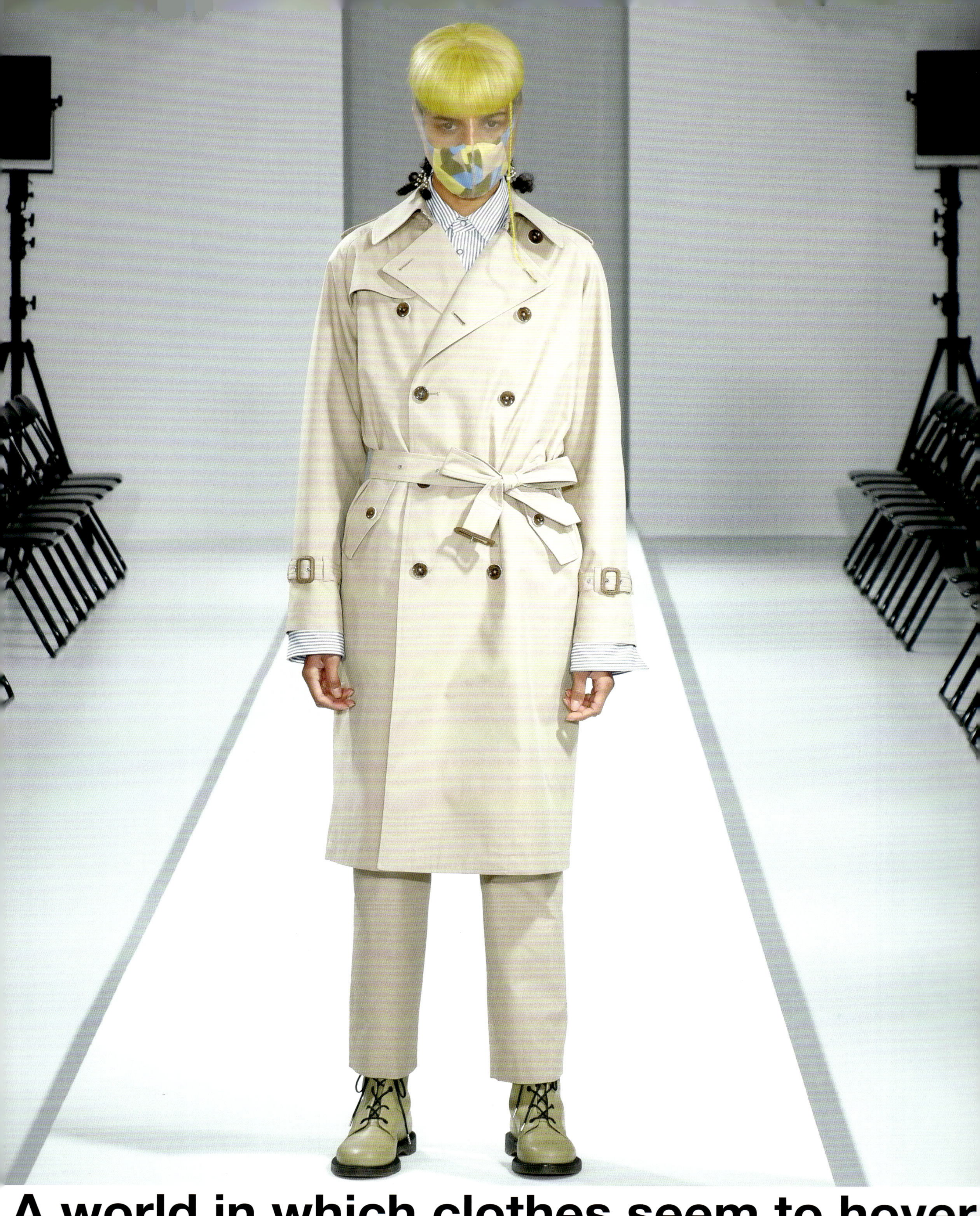

A world in which clothes seem to hover

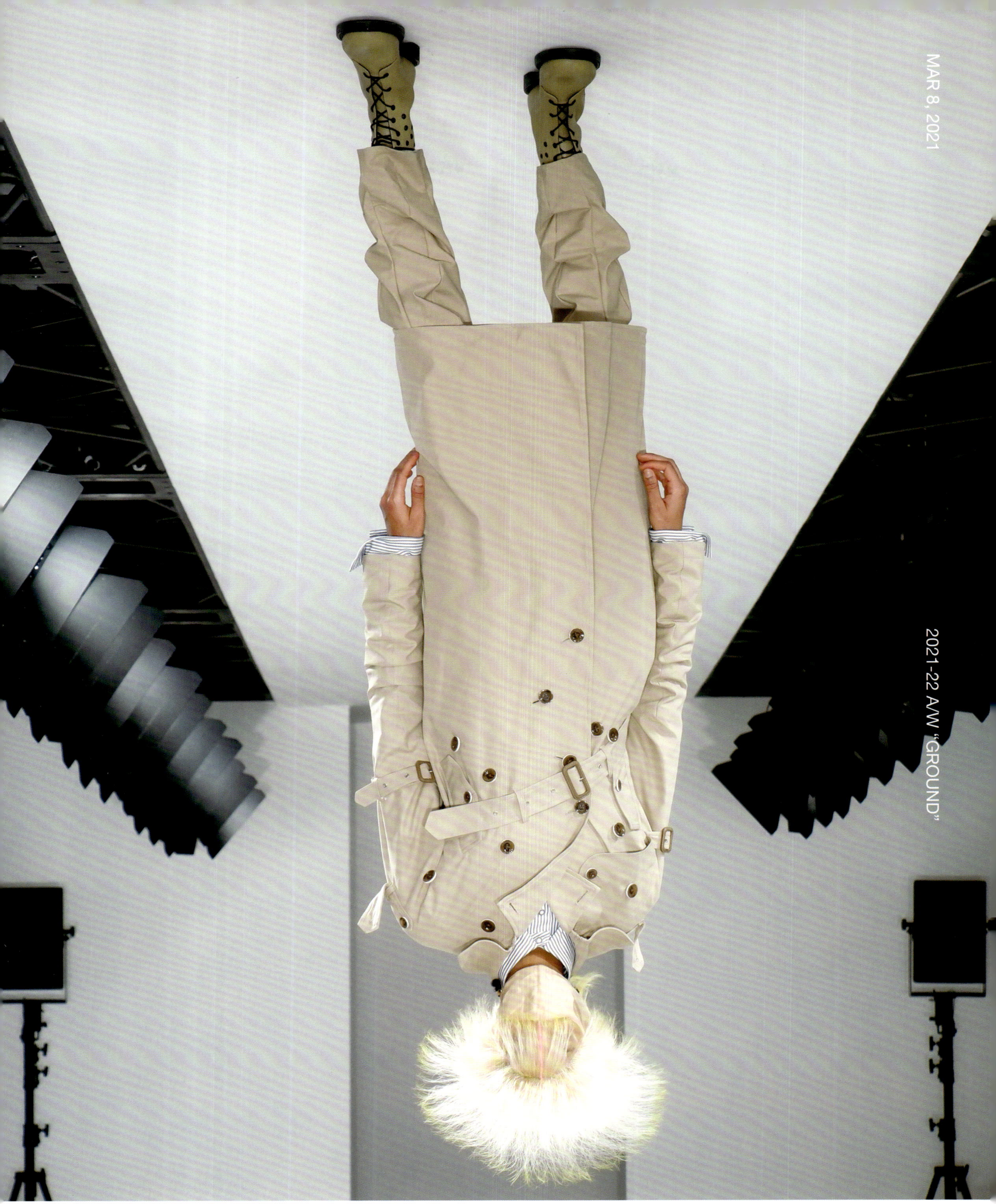

or fall depending on the perspective

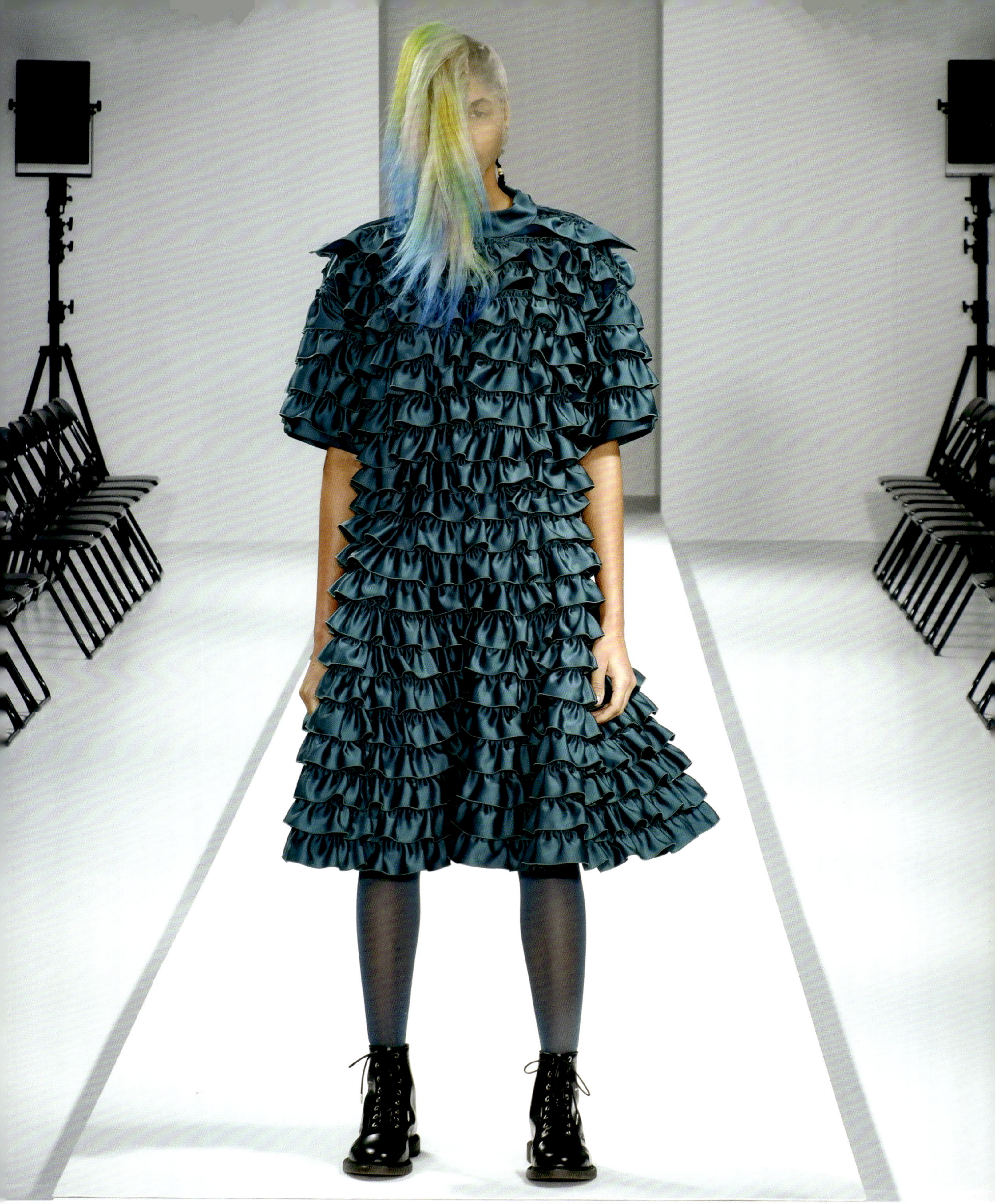

Treading a new ground

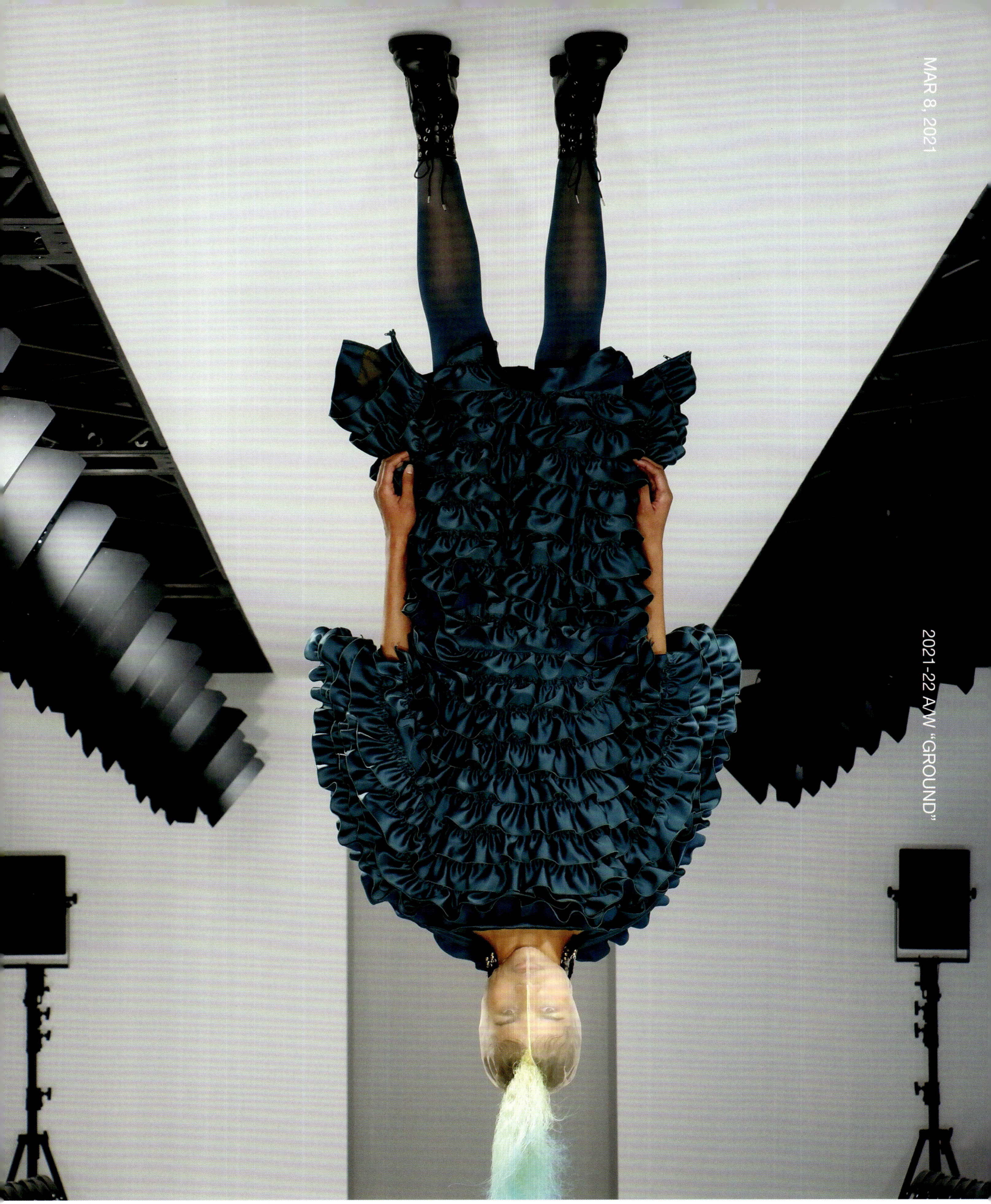

MAR 8, 2021

2021-22 A/W "GROUND"

home [noun]

the place where you live:

He wasn't at home.

a place where people who need special care live:

an old people's home

home [adverb]

to or in the place where you live

home [adjective]

made or used in the place where someone lives:

home cooking

a home computer

HOME

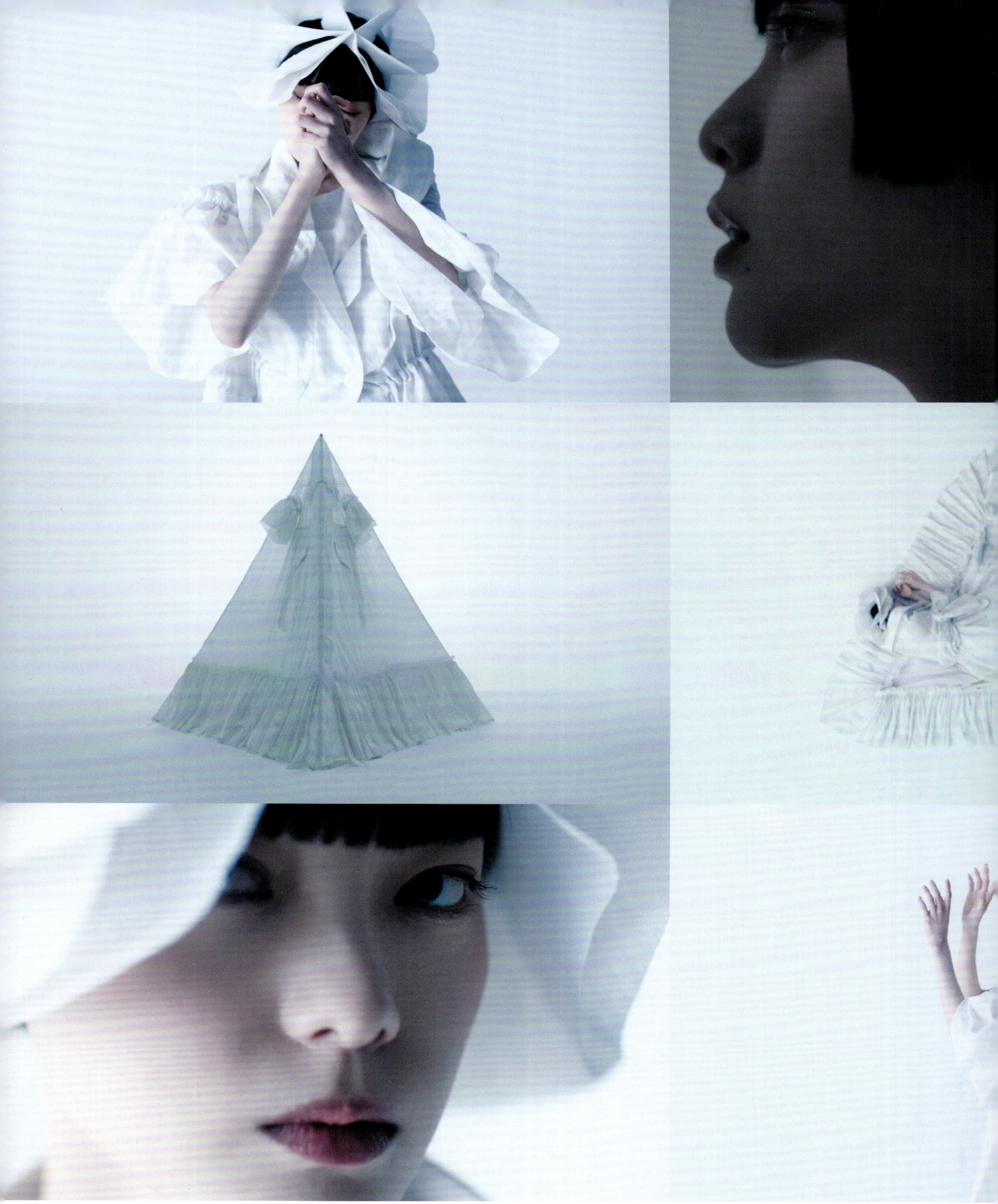

A "home ground" is a place that gives y

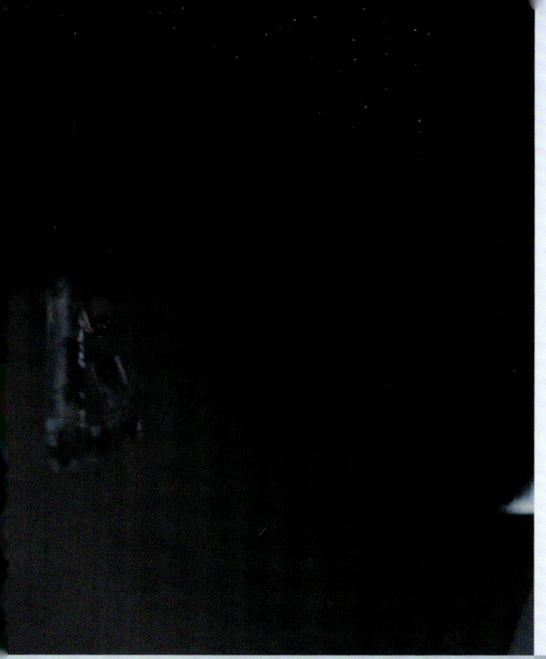

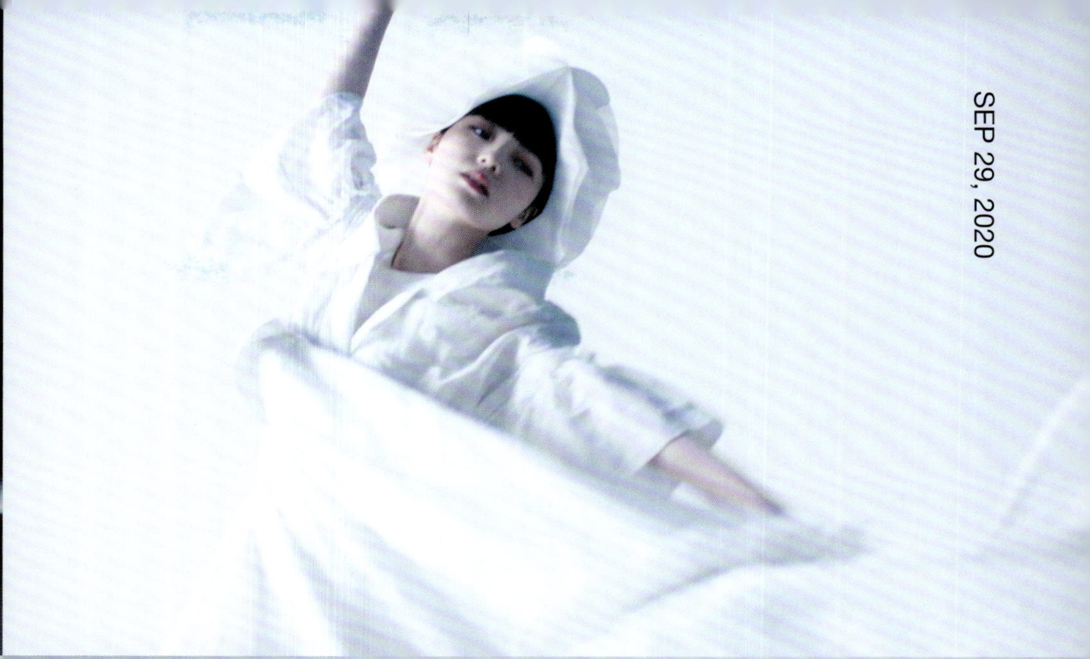

SEP 29, 2020

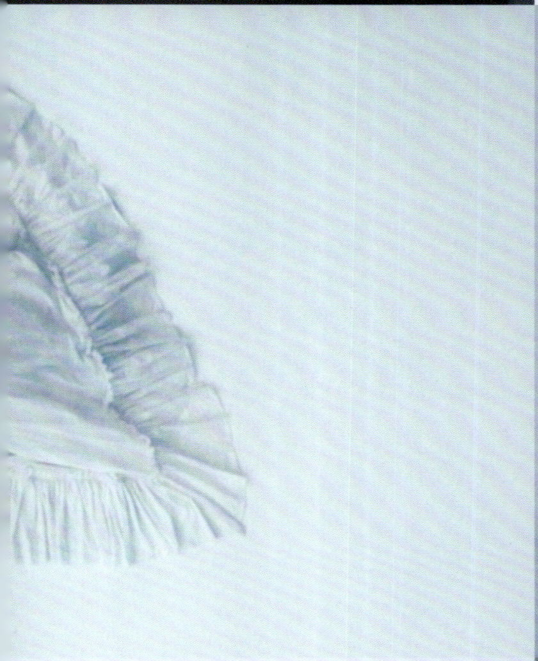

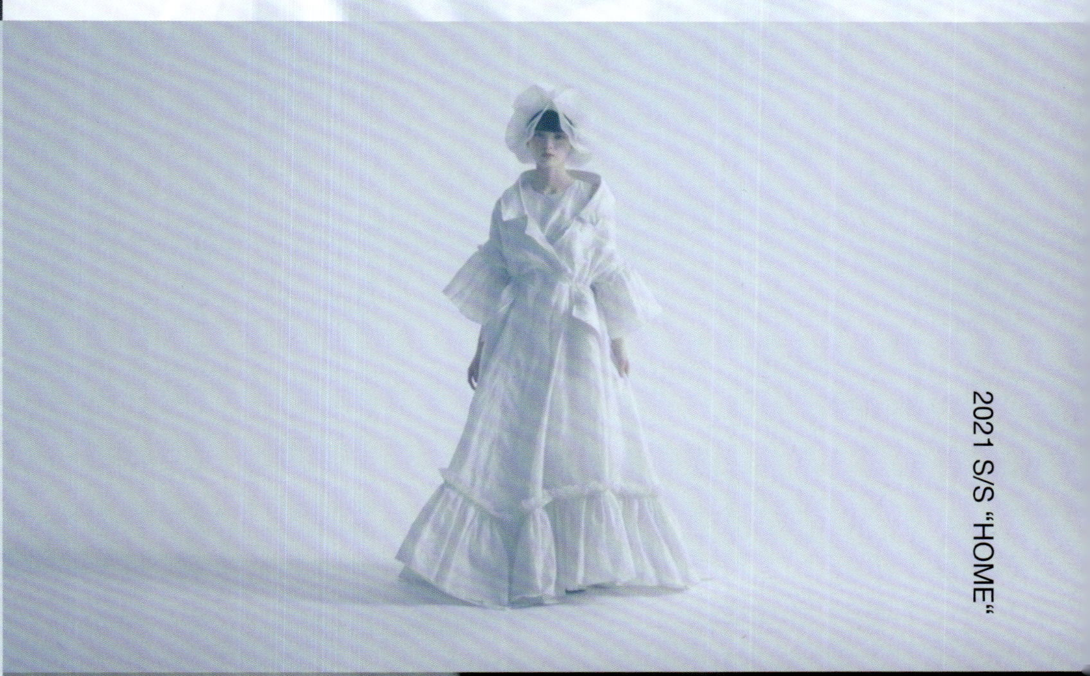

2021 S/S “HOME”

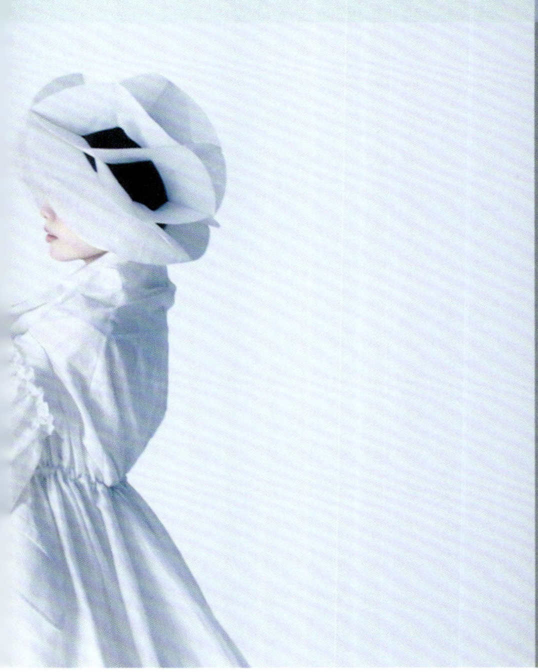

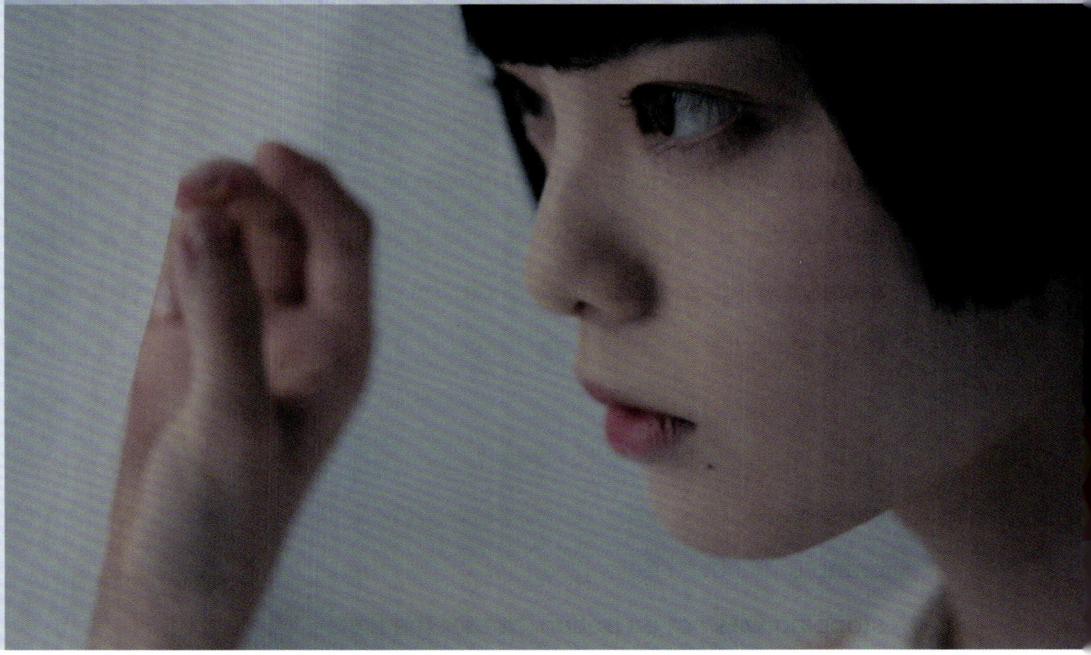

ou an absolute sense of security

HOME

Daily Life

A year and a half had passed since our flagship shop in Minami Aoyama, Tokyo, shifted from a physical operation to an online business. I didn't want fashion, which encourages communication between people, to become the cause of the spread of infection. I had to prioritize the safety of our customers and employees. The idea that merely selling and distributing fashion could be life-threatening broke my heart.

I continued to think about what fashion can do at such a time. Since I started my brand until now, I belonged to a world where stopping was not an option, but for the first time, I paused and thought about my daily life. What should we value moving forward? Today, the human instinct to be close to others is denied outright and being there for someone's death or birth has become increasingly complex. Will we be able to return to the days when such a life was considered extraordinary?

As a brand, Anrealage was forced to reconsider our basic concept that "fashion can be a device to change everyday life." Now that our daily life has become something extraordinary, we needed to reposition fashion as "a device to recover everyday life."

In the spring of 2020, fabric vendors and sewing factories shut down completely. Even if we wanted to create something, we couldn't purchase any materials. We had no choice but to use the materials left in our atelier. Our atelier had accumulated textiles from every season over the last twenty years. We connected these textiles one by one into a patchwork, unconcerned about keeping each season together. For Anrealage, this was a way to tether what was quickly getting lost and mend the daily life that had torn into pieces.

The masks sold out in two minutes. I felt the anxiety that many people were living with all the more deeply. I became more motivated to protect people through fashion.

Of course, fashion cannot kill the virus. So how can everyday fashion protect people in a way that is different from healthcare and medical supplies?

I felt that the times were changing. Such a moment of change anticipates the arrival of clothes that can change a generation. A time that heralds a new concept of clothes, a new way to communicate, and a new way to live each day. If fashion designers cannot rise to the challenge of confronting our creations now, why did we choose to become designers in the first place?

Social distancing requires us to maintain two meters from other people. We must wear masks or face shields to prevent infection. We must refrain from going out and stay home. How can a fashion designer contribute to this new lifestyle? If we look at the limitations in another way, it means we can approach others up to two meters. Although we are not allowed to touch, we can be nearby. We can see other people if we wear a mask. There is a world of difference between being completely cut off and working within restrictions. Just as we can still communicate between a distance of two meters, I believe fashion that accommodates this same distance is achievable.

I began by pondering the meaning of the word "home" in the ubiquitous phrase, "Stay Home." If there is one place that can protect people from viruses, it is our homes.

Since the state of emergency was declared in Japan, all I heard on the news were the words "stay home." I felt oppressed, as if fashion itself were under lockdown. Home is by no means a positive word for fashion designers. As represented by "homewear," it calls to mind loungewear and sleepwear. These are different from the clothes you wear on the premise of going out and meeting people. You cannot fully demonstrate the power of fashion with homewear.

But the coronavirus made me rediscover the meaning of "home." I thought of words such as "home button" and "home ground," and realized that home is a place that you can always return to, a place that provides you with an absolute sense of security.

Clothes and Shelter

I decided that the theme of Anrealage's 2021 Spring/Summer Paris Fashion Week show will be *Home*.

There was something I realized as the coronavirus crisis grew more serious. Clothes don't always cover the whole body. No matter what we wear, a part of us will always be exposed. The only time human beings are entirely covered is when are in the womb or in a coffin after we die. The feeling of being completely covered must be similar to the feeling of being completely protected. The walls of a house also shelter our bodies. A home protects us. Yet the walls of a house don't give us the warmth and sense of comfort we feel in the presence of another person.

A home that feels like clothes, clothes that feel like a home. Something that exists between the two. Can we not wear a home like wearing clothes? Can we not wear clothes like living in a home? Clothes that cover us from the top of our heads to the tips of our toes. Clothes that function as a small house. I thought using antivirus material would be ideal.

I found a clue in a hermit crab. Hermit crabs fit inside a shell, but they need to find larger shells when their bodies grow larger. In this case, is the shell shelter or clothes? Do they live inside it, or do they wear it? Both are likely, but neither seemed right.

It was something between clothes and shelter, between the real and the unreal.

Clothes that secure a physical distance of two meters and can transform into a home. When you remove the framing and pull on the string, the home transforms into clothes. Clothes that function as a tent, and a tent that can also turn into clothes. It is a piece that incorporates two functions and forms. In addition to the tetrahedron that could be used as a tent, the clothes were also made as mobile homes based on the shapes of spheres, hexahedrons, octahedrons, dodecahedrons, and icosahedrons. Each piece can be folded up. When it is folded flat, the string returns to being a part of the clothes. When the piece is a home it feels solid, and when it is clothes it features lightly flowing drapes and a gentle volume.

Online and Offline

Paris Fashion Week 2020, held for nine days from late September, had a very different participation format from its past editions. General admissions for fashion shows were severely restricted, and in an unprecedented move, the shows were streamed online. Saint Laurent and Celine called off their shows, spreading further confusion.

One month before Paris Fashion Week, I agonized over how we should present our new collection, *Home*. Should we go to Paris and have a show in front of the audience with models walking down the runway as usual? Or should we stream the show online for the first time? There was no sign that the spread of the new coronavirus would subside in Europe. If I forced myself to have a show in Paris, I would put the hundred plus staff members supporting Anrealage at risk. Then should I shoot a video of the show in Tokyo and present it in Paris instead? My mind wavered. I knew that I could never outdo my past self if I streamed the show in a simple way. I began to think that the only way to triumph was to stay true to the Anrealage's way of doing things—even online.

Both the runway shows that would take place in Paris and the online streaming shows were officially authorized as part of Paris Fashion Week. But there was still a big difference between the two. A show that occurs live before an invited audience, for example, has a rarity that a streaming show that can be seen by anyone cannot replicate. There is also a sense of realism that a live performance can impart. Offline shows offer audiences the thrill of improvisation and excitement of seeing things happen only once. On the other hand, streaming shows can be viewed anywhere and as many times as you like.

A fashion show always involves a lot of people. People who wear the clothes, people who put on the clothes, people who display the clothes, people who come to see the clothes. It is collaborative work among all these people. For every ten minutes, an Anrealage show needs a staff of over a hundred. It takes an expansive range of work by show producers, musicians, lighting technicians, sound artists, stage artists, cameramen, as well as stylists, hair and makeup artists, models, fitters, ushers, and receptionists. A show streamed online, which can incorporate CG and animation, makes it possible to reduce the number of people needed to the utmost limit. A physical fashion show wouldn't go that way.

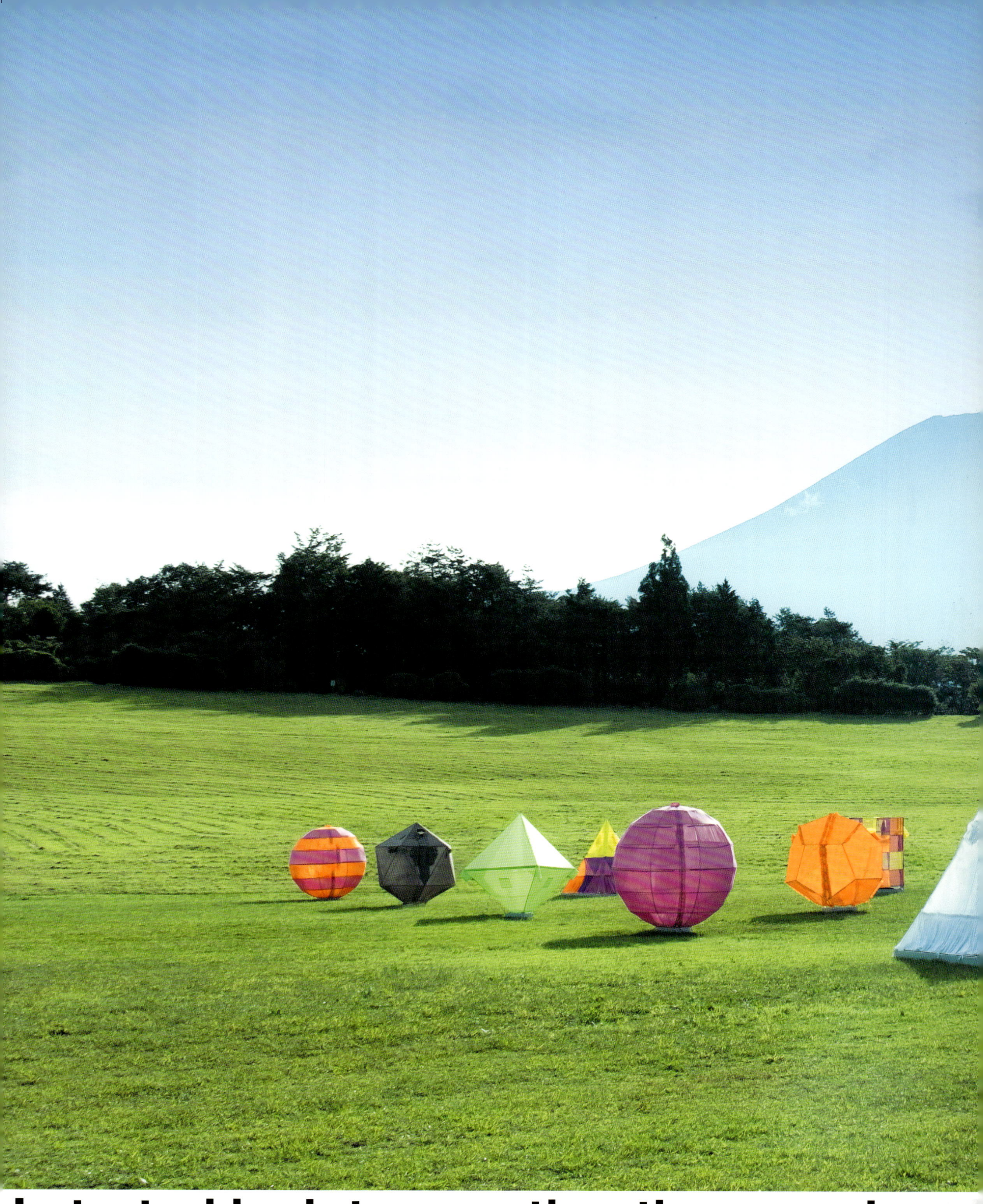

I started by interrogating the meaning o

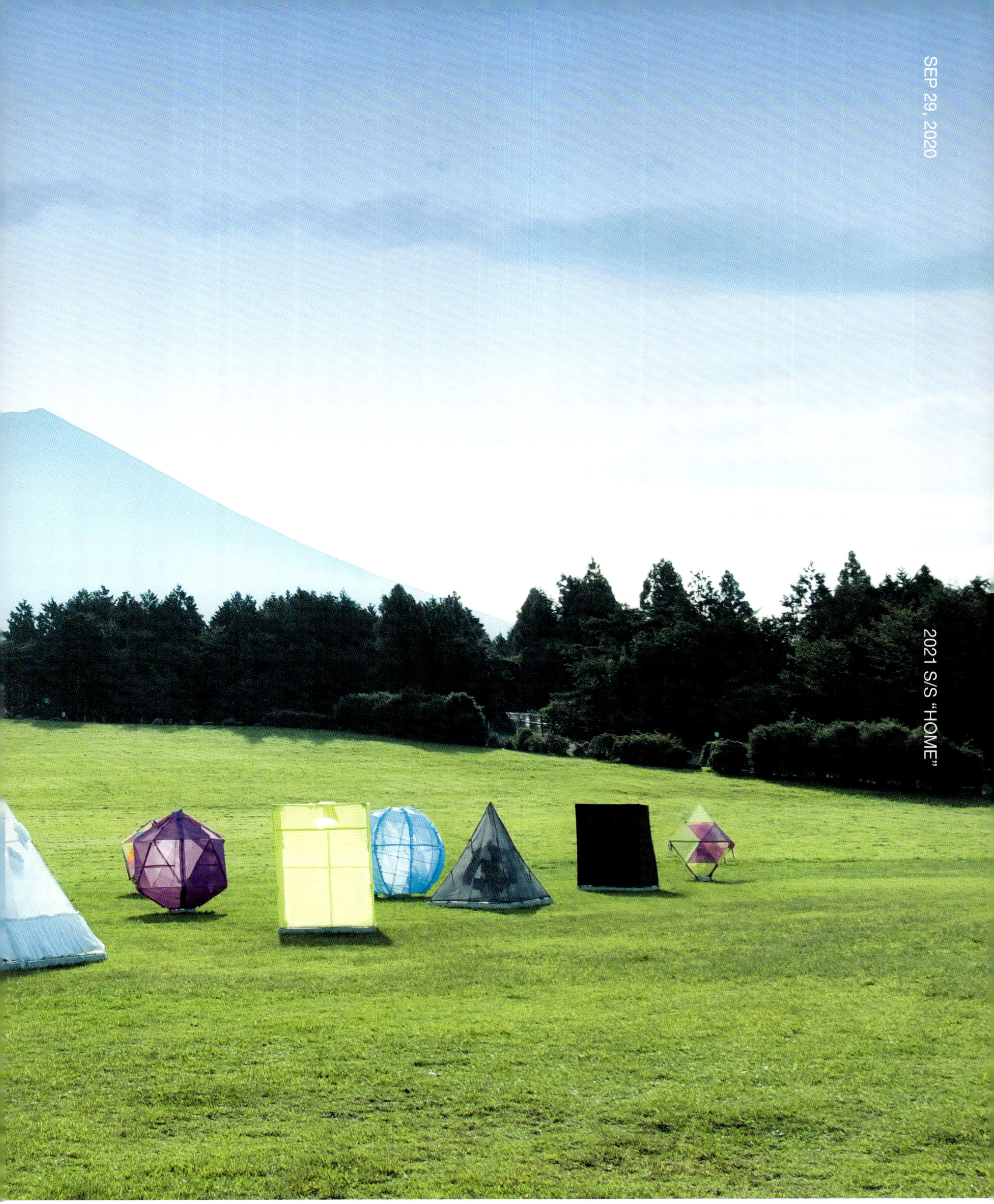

f "Home" in the phrase "Stay Home"

Which way should Anrealage take? Online or off?

Mt. Fuji

It was August 20, one month until the start of Paris Collection in late September. Riding in a car driven by Shigetaka Kaneko, the show director, we searched for a suitable location for our streaming show. I wanted to find a place where fashion shows aren't usually held. I wanted to take the antithesis of the show's theme, *Home*, and have it outdoors. I narrowed down my choices and decided on campsites, since we could take drone shots there and they would also enhance the tent-like clothes in the collection.
The five campgrounds in Shizuoka Prefecture that we previewed were overrun with weeds, and they also had restrictions on drone use and could not be rented out. Unable to find a suitable site, we gave up and started to drive back to Tokyo when we spotted a billboard for Asagiri Nature Park. We stopped by and discovered that the park offered a large expanse of grassland, and that it was possible to see Mt. Fuji in good weather. I immediately contacted Fujinomiya City, which had jurisdiction over the park. They replied that it was possible to set up tents, rent out the area, and even shoot with a drone. I made up my mind to stream our show from Asagiri Nature Park, using Mt. Fuji as the only set design. I could already imagine it: colorful clothes shaped like tents lining up in a V formation against the majestic backdrop of Mt. Fuji, the V reflecting the mountain upside down.

I sent one of my employees to Asagiri Nature Park to observe the view of Mt. Fuji for a week. I asked her to give me an hourly report on how the landscape and weather conditions change. There was a possibility that we would be able to see the entire view of the mountain early in the morning. A fashion show against the backdrop of Mt. Fuji could be realized if we began shooting at 6 AM. The employee told me, "I could only see Mt. Fuji one out of the seven days I was there, and I could only see half of the mountain. Our only chance to see it is until seven in the morning. That means we have one hour to do the show."

Anrealage's online show was scheduled to be streamed on September 29. Filming took place one week prior to this date. We began setting up the clothes at five in the morning. A stunning panoramic view of Mt. Fuji appeared before us. We all held our breath, awed by the mountain's perfect, cloudless silhouette. We had one hour before shooting. Then, something unexpected occurred. Due to the effect of Typhoon No. 12, our campground was hit directly by a strong wind. The wind blew down the tents and pillars and wrecked the frames. It would take more than half a day to reinforce the pillars. But we only had one hour to shoot in front of Mt. Fuji. "There's nothing we can do now. We need to give up." As I was about to say this, Kaneko asked me how many staff members I had with me. "I have at least a hundred," I answered. Kaneko said, "We have eighteen tent-shaped clothes, and they can all be supported by people. Gather everyone at once." We realized that the people supporting the tent would appear on screen, but the film editor immediately explained that they can be digitally removed later. Hence filming began on schedule, with people supporting the tent-shaped clothes. We continued to shoot until seven in the evening. Miraculously, Mt. Fuji showed itself the entire time.

Without Kaneko's quick thinking and our staff members' support, the collection *Home* would not have been possible. Even though our show format changed to streaming, fashion shows are made up of people. This will always stay the same.

The Origin

I had hoped to move away from my past collections and venture far with the collection *Home*. However, I realized that the collection encapsulates many of the themes that could be described as the origin of Anrealage.

The shapes seen in this collection echo those in the 2009 Spring/Summer collection, ○△□. The clothes are not structured to conform to the human body.

The forms in this collection evoke the 2013 Spring/Summer collection, *Bone*. The clothes consist of frameworks, as well as the skin and membrane that cover them.

This collection is also similar to the concept behind the 2016 Spring/Summer collection, *Reflect*. Like a reflection of light, a single form is amplified into multiple facets, creating a realm unlike any other.

Finally, this collection harkens back to the functional transformation seen in the 2019 Fall/Winter collection, *Detail*. Just as a cuff is transformed into a waist, by shifting dimensions, "clothes" are transformed into "shelter."

The last piece in *Home* is a shining patchwork. Patchwork is at the heart of Anrealage. The piece was my attempt at narrating everyday life through my collection and connect people. I wanted to light up the clothes, just as you would turn on the light inside a home. A home is a place that you eventually return to. I thought I would find such a place somewhere far into the future, but I realized that the origin of Anrealage was my home.

SEP 29, 2020

2021 S/S “HOME”

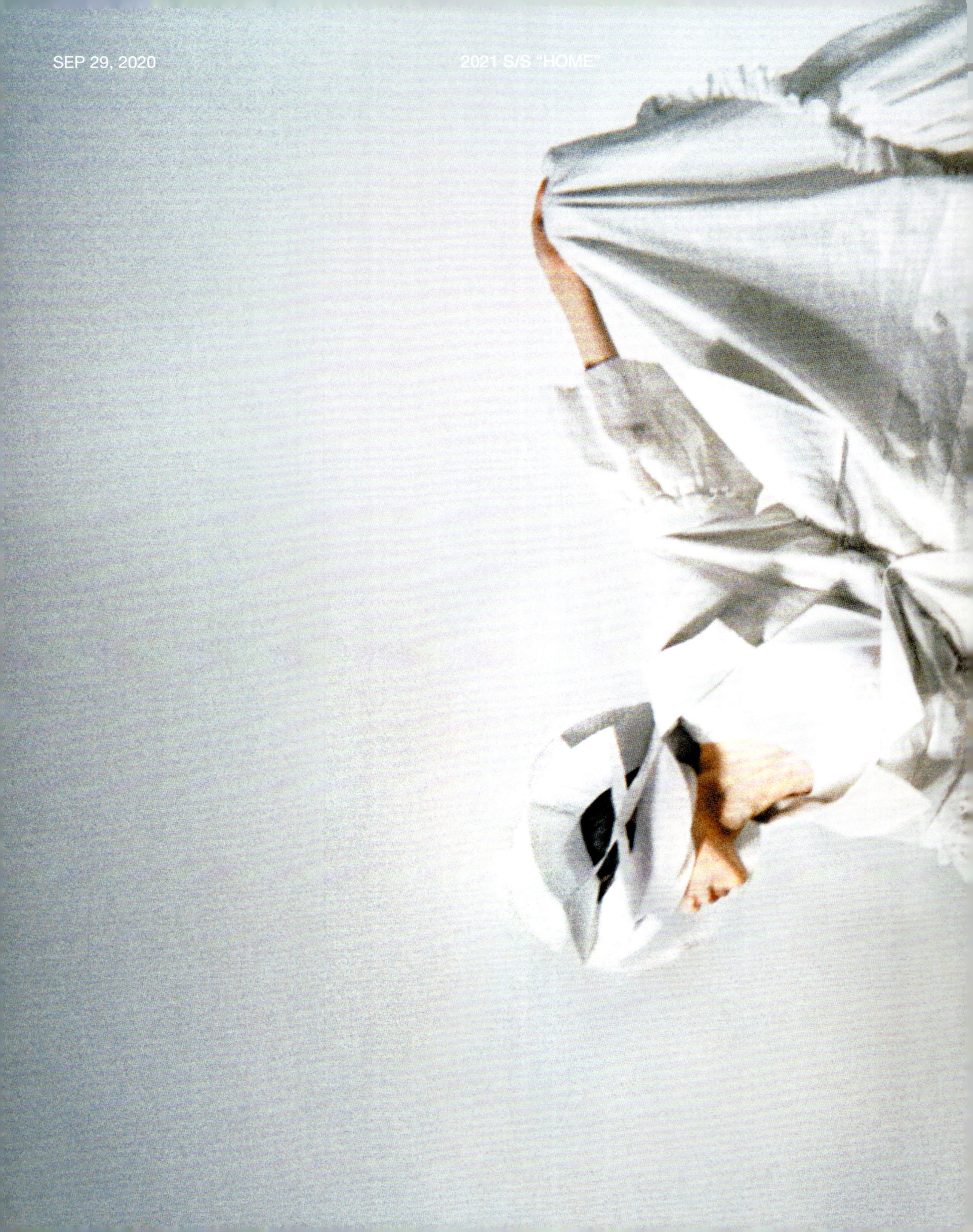

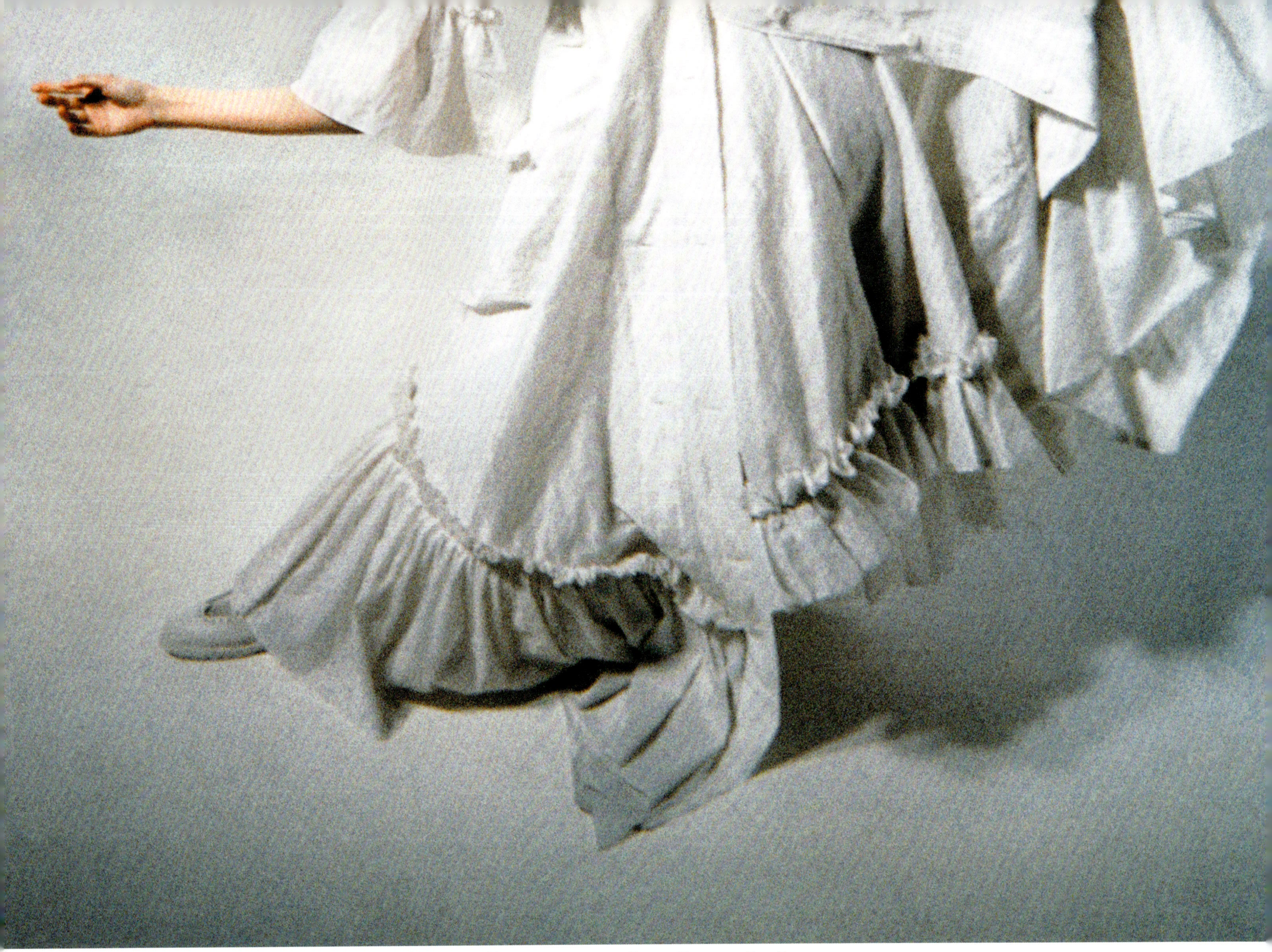

To protect people through fashion

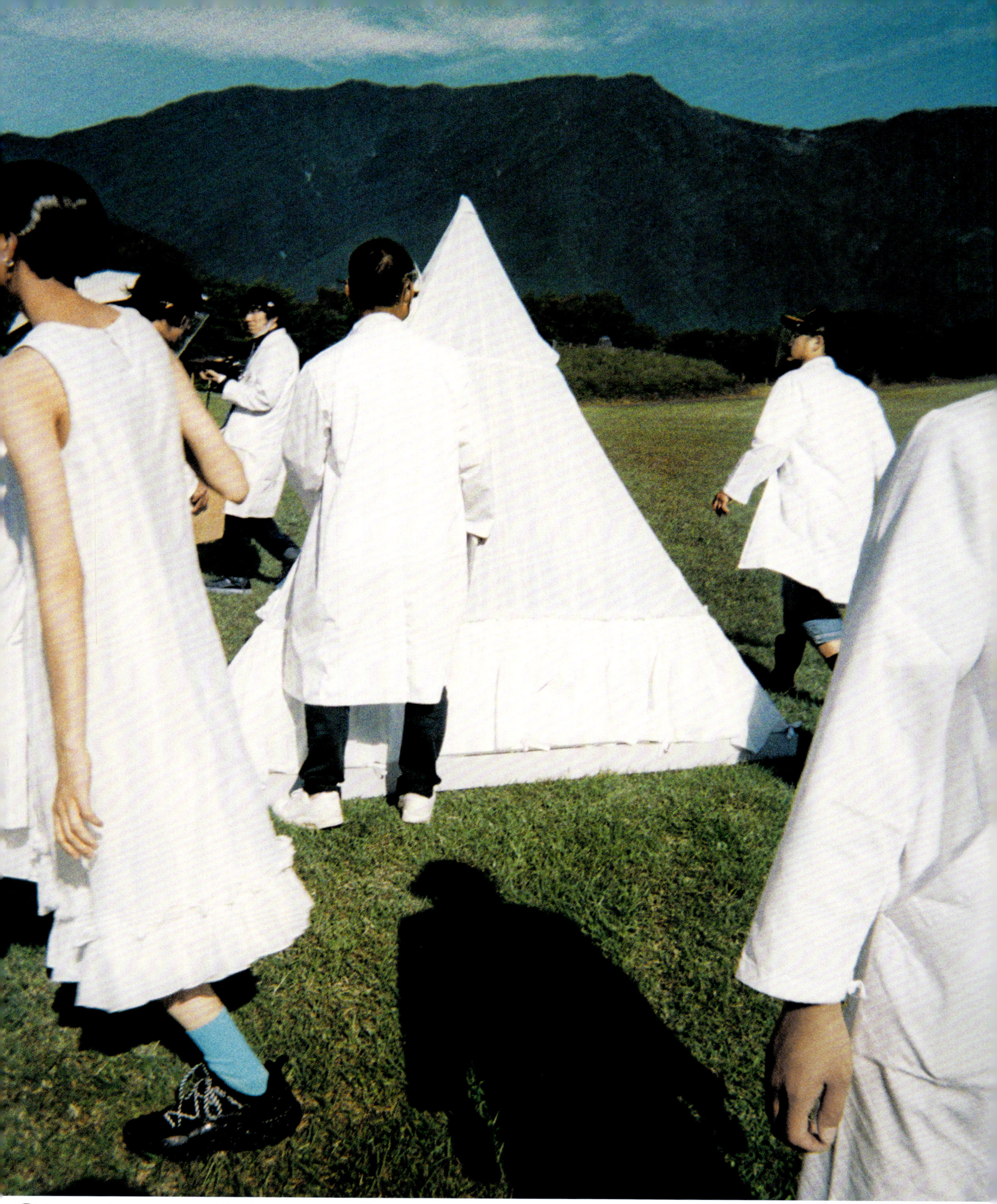

Clothes like a home, or a home like clot

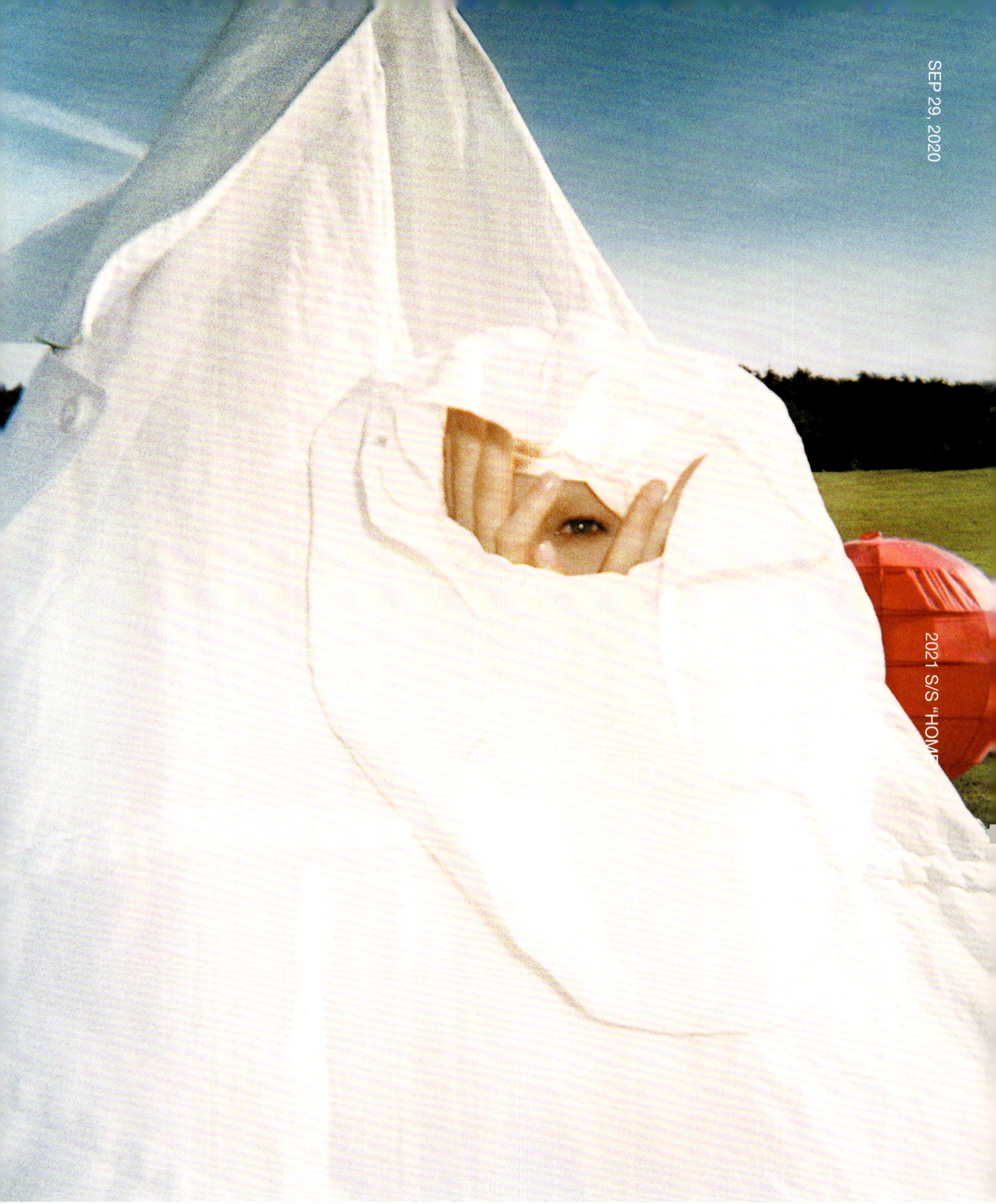

nes

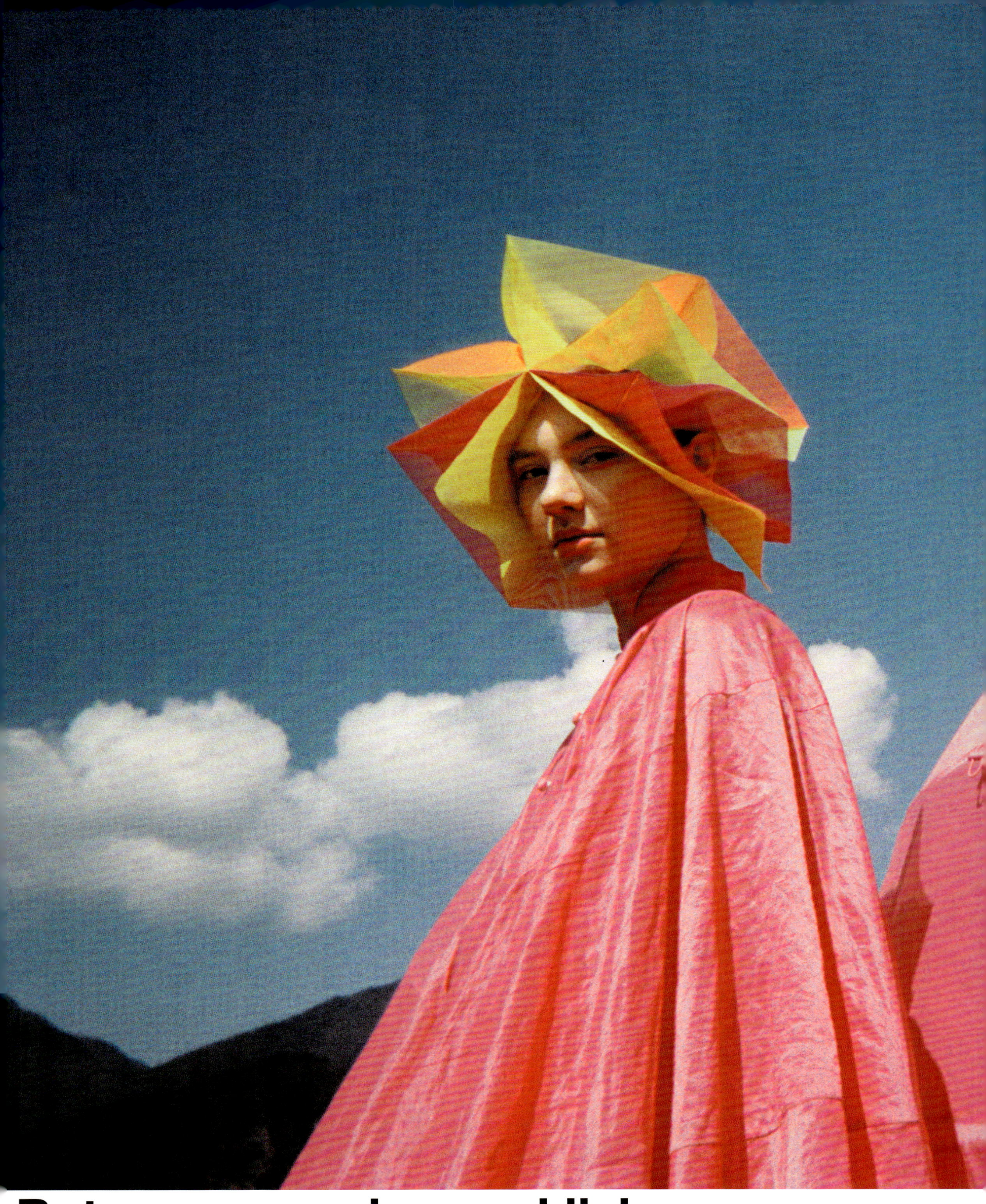

Between wearing and living

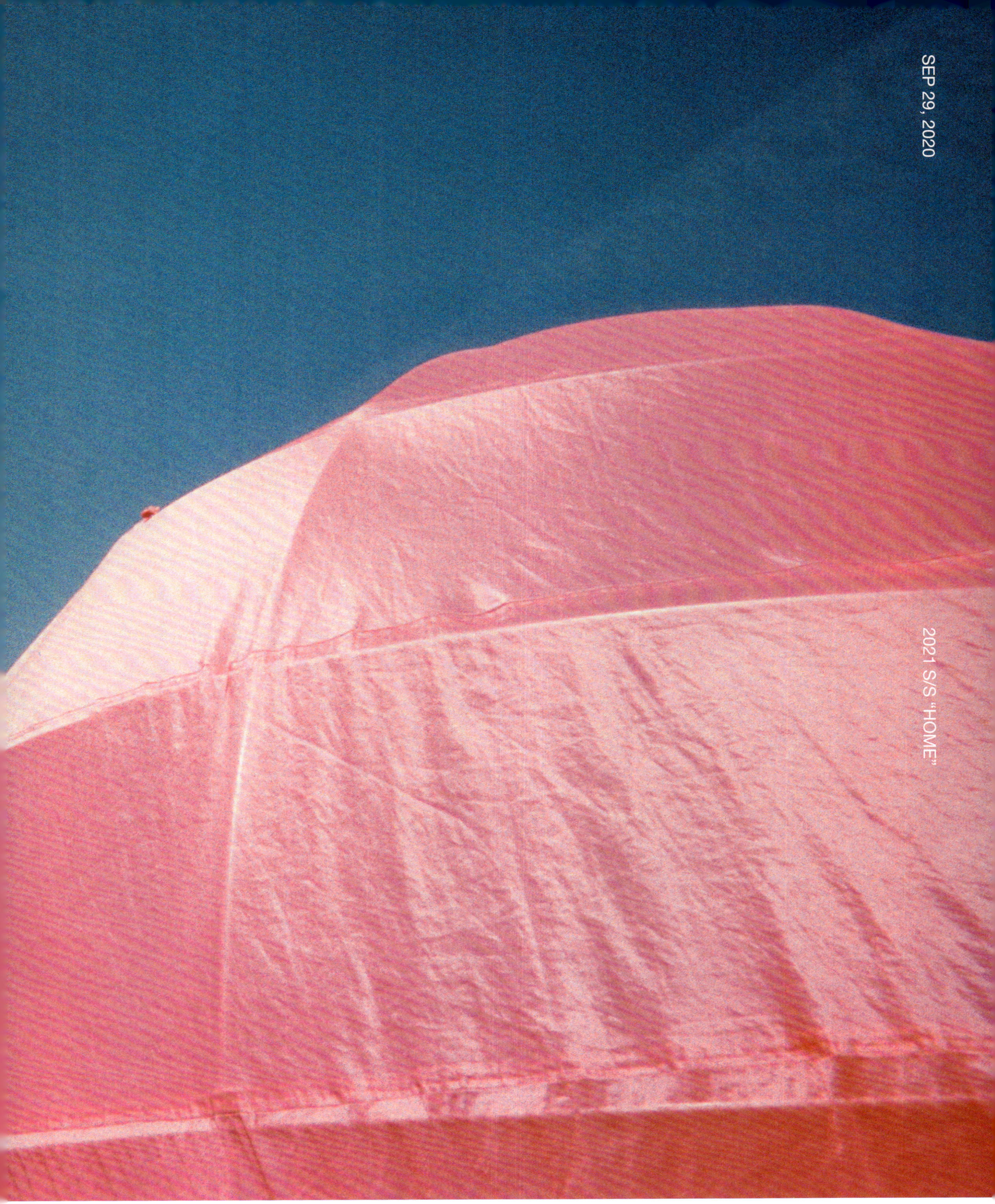
SEP 29, 2020
2021 S/S "HOME"

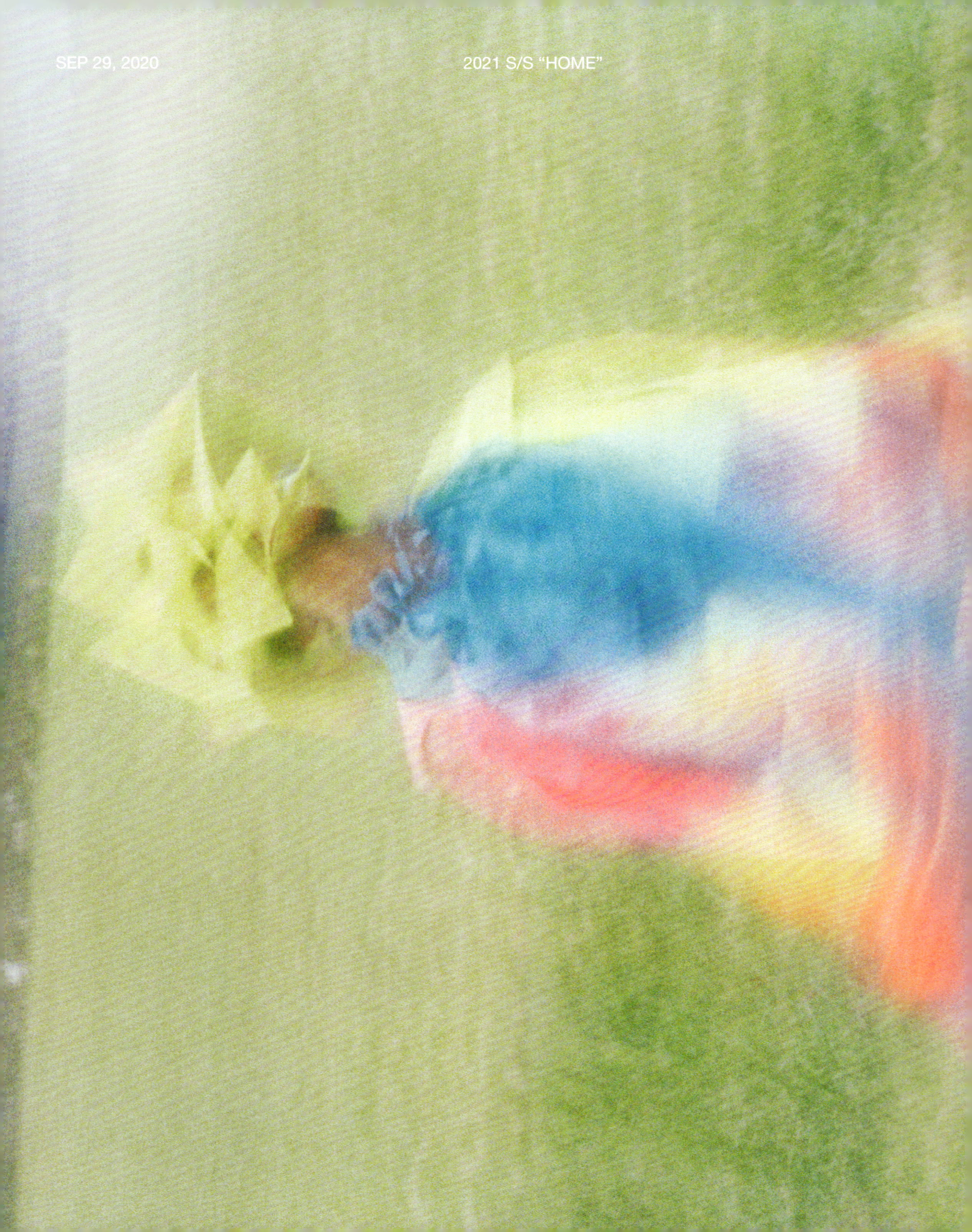

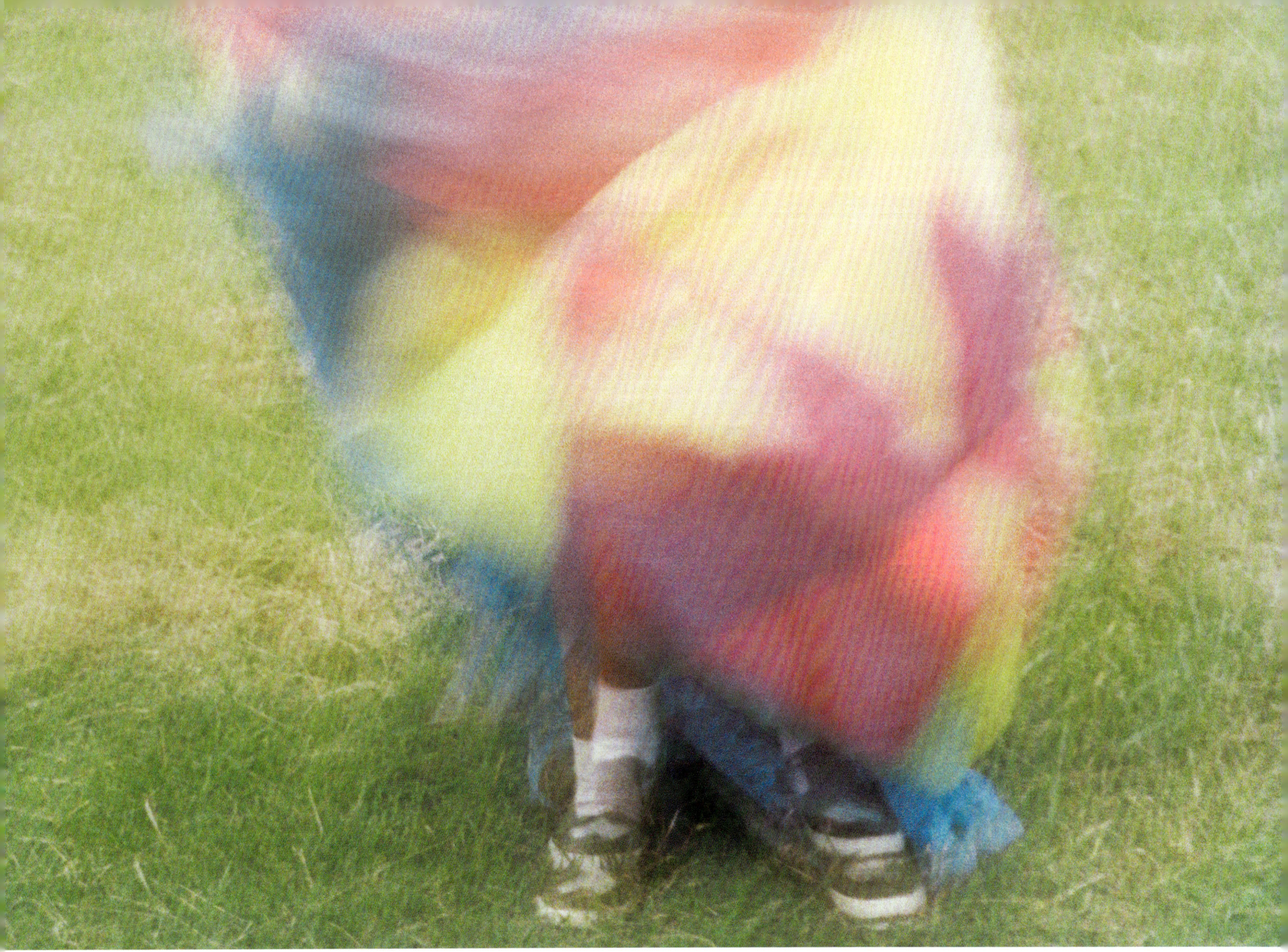

A place to come back to

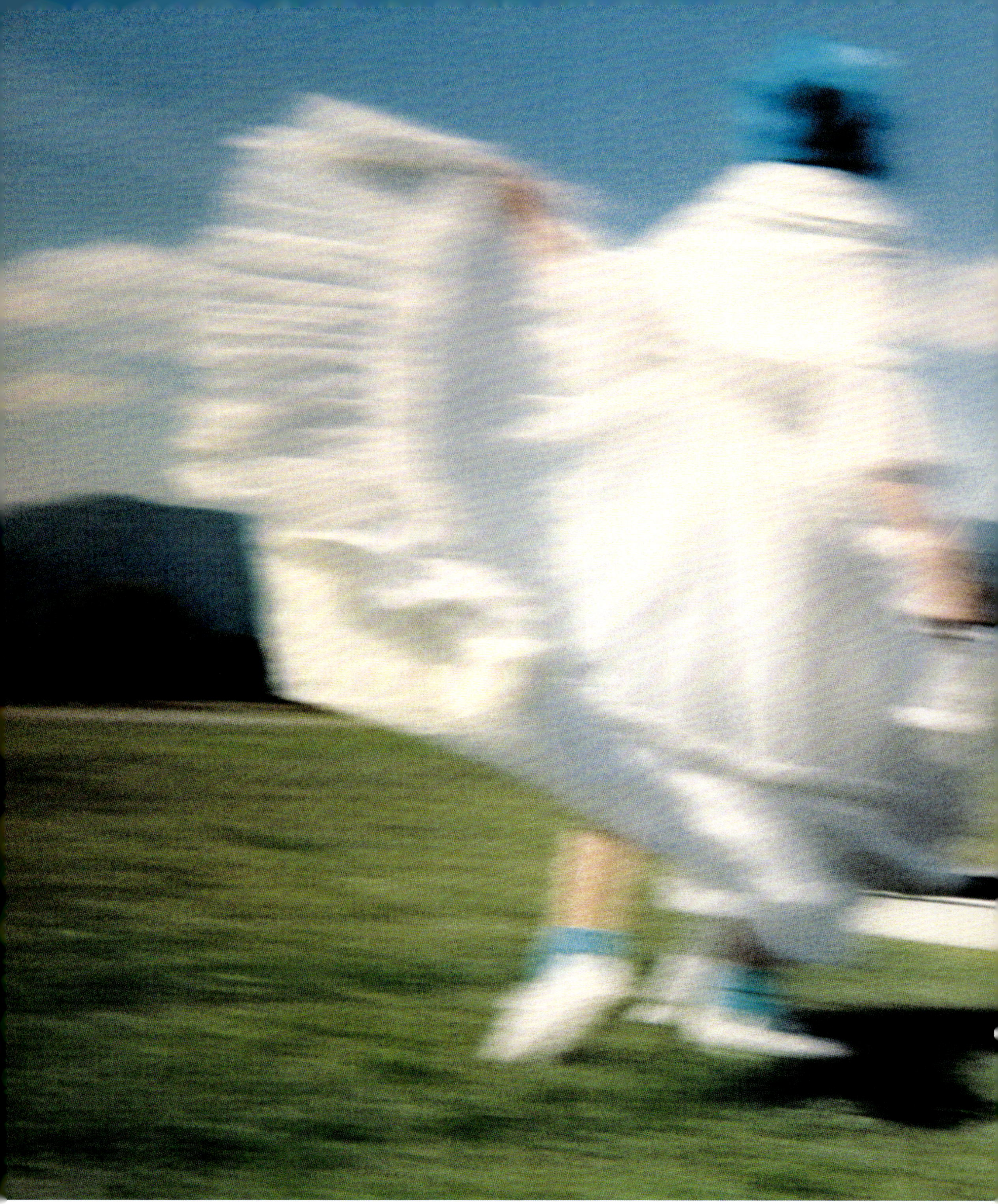

Fashion can be a device to change ever

yday life

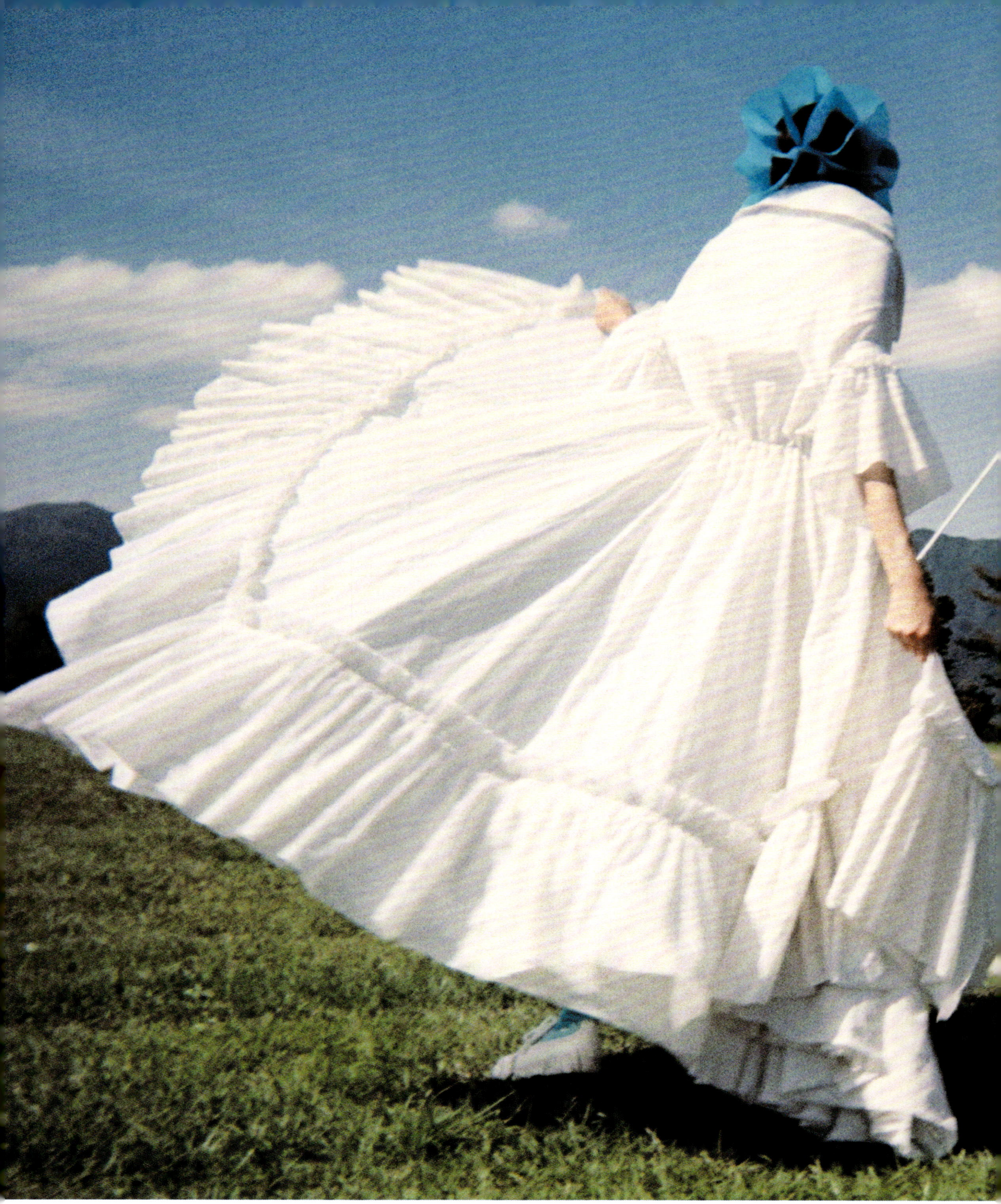

Fashion can be a device to retrieve eve

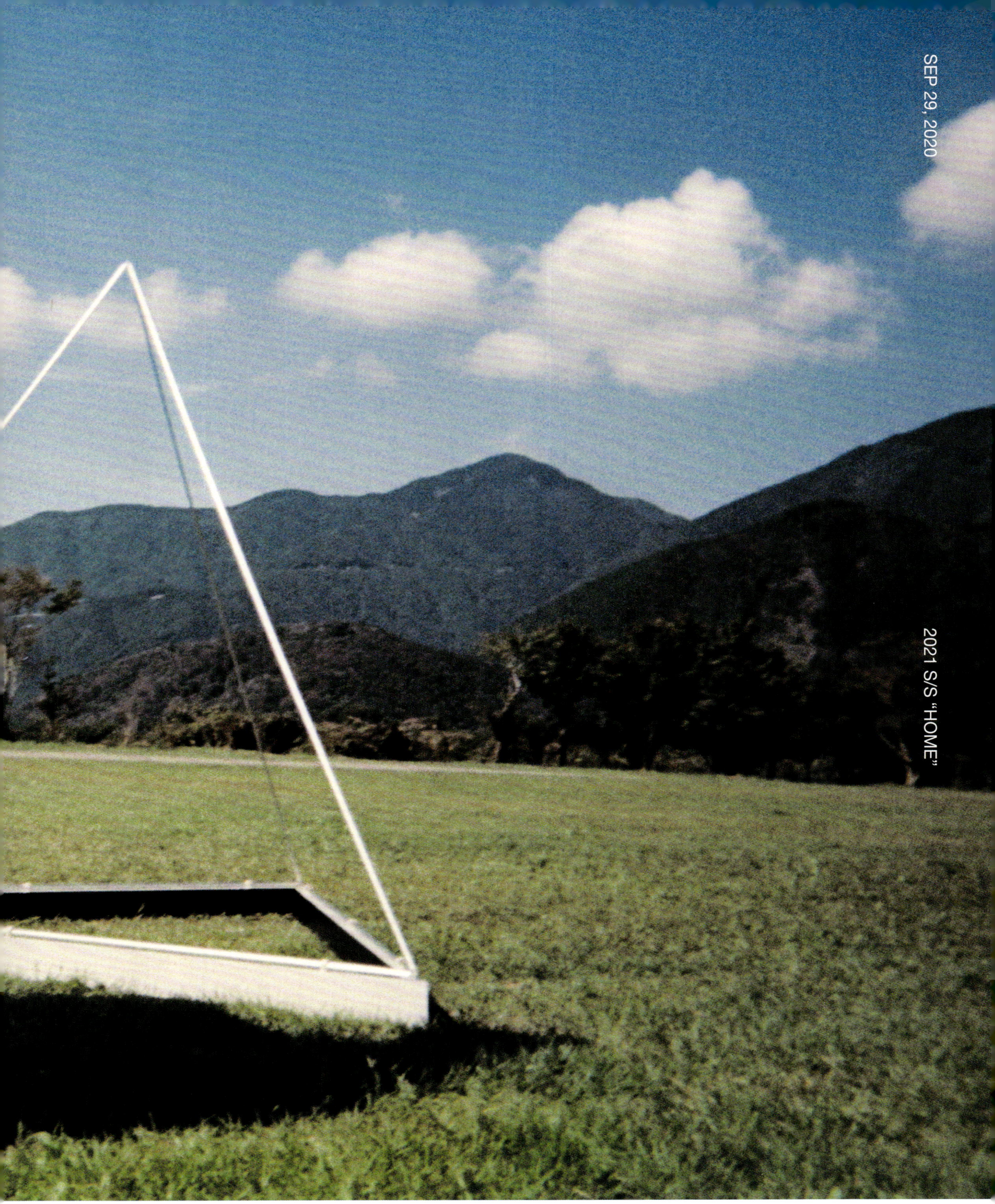

SEP 29, 2020

2021 S/S “HOME”

yday life

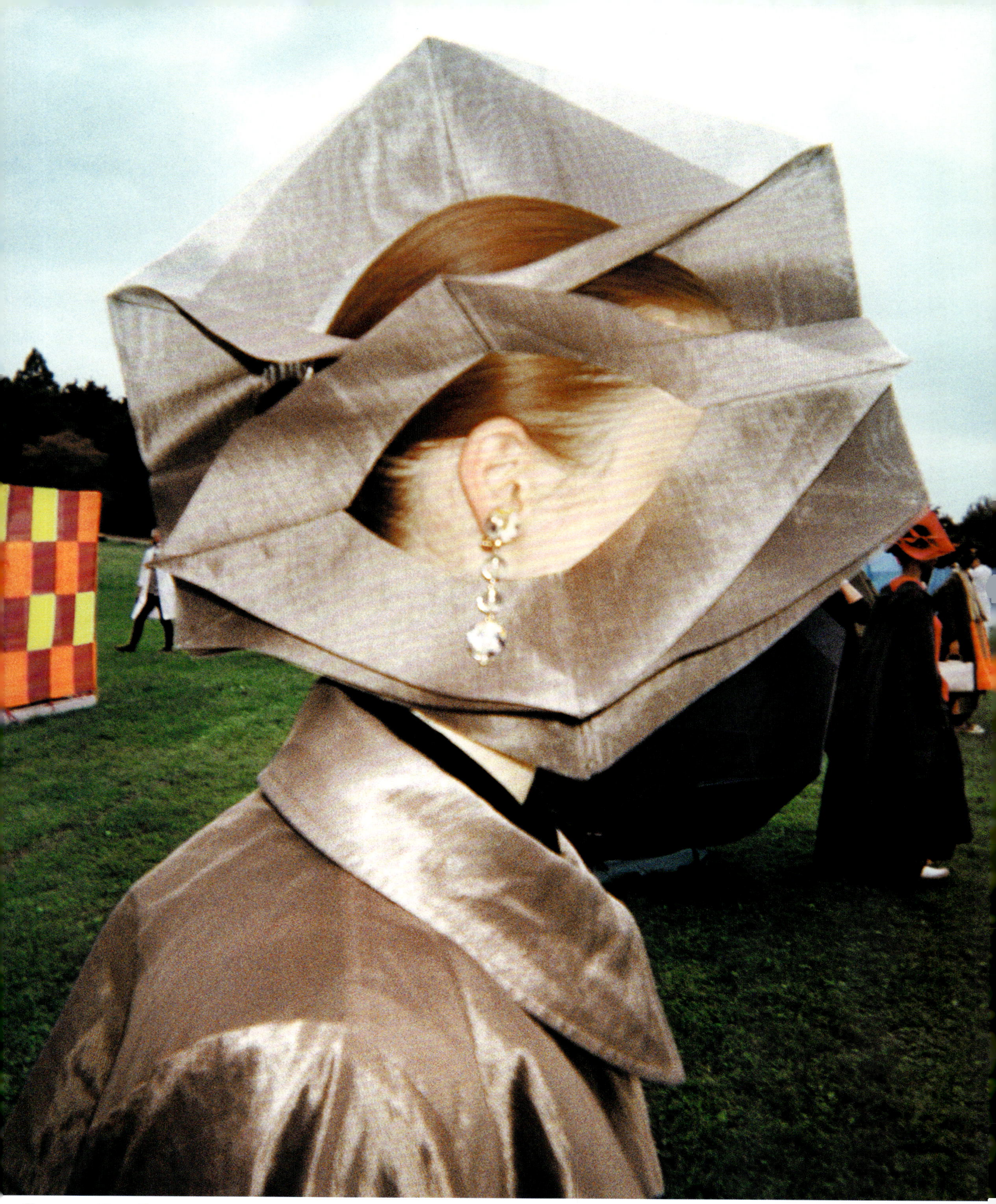

Antivirus material dress, antivirus mate

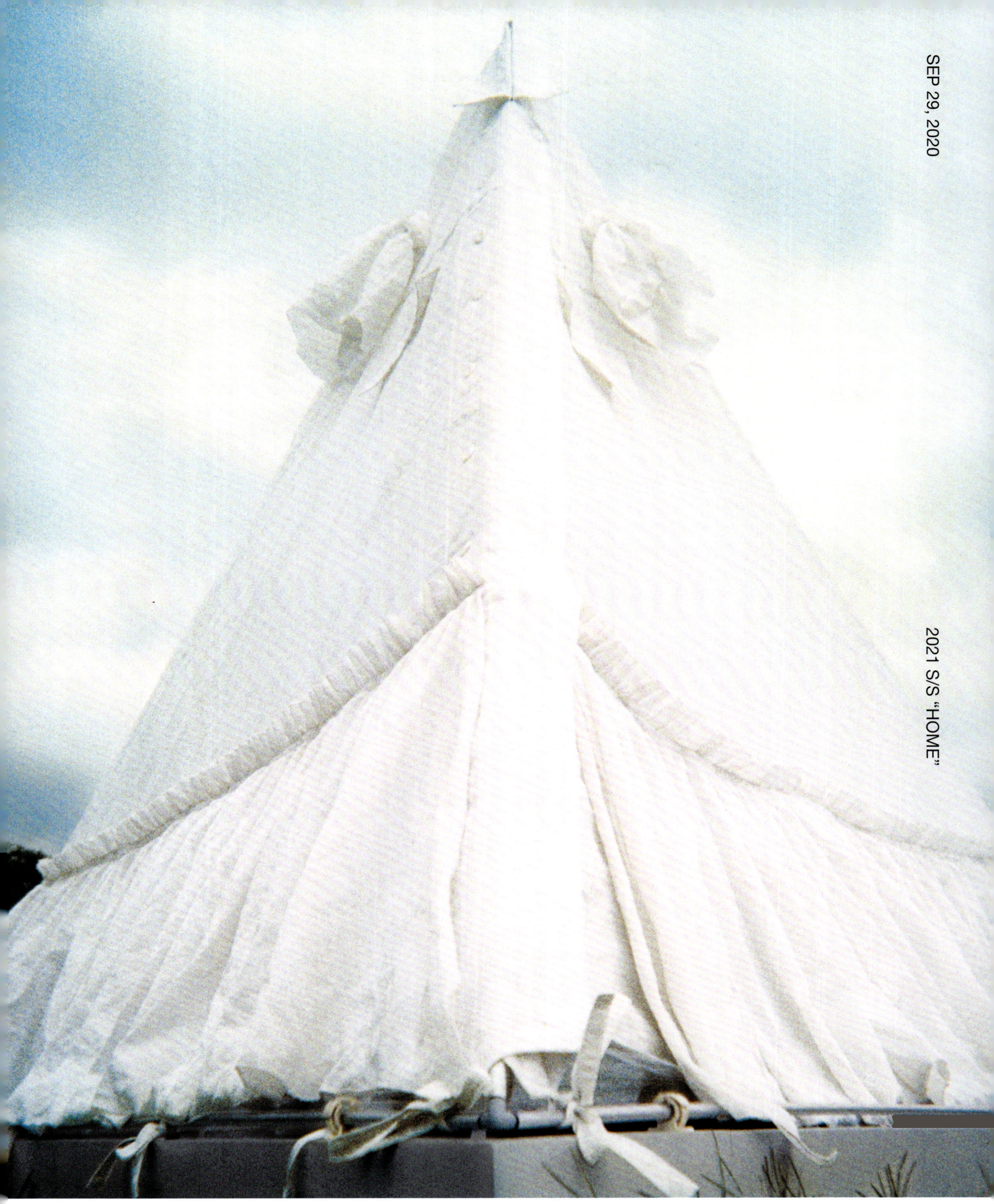

SEP 29, 2020

2021 S/S “HOME”

ial home

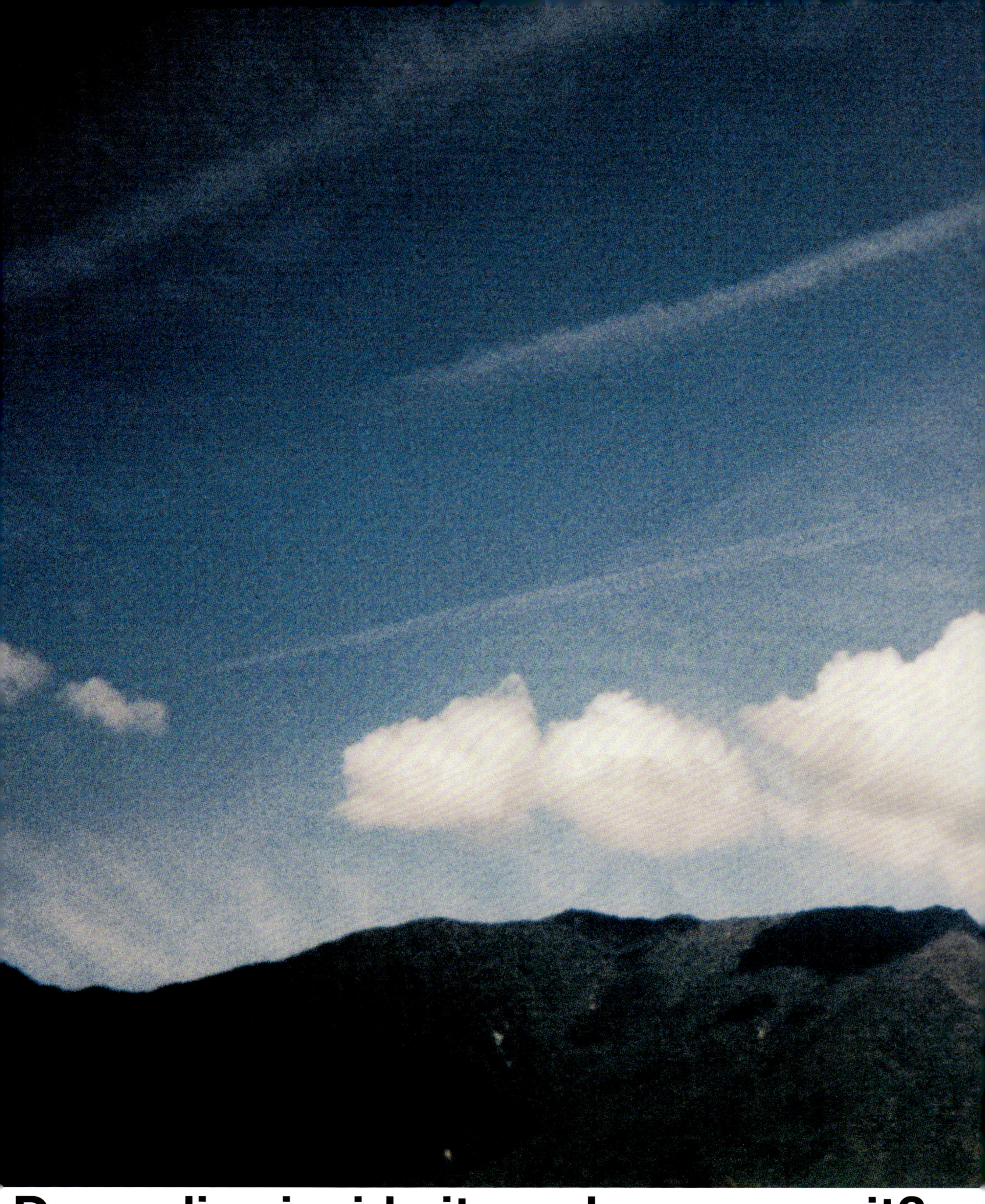

Do we live inside it, or do we wear it?

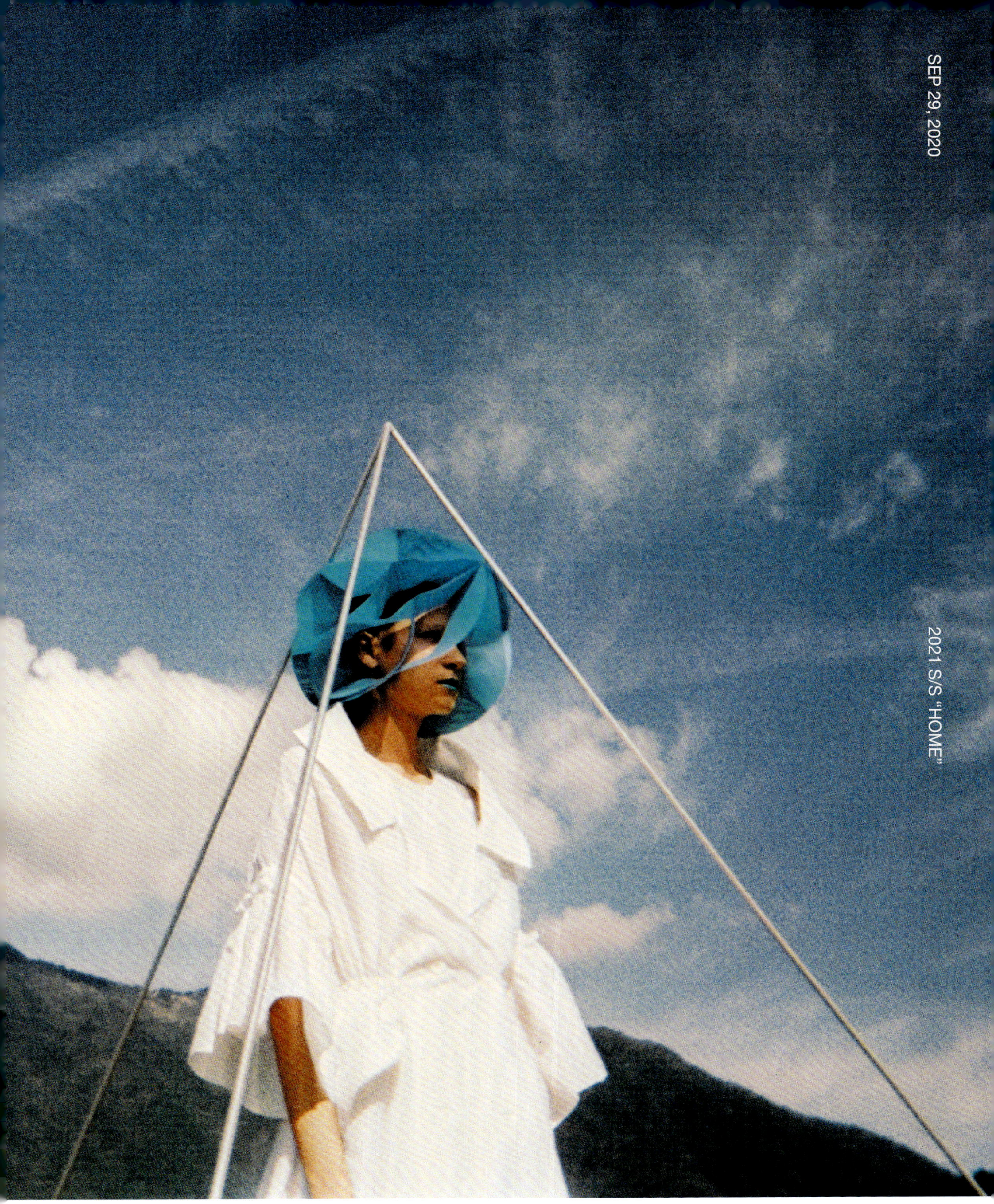
SEP 29, 2020
2021 S/S "HOME"

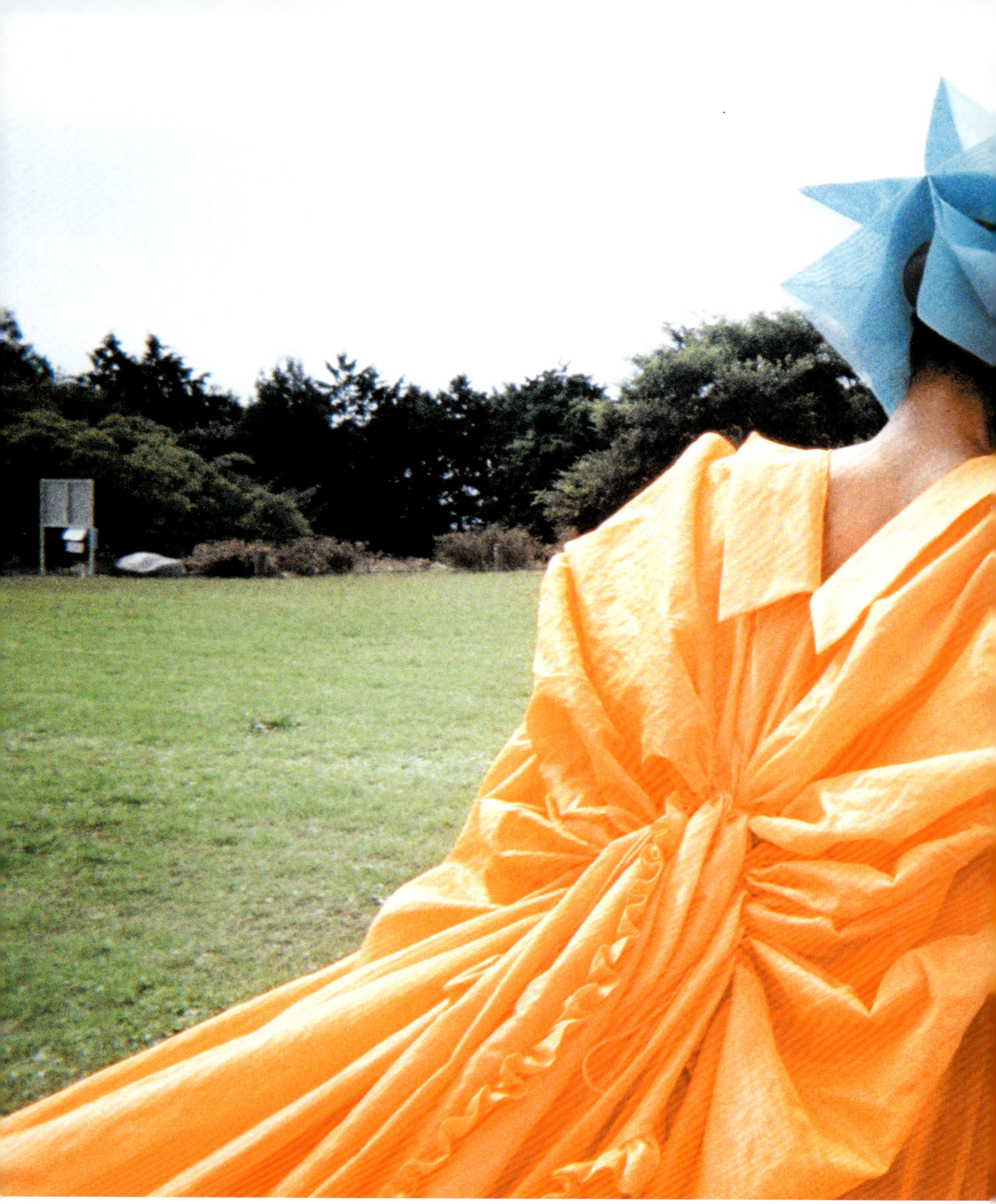

Can we not wear a home like wearing c

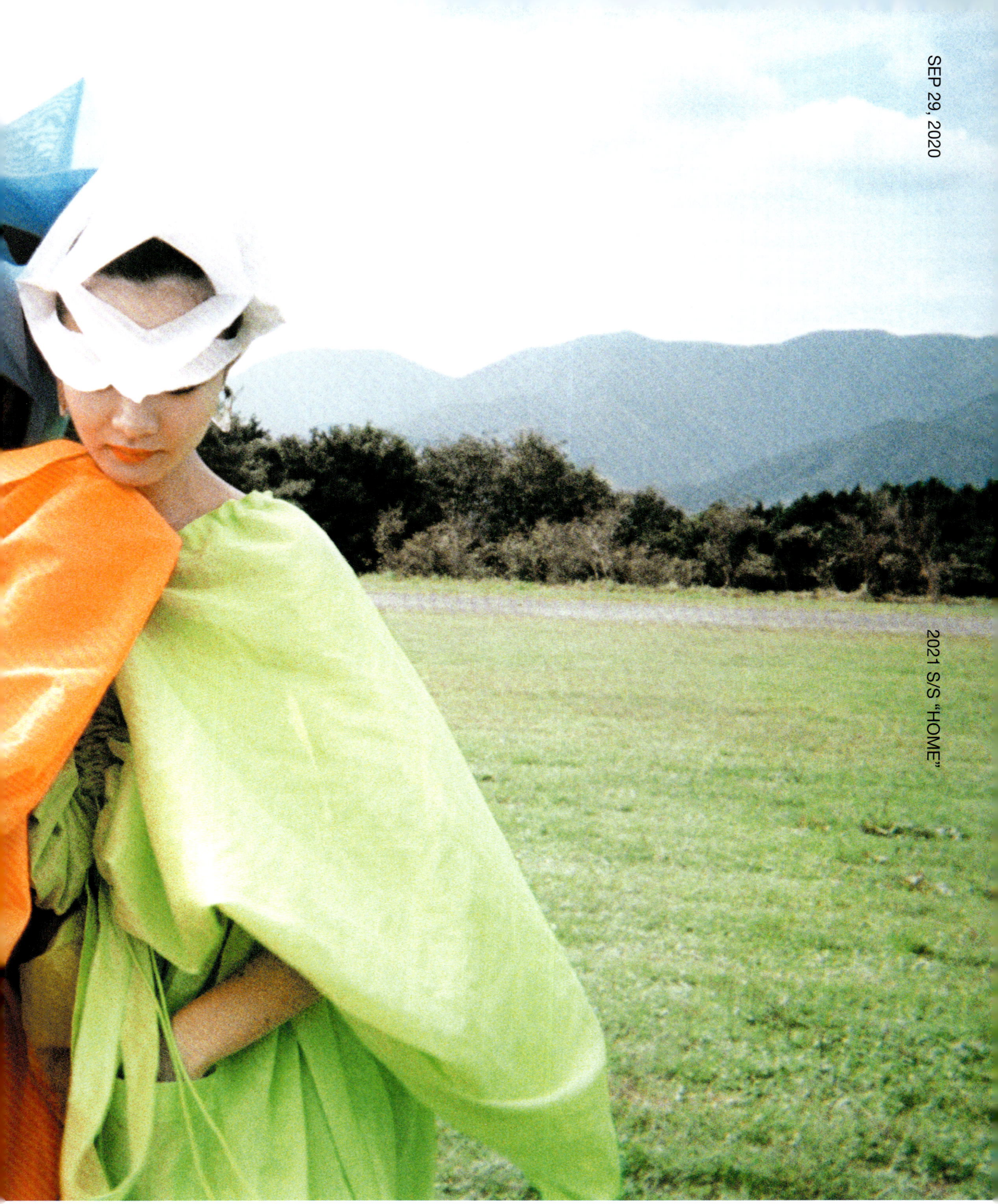

SEP 29, 2020

2021 S/S "HOME"

othes?

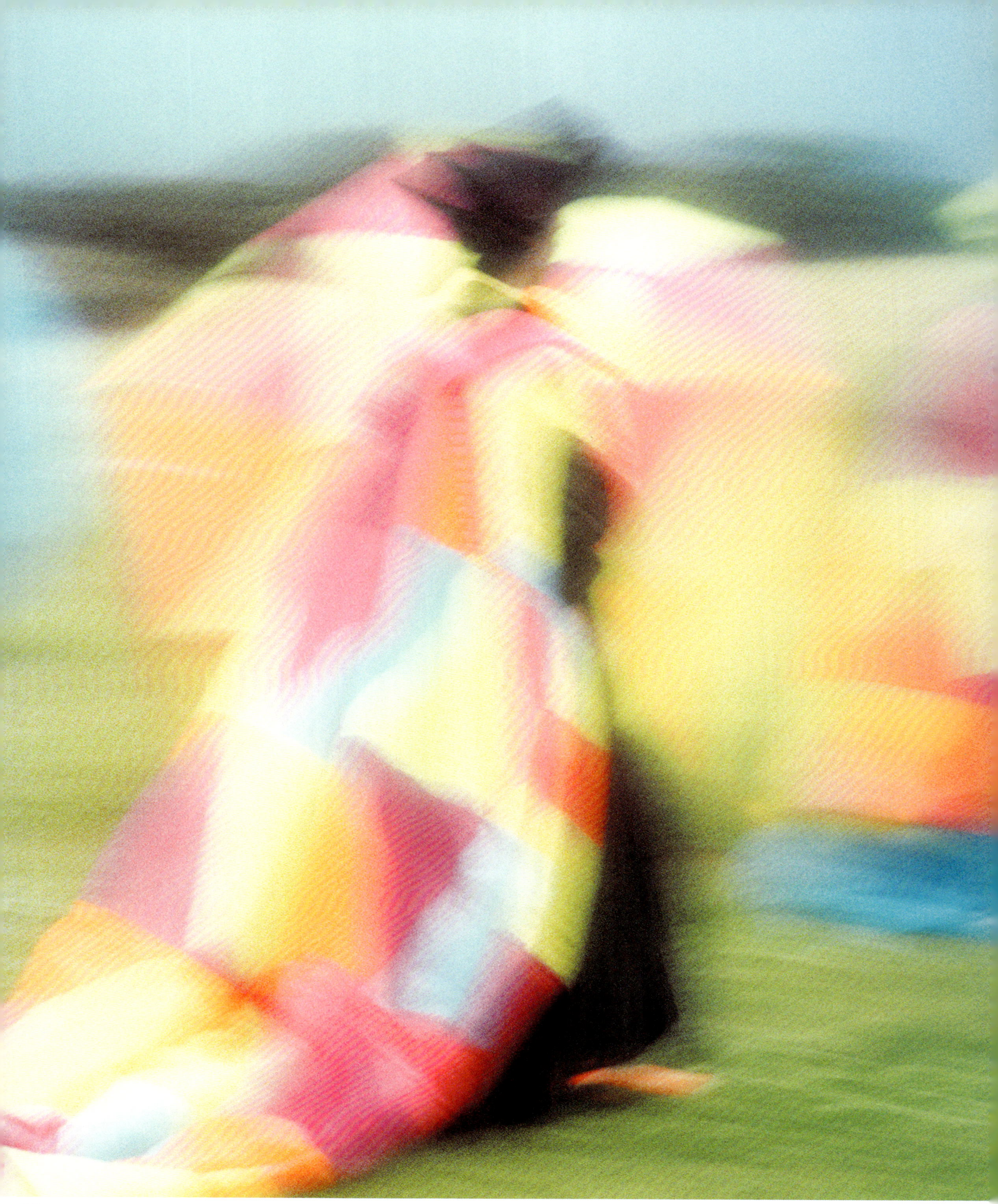

Can we not wear clothes like living in a

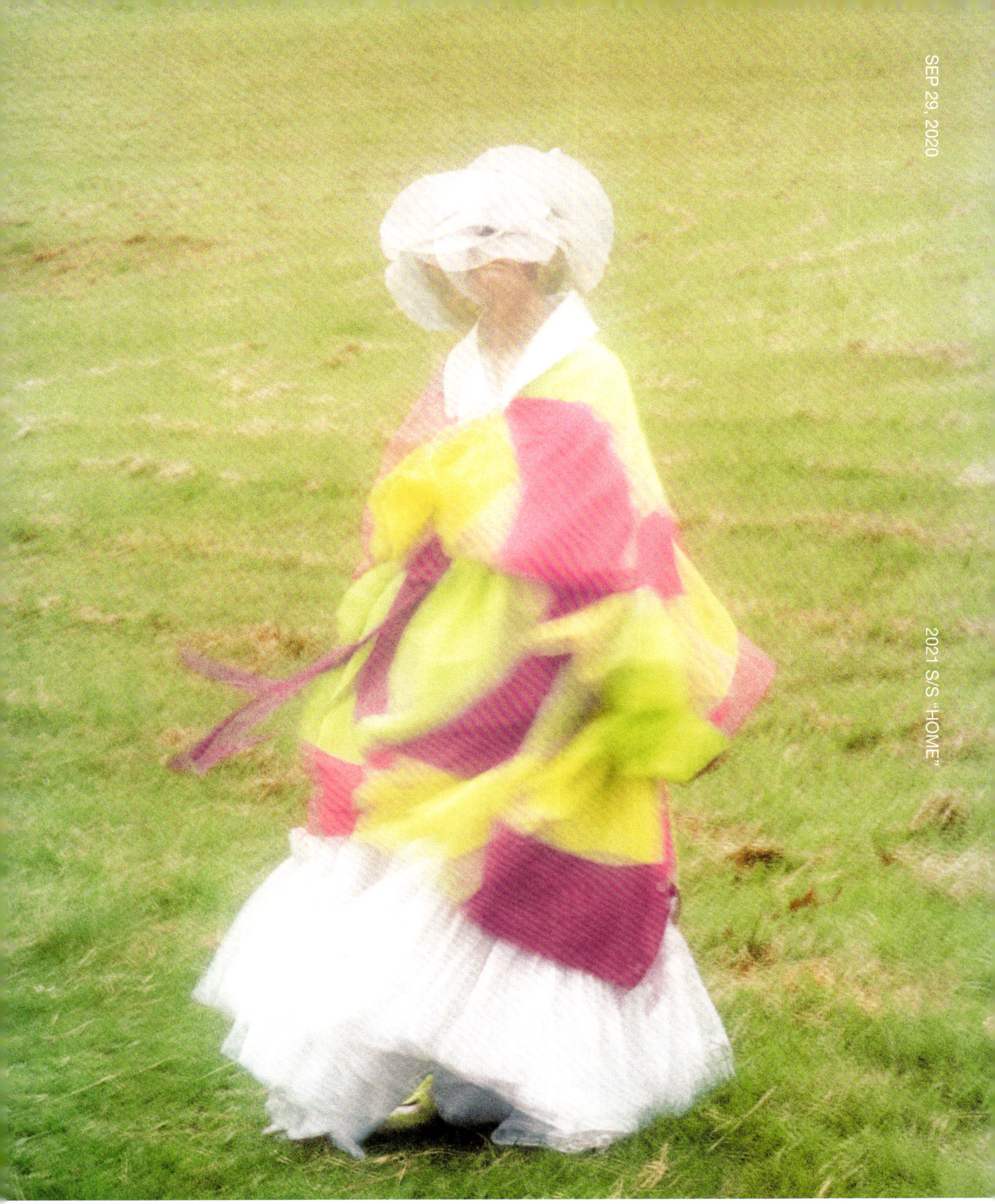

nome?

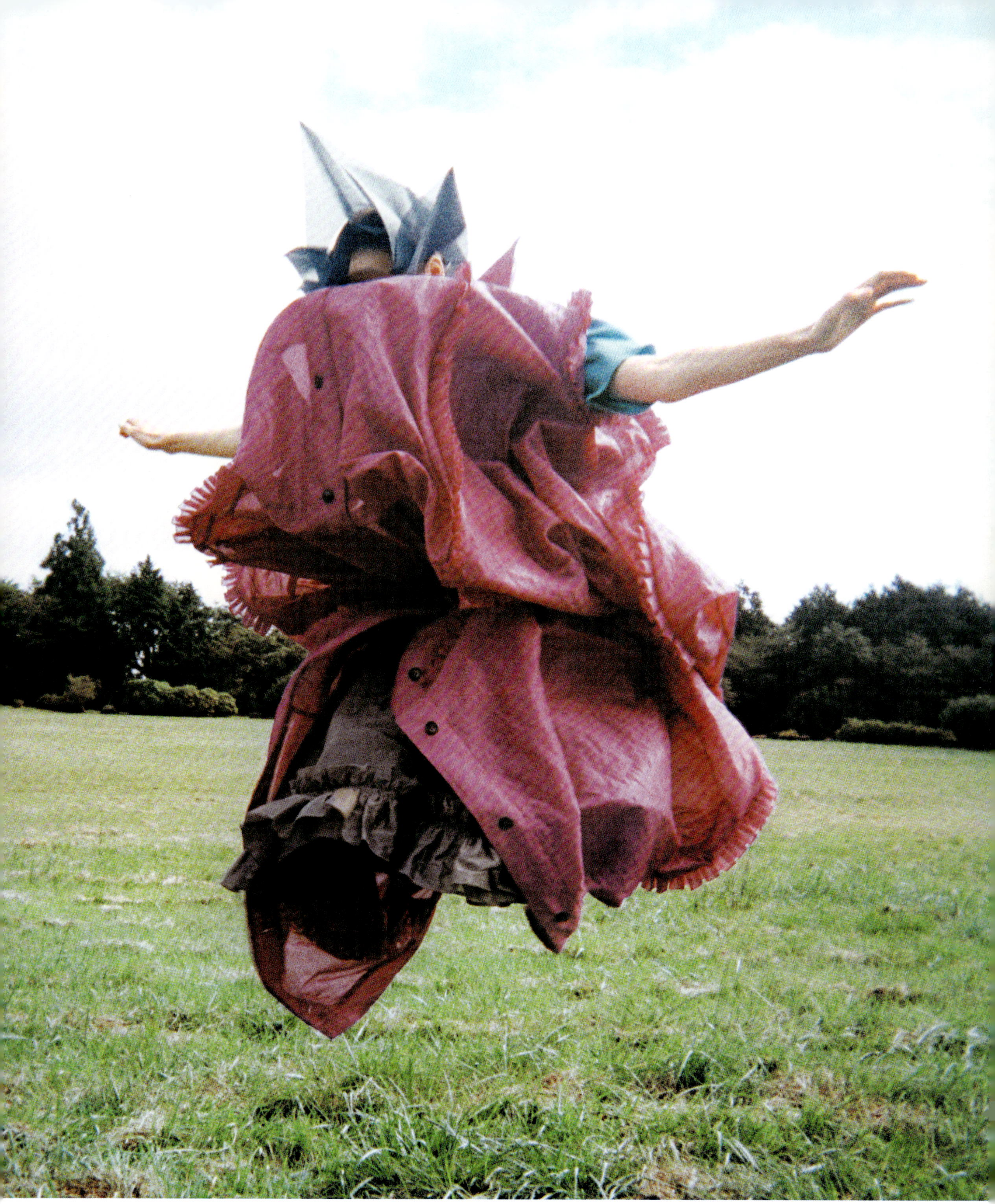

The clothes were made as mobile home

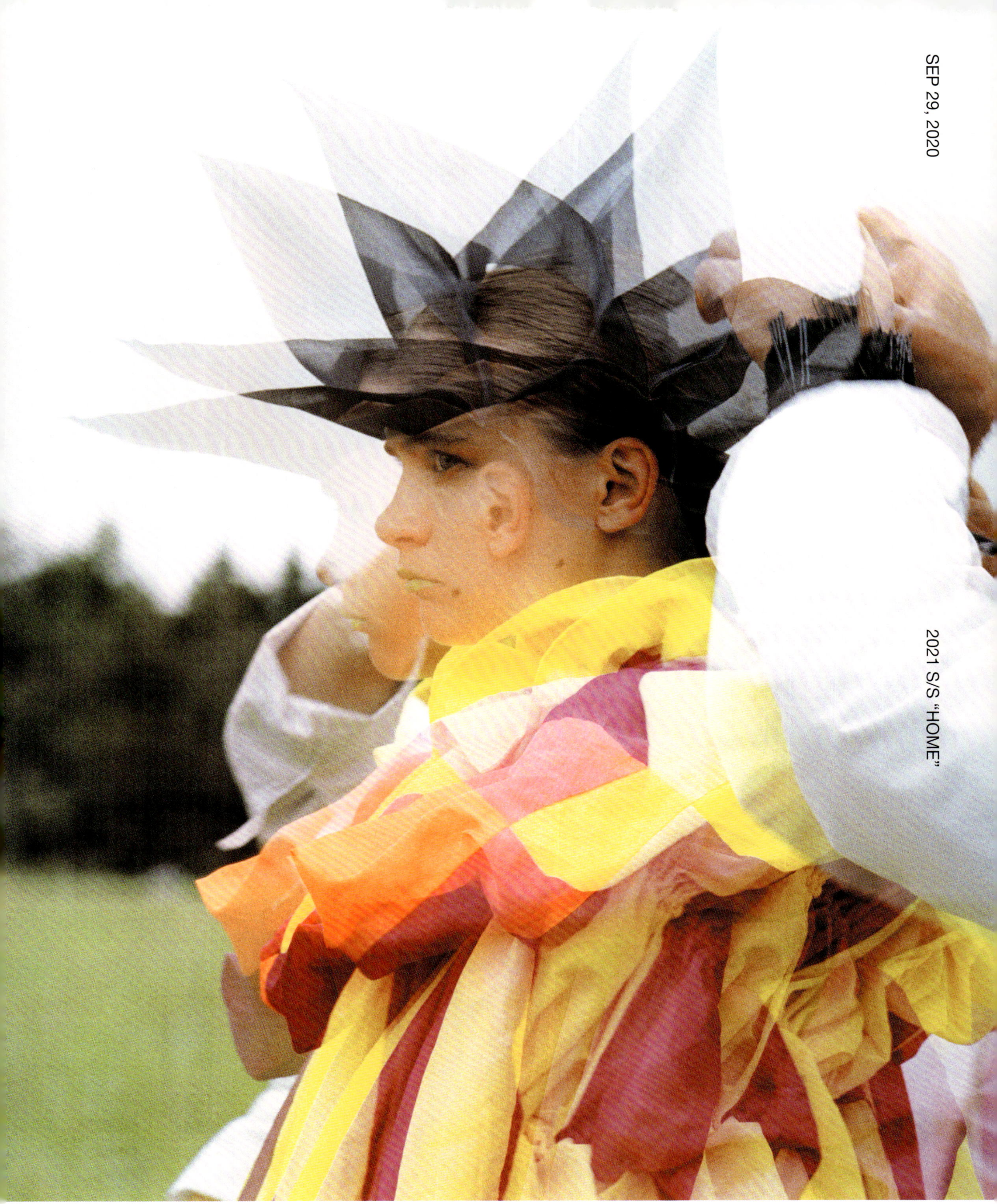

SEP 29, 2020

2021 S/S “HOME”

S

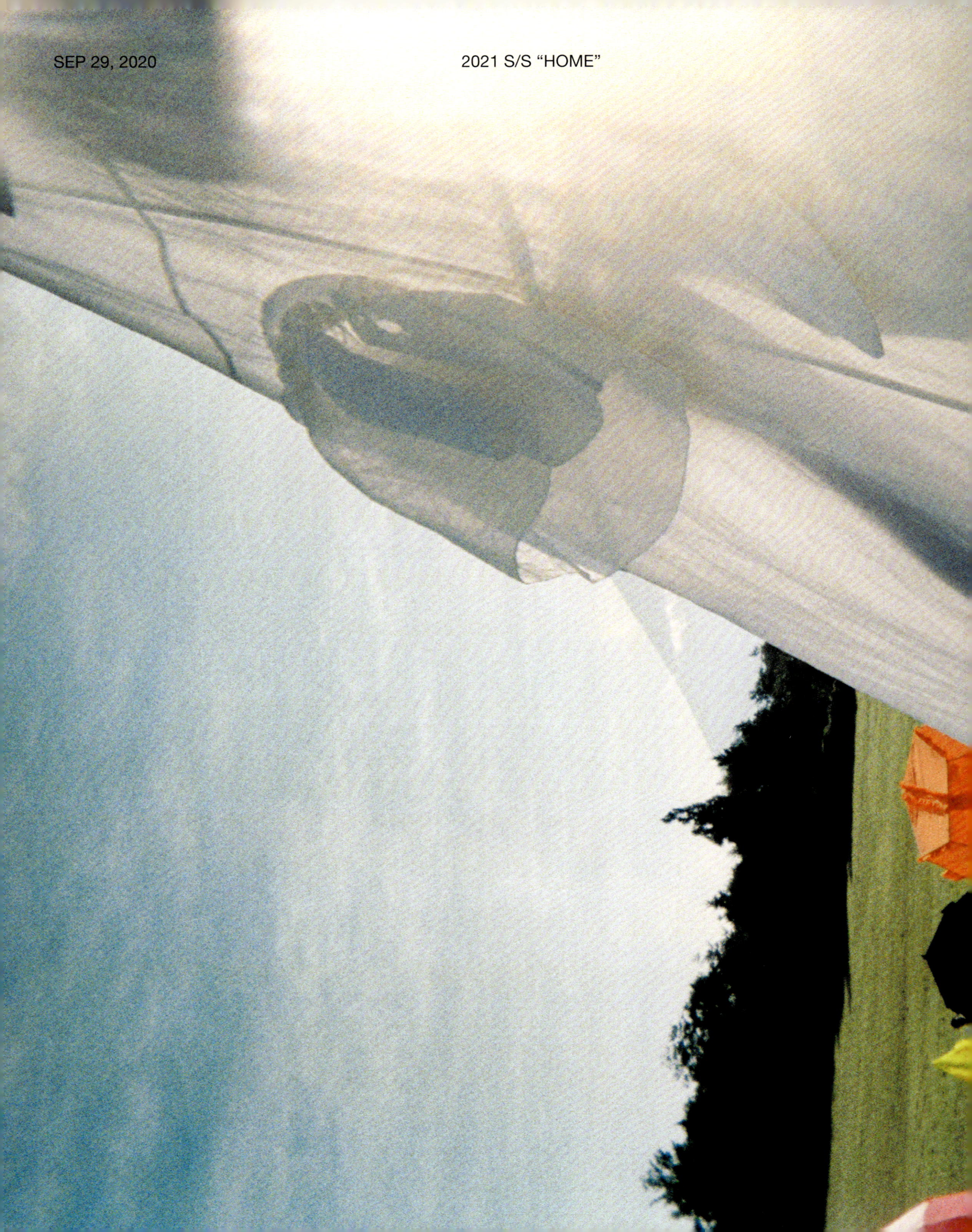

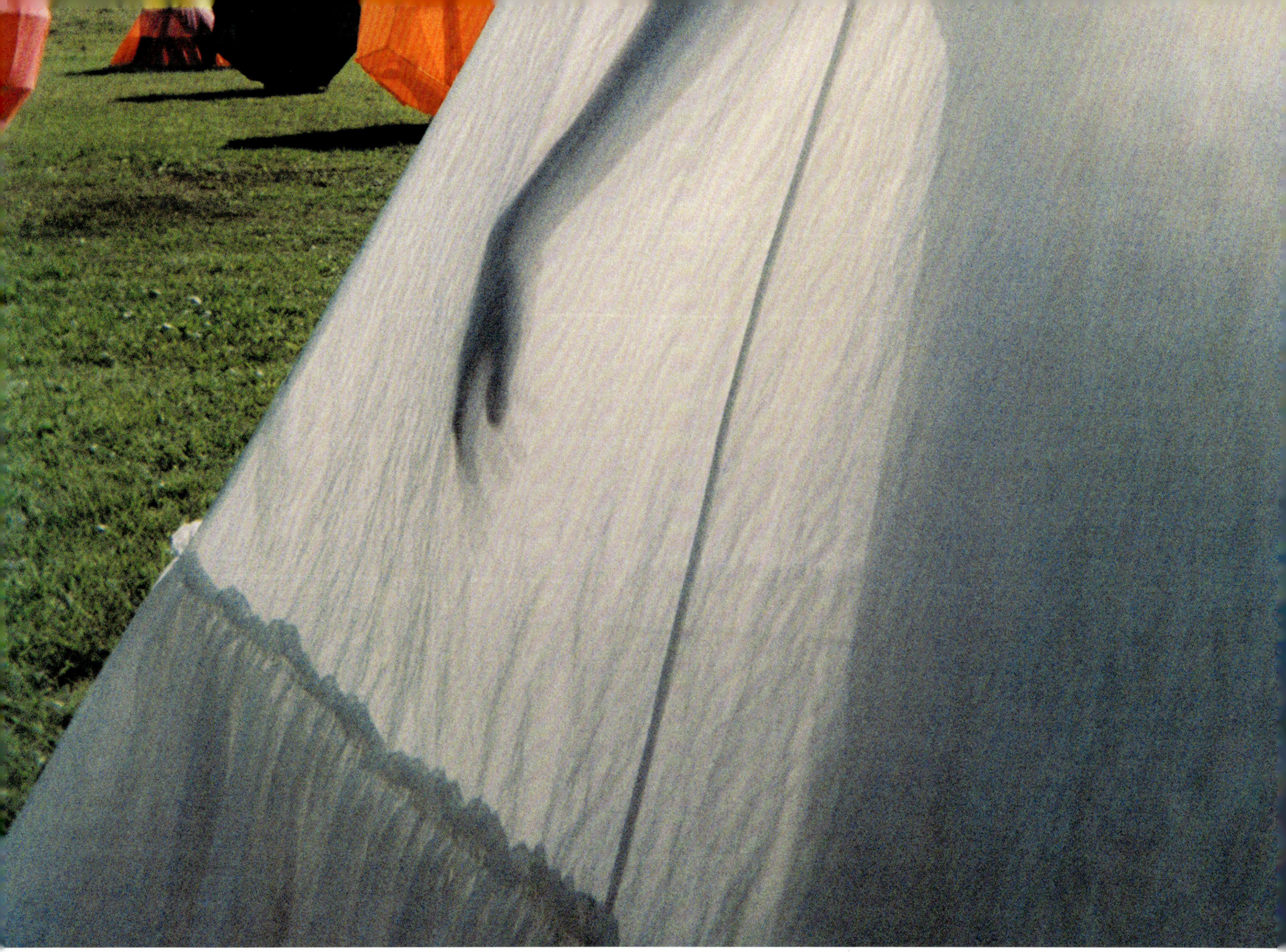

The feeling of being completely covered

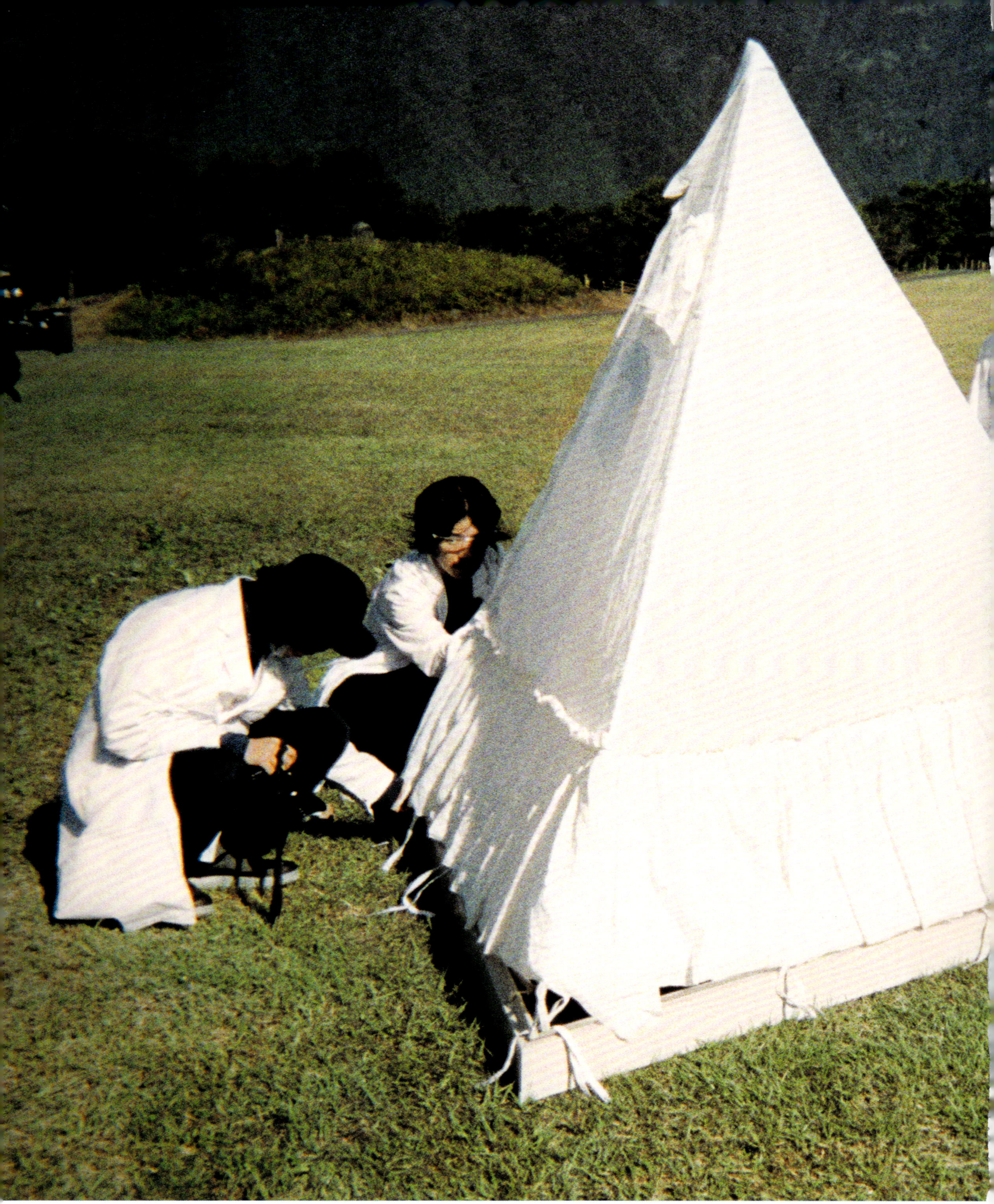

Fashion shows are made up of people

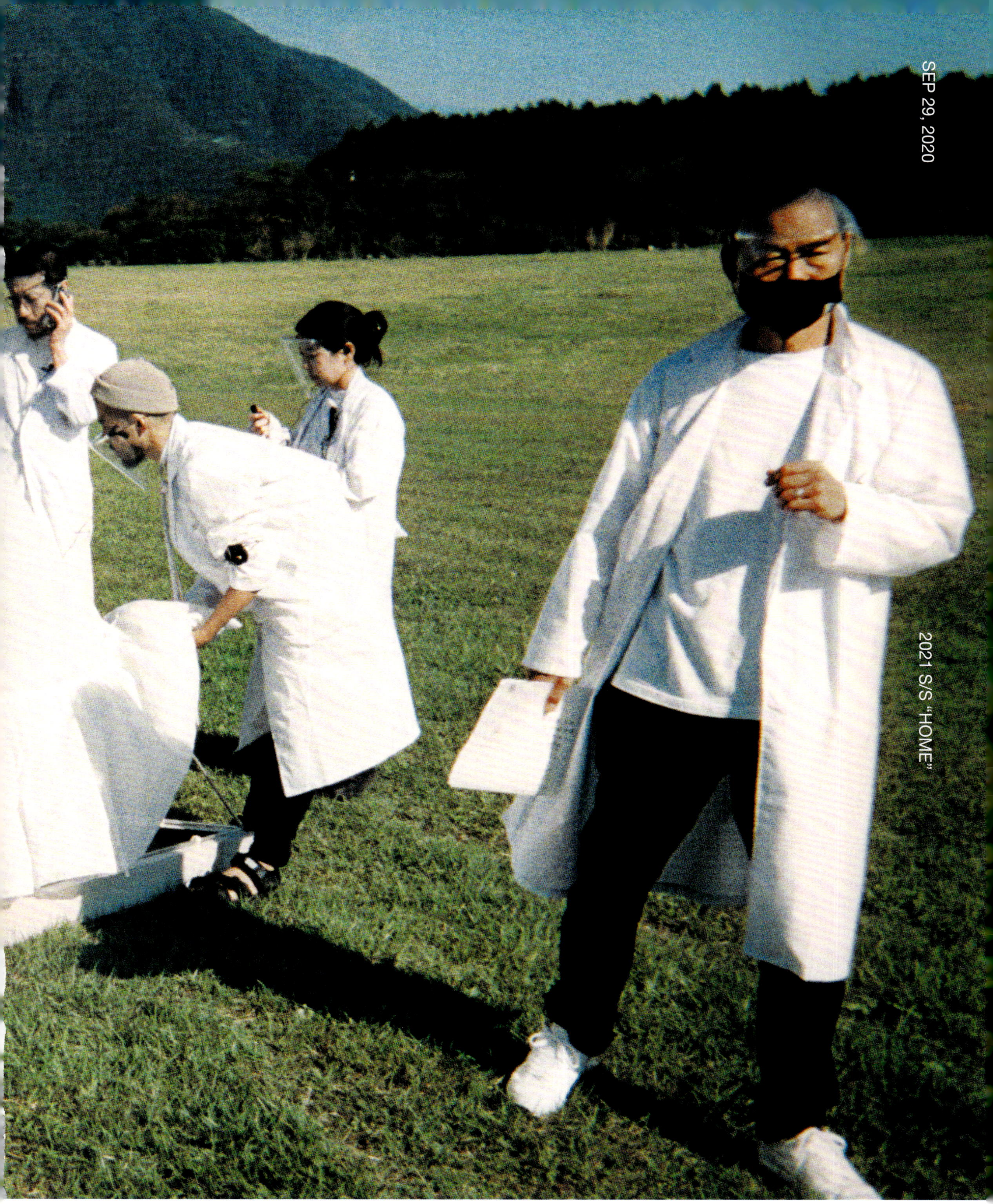

SEP 29, 2020

2021 S/S “HOME”

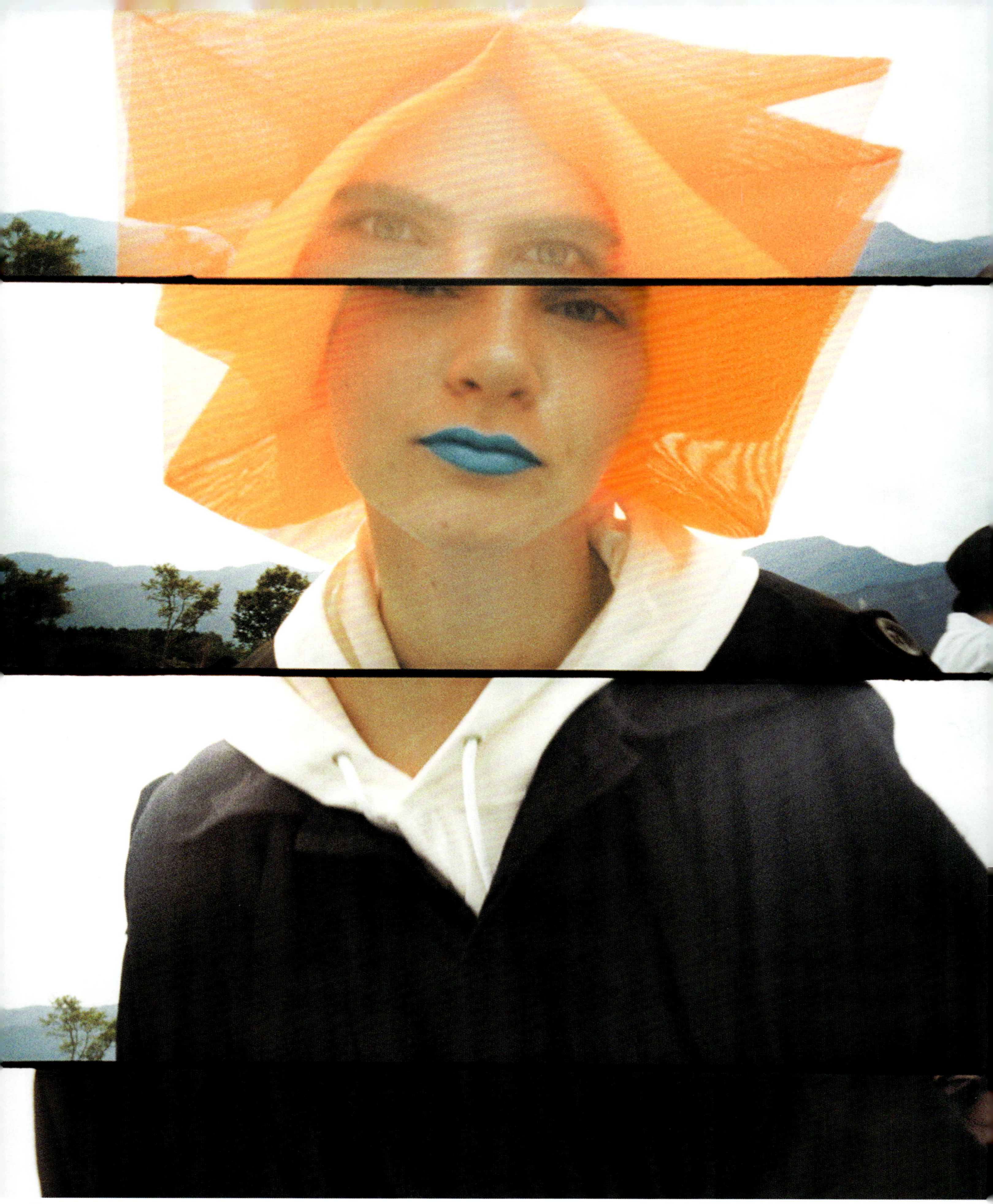

Clothes that secure a social distance of

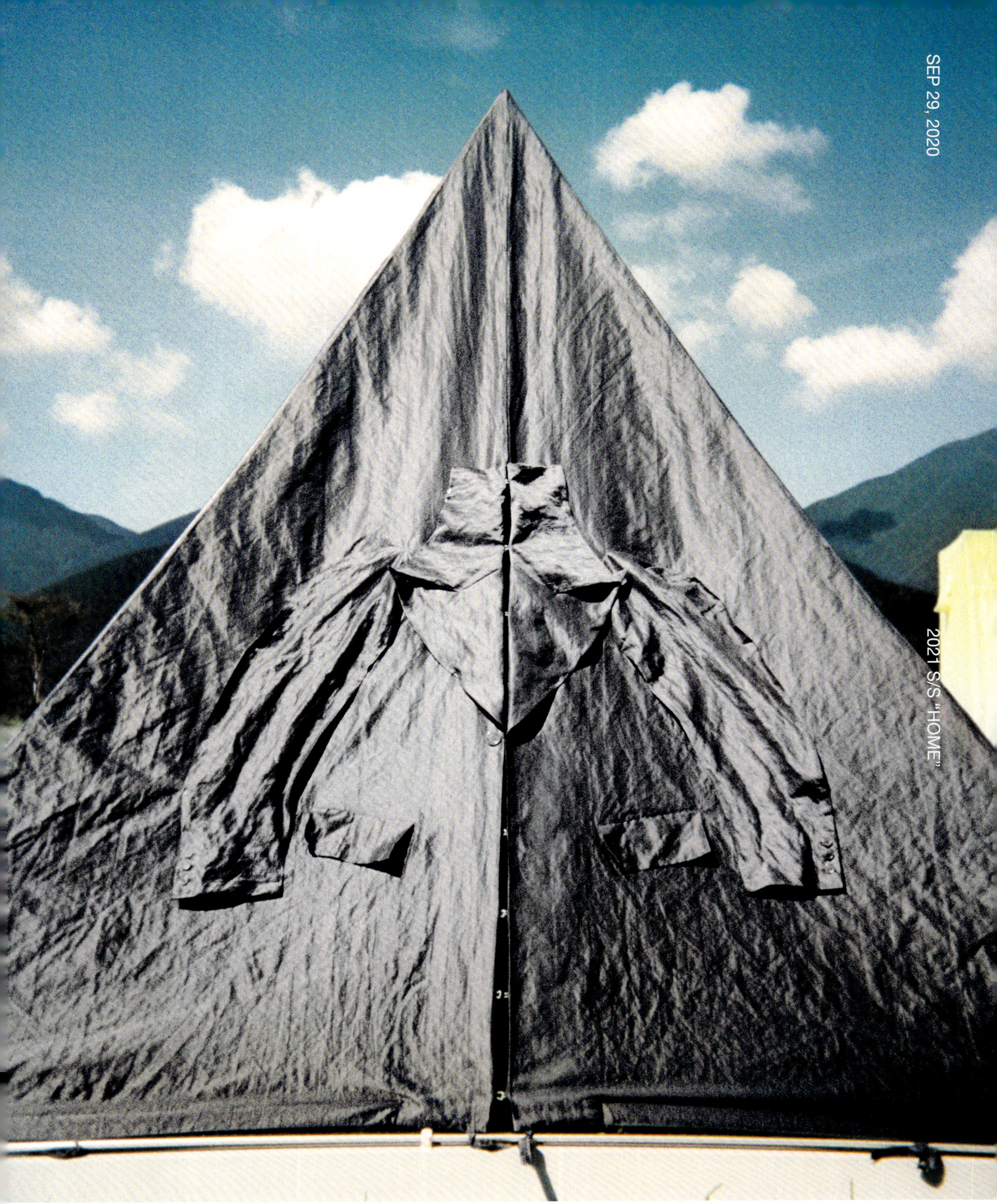

two meters

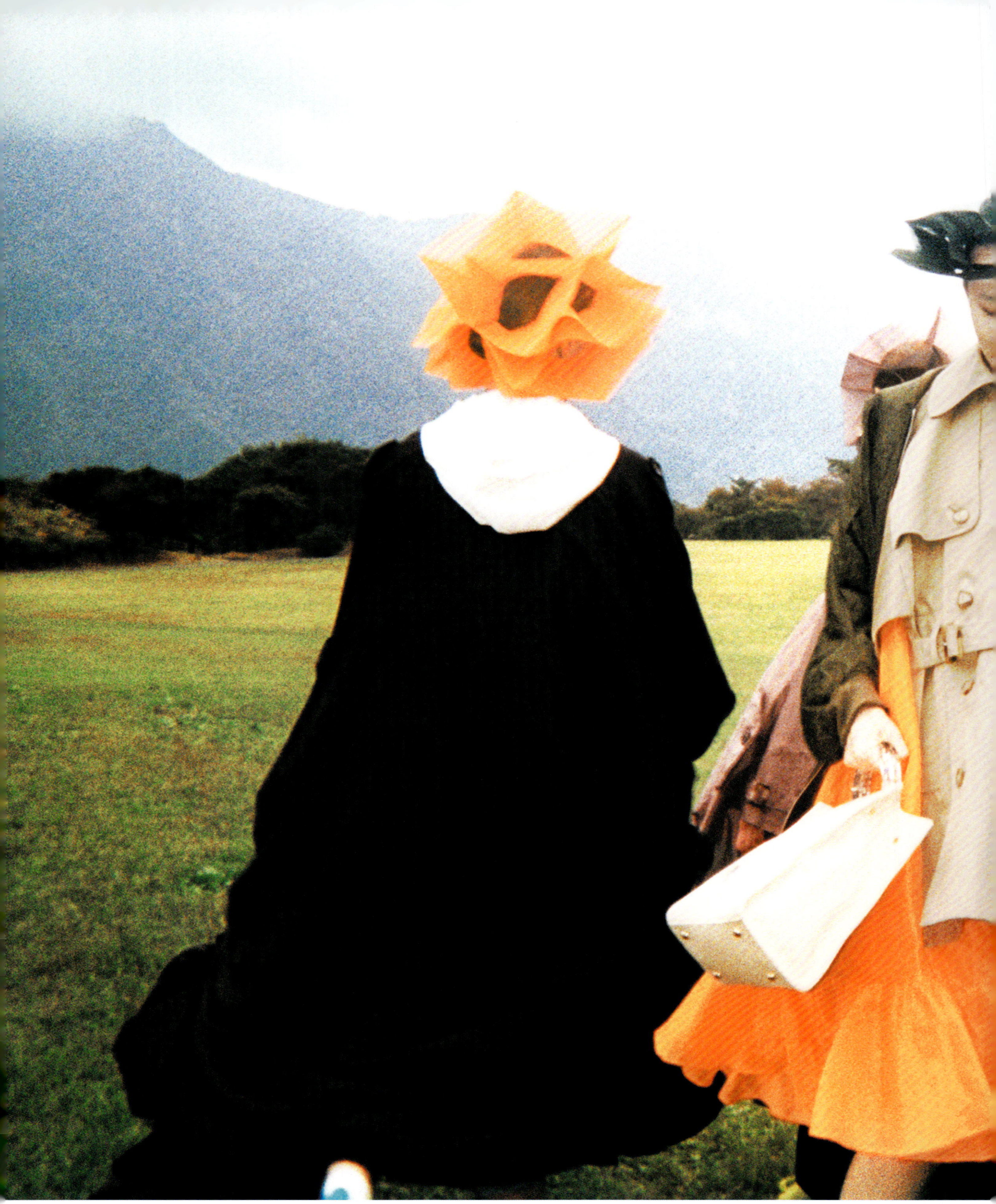

Between the ordinary and extraordinary

SEP 29, 2020

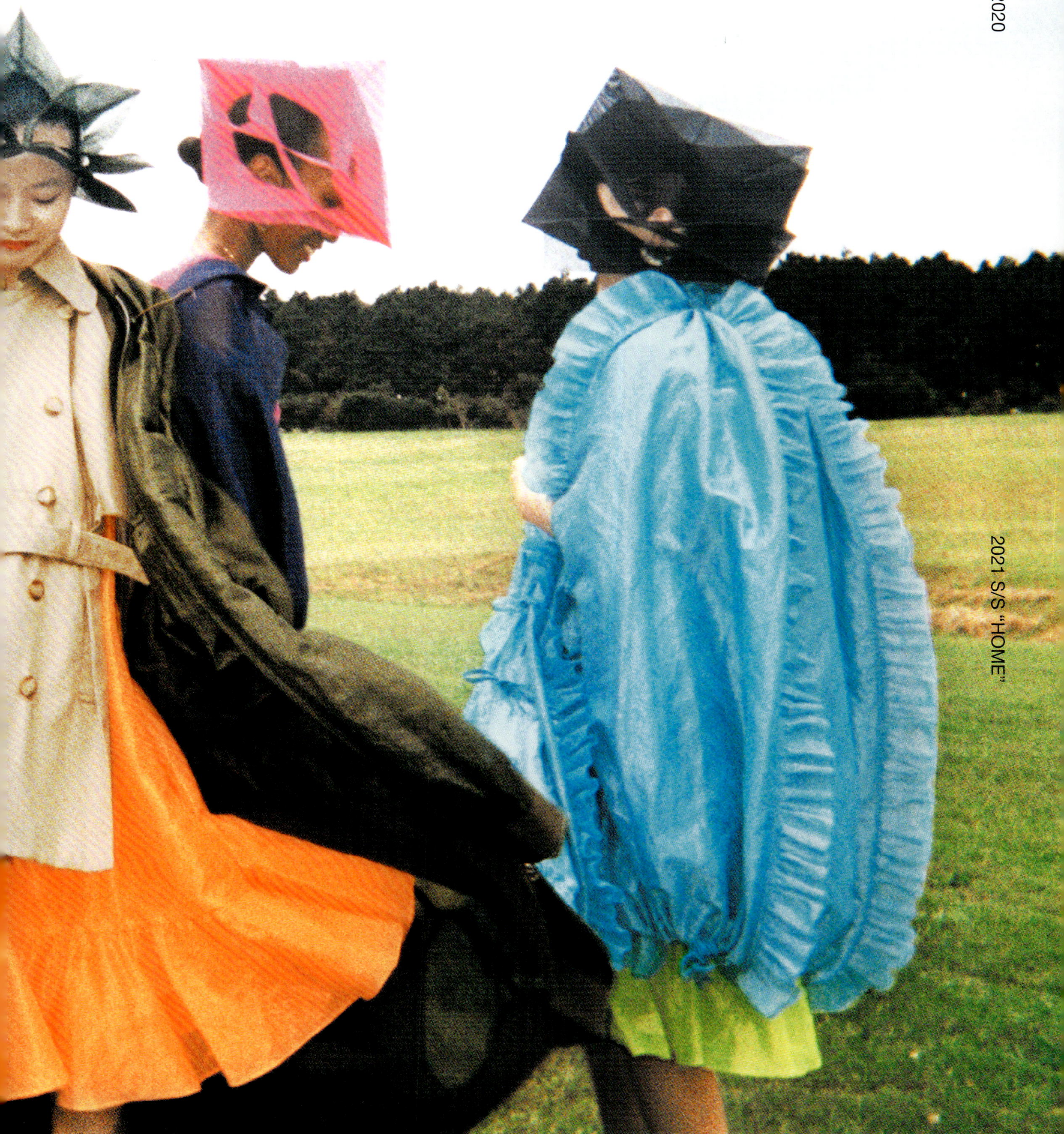

2021 S/S "HOME"

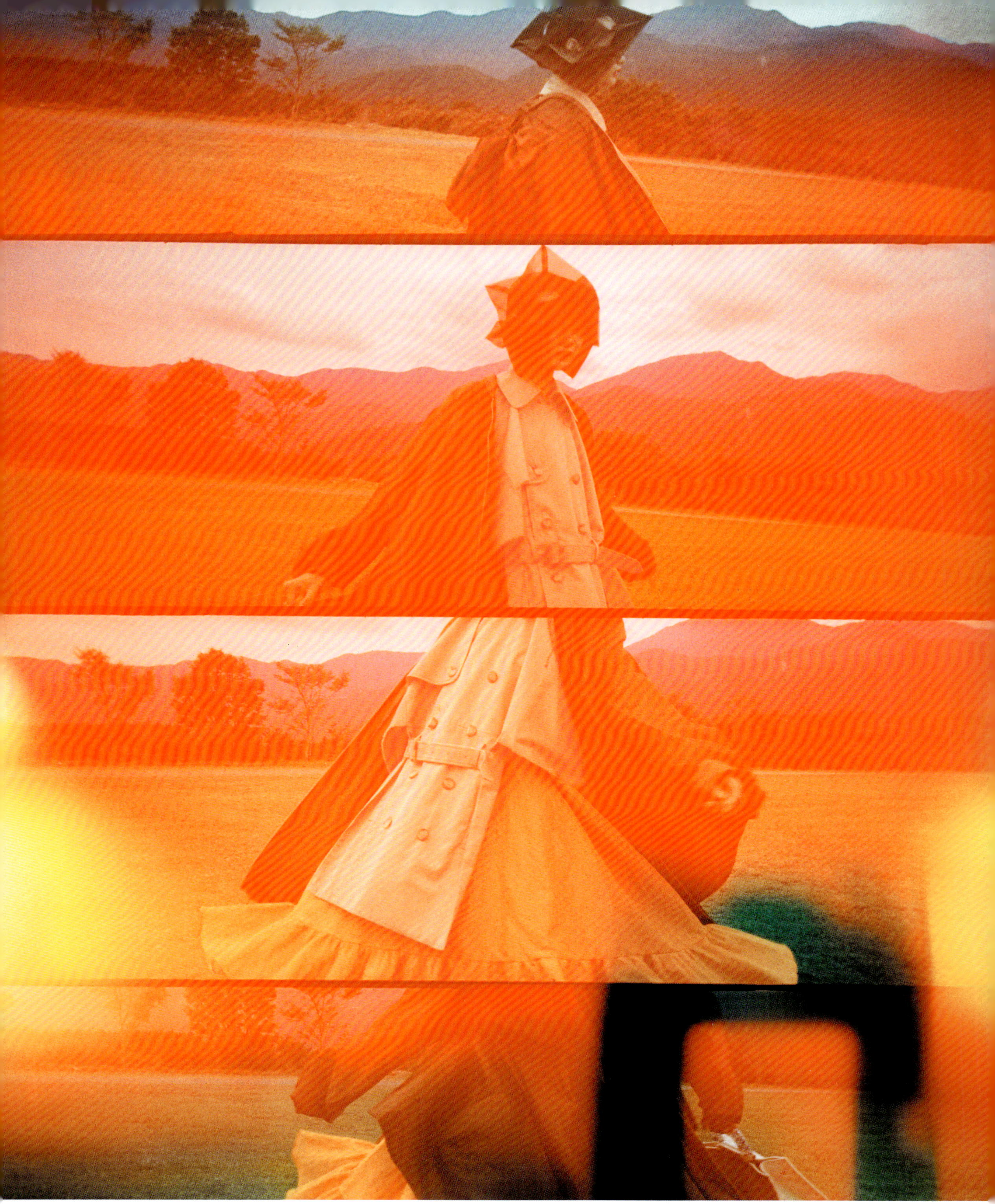

By praying and hoping, it reveals its out

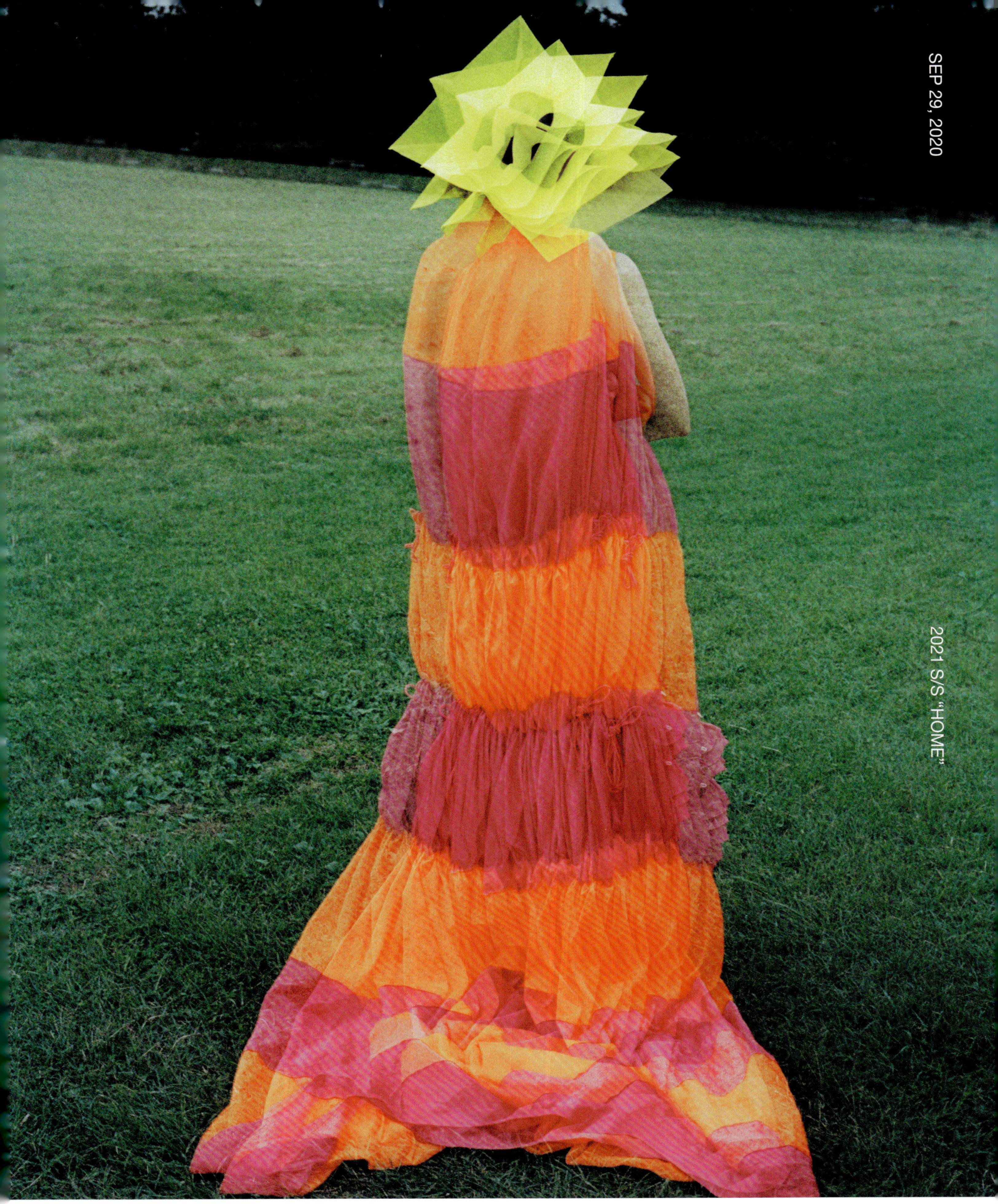

ine, for the first time

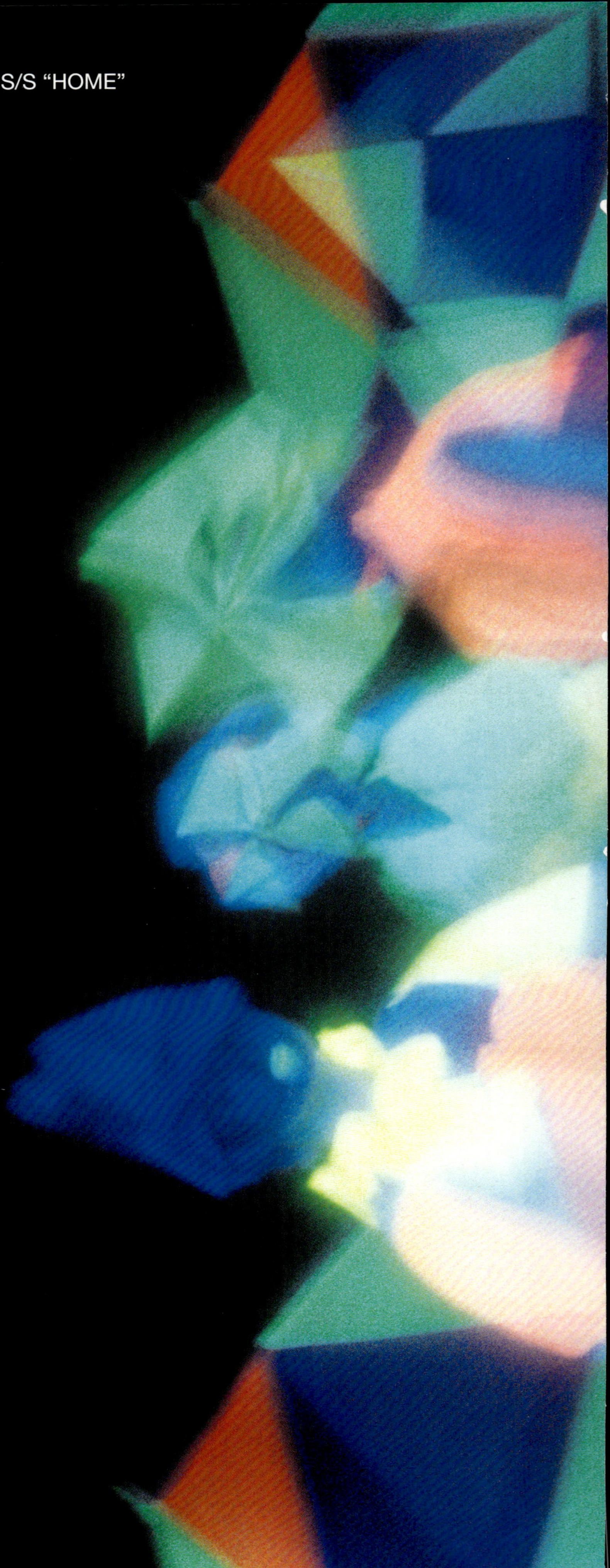

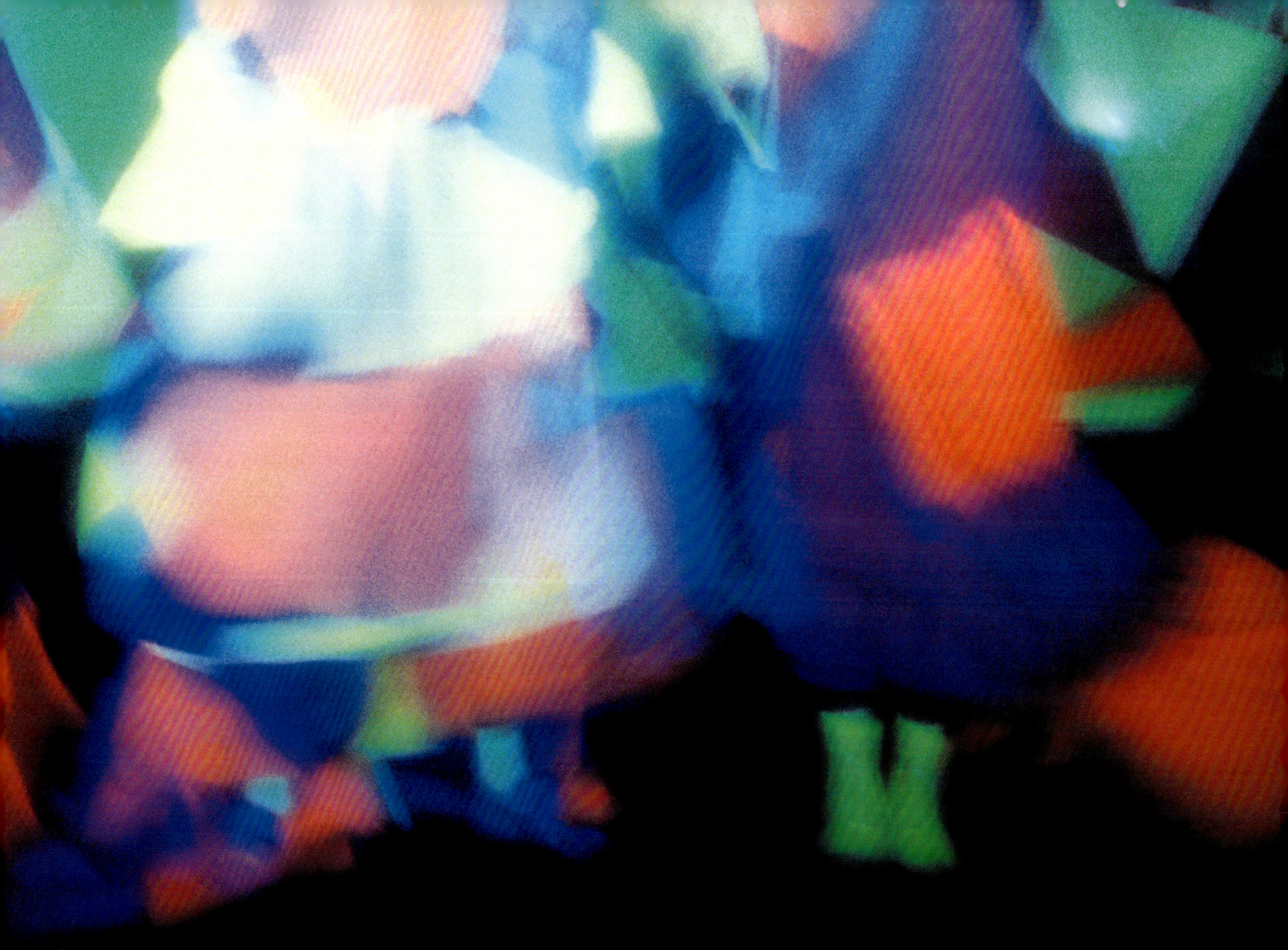

What is different between the unreal and the real?

history [noun]

events that happened in the past

history [noun]

the study of events in the past

8

HISTORY

◆Jul 1999 Morinaga saw the fashion show held on the train (Keio Inokashira Line) by Keisuke Kanda on July 4th. The show made him electrified, and made him decide to become a fashion designer. ◆May 2000 Morinaga

2003

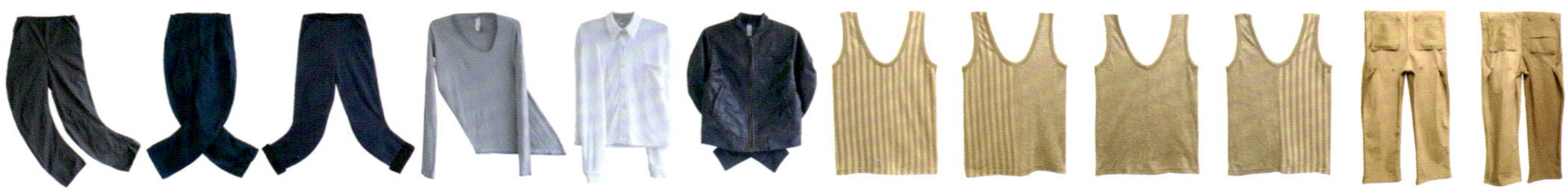

announced his fashion brand "人原理有 (ningen real)," which meant human, logic, reality, and existence. ◆Jan 2002 The brand was renamed as "ANREALAGE." ◆Mar 2002 Announced the 2002 AW collection "fragments of mind"

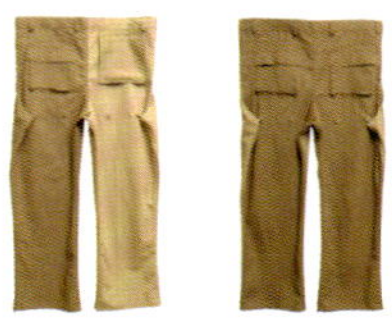

2004

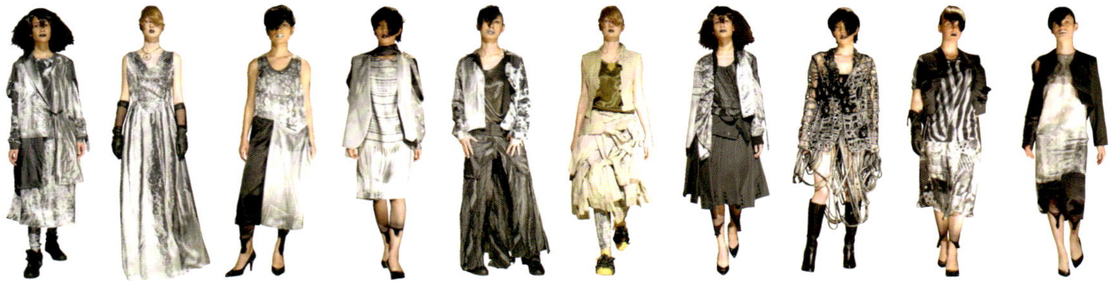

(Aoyama Round Theatre, Tokyo). ◆Apr 2003 Founded ANREALAGE as a business entity. ◆Apr 2003 Announced the 2003 AW collection "A Non-Descriptive" (Aoyama Bell Commons, Tokyo). ◆Sep 2003 Announced the 2004

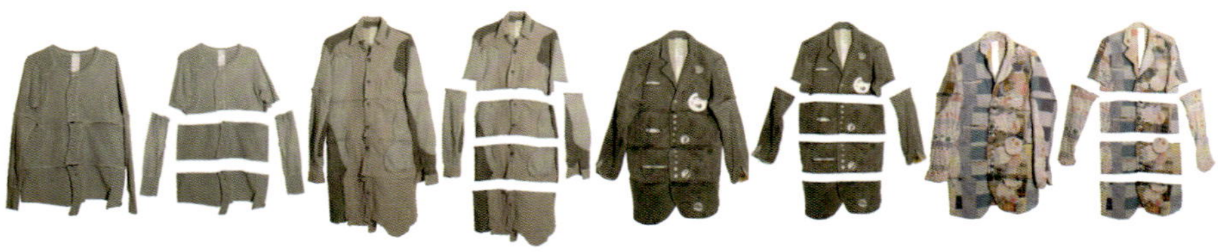

2005

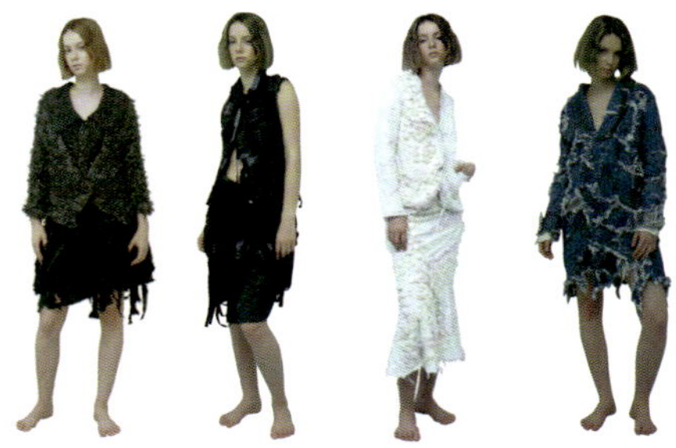

SS collection "WHERE FRONT IS?" (Tokyo Tower Amusement Hall, Tokyo). ◆May 2004 Announced the 2004 AW collection "LEMON" (East Gallery, Tokyo). ◆Sep 2004 Announced the 2005 SS collection "KIREHITO SANKA"

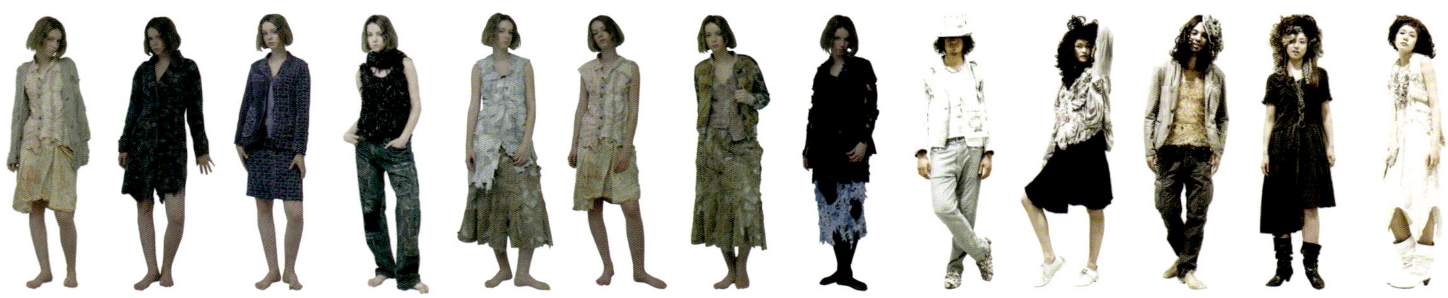

(Yoyogi National Stadium, Tokyo). ◆Aug 2005 Founded ANREALAGE CO., LTD. ◆Apr 2005 Announced the 2005 AW collection "SUZUMENO NAMIDA" (Gallery Site, Tokyo). ◆May 2005 Won the Design Vision Award For Avant

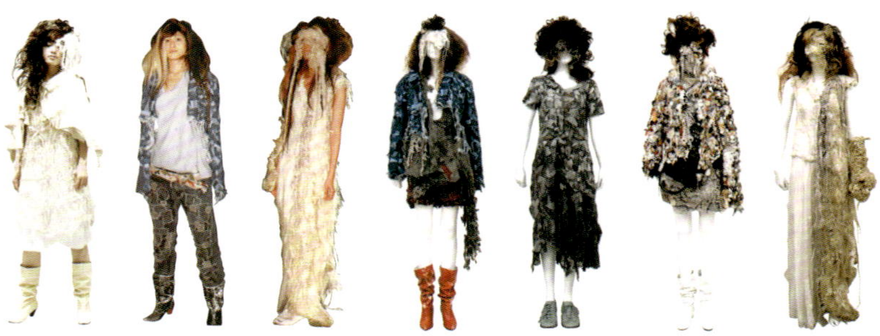

2006

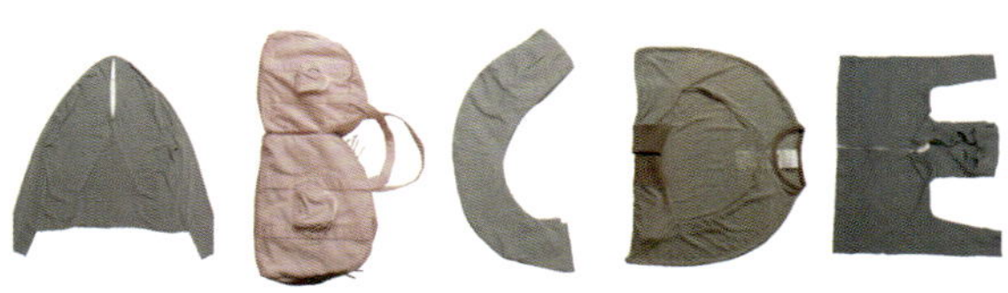

Garde at Gen Art competition for new designers in New York. ◆Nov 2005 Started to participate in Tokyo Fashion Week, and announced the 2006 AW collection "BUTTER" (Tokyo Tower, Tokyo). ◆Apr 2006 Announced the 2006

AW collection "CANON" (STUDIO BYBROS, Tokyo). ◆Nov 2006 Announced the 2007 SS collection "PRAYER" (EBiS303, Tokyo). ◆Apr 2007 Announced the 2007 AW collection "HARUKAHARU" (EBiS303, Tokyo). ◆Nov 2007

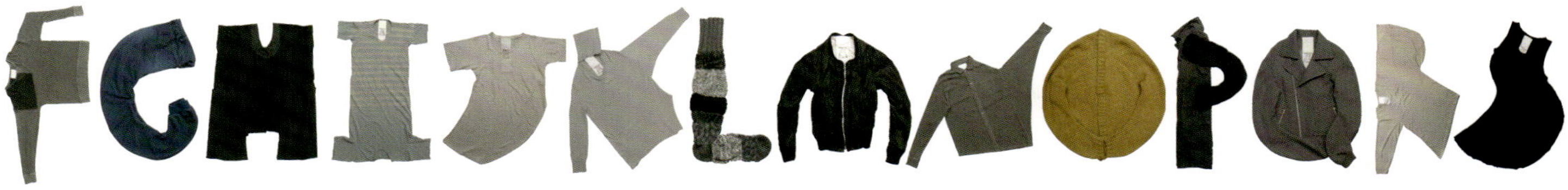

Announced the 2008 SS collection "NO MORE" (EBiS303, Tokyo). ◆Apr 2008 Announced the 2008 AW collection "MUTYU" (Shin-Marunouchi Bldg., Tokyo). ◆Oct 2008 Announced the 2009 SS collection "○△□" (Sakaesou

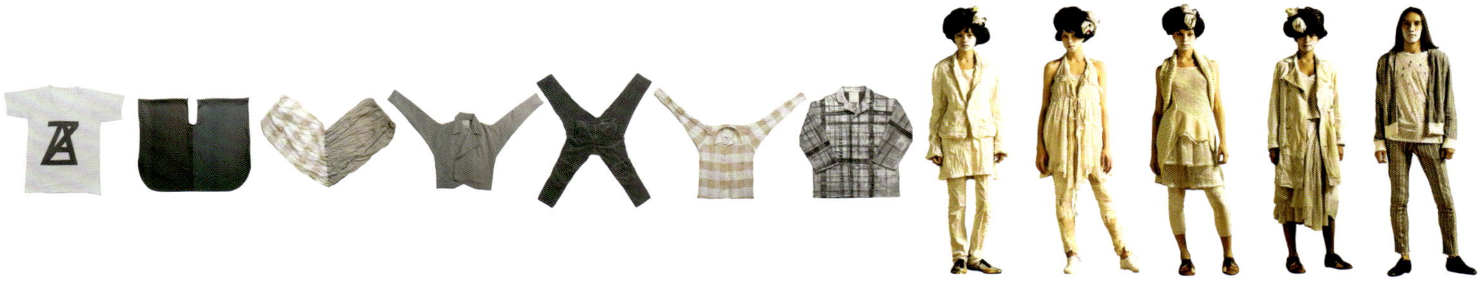

studio, Tokyo). ◆Apr 2009 Announced the 2009 AW collection "凹凸" (LION BUILDING, Tokyo). ◆Oct 2009 Announced the 2010 SS collection "SILHOUETTE" (Gotanda Abandoned Building, Tokyo). ◆Oct 2009 Showcased works

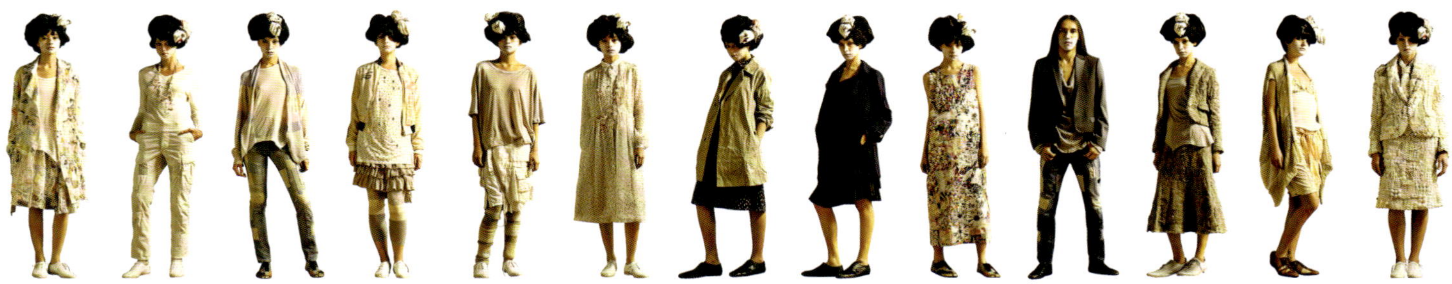

at The Museum of Far Eastern Antiquities (Stockholm, Sweden). ◆Apr 2010 Announced the 2010 AW collection "WIDESHORTSLIMLONG" (AOYAMA STUDIOS, Tokyo). ◆Oct 2010 Announced the 2011 SS collection "AIR" (Belle

2007

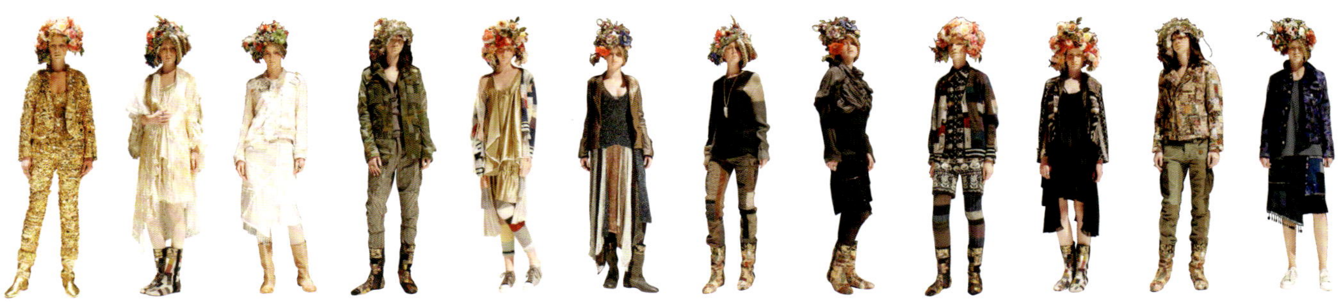

Salle Shibuya First, Tokyo). ◆Oct 2010 Participated in the exhibition "Future Beauty—30 Years of Japanese Fashion" at the Barbican Centre, London, curated by the Kyoto Costume Institute. The exhibition also traveled to Haus

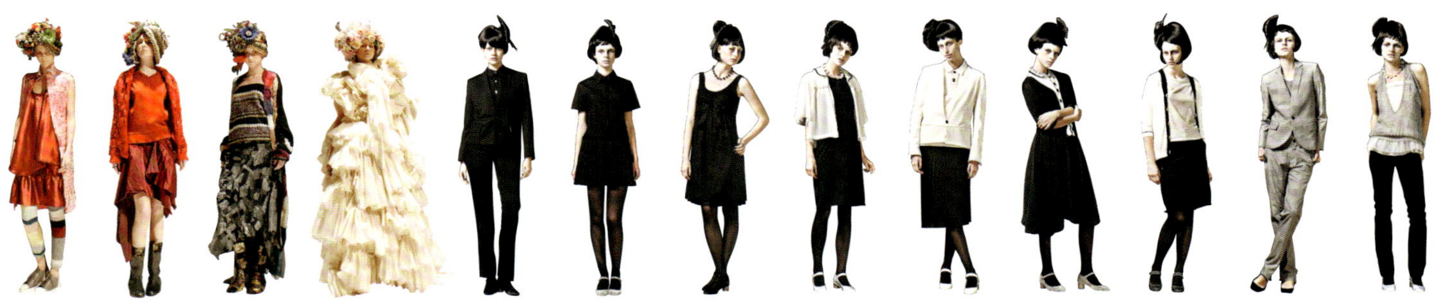

der Kunst (Munich, Germany) in 2011, and The Museum of Contemporary Art, Tokyo (Tokyo, Japan) in 2012. ◆Mar 2011 Opened the flagship shop "ANREALAGE ONLY SHOP" in Jingumae, Harajuku, Tokyo. ◆Apr 2011

Participated in the exhibition “Miffy in Fashion” at the Centraal Museum (Utrecht, The Netherlands). ◆Apr 2011 Announced the 2011 AW collection “LOW” (Laforet Museum Roppongi, Tokyo). ◆May 2011 Participated in the charity

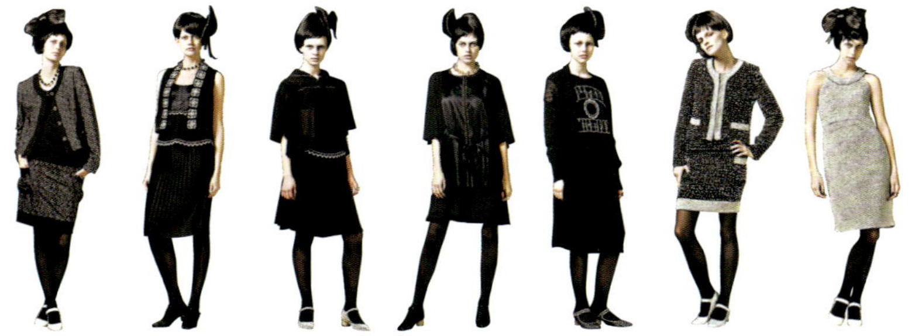

2008

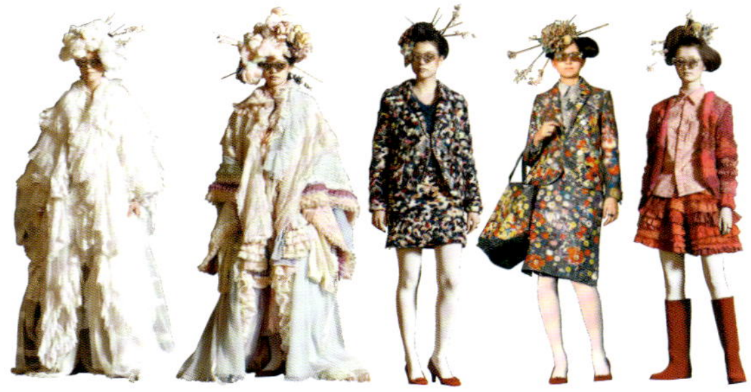

exhibition for East Japan reconstruction support, “SAVE TOKYO CREATION supported by NARS” (EYE OF GYRE, Tokyo). ◆Oct 2011 Participated in the exhibition “Feel and Think: A New Era of Tokyo Fashion” at the Tokyo Opera

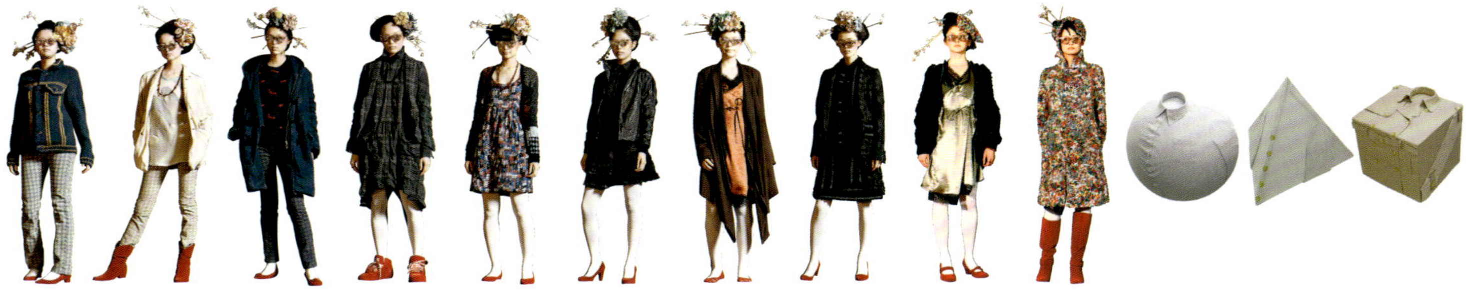

City Art Gallery. The exhibition also traveled to the National Art School Gallery (Sydney, Australia) in 2013. ◆Oct 2011 Won the 29th Mainichi Fashion Grand Prix for the Best New Designer and Shiseido Incentive Award. ◆Oct

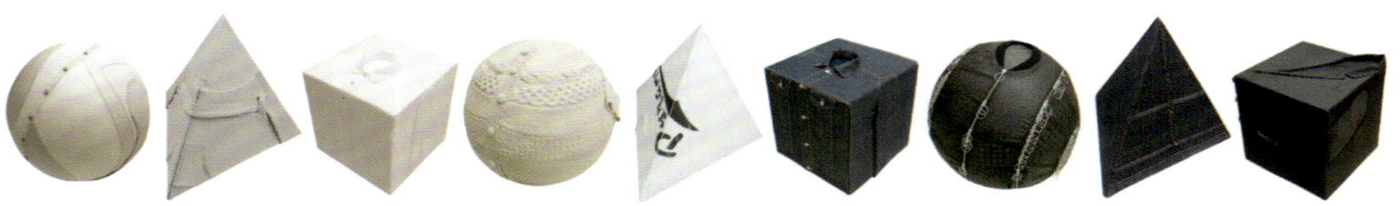

2009

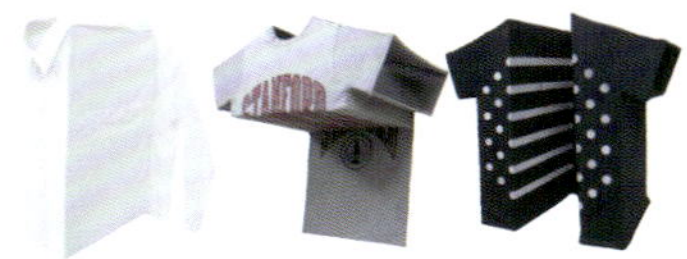

2011 Announced the 2012 SS collection “SHELL” (Belle Salle Shibuya First, Tokyo). ◆Feb 2012 Participated in “TOKYO FASHION WEEK in INDIA” (New Deli, India). ◆Mar 2012 Announced the 2012 AW collection “TIME” (Laforet

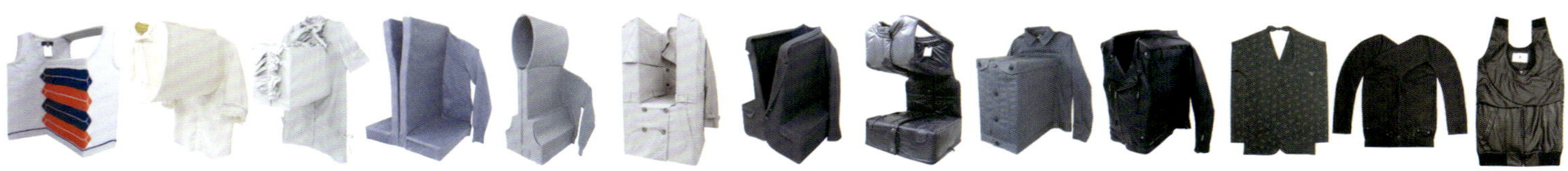

Museum Roppongi, Tokyo). ◆Jun 2012 Showcased the exhibition “I.T BEIJING MARKET COMME des GARÇONS” (Beijing, China). ◆Sep 2012 Launched “AA PROJECT” in collaboration with Adlens Japan. ◆Oct 2012 Announced

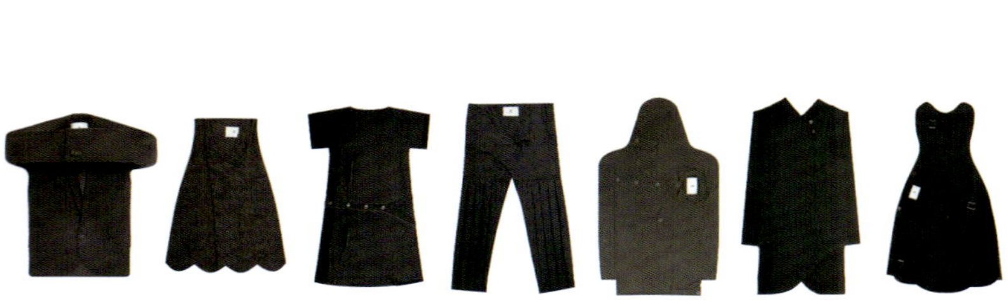

2010

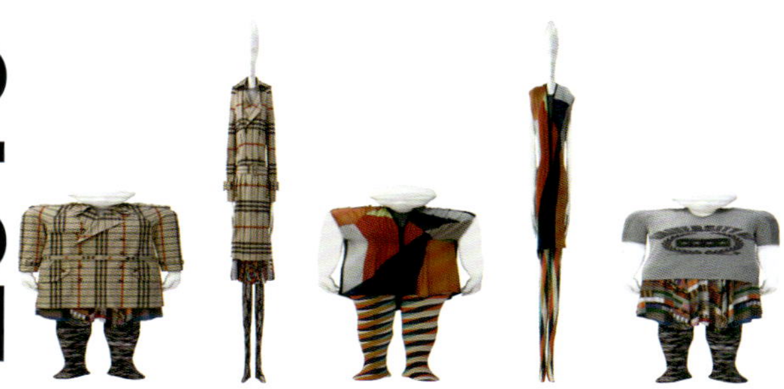

the 2013 SS collection “BONE” (Laforet Museum Roppongi, Tokyo). ◆Dec 2012 Announced “FANTASY COUTURE” in collaboration with artist Yoshitaka Amano, the character designer for FINAL FANTASY. ◆Dec 2012 Held the solo exhibition "A REAL UN REAL AGE" at Parco Museum, Tokyo, which commemorated the brand's first monograph titled "A REAL UN REAL AGE," that compiled the 10 years history of the brand. The exhibition also traveled to

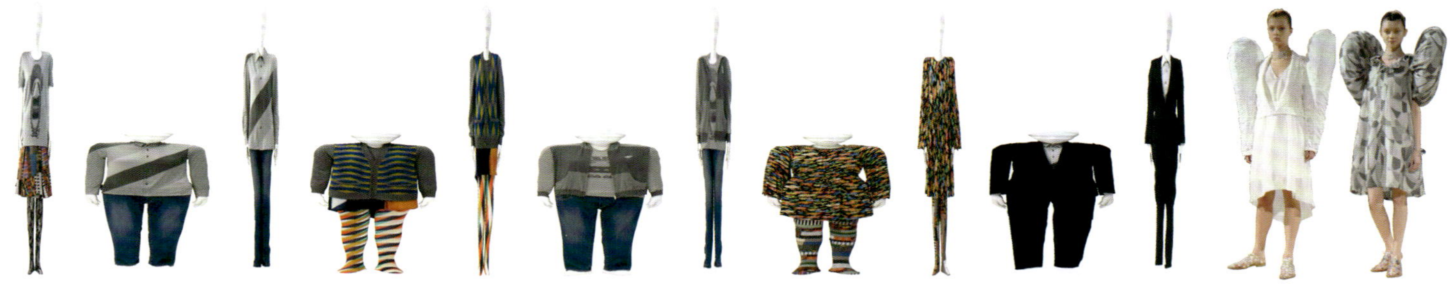

Paris in 2014 (L'ECLAIREUR SEVIGNE, Paris). ◆Feb 2013 Participated in "HELLO, SHIBUYA TOKYO with Singapore" (Orchard Road, Singapore). ◆Mar 2013 Announced the 2013 AW collection "COLOR" (Garden hall room,

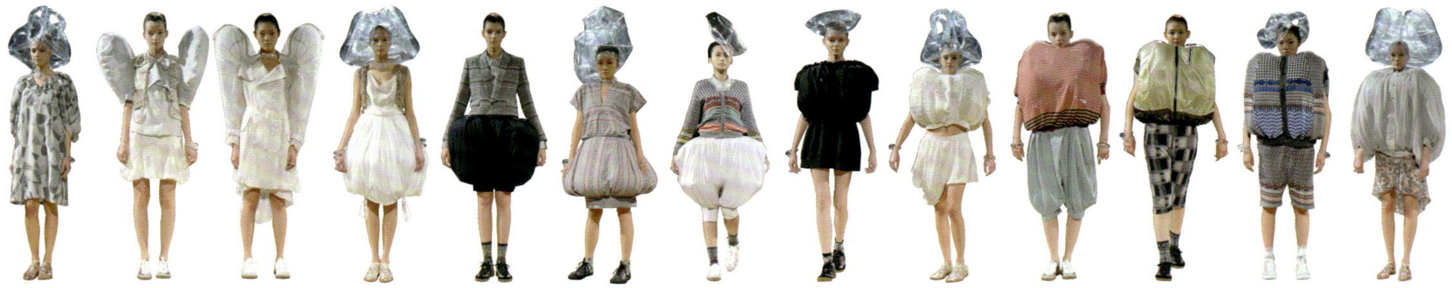

Tokyo). ◆Jun 2013 Designed stage costumes for the concert by SAKANACTION "SAKANAQUARIUM2013." ◆Jun 2013 Designed stage costumes for the concert by AKB48 "2013 A Midsummer Dome Tour." ◆Jun 2013

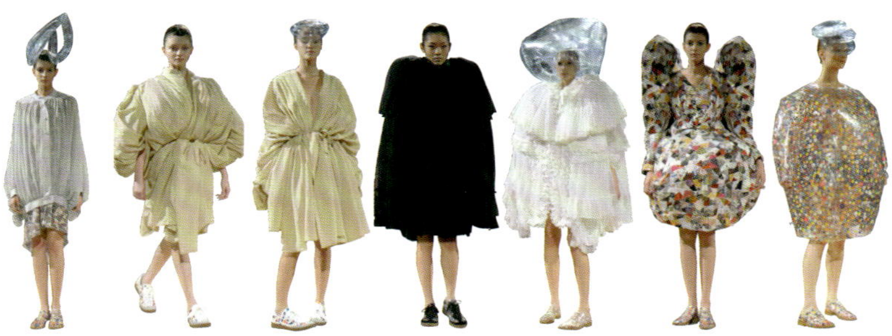

2011

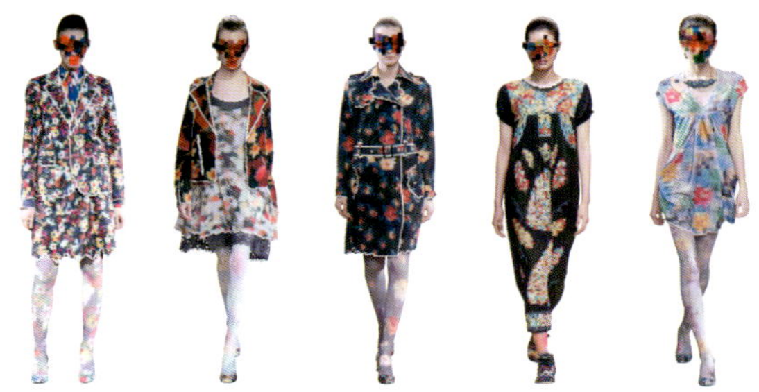

Announced *yukata* (Japanese casual summer clothing) in collaboration with HINAYA KYOTO (Isetan Shinjuku, Tokyo). ◆Jul 2013 Designed "design shuffle" in collaboration with MINTDESIGNS. ◆Jul 2013 Held the solo exhibition

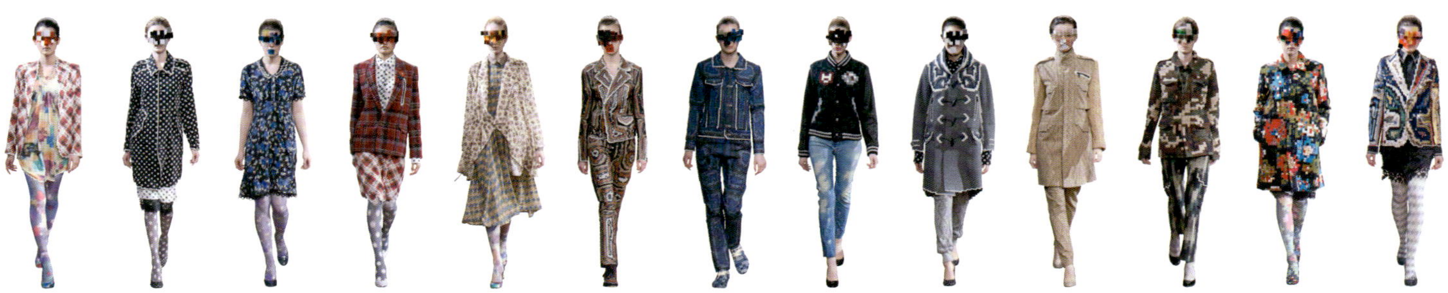

"Philosophical Fashion 2: ANREALAGE 'A COLOR UN COLOR'" (Design Gallery, 21st Century Museum of Contemporary Art, Kanazawa). ◆Jul 2013 Published *A COLOR UN COLOR* in parallel with the exhibition at 21st Century

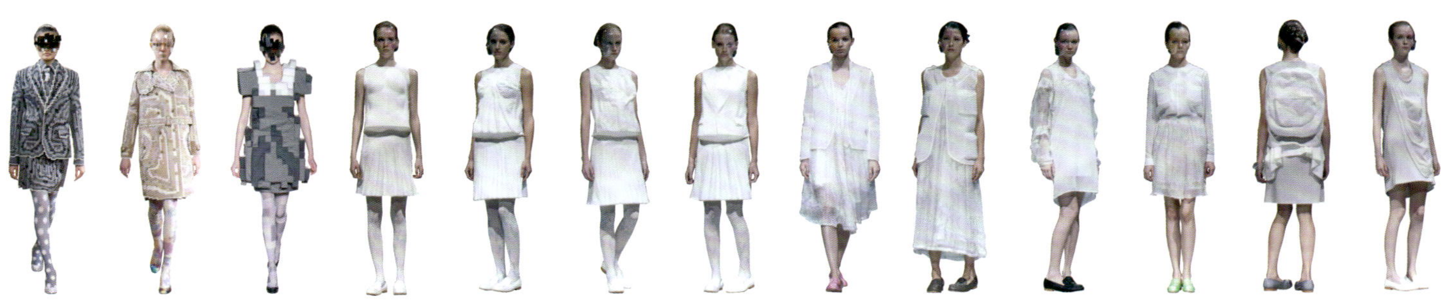

Museum of Contemporary Art, Kanazawa. ◆Sep 2013 Participated in the pop-up store "JAPAN CREATOR'S TEXTILE" produced by Mika Ninagawa (Isetan Shinjuku, Tokyo). ◆Oct 2013 Announced the 2014 SS collection "SIZE"

Refiguring Perception: Clothes as Actors of Micropolitics

By Yuko Hasegawa (Curator, Critic)

These technologies are ways of life, social orders, practices of visualization. Technologies are skilled practices. How to see? Where to see from? What limits to vision? What to see for? Whom to see with? Who gets to have more than one point of view? Who gets blinkered? Who wears blinkers? Who interprets the visual field? What other sensory powers do we wish to cultivate besides vision? Moral and political discourse should be the paradigm of rational discourse in the imagery and technologies of vision.

Simians, Cyborgs, and Women: The Reinvention of Nature
Donna J. Haraway

Fashion is an experience mediated by the body, a visual occurrence, an act made upon our society and the environment.

On the topic of clothing that changes, what immediately comes to mind is Hussein Chalayan's moving dresses. His dresses move like sophisticated robots, their skirts getting shorter or zippers opening of their own accord. The performance of a dress that condenses the century of fashion history (that is the history of the skirt length from long to mini) enraptured the audience with its fluid movements, as if orchestrated by an invisible hand. Chalayan reveals the hyper-conscious and organic object-ness of history and the female body. The dresses are beautiful armors wherein clothing, as robots, fuse with the living body. They express the character of the subject as a muse, as a warrior.

Tricks that animate clothing, making them transform like living things, startle us. Anrealage also transforms clothing while occupying a different space from Chalayan's. Anrealage's founder, Kunihiko Morinaga, came up with the brand's name—a combination of the words "real," "unreal," "age"—with the intention to "surprise and enchant," to traverse the real and the unreal and shift from one to the other.

Morinaga, who was influenced by Commes des Garçons and the designer Keisuke Kanda and known for his unique and spontaneous one-of-a-kind pieces, aspired toward his own "metamorphoses," achieved not on a mechanical level but by altering the DNA of materials or by rearranging information.

Morinaga employs various technical materials. The wearer is present, and when the surface of the garment changes, its surrounding is altered. Morinaga's pieces are neither driven by the individuality nor the character of the person; rather, they make personality anonymous. The visual surprise rendered by the changes to the garment and the accompanying transformation of its surroundings are what create a new "place" with the garment at its center. In this sense, Anrealage's pieces are akin to Bruno Latour's "actors." By bringing about a change to our perception, clothing transforms the senses directed upon our everyday life, and this process can occur in any place where clothing might appear. This can be described as a micropolitics, made possible by the influence of visual technology.

Things that do not register in our consciousness—abstract concepts or things that surround us and yet somehow remain invisible—are visualized, coded into clothes, and then become objects of description. Examples include Anrealage's collections *Noise* (as in white noise), *Shadow* (darkness), *Prism*, *Light*, *Reflect*, and *Bone*. While transforming the wearer is one of the motivations behind the clothing, what transforms the environment is the change that occurs on the clothing, or rather the sensibility that is evoked and awakened after the code hidden into the clothing is deciphered.

The collections *Prism* and *Reflect* translate in various ways the functions of optical light on our perception into the language of fashion. The collections also include Morinaga's experiments with the relationship between light and color. The effect of combining special fabrics with varying light sources becomes all the more dramatic on the runway. The micro effects of the clothing continue to lend moments of surprise to everyday life.

Morinaga also attempts a symbolic deconstruction as a way to transition from the ordinary to the extraordinary, as a way to symbolically present ambivalence. The collection *Shadow* presents all-white garments that are the antithesis of the theme suggested by its title. Upon this blank palette the temporary shadows appear, suggesting the vestiges of the body. In order to develop the dye used in the collection, Morinaga worked with a company that produces a special ink.

"The dye is made of molecules. We see color when light is reflected, and an object appears white when the molecules reflect all light. While photochromic technology (dyes similar to photosensitive paper that responds to light) made it possible to alter the degree of the reflection of light, so that we can selectively reflect only red or blue and subtly manipulate the differences in degrees, the black used in this collection absorbs all light, so we took it as an opportunity to work with UV light, an extremely difficult challenge."

These words underscore how Morinaga's contemplation of materials extends to the level of molecules and particles of light. His process, as if working in a laboratory, creates a certain condition or event—an event that must always occur upon wearable pieces of clothing.

Morinaga's work brings our attention to the ordinary: that the parts and movements of bodies continually cast shadows. He uses clothing as both equipment and medium to transform what regularly occurs around us into causes for wonder. The symbolic meaning is reversed when under the theme of "Light," the black garments are illuminated to reveal a pattern—a performance design that symbolizes not light itself but lighting as an event.

A common criticism against Anrealage is that their concept of clothes is superficial and too dependent on changes that stimulate our perception. On what criteria do we base our critique of fashion? Fashion constantly adapts and responds to our environment. There are so many more things around us that undergo constant change than things that remain in stasis. Videos and images continuously stream into our devices, while countless digital services are conducted on incorporeal interfaces. The physical and the Cloud, and our internal senses of the real and the unreal are in a constant state of active and complex exchange.

Against a time when the line between the real and the unreal have become ambivalent, Morinaga uses our bodies as real foundations to create events that act as clear markers of differences and borders, so that he can delight and excite our consciousness and awareness. Anrealage's clothing evokes a sensibility that is tied to the brand's hope to always retain a fresh and fluid approach. The experiences that Anrealage provides delight the wearer in the same way that embellishments such as a frill, a cut, or a color used to.

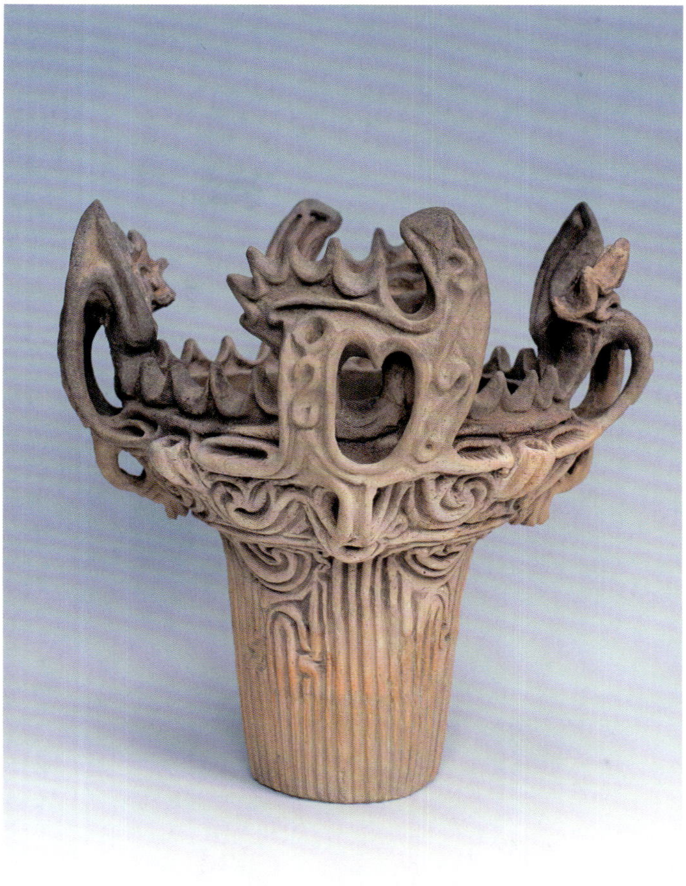

Tokamachi City Museum, National Treasure, Flame Style Vessel

Lastly, let's discuss the object-ness of Anrealage's clothing. The dynamic collection *Roll*, in which garments are carved from rolls of denim fabric, was a collaboration with the sculptor Kohei Nawa. Presenting the dresses alongside pottery from the Jomon period, the artists established a conversation on Japanese beauty between works separated by a history of five thousand years. Morinaga never allows his concepts to become meta; instead, his strength lies in his ability to turn his leap between the real and the unreal into an event before our eyes and offer them as tangible products.

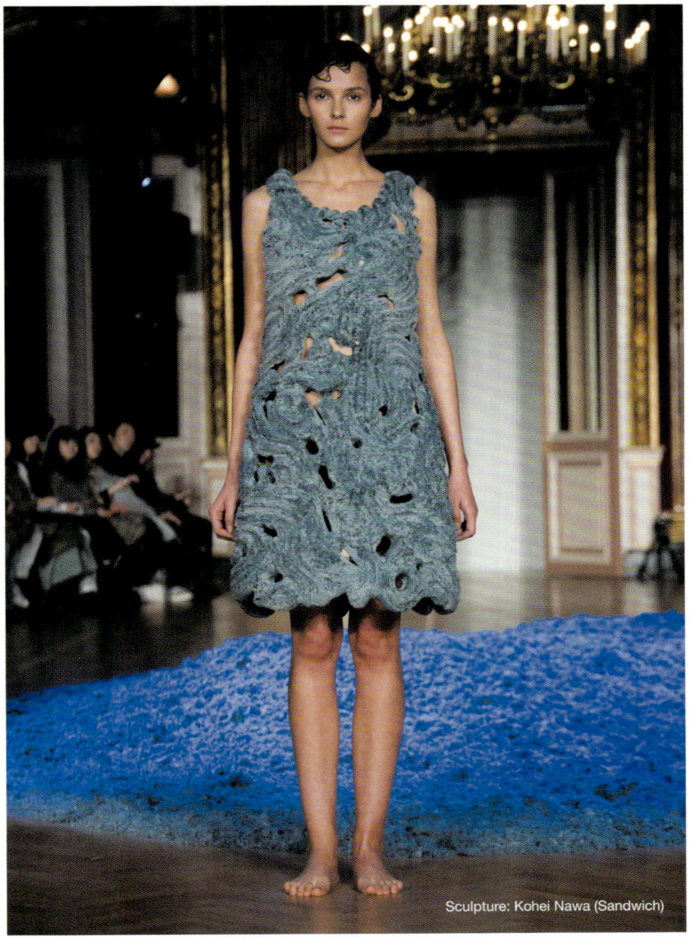

Sculpture: Kohei Nawa (Sandwich)

(Laforet Museum Roppongi, Tokyo). ◆Nov 2013 Participated in the public talk "Kunihiko Morinaga × Kiyokazu Washida: Body × Clothes × Sexuality" (Sendai Mediatheque, Miyagi, Japan). ◆Nov 2013 Designed the gift item line

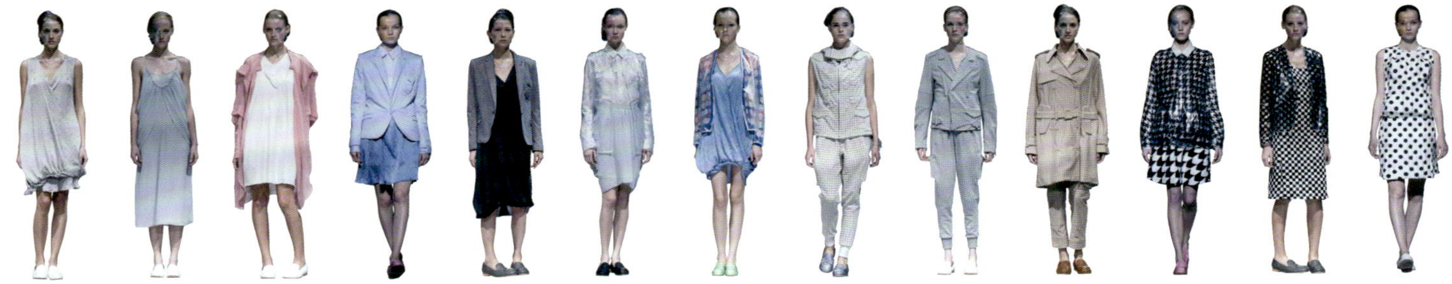

"HAVE A POP CLASSICO HOLIDAY" in collaboration with Yumi Matsutoya (BARNEYS NEW YORK). ◆Dec 2013 Participated in "7 Hair and Makeup Artists, and Tokyo Fashion Exhibition" (Shiseido Hanatsubaki Hall, Tokyo). ◆Jan

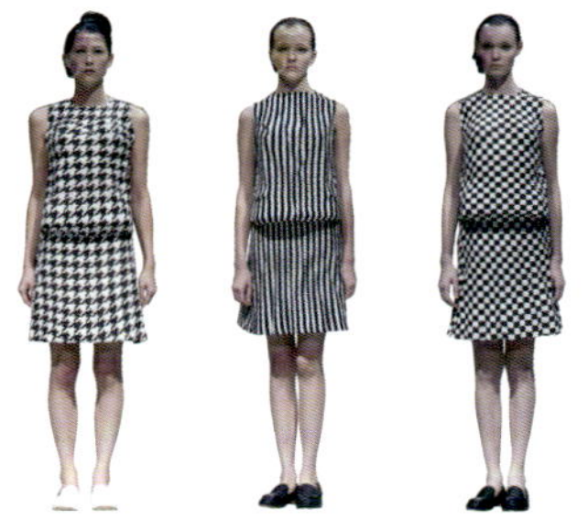

2012

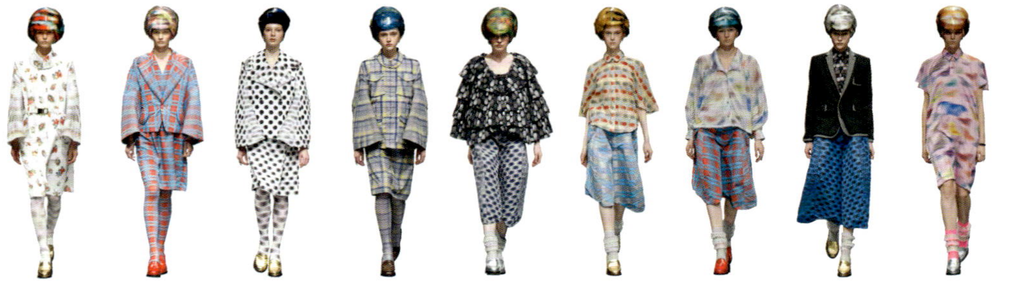

2014 Participated in the East Japan reconstruction support art and charity program "KISS THE HEART#3" (Isetan Shinjuku, Tokyo). ◆Feb 2014 Opened ANREALAGE LIMITED SHOP named "Hikari (Light)" in Shibuya PARCO

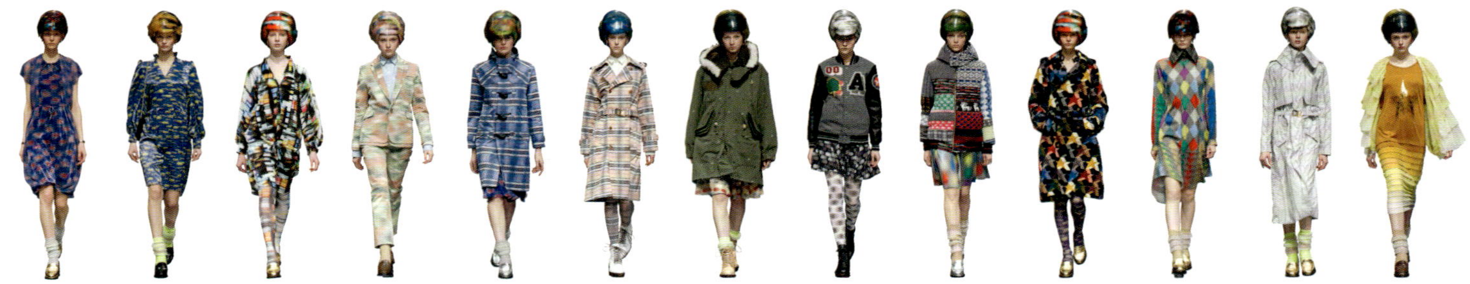

(Shibuya PARCO, Tokyo). ◆Feb 2014 Participated in the pop-up store "NIPPONISTA" held at Green Street, Soho (New York). ◆Feb 2014 Announced the collaboration with Hobonichi Techo, and released a design for "Hobonichi

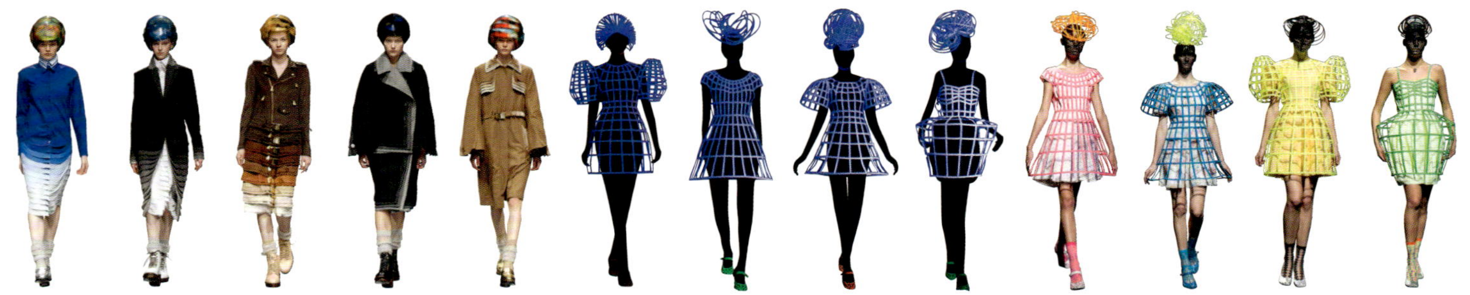

Techo WEEKS 2014 spring." ◆Mar 2014 Participated in the project "Creative Piece: LEXUS × TOKYO FASHION" (Intersect by LEXUS Tokyo, Tokyo). ◆Mar 2014 Announced the 2014 AW collection "SEASON" (Laforet Museum

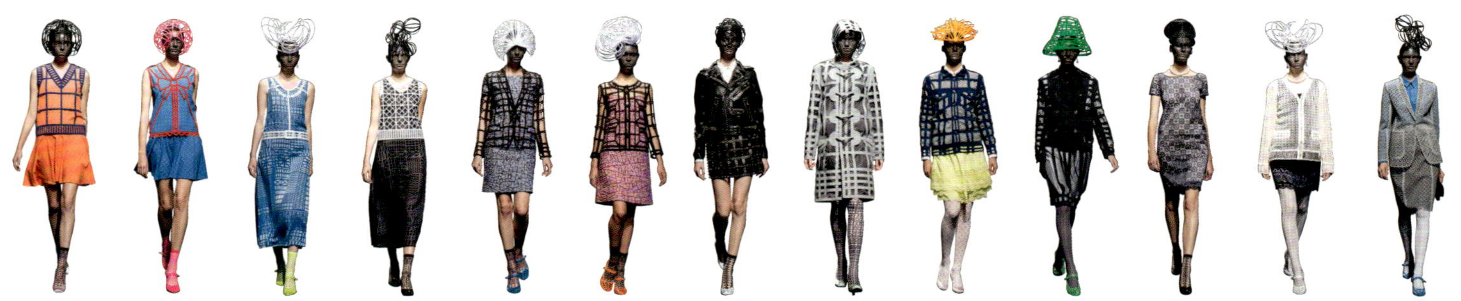

Roppongi, Tokyo). ◆Mar 2014 Announced the collaboration with Creative Laboratory PARTY and AID-DCC Inc., and released "FOCUS: Life Gear," a collection that focused to shut out and control the wearer from storms of

information (Toronto Fashion Week, Canada). ◆Mar 2014 Launched the second line "ANSEASON ANREALAGE" (women's and men's). ◆Mar 2014 Participated in the exhibition, "Future Beauty: The Tradition of Reinvention in

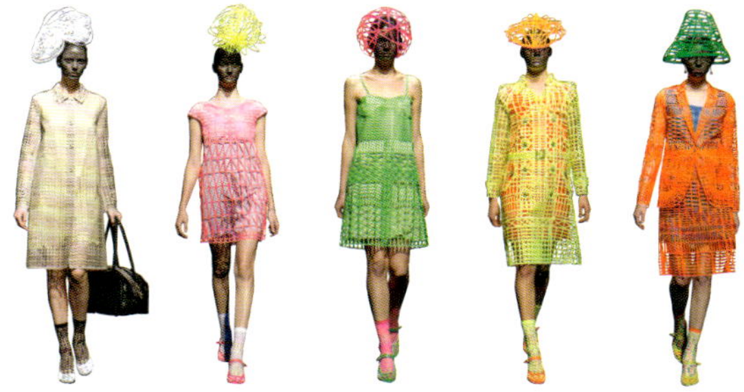

2013

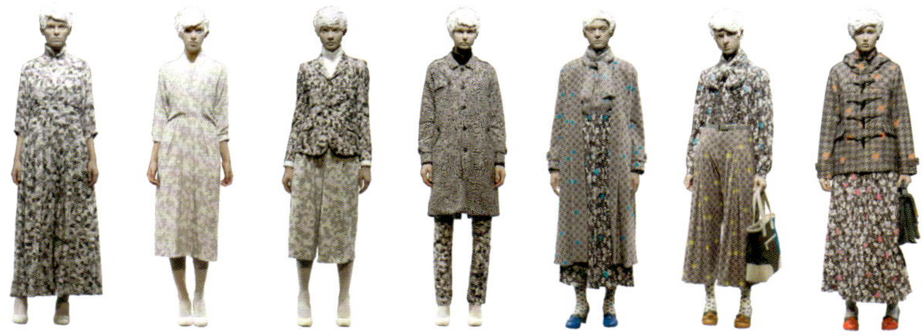

Japanese Fashion" curated by Kyoto Costume Institute (The National Museum of Modern Art, Kyoto). ◆May 2014 Participated in "ADIDAS ORIGINALS ENJIN COLLECTION" (Isetan Shinjuku, Tokyo). ◆May 2014 Participated in

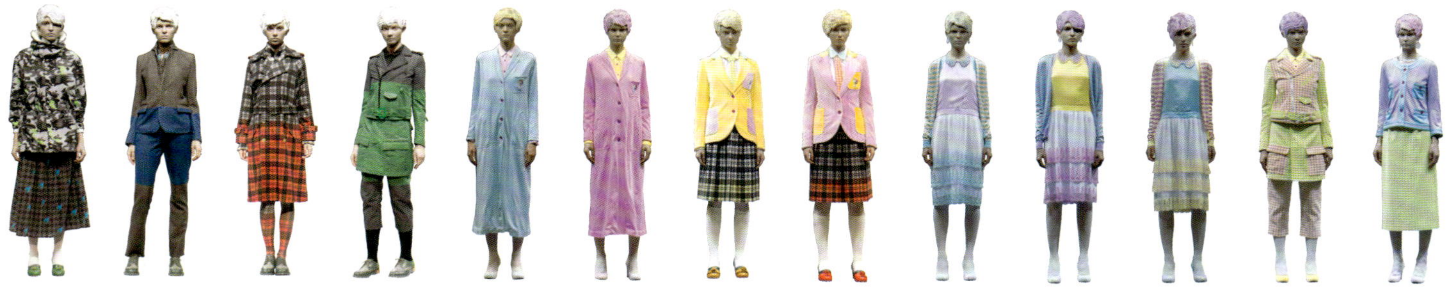

"Yuki Onodera + Kunihiko Morinaga (Anrealage) 'Special Edition'" (G/P gallery, Tokyo). ◆Jun 2014 Participated in "ISETAN YUKATA SELECTION 2014" (Isetan Shinjuku, Tokyo). ◆Aug 2014 Participated in Yokohama Paratriennale

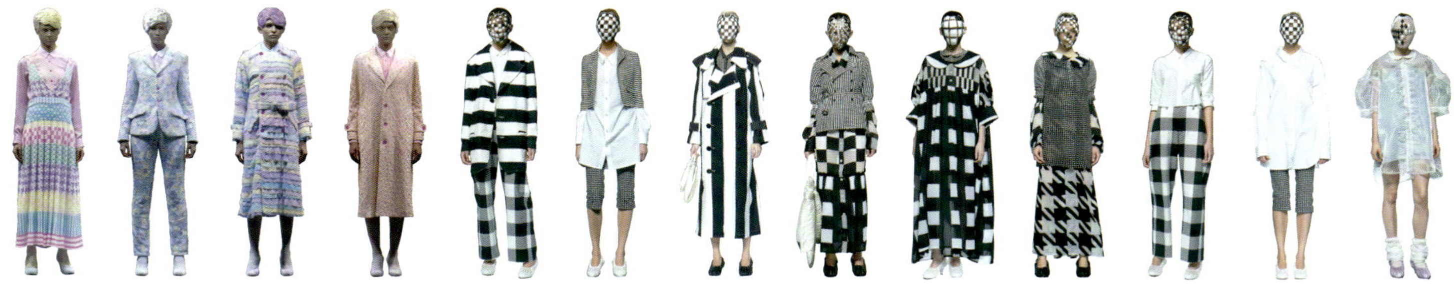

and showcased the artwork "Listening to the Clothes" (ZOU-NO-HANA TERRACE, Kanagawa). ◆Sep 2014 Released "SWITCH October Issue" directed by Kunihiko Morinaga. ◆Sep 2014 Debuted in Paris Fashion Week, and

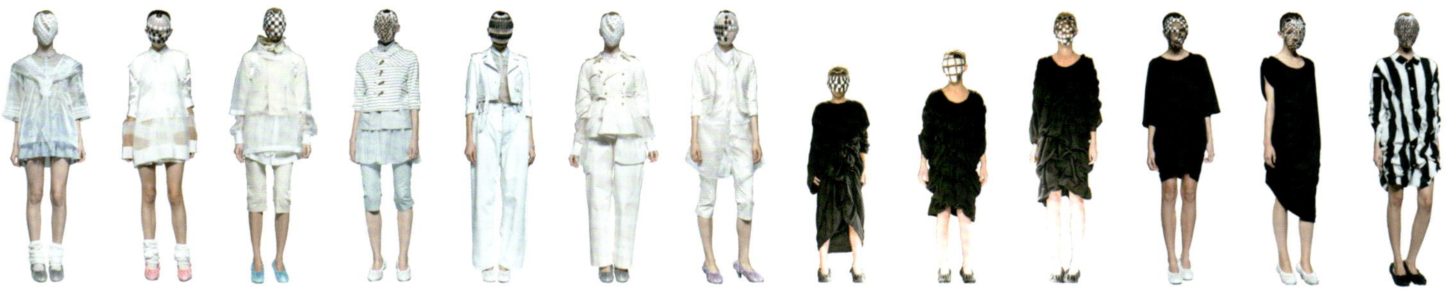

announced the 2015 SS collection "SHADOW" (Beaux-Arts Salle Melpoméne, Paris). ◆Sep 2014 Participated in the program "TOKYO DESIGNERS meets TOHOKU." ◆Oct 2014 Participated in the exhibition "Wardrobe Memories"

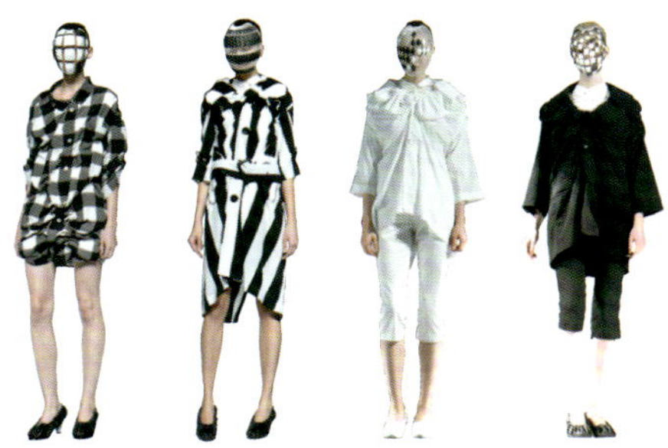

2014

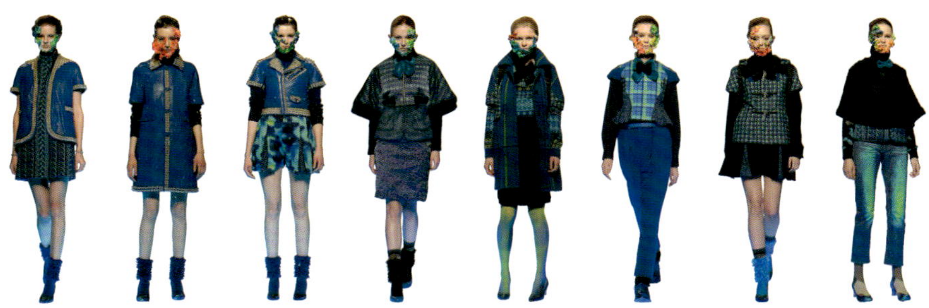

(Arts Maebashi, Gunma). ◆Oct 2014 Morinaga was featured in the documentary TV program, "JOUNETSU - TAIRIKU." ◆Oct 2014 Participated in the exhibition "SHOWCASE" (Daikanyama Loveria Annex, Tokyo). ◆Nov 2014

Announced the collaboration "ANREALAGE × Attack On Titan." ◆Nov 2014 Designed the costume for "DISNEY Collection created by Zoff." ◆Dec 2014 Released the inaugural issue of "W _ _ K W _ _ K," created as a collaboration

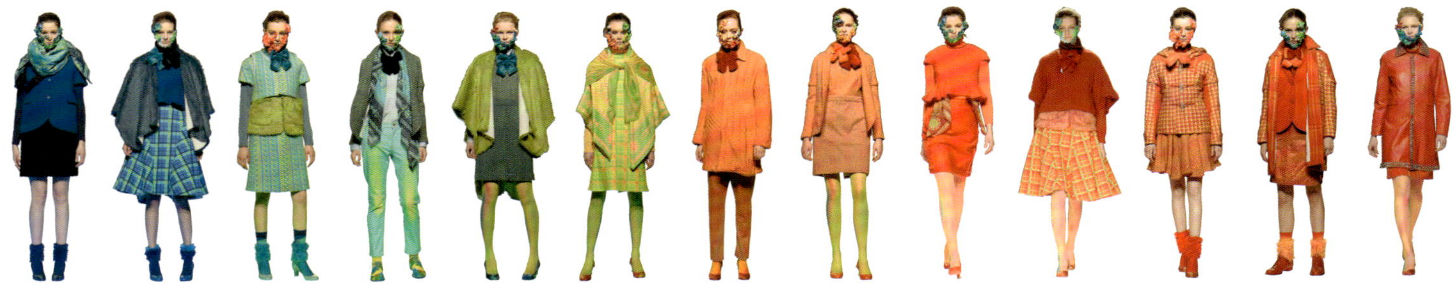

with the Singaporian graphic designer, Theseus Chan, and photographer, Yoshiyuki Okuyama. ◆Dec 2014 Held the exhibition "W _ _ K W _ _ K" (GALLERY X BY PARCO, Tokyo). ◆Jan 2015 Participated in the TV program "NHK

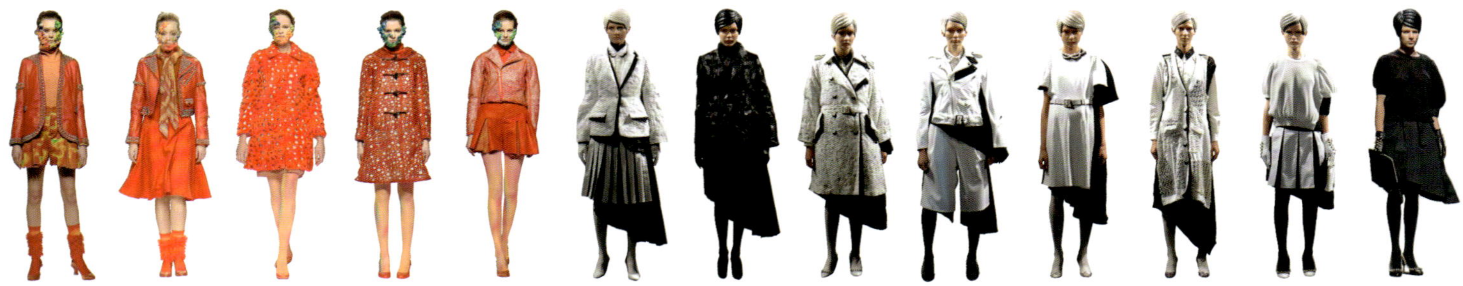

Special: NEXT WORLD - Our Future." ◆Feb 2015 Produced "WEARABLE INFOBAR PATTERN GENERATOR" in collaboration with KDDI and RHIZOMATIKS. ◆Mar 2015 Announced the 2015 AW collection "LIGHT" (Beaux-Arts

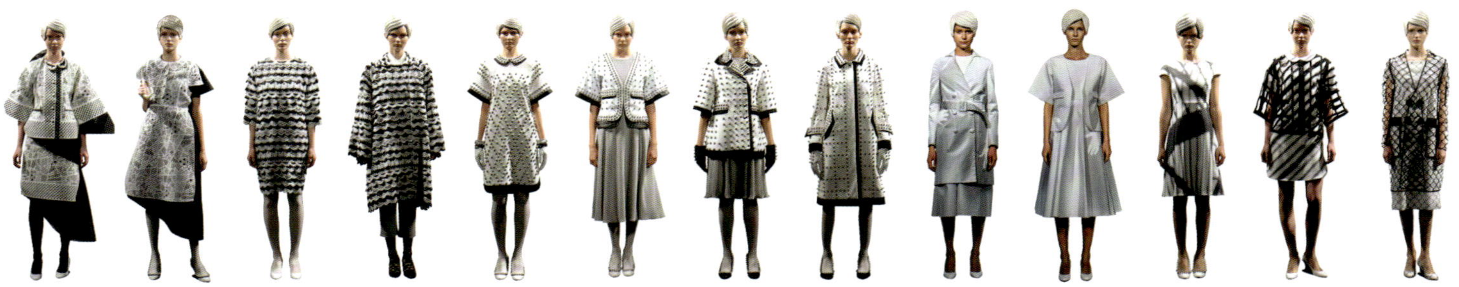

Salle Melpomène, Paris). ◆Mar 2015 Opened "ANREALAGE LIMITED SHOP & WINDOW DISPLAY IN SEIBU SHIBUYA" in collaboration with Rhizomatiks (Seibu Shibuya, Tokyo). ◆Apr 2015 Participated in the exhibition

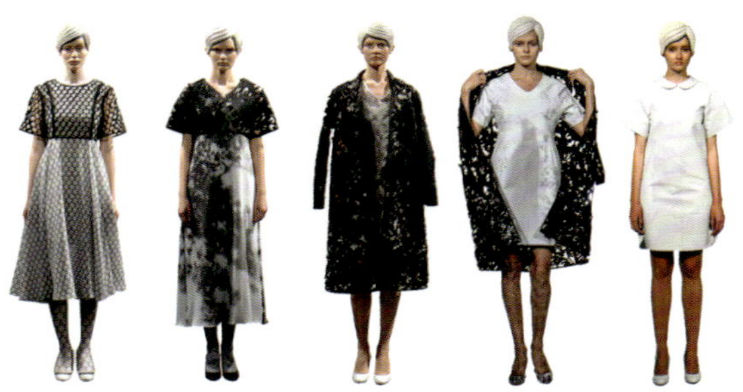

2015

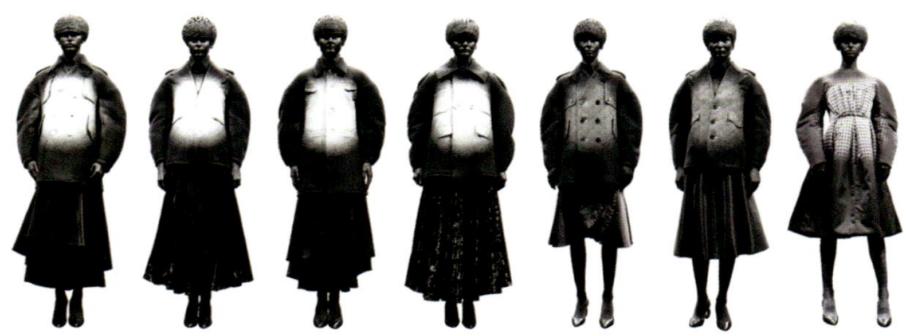

"Transcendent Artful Embroidery II" (Kobe Fashion Museum, Hyogo, Japan). ◆May 2015 Showcased archived works at "DRESSING FOR FUN EXHIBITION" (DRESSING FOR FUN, China). ◆Jun 2015 Shortlisted at "ANDAM

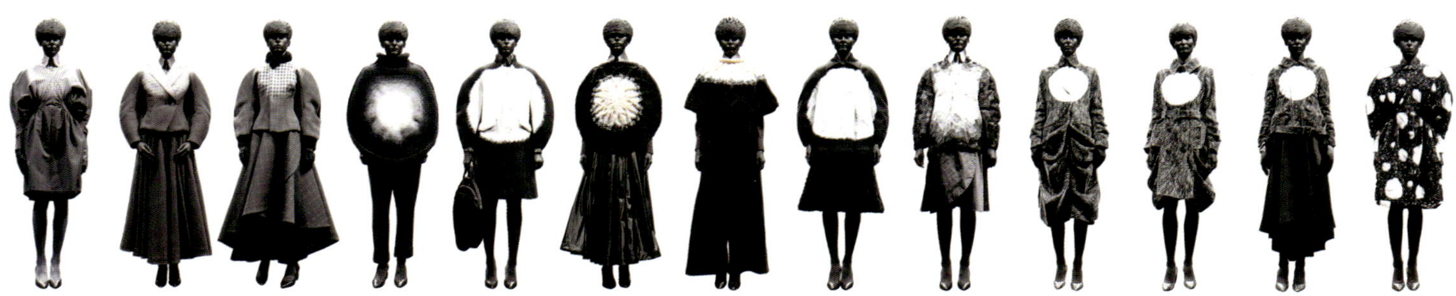

fashion award" by the French Haute Couture and Fashion Federation. ◆Jun 2015 Held the exhibition "ANREALAGE T-shirts Line AZ" in collaboration with the designers' collective NO DESIGN (SFT Gallery, The National Art Center,

Tokyo). ◆Jun 2015 Released "ANDROID WEAR" in collaboration with Google. ◆Jul 2015 Participated in the exhibition "DIGITAL × FASHION" (Kobe Fashion Museum, Hyogo, Japan). ◆Sep 2015 Announced the 2016 SS

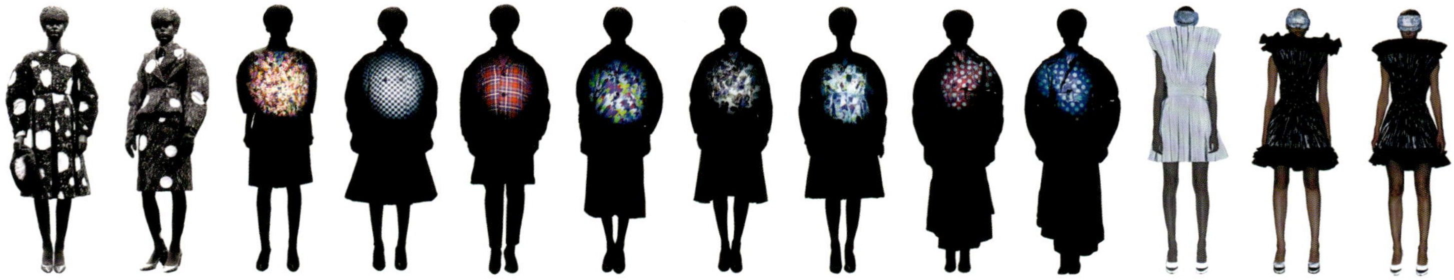

collection "REFLECT" (Palais de Tokyo, Paris). ◆Nov 2015 Announced Circle Case "ANREALAGE × Hobonichi Techo" in collaboration with PORTER. ◆Nov 2015 Participated in "NEO TOKYO BRANDS in THAILAND" (M floor,

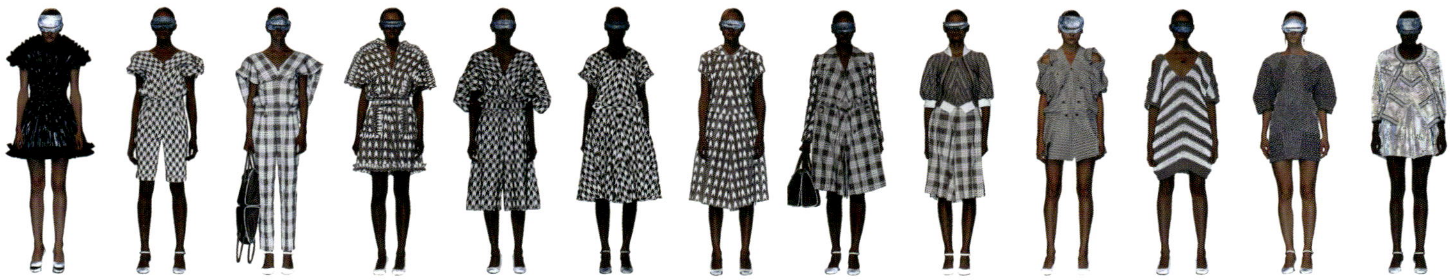

EmQuartier, Bangkok). ◆Dec 2015 Announced "ANREALAGE × STARWARS COLLABORATION COLLECTION." ◆Feb 2016 Designed the main image for "2016 HANABANASAI" in collaboration with photographer/film director

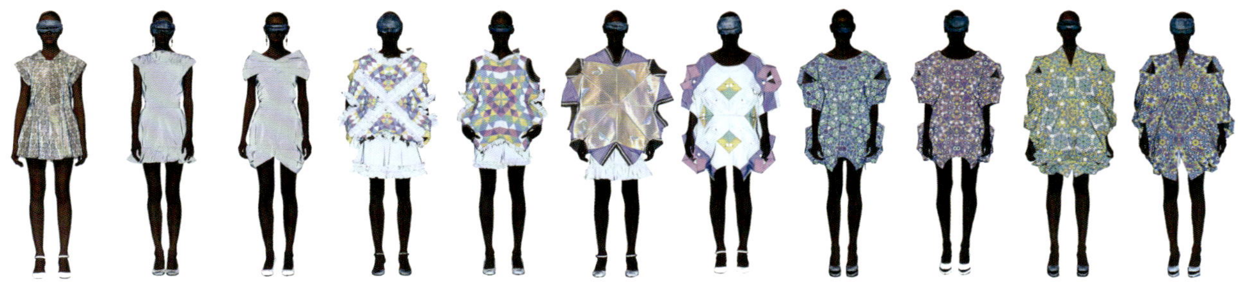

2016

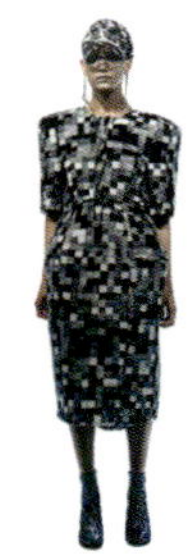

Mika Ninagawa (Isetan Shinjuku, Tokyo). ◆Mar 2016 Announced the 2016 AW collection "NOISE" (Palais de Tokyo, Paris). ◆Mar 2016 Announced the collaboration with the UK based Collaborative Practice, TOMATO, and released

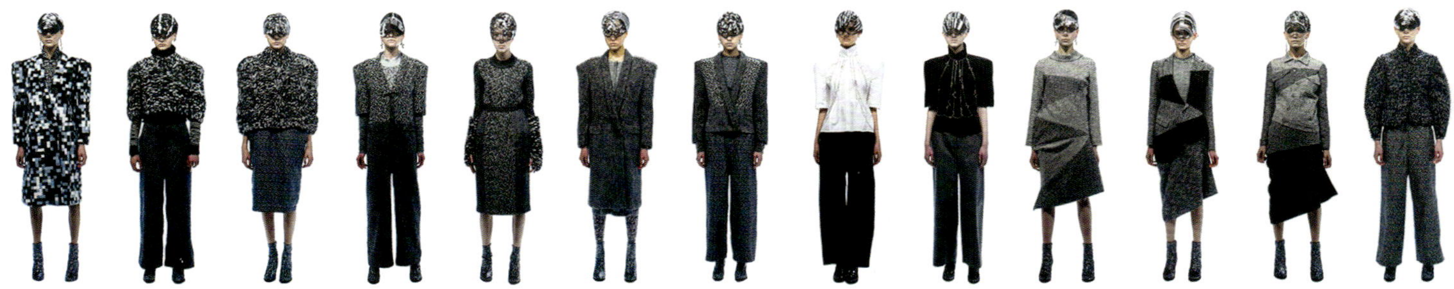

limited items for "THE TOMATO PROJECT 25TH ANNIVERSARY EXHIBITION 'O'" (Parco Museum, Tokyo). ◆Mar 2016 Designed the workwear dedicated to traditional craftsmen "POWER of COTTON." ◆Jun 2016 Announced

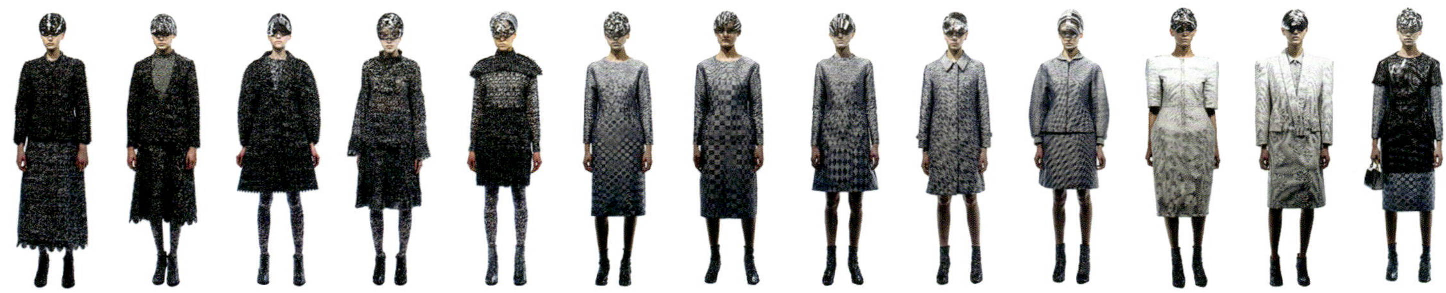

the limited model of "SmartWatch3" in collaboration with SONY SMART WATCH. ◆Jul 2016 Held "BMW COLLABORATION SHOW" (BMW GROUP Tokyo Bay, Tokyo). ◆Aug 2016 Announced "JERSEY MEETS SUITS," the

ANREALAGE

Alexandre Samson (Fashion Curator, Historian)

At the time of writing this, more than ten fashion seasons have passed since the appearance of the first Anrealage collection in Paris, which was shown on September 23, 2014, as part of the spring-summer 2015 womenswear fashion week.

If we assume that each season during fashion week designers show nearly 4,000 looks in the French capital alone (to say nothing of the collections produced in London, New York and Milan), it is possible to estimate that, in the almost five years since that first show, nearly 40,000 outfits have been created.

Such profusion questions the notion of creation itself. In the midst of this aesthetic cacophony, how are we to distinguish between the most compelling and innovative designs, those which hold a mirror up to our times, and those of lesser importance? This is the question which editors, stylists and fashion museums across the globe are continually seeking to answer.

In this respect, the Palais Galliera, Paris Fashion Museum, is proud to be among the first to collect Anrealage by Kunihiko Morinaga, having added the brand to its historic archives in 2016. Alongside pieces dating from the 18th century right up to today, from the illustrious Charles-Frédérick Worth to Madeleine Vionnet or Cristobal Balenciaga, the inclusion of Anrealage's designs enriches the museum's collection and places him in the context of that great cohort of designers from the end of the 20th century known as the Japanese School. Kenzo Takada, Issey Miyake, Rei Kawakubo and Yohji Yamamoto: these different personalities with different creative identities revolutionised the fashion of their time and influenced the generations that followed them, among them Martin Margiela and Helmut Lang.

Similar but singular, Anrealage has carved out his path in the wake of his predecessors and written his own vocabulary.
His new approach to technique, by questioning light, volume and movement by performing cut and fabric, is now one of his recognised trademarks. His negation of the human body, seeming at first to be the very antithesis of conventional fashion creation, is what has come to define the accuracy of his work, just as his shows transformed into a unique sensory experience.
Collection after collection, Anrealage questions not just fashion trends, but the very essence of creation itself.

collaborative project with ASICS and keisuke kanda. ◆Aug 2016 Opened the shop "ANREALAGE AOYAMA" in Minami Aoyama, Tokyo. ◆Sep 2016 Announced "Acrylic Flower Band for AppleWatch." ◆Sep 2016 Designed

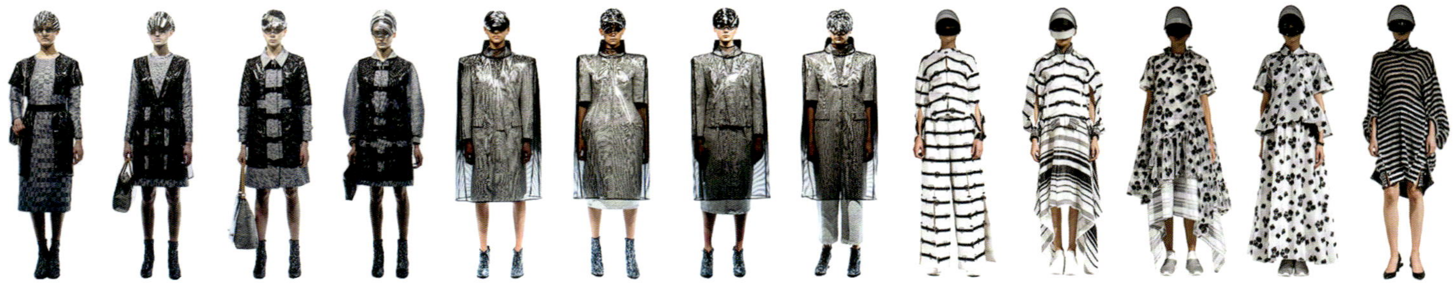

"PLAYSTATION VR COSTUME." ◆Sep 2016 Announced the 2017 SS collection "SILENCE" (Palais de Tokyo, Paris). ◆Feb 2017 Announced the 2017 AW collection "ROLL" (Palais de Tokyo, Paris). ◆Feb 2017 Designed the

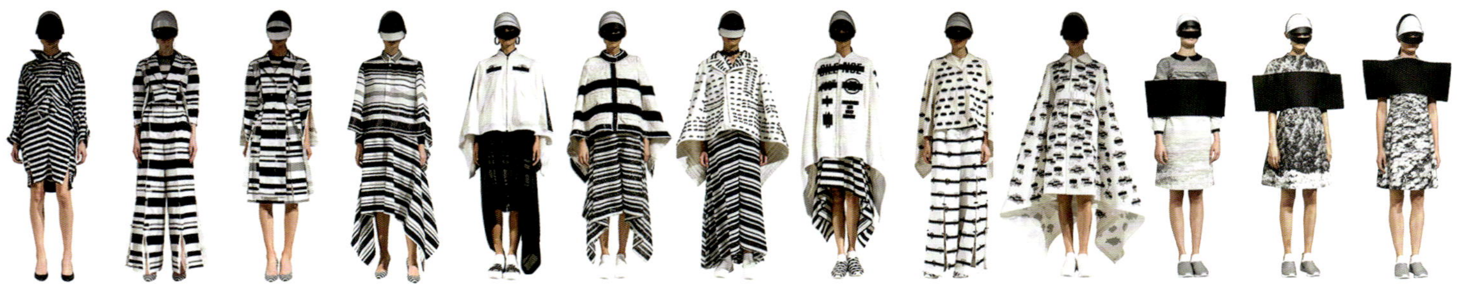

uniform for the ramen restaurant, IPPUDO. ◆Apr 2017 Announced the collaboration ORPHE × ANREALAGE, and released the collaboration model shoes. ◆Jun 2017 Announced the collaboration ONITSUKA TIGER ×

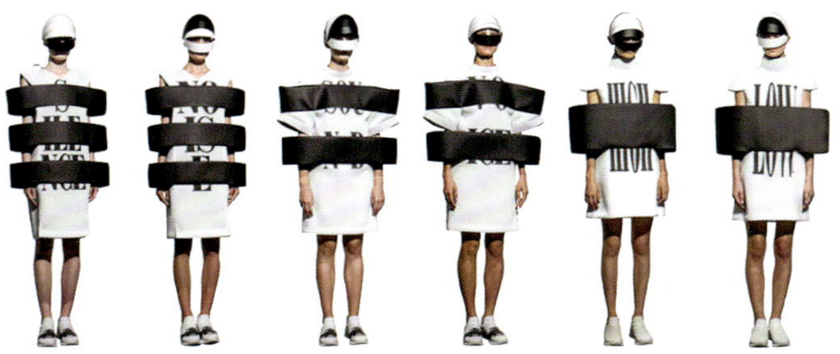

2017

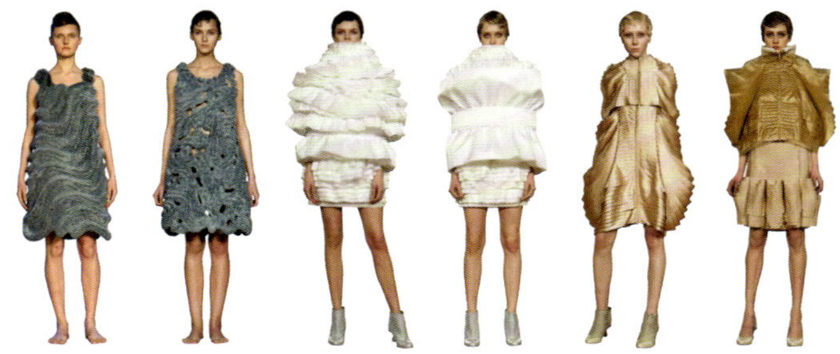

ANREALAGE, and released MONTE Z. ◆Jun 2017 Announced the collaboration ANREALAGE × CANTON OVERALLS, and released WIDE SHORT DENIM PANTS. ◆Jun 2017 Announced the collaboration with Fashion

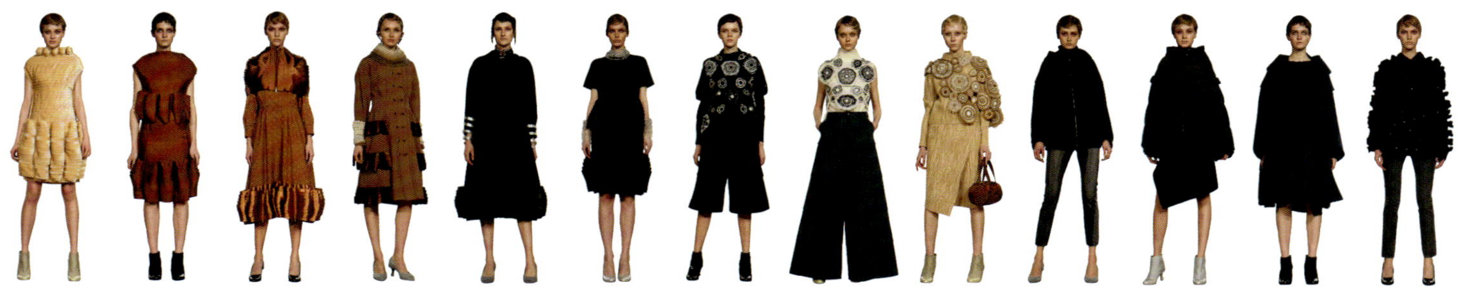

Entertainments (SONY), and released a FES WATCH U design for Tokyo Monochrome. ◆Jun 2017 Participated in Google's new project, "We Wear Culture." ◆Jun 2017 Relocated ANREALAGE FLAGSHIP SHOP from Jingumae

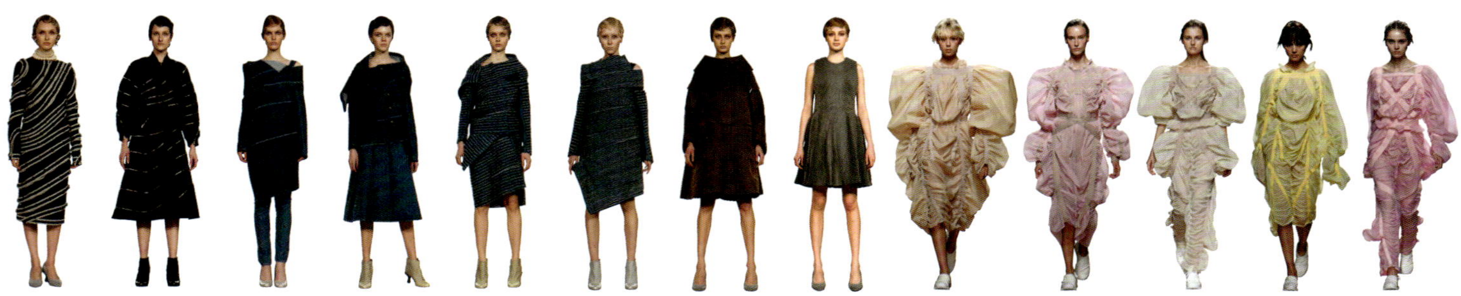

to Minami Aoyama. ◆Jun 2017 Announced the collaboration RADO × ANREALAGE, and released "TRUE SHADOW." ◆Jun 2017 Announced the collaboration "Keisuke Kanda × ANREALAGE," and held the joint-exhibition "Ano

Fuku" at Maison de la Culture du Japon à Paris (Paris, France). ◆Sep 2017 Announced the 2018 SS collection "POWER" (Palais de Tokyo, Paris). ◆Oct 2017 Announced the collaboration ASICS × ANREALAGE, and released

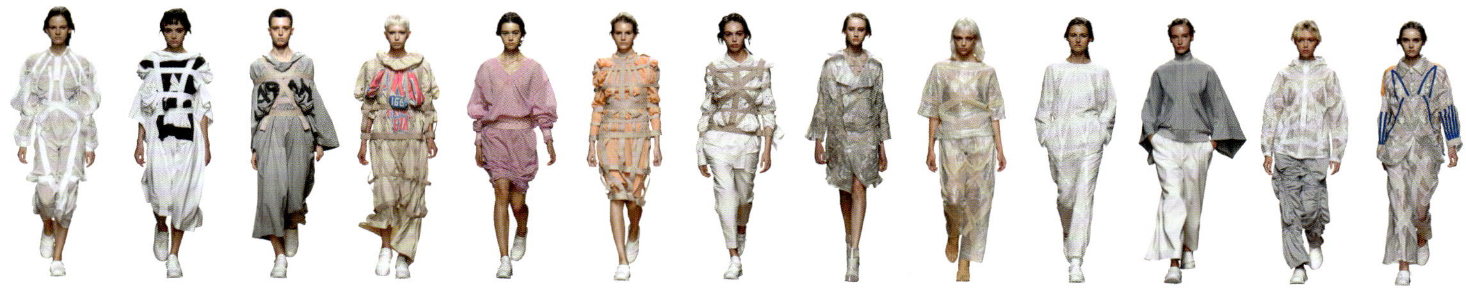

"KALEIDOSCOPE COLLECTION." ◆Oct 2017 Announced the collaboration TOYOTA × ANREALAGE, and released "WONDER-CAPSULE CONCEPT." ◆Nov 2017 Announced the collaboration PANASONIC × ANREALAGE, and

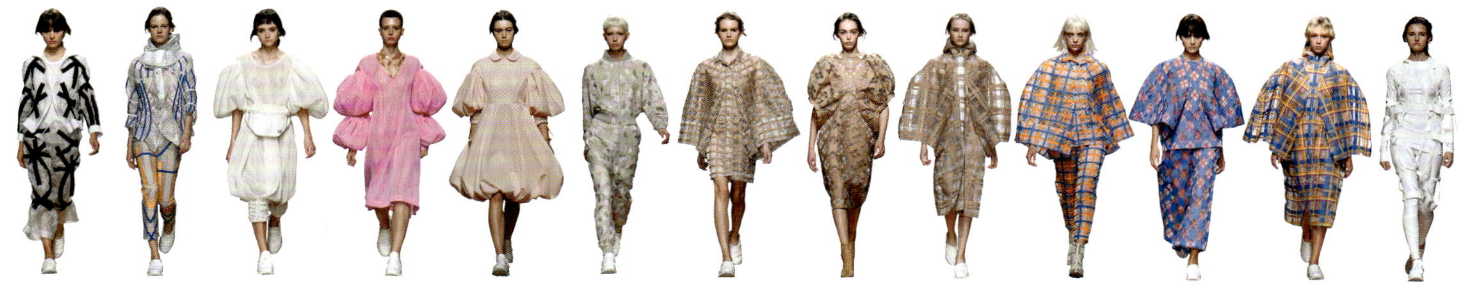

released "WEAR SPACE." ◆Nov 2017 Held the solo exhibition "A LIGHT UN LIGHT," which commemorated the brand's second monograph titled "A LIGHT UN LIGHT." The exhibition also traveled to PARCO GALLERY (Nagoya)

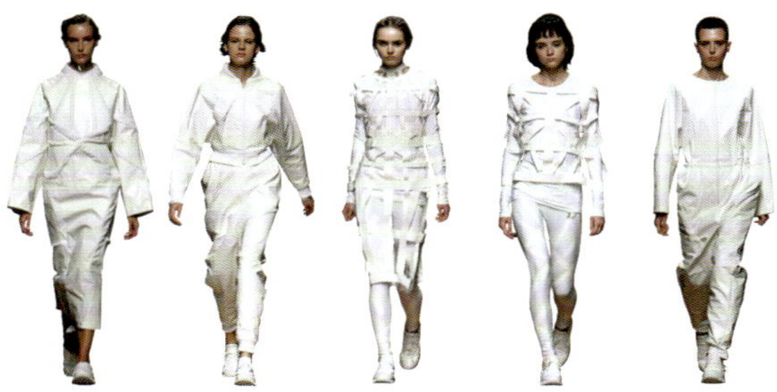

2018

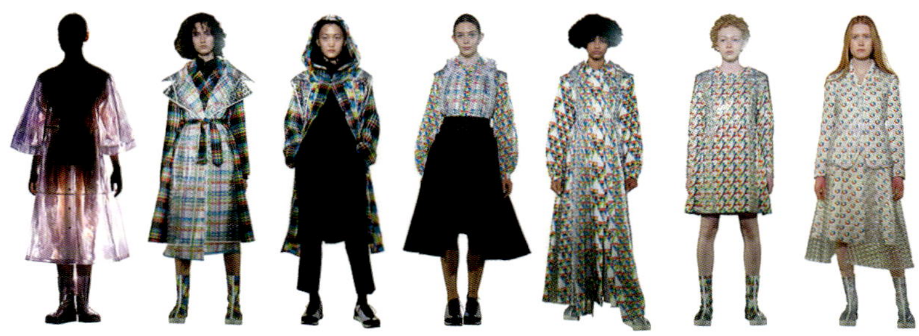

and the JAPAN HOUSE Los Angeles (USA) in 2018. ◆Nov 2017 Participated in the exhibition "Art and Design: dialogue with materials" at the Toyama Prefectural Museum of Art and Design (Toyama, Japan). ◆Jan 2018 Started

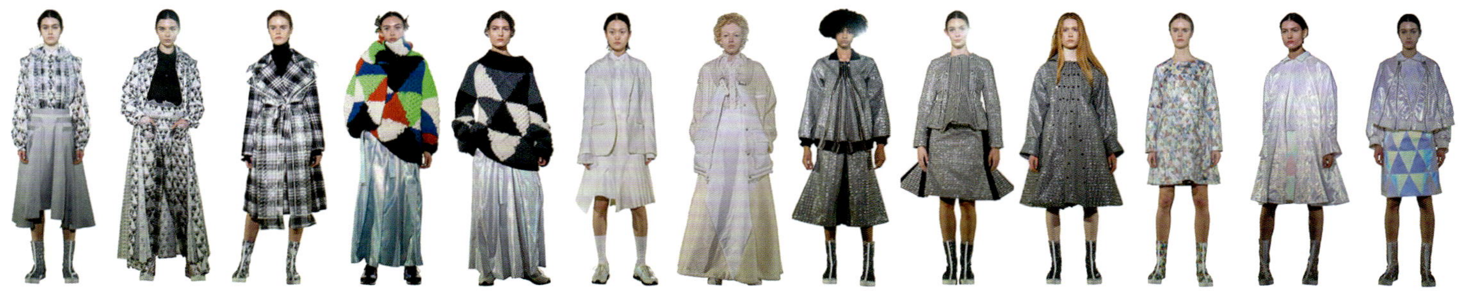

the project "AROUND THE WORLD" that themes on clothes that travels across the bodies of the world. Participators would 1) receive the shirt, 2) draw or color a patchwork, 3) take a photo, and 4) pass it on. More than 170 people

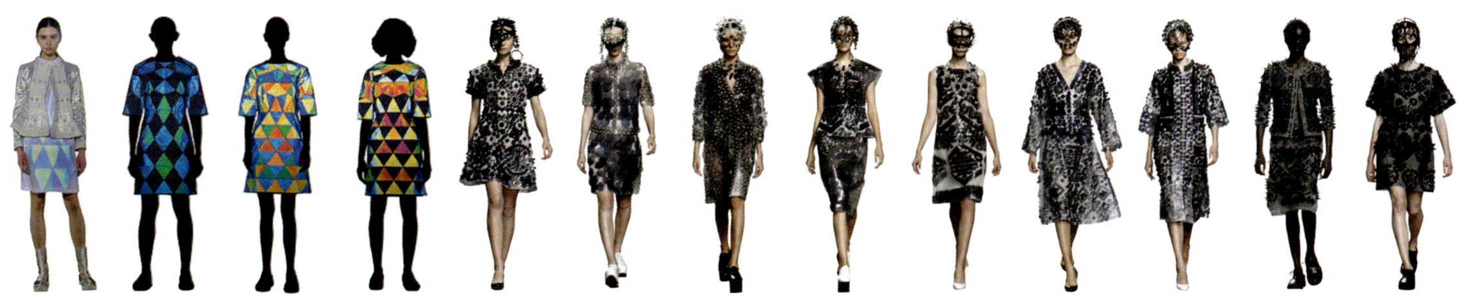

have participated so far from around the world. ◆Feb 2018 Announced the 2018 AW collection "PRISM" (Le Centorial, Paris). ◆Apr 2018 Collaborated with the renowned restaurant GAGGAN, and announced the new uniform at

"Cuisine Saga." ◆May 2018 Announced the collaboration APPLE WATCH × ANREALAGE, and released "ANREALAGE FLOWER APPLE WATCH BAND." ◆May 2018 Announced the collaboration MEDICOM TOY × ANREALAGE,

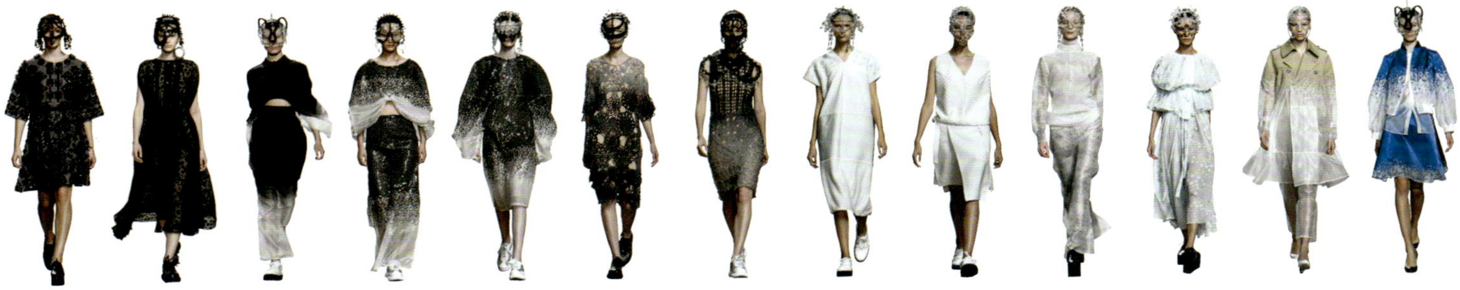

and released "ANREALAGE FLOWER BE@RBRICK 100% & 400%" and "ANREALAGE FLOWER B@RBRICK 1000%." ◆Jun 2018 Participated in the exhibition "ROCK: POWER, SPIRIT & LOVE" (Museum "EKi" Kyoto). ◆Jul 2018

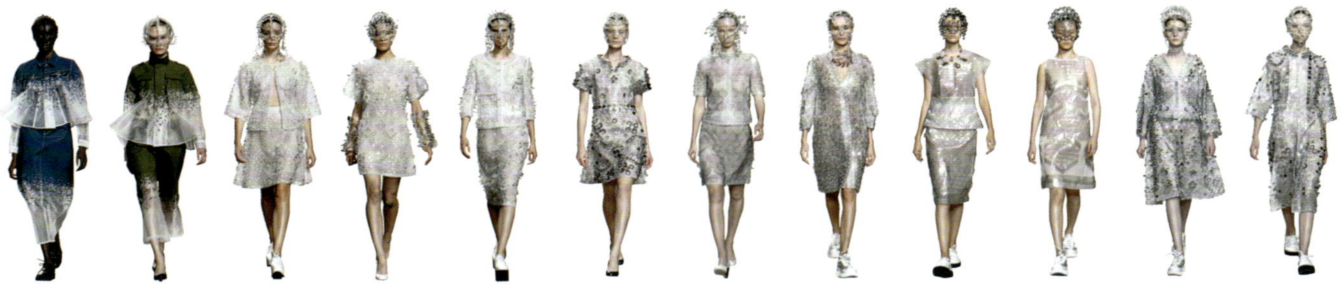

2019

Showcased "echo" at the Miraikan (National Museum of Emerging Science and Innovation), Tokyo. The presentation showcased the "echo wear," which was a special clothing that allowed the wearer recognize space in darkness.

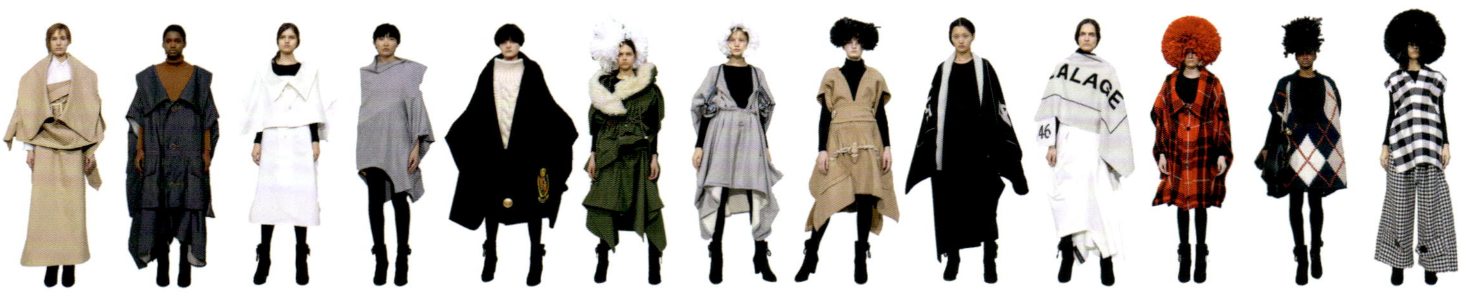

◆Jul 2018 Participated in the exhibition "JAPONISMES 2018: FUKAMI—une plongée dans l'esthétique japonaise" curated by Yuko Hasegawa (Hôtel Salomon de Rothschild, Paris). ◆Jul 2018 Held the collaboration exhibition

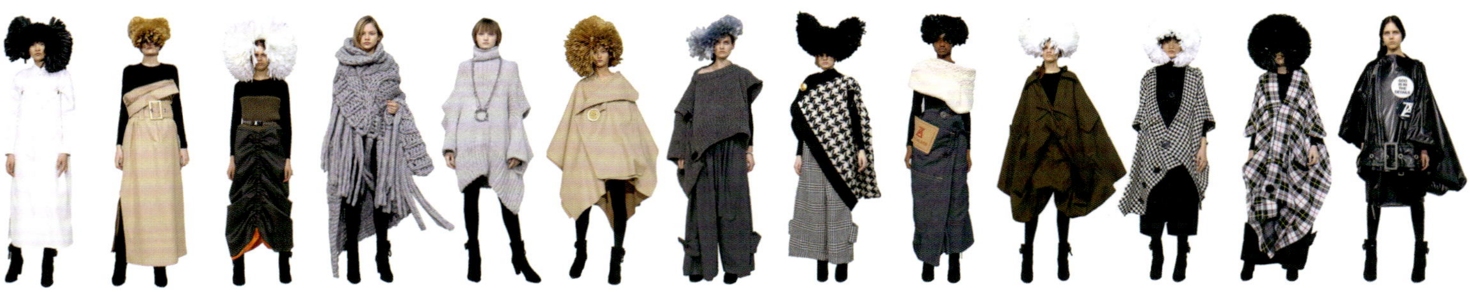

"BMW i8 × ANREALAGE" (BMW GROUP STUDIO, Tokyo). ◆Sep 2018 Announced the 2019 SS collection "CLEAR" (Palais des Beaux-Arts, Paris). ◆Oct 2018 Participated in AT TOKYO held by Amazon Fashion, and showcased

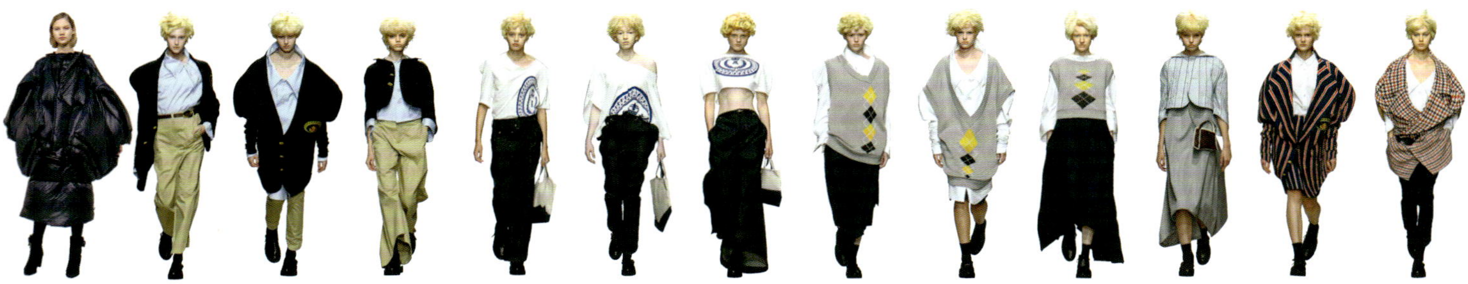

the brand's 15th anniversary collection "A LIGHT UN LIGHT COLLECTION" that showcased 100 looks from the brand's very first collection (Amazon Studio, Tokyo). ◆Feb 2019 Participated in the exhibition "Mori Art Museum 15th

Anniversary Exhibition—Roppongi Crossing 2019: Connexions" (Mori Art Museum, Tokyo). ◆Feb 2019 Announced the 2019 AW collection "DETAIL" (Espace Commines, Paris). ◆Mar 2019 Participated in Amazon Fashion Week

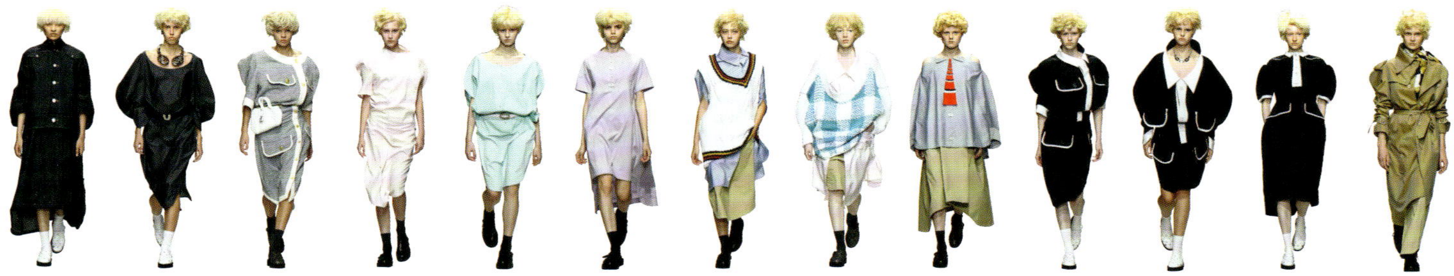

Tokyo, and announced the 2019 AW collection "DETAIL" (Shibuya Hikarie, Tokyo). ◆Jul 2019 Held the exhibition "The 19th Future of Creation 'more than Reason' by Kengo Kuma, Ichiro Yamaguchi (NF/sakanaction) & Kunihiko

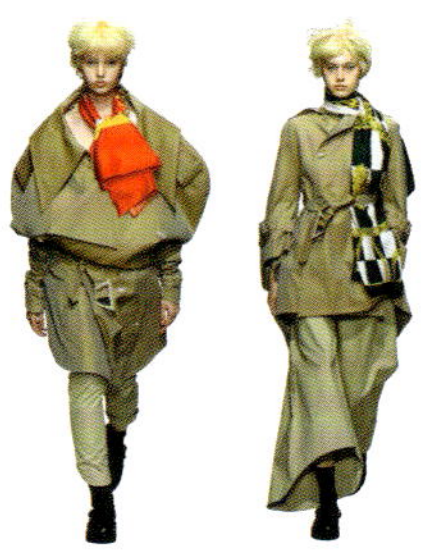

2020

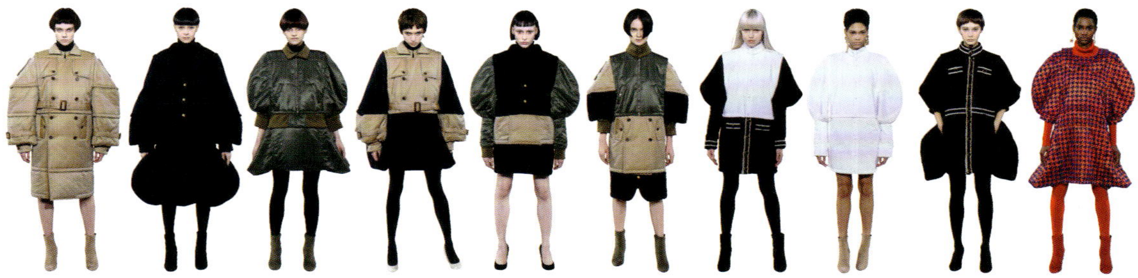

Morinaga (ANREALAGE)" (LIXIL Gallery, Tokyo). ◆Sep 2019 Selected as the Finalist for "LVMH Prize for Young Fashion Designers 2019." ◆Sep 2019 Announced the 2020 SS collection "ANGLE" (Palais de Tokyo, Paris). ◆Nov

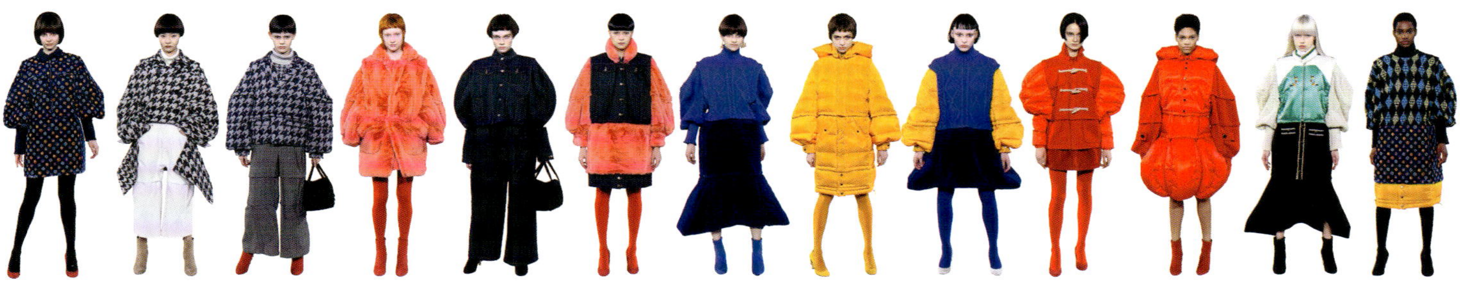

2019 Won the Grand Prize of the 37th Mainichi Fashion Grand Prix. ◆Nov 2019 Announced the 2020 SS Men's collection "AGE" (Shibuya PARCO, Tokyo). ◆Jan 2020 Announced the capsule collection "TOKYO KNIT ×

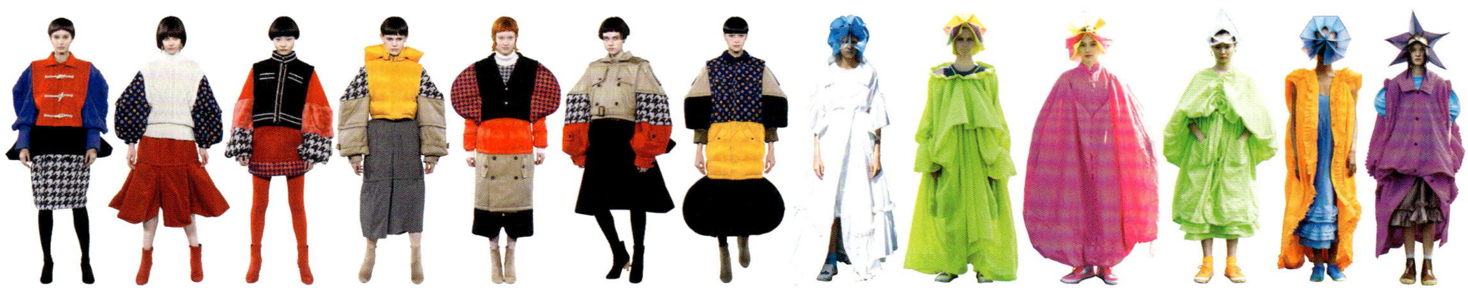

ANREALAGE" at the Pitti Immagine Uomo, Italy. ◆Jan 2020 Collaborated with FENDI, and showcased the collaboration items at the FENDI 2020AW collection titled "FENDI-field classicism" during the Men's Milan Fashion Week.

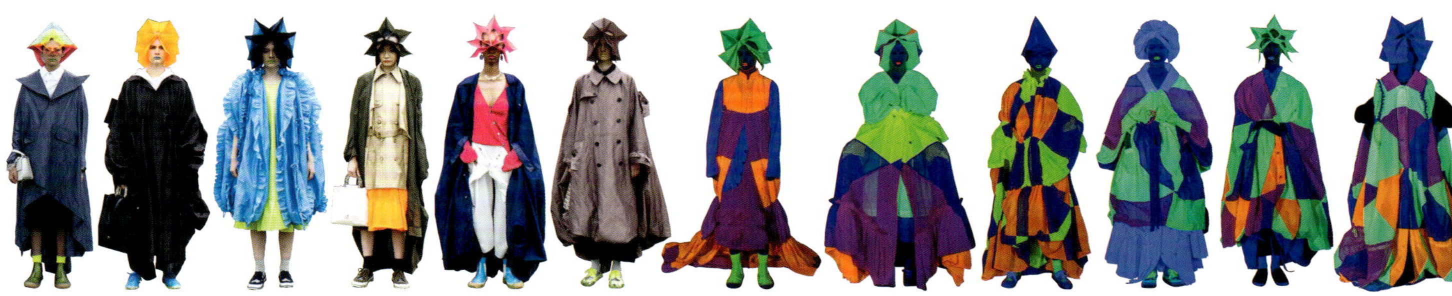

◆Feb 2020 Announced the 2020 AW collection "BLOCK" (Pavillon Cambon Capucines, Paris). ◆Mar 2020 Announced the uniform design for EXPO 2020 Dubai. ◆Sep 2020 Announced the 2021 SS collection "HOME."

Real / Unreal

At dawn, stars were still shining in the sky above Mt. Fuji.
Even after the sun rose, no clouds covered the sky and the silhouette of the mountain remained clear and beautiful.

Inside Asagiri Nature Park at the foot of Mt. Fuji, people rushed around to prepare for the collection, Home.
An unexpectedly strong wind was blowing through the area.

Despite what we thought at first, there were things we could do.
So many things that needed to be done.

I kept my eyes on the sky.
Will Mt. Fuji continue to show its silhouette?

Clothes that looked like small homes were carried out to the site.
The pillars collapsed in the strong wind.
People holding up the pillars were nearly blown away.

Home was supported by so many people.
They were protecting the collection from the fierce wind.
Beautiful Mt. Fuji watched over us the entire time.

There are things beyond human understanding.

Whether the sky will be clear.
Whether the clouds will roll in.
Whether the wind will blow.

Whether one will be born.
Whether one will die.

These things are beyond human control.
Even then, there are things we can do.

To pray that the unreal changes to the real.
To hope that the real changes to the unreal.

What is the difference between the unreal and the real?

What separates A and Z?

By praying and hoping, it reveals its outline, for the first time.

First published in the United States of America in 2021
by Rizzoli International Publications, Inc.
300 Park Avenue South
New York, NY 10010
www.rizzoliusa.com

Anrealage: A and Z

Texts: Kunihiko Morinaga, Yuko Hasegawa and Alexandre Samson

For Anrealage:

Editor: Kana Kawanishi
Proofreading: Jun Orikasa (Kana Kawanishi Art Office)

Art Direction and Graphic Design: Masaya Muto

For Rizzoli:

Editor: Ian Luna
Project Editor: Meaghan McGovern
Production Managers: Barbara Sadick and Maria Pia Gramaglia
Copy Editor/Translator: Marie Iida
Design Coordination: Eugene Lee and Olivia Russin

Publisher: Charles Miers

Photography Credits

© Yoshiyuki Okuyama
Cover, P. 6-17, 24-25, 28-35, 40-47, 50-51, 78-85, 98-103, 112-137, 184-217

© Shinya Fujiwara
P. 8-17, 62-63
Take a look at Leica Digital, analog strata are visible

© ANREALAGE
P. 18-19, 36-39, 56-57, 60-61, 76-77, 86-89, 92-93, 144-163, 174-175, 180-181, 220-237

© Seiji Ishigaki
P. 64-65, 164-171

© Leslie Kee
P. 66-69

© Mareo Suemasa, courtesy 21st Century Museum of Contemporary Art, Kanazawa
P. 94-97
"Philosophical Fashion 2: ANREALAGE "A COLOR UN COLOR"
July 12, 2013–November 24, 2013
Design Gallery, 21st Century Museum of Contemporary Art, Kanazawa

© FENDI
P. 104-109

Definitions of words used for the titles of each chapter have been cited from the online version of the Cambridge Dictionary.

Acknowledgments:

Anrealage would like to thank Silvia Fendi (FENDI), Shigetaka Kaneko (Shige Kaneko Co., Ltd), Katsuya Kamo (Kamo Head), Hiromi Otsuka, Natalie Ours (PR Consulting), Kanako B. Koga, Teppei, Ichiro Yamaguchi (Sakanakushon/NF), Shotaro Aoyama (NF), Kengo Kuma (KKAA), Kohei Nawa (Sandwich), Daito Manabe (Rhizomatiks), Yoshiyuki Okuyama (band), Tomohiro Kono, Souta Yamaguchi, Ippei Sugihara, Toshihiro Tani (Waseda University Press), Koichi Suga (Waseda University Press), Seiji Ishigaki, Tomoyuki Kujirai, Kayo Itagaki (Infas Publications), Hisashi Abe (Studio 44), Kose Shinichiro (One O), Rena Takeda (Shiseido), Kiyoko Odo (Bryant Artists), Nami Yoshida (Bryant Artists), Sylvie, Takahiro Komatsu, Tatsuya Miura, Rei Yuzurihara (Shige Kaneko Co., Ltd.), Moe Rachel Hoshima (Shige Kaneko Co., Ltd.), Koji Hirano, Yuri Iwatsuki, Hirofumi Kera (Shiseido), Satoshi Takahashi (NION), Yusuke Tanaka (Caviar), Misa Nakamura (Caviar), Yoshiko Suehiro, Noriko Shimizu, Tsuyoshi Oikawa, Shinichi Yokota, Jaeyong Lee, Shin Yoshida (Moririn), Hiromasa Asano (Sunace), Takashi Aoki (Macronic), Yasuhiro Hara (Lim), Porter, Authentic Shoe & Co., Onward, Mitsui Chemicals, Sure Corporation, Fujibo, Proud, Mudsnail, Shikibo, Hiroshi Morinaga, Shoji Nishitani, and Keisuke Kanda.
Kunihiko Morinaga would like to extend his sincere gratitude to the team of Anrealage Co., Ltd, and his family.

A special appreciation is extended to Yurina Hirate, who appears on the cover of the Anrealage edition.

Rizzoli would like to thank Kunihiko Morinaga for his generosity, and to Masaya Muto, Emi Komatsu and Eiji Kagawa.

This book includes the English translation of text published in *A and Z: The Fashion of Anrealage* (Waseda University Press, 2020).

Printed in China

2021 2022 2023 2024 2025 / 10 9 8 7 6 5 4 3 2 1

ISBN: 978-0-8478-6486-7
Library of Congress Control Number: 2021938045

Visit us online: Facebook.com/RizzoliNewYork
Twitter: @Rizzoli_Books
Instagram.com/RizzoliBooks
Pinterest.com/RizzoliBooks
Youtube.com/user/RizzoliNY
Issuu.com/Rizzoli